Julie C. Meloni

Sams **Teach Yourself**

PHP, MySQL® and Apache in All One

SAMS   800 East 96th Street, Indianapolis, Indiana, 46240 USA

Sams Teach Yourself PHP, MySQL® and Apache All in One

ISBN-13: 978-0-672-33543-3
ISBN-10: 0-672-33543-3

Library of Congress Cataloging-in-Publication Data

Meloni, Julie C.
  Sams teach yourself PHP, MySQL and Apache : all in one / Julie C. Meloni.
      p. cm.
  Includes index.
  ISBN-13: 978-0-672-33543-3 (pbk. w/cd)
  ISBN-10: 0-672-33543-3
 1. Web site development. 2. PHP (Computer program language) 3. Apache (Computer file : Apache Group) 4. MySQL (Electronic resource) I. Title.
  TK5105.888.M45 2012
  005.13–dc23

                         2012016353

Printed in the United States of America
First Printing May 2012

Trademarks

Warning and Disclaimer

Bulk Sales

Sams Publishing offers excellent discounts on this book when ordered in quantity for bulk purchases or special sales. For more information, please contact

U.S. Corporate and Government Sales
1-800-382-3419
corpsales@pearsontechgroup.com

For sales outside of the U.S., please contact

International Sales
international@pearsoned.com

Acquisitions Editor
Mark Taber

Development Editor
Songlin Qiu

Managing Editor
Sandra Schroeder

Project Editor
Mandie Frank

Copy Editor
Keith Cline

Indexer
Heather McNeill

Proofreader
Paula Lowell

Technical Editor
Timothy Boronczyk

Publishing Coordinator
Vanessa Evans

Media Producer
Dan Scherf

Designer
Gary Adair

Compositor
Studio Galou, LLC

Contents at a Glance

Table of Contents

About the Author

Julie C. Meloni is a technical consultant who has been developing web-based applications since the Web first saw the light of day. She has authored numerous books and articles on web-based programming and scripting languages and database topics, and you can find translations of her work in 18 different languages. She blogs at thickbook.com and nerdtripping.com—the latter reserved for tips and tricks for traveling while nerdy.

Acknowledgments

The Apache Software Foundation, the PHP Group, and MySQL AB deserve much more recognition than they ever get for creating these super products that drive the vast majority of the Web.

Although this book is several editions removed from the original text by Daniel Lopez (author of *Sams Teach Yourself Apache 2 in 24 Hours*) and Matt Zandstra (author of *Sams Teach Yourself PHP in 24 Hours*), this book would not exist without their work oh so many years ago.

We Want to Hear from You!

As the reader of this book, *you* are our most important critic and commentator. We value your opinion and want to know what we're doing right, what we could do better, what areas you'd like to see us publish in, and any other words of wisdom you're willing to pass our way.

You can email or write directly to let us know what you did or didn't like about this book—as well as what we can do to make our books stronger.

Please note that we cannot help you with technical problems related to the topic of this book, and that due to the high volume of mail we receive, we might not be able to reply to every message.

When you write, please be sure to include this book's title and author as well as your name and phone number or email address.

E-mail: feedback@samspublishing.com

Mail: Reader Feedback
Sams Publishing
800 East 96th Street
Indianapolis, IN 46240 USA

Reader Services

Visit our website and register this book at informit.com/register for convenient access to any updates, downloads, or errata that might be available for this book.

Introduction

Welcome to *Sams Teach Yourself PHP, MySQL, and Apache All in One, Fifth Edition*. I'm happy to report that the PHP language and its community of developers and users continues to grow every day—hence the need for a refresh of this book.

Since the previous edition of this book, the "end of life" of PHP 4 finally set in; with the help of a GoPHP5 initiative, web hosting providers and application developers migrated their services and code away from PHP 4-specific features and coding practices and into the world of PHP 5—full of speed and an even greater feature set. As with the previous edition, all the code in this edition is based on the latest version of PHP available at the time of this writing (5.4.0, in this case).

Some of you might have heard of PHP 6 or have seen books touting PHP 6 as the core language used. Well, a version of the language called PHP 6 never materialized—the functionality planned for a version 6 release was added to PHP 5.3 and PHP 5.4. So, have no fear; you're not missing anything if you hear PHP 6 and cannot find anything about it online or at the PHP.net website.

Over the course of this book, you learn the concepts necessary for configuring and managing the Apache web server, the basics of programming in PHP, and the methods for using and administering the MySQL relational database system. The overall goal of the book is to provide you with the foundation you need to understand how seamlessly these technologies integrate with one another and to give you practical knowledge of how to integrate them into functioning websites and web applications. This book should be a first step—not your only step—to more advanced site development.

Who Should Read This Book?

This book is geared toward individuals who possess a general understanding of the concepts of working in a web-based development environment, be it Linux/UNIX, Windows, or Mac OS X. Installation and configuration instructions assume that you have familiarity with your operating system and the basic methods of building (on Linux/UNIX systems) or installing (on Windows and Mac OS X systems) software.

The lessons that delve into programming with PHP assume no previous knowledge of the language. However, if you have experience with other programming languages, such as ASP (Active Server Pages), JSP (JavaServer Pages), Ruby, or Perl, you will find the going much easier because of your familiarity with such programming elements as variables, control structures, functions, objects, and the like. Similarly, if you have worked with other databases, such as Oracle or Microsoft SQL Server, you already possess a solid foundation for working through the MySQL-related lessons.

The only real requirement is that you already understand static web content creation with HTML. If you are just starting out in the world of web development, you will still be able to use this book, but you should consider working through an HTML tutorial. If you are comfortable creating basic pages, you will be fine.

How This Book Is Organized

This book is divided into six parts, corresponding to particular topic groups. You should read the chapters within each part one right after another, with each chapter building on the information found in those before it:

▶ Part I, "Getting Up and Running," provides a quick-start guide to installation and walks you through the installation and configuration of MySQL, Apache, and PHP in depth. You need to complete at least one version of these instructions—either the quick-start installation or the longer instructions—before moving on *unless you already have access to a working installation of these technologies through a hosting provider*. Even if you do not need to install and configure MySQL, Apache, and PHP in your development environment, you should still skim these lessons so that you understand the basics of their interaction.

▶ Part II, "PHP Language Structure," is devoted to teaching you the basics of the PHP language, including structural elements such as arrays and objects. The examples will get you in the habit of writing code, uploading it to your server, and testing the results.

▶ Part III, "Getting Involved with the Code," consists of chapters that cover intermediate-level application development topics, including working with forms and files, restricting access, and completing other small projects designed to introduce a specific concept.

- ▶ Part IV, "PHP and MySQL Integration," contains chapters devoted to working with databases in general, such as database normalization, as well as using PHP to connect to and work with MySQL. Included is a basic SQL primer, which also includes MySQL-specific functions and other information.

- ▶ Part V, "Basic Projects," consists of chapters devoted to performing a particular task using PHP and MySQL, integrating all the knowledge gained so far. Projects include an address book, a discussion forum, and a basic online store-front, among others. These examples are built in a black-and-white environment, meaning the aesthetic display is minimal. This allows you to focus on the programming and logic involved in building the structures rather than making these items aesthetically pleasing.

- ▶ Part VI, "Administration and Fine-Tuning," is devoted to administering and tuning Apache and MySQL. It also includes information on virtual hosting and setting up a secure web server.

If you find that you are already familiar with a topic, you can skip ahead to the next chapter. However, in some instances, chapters refer to specific concepts learned in previous chapters, so be aware that you might have to skim a skipped chapter so that your development environment remains consistent with the book.

At the end of many chapters, a few quiz questions test how well you've learned the material. Additional activities provide another way to apply the information learned in the chapter and guide you toward using this newfound knowledge in the next chapter.

About the Book's Source Code

All the code that appears in listings throughout the chapters is also available on the accompanying CD-ROM. You may also download the source code bundle from the author's website at http://www.thickbook.com/.

Typing the code on your own provides useful experience in making typos, causing errors, and performing the sometimes mind-numbing task of tracking down errant semicolons. However, if you want to skip that lesson and just upload the working code to your website, feel free!

Conventions Used in This Book

This book uses different typefaces to differentiate between code and plain English and to help you identify important concepts. Throughout the chapters, code, commands, and text you type or see onscreen appear in a `computer typeface`. New terms appear in italics at the point in the text where they are defined. In addition, icons accompany special blocks of information:

NOTE

A Note presents an interesting piece of information related to the current topic.

TIP

A Tip offers advice or teaches an easier method for performing a task.

CAUTION

A Caution warns you about potential pitfalls and explains how to avoid them.

CHAPTER 1

Installation QuickStart Guide with XAMPP

In case you want to get started quickly, this short chapter steps you through installation from the all-in-one cross-platform installation package, XAMPP. Then, the next three chapters explain how to obtain and install MySQL, Apache, and PHP, respectively, from the Internet so that you can make sure that your versions are up-to-date. In addition, those next three chapters contain extended explanatory information about each step and other important information relevant to understanding how these technologies work together.

You should familiarize yourself with the extended information for each technology in those next three chapters. However, if you just want to *get started* working on your local machine, that's fine, too.

Using Third-Party Installation Packages

Third-party installation packages are those bundles of programs that are provided by a company or organization other than the original creator. In this chapter, you learn how to use the XAMPP installation package to install PHP, MySQL, and Apache simultaneously, on whichever operating system you are using (Linux/UNIX, Windows, or Mac).

Besides my own experience as an XAMPP user for several years, I selected it for use in this chapter because of the X in its name: The X indicates it is a cross-platform installation of AMPP (or Apache, MySQL, PHP, and Perl). (Perl is not a topic of this book, so just consider it a bonus.)

There are two other very good third-party installation packages for Apache, MySQL, and PHP that are specific to operating systems:

▶ **WAMP**—Installation of Apache, MySQL, and PHP on Windows. See http://www.wampserver.com/ for more information.

▶ **MAMP**—Installation of Apache, MySQL, and PHP on Mac. See http://www.mamp.info/ for more information.

One potential drawback to using third-party installation packages is that the version of the core technologies that are bundled together will always be a few revision versions behind. This happens because of the work that goes into creating and testing the bundle itself, to ensure that no conflicts exist between the latest versions of the technologies; it also has to go through a quality-assurance process. The upside of this process, however, is that when you install these technologies using a bundled installer, the upgrade process requires nothing more than running the new installer—it takes care of removing and updating all the files for you.

The next three sections describe the basic installation process of XAMPP. You only need to read the section that applies to your operating system. However, be sure to read the "Securing XAMPP" at the end of this chapter; it applies to all operating systems.

Installing XAMPP on Linux/UNIX

Although the following instructions were tested on an Ubuntu Linux system, the steps are the same for a default installation of all other Linux or commercial UNIX distributions. Should you encounter unexpected error messages during compilation, contact your systems administrator or refer to the documentation for your particular operating system.

If you are using the version of XAMPP included on this book's CD-ROM, begin as the superuser (either log in as root or su from a regular system user) and mount the CD-ROM under /mnt on your filesystem:

```
# mount /dev/cdrom /mnt -t iso9660
```

Now that you have access to the XAMPP file on the CD-ROM, or if you have downloaded the latest version from http://www.apachefriends.org/en/xampp-linux.html, continue to the specific installation steps.

As the superuser, copy the file from the XAMPP directory on the CD-ROM (or from your download location) to the /opt directory. Within the /opt directory, extract the files you have downloaded:

```
# tar xvfz xampp-linux-VERSION-NUMBER.tar.gz -C /opt
```

NOTE

The XAMPP version number at the time of this writing is 1.8.0-beta2, so the filename is xampp-linux-1.8.0-beta2.tar.gz. Later versions will have a different filename, so adjust the command accordingly.

This creates a directory called /opt/lampp, in which XAMPP is installed. To start XAMPP, first change directories to the new directory:

```
# cd lampp
```

Issue the following command to start XAMPP (which starts Apache and MySQL):

```
# ./lampp start
```

You will see a message such as this:

```
Starting XAMPP for Linux 1.8.0...
XAMPP: Starting Apache with SSL (and PHP5)...
XAMPP: Starting MySQL...
XAMPP: Starting ProFTPD...
XAMPP for Linux started.
```

To test whether the web server is running, open a web browser and enter **http://localhost/xampp/index.php**. The menu for the XAMPP service should display, as shown in Figure 1.1.

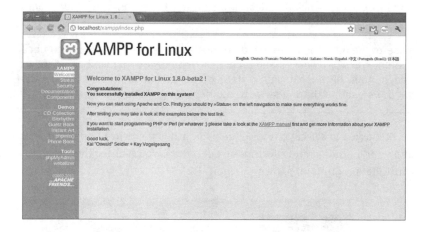

FIGURE 1.1
The XAMPP menu page.

That's all there is to it; XAMPP has installed Apache, PHP, and MySQL on your machine, and you can see the status of services and read more information about it through the links in the left column when viewing http://localhost/xampp/index.php.

To stop XAMPP and its services, you can issue the following command at any time from the command line:

```
# /opt/lampp/lampp stop
```

Be sure to read "Securing XAMPP" at the end of this chapter for more information about locking down your XAMPP-powered machine (even if it is only for development).

Installing XAMPP on Windows

The XAMPP installation file included on the CD-ROM has been tested and is suitable for Windows operating systems from XP through Windows 7. Earlier versions of Windows are not supported.

To use the XAMPP installation file from the CD-ROM, first insert the CD-ROM into your PC; it should play automatically. If it does not, double-click the drive icon for your CD-ROM under My Computer, and navigate to the directory containing the XAMPP installer files.

Now that you have access to the XAMPP file on the CD-ROM, or if you have downloaded the latest version from http://www.apachefriends.org/en/xampp-windows.html, double-click the file to launch the wizard-based installer program.

NOTE

> Because of the nuances in the Windows operating system releases, and because of different security practices and programs that may be installed on Windows machines, if any of the installation steps do not go smoothly, visit the XAMPP FAQ for Windows users at http://www.apachefriends.org/en/faq-xampp-windows.html.

You are first asked to select your language; English is the default selection. After selecting your language and clicking the OK button, you will see the welcome screen of the installer program, as shown in Figure 1.2.

FIGURE 1.2
The XAMPP installation main screen.

The XAMPP version number at the time of writing is 1.7.7, so the installation wizard displays that number. Later versions will have a different number, but the process will be similar.

Click the Next button to continue the installation process. As with most wizard-like installations, you are asked to select an installation location and some installation options before moving to the next step. The XAMPP installation is no different; you should leave the default installation location and the default installation options as marked and click the Next button to move on past each screen. At this point, the installation process itself happens, as shown in Figure 1.3.

FIGURE 1.3
The XAMPP installation continues as the files are extracted.

When the installation process finishes, the installer alerts you to this status; click the Finish button to complete the installation. Before the XAMPP installation process completely closes, it asks whether you want to start the Control Panel for managing the installed services, as shown in Figure 1.4.

FIGURE 1.4
The XAMPP
installation is
complete.

The XAMPP Control Panel, as shown in Figure 1.5, provides you with one-click access to starting and stopping the Apache and MySQL server processes running on your machine. If you are running these server processes on your local machine for development purposes only, you might want to turn them on only when you need them; the Control Panel allows quick access to do just that.

FIGURE 1.5
The XAMPP
Control Panel.

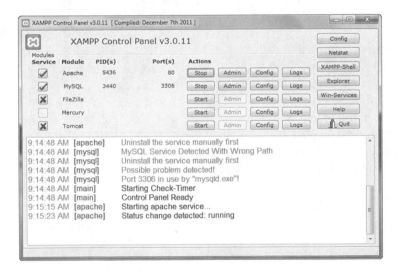

To test whether the web server is running, open a web browser and enter **http://localhost/xampp/xampp.php**. The menu for the XAMPP service should display, as shown in Figure 1.6.

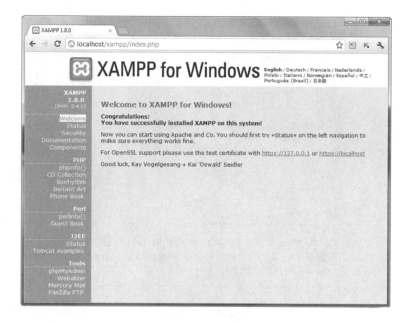

FIGURE 1.6
The XAMPP
menu page.

That's all there is to it; XAMPP has installed Apache, PHP, and MySQL on your machine, and you can see the status of services and read more information about it through the links in the left column when viewing http://localhost/xampp.

Be sure to read "Securing XAMPP" at the end of this chapter for more information about locking down your XAMPP-powered machine (even if it is only for development).

Installing XAMPP on Mac OS X

The XAMPP installation file included on the CD-ROM has been tested and is suitable for Mac OS X 1.4 and later. Earlier versions of Mac OS X are not supported.

To use the XAMPP installation file from the CD-ROM, first insert the CD-ROM into your Mac; it should play automatically. If it does not, double-click the drive icon for your CD-ROM and navigate to the directory containing the XAMPP installer files.

Now that you have access to the XAMPP file on the CD-ROM, or if you have downloaded the latest version from http://www.apachefriends.org/en/xampp-mac.html, double-click the DMG image. You will see a screen like that shown in Figure 1.7.

FIGURE 1.7
Instructions for
installing
XAMPP on a
Mac.

Follow the onscreen instruction to drag the XAMPP folder to the Applications folder.
After the folder and files are copied, you can find a link to the XAMPP Control Panel
in the /Applications/XAMPP folder, as shown in Figure 1.8.

FIGURE 1.8
Find the link to
the XAMPP
Control Panel.

Double-click this link to start the XAMPP Control Panel, through which you can
start and stop the Apache and MySQL server processes running on your machine. If
you are running these server processes on your local machine for development purposes only, you might want to turn them on only when you need them; the Control
Panel allows quick access to do just that.

To test whether the web server is running, open a web browser and enter
http://localhost/xampp/index.php. The menu for the XAMPP service should
display, as shown in Figure 1.9.

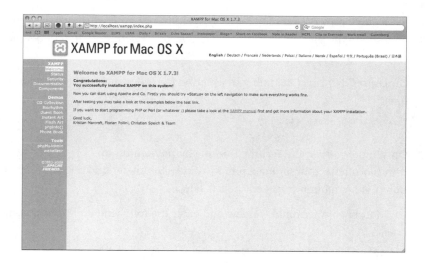

FIGURE 1.6
The XAMPP
menu page.

That's all there is to it; XAMPP has installed Apache, PHP, and MySQL on your machine, and you can see the status of services and read more information about it through the links in the left column when viewing http://localhost/xampp/index.php.

Be sure to read "Securing XAMPP," next, for more information about locking down your XAMPP-powered machine (even if it is only for development).

Securing XAMPP

The primary purpose of XAMPP is to provide a quick-and-easy installation method for Apache, MySQL, and PHP within a development environment. One of the trade-offs for this quick-and-easy installation is that some security settings are left incomplete—or, at least, up to the user to determine whether they are important enough to set.

Using the installation right out of the (virtual) box, the following are some potential security issues:

▶ The MySQL administrator user has no password. (You can use a blank password.)

▶ MySQL and Apache run as the same user (nobody; relevant for Linux/UNIX and Mac only).

▶ Some services are accessible to the network unless you specifically disallow access through your personal firewall.

However, XAMPP provides a utility for each operating system, which you can run and step through the process of securing your XAMPP system even in a development environment, as follows:

▶ On Linux/UNIX, run the utility by entering the following on the command line:

```
# /opt/lampp/lampp security
```

▶ On Windows, open the Security Console by navigating to http://localhost/xampp/index.php in your web browser and selecting Security from the navigation menu on the left side.

▶ On Mac, open a terminal window and enter the following on the command line:

```
# /Applications/XAMPP/xamppfiles/xampp security
```

Troubleshooting

The steps in this chapter have been tested with the versions of the software supplied on the CD-ROM that accompanies this book. If you experience installation problems, first check that you have followed the steps exactly as given in this chapter. Then, check the XAMPP website at http://www.apachefriends.org/ for FAQs specific to this installation package.

If these processes still don't work and you want to try another all-in-one third-party installation package, feel free to try WAMP and MAMP (mentioned at the beginning of this chapter).

You could also try the installations the "long" way, using the extended information found in the next three chapters. Those chapters provide troubleshooting tips and links to additional sites that can help you work through your installation issues.

CHAPTER 2

Installing and Configuring MySQL

In this chapter, you learn the following:

► How to install MySQL
► Basic security guidelines for running MySQL
► How to work with the MySQL user privilege system

This is the first of three installation-related chapters in which you learn how to set up your development environment. We tackle the MySQL installation first because on some systems building the PHP module requires bits of the MySQL installation to be complete if you're going to use MySQL with PHP.

Current and Future Versions of MySQL

The installation instructions in this chapter refer to MySQL Community Server 5.5.21, the current production version of the software. This version number can be read as "revision number 21 of minor release 5, of the major version 5 of the MySQL server software." Revisions and minor releases do not follow a set release schedule. When enhancements or fixes are added to the code and thoroughly tested, a new version is released with a new revision or minor version number.

By the time you purchase this book, the version number might have changed to 5.5.22 or later. If so, read the list at http://dev.mysql.com/doc/refman/5.5/en/news-5-5-x.html for any installation/configuration process changes. These processes make up the bulk of this chapter.

Although it is unlikely that any installation instructions will change between minor version updates, always check the changelog of software that you install and maintain. If a minor version change does occur while you are reading this book but the changelog notes no installation changes, just make a mental note and substitute the new version number wherever it appears in the installation instructions and accompanying figures.

How to Get MySQL

MySQL AB was the name of the company that developed, maintained, and distributed the MySQL database server; through a series of acquisitions (Sun Microsystems purchased MySQL AB, and Oracle Corporation purchased Sun Microsystems), database giant Oracle now owns MySQL. However, the MySQL Community Edition of the software remains open source, is supported by open source developers, and is freely available on the MySQL website at http://www.mysql.com/. Binary distributions for all platforms, installer packages for Mac OS X, and RPMs and source code files for Linux/UNIX platforms are all available.

NOTE

Linux and Mac OS X distributions usually contain some version or another of the open source MySQL software, although these are usually several revision or minor versions behind the current release.

The installation instructions in this chapter are based on the official MySQL 5.5.x Community Server distribution. You can download all files from http://dev.mysql.com/downloads/mysql/5.5.html, and you can find all the current versions as of the time of this writing on the CD included with this book.

Installing MySQL on Linux/UNIX

The process of installing MySQL on Linux/UNIX is straightforward, whether you use RPMs or install the binaries. If you are installing from RPMs, there are platform-specific RPMs such as those for SuSE and generic Linux running on different processor types, such as x86 32- and 64-bit.

For a minimal installation from RPMs, you need two files from the downloads page at http://dev.mysql.com/downloads/mysql/5.5.html (or obtained from the CD-ROM that accompanies this book):

▶ **MySQL-server-type-**_VERSIONNUMBER_**.**_PLATFORM_**.rpm**—The MySQL server

▶ **MySQL-client-type-**_VERSIONNUMBER_**.**_PLATFORM_**.rpm**—The standard MySQL
   client libraries

To perform a minimal installation from RPMs, type the following at your prompt:

```
# rpm -i MySQL-server-VERSION.i386.rpm MySQL-client-VERSION.i386.rpm
```

NOTE

Replace _VERSIONNUMBER_ in the filename with the actual version you downloaded,
and _PLATFORM_ with the short name of the platform you are using. For example,
the current MySQL 5.5 server RPM for generic Linux distributions is `MySQL-`
`server-5.5.21-1.linux2.6.i386.rpm`, and the client libraries RPM is `MySQL-`
`client-5.5.21-1.linux2.6.i386.rpm`.

For an installation from Debian packages, you need the `*.deb` file from the downloads page at http://dev.mysql.com/downloads/mysql/5.5.html (or obtained from
the CD-ROM that accompanies this book). Then type the following at your prompt:

```
# dpkg -i mysql-VERSION-debian6.0-i686.deb
```

Another painless (and very common) installation method is to install MySQL from a
binary distribution. This method requires the `gunzip` and `tar` utilities to uncompress
and unpack the distribution, and also requires the ability to create groups and users
on the system. The first series of commands in the binary distribution installation
process has you adding a group and a user and unpacking the distribution, as follows:

```
# groupadd mysql
# useradd -r -g mysql mysql
# cd /usr/local
# tar zxvf /path/to/mysql-VERSION-PLATFORM.tar.gz
```

NOTE

Replace _VERSION-PLATFORM_ in the filename with the actual version you
downloaded. For example, the current MySQL 5.5 generic Linux binary is
`mysql-5.5.21-1-linux2.6.i386.tar`.

Next, the instructions tell you to create a symbolic link with a shorter name:

```
# ln -s mysql-VERSION-PLATFORM mysql
# cd mysql
```

After you unpack them, the README and INSTALL files walk you through the remainder of the installation process for the version of MySQL you've chosen. In general, the following series of commands are used:

```
# scripts/mysql_install_db --user=mysql
# chown -R root  .
# chown -R mysql mysql_data
# chgrp -R mysql .
# bin/mysqld_safe --user=mysql &
```

You're now ready to start the MySQL server, so skip ahead in this chapter to the "Basic Security Guidelines" section to learn how to add passwords and users. If you experienced any issues with your installation, check the "Troubleshooting Your Installation" section.

Installing MySQL on Mac OS X

The MySQL installation process for Mac OS X is fairly straightforward—there is an installation package for Mac OS X. Go to the MySQL downloads page at http://dev.mysql.com/downloads/mysql/5.5.html and select Mac OS X from the drop-down list (or use the files from the CD-ROM that accompanies this book).

If you are going to the website, be sure to download the appropriate DMG archive for your system: either 10.5 or 10.6, and either 32- or 64-bit.

When you have the file, double-click the DMG archive. After you open the DMG archive, you will see a folder with a few files in it, as shown in Figure 2.1.

FIGURE 2.1
Showing the contents of the MySQL DMG archive.

Double-click the *.pkg file in that folder and follow these installation steps to complete the process:

1. The MySQL installer launches automatically, as shown in Figure 2.2. Click Continue to move to the next step.

FIGURE 2.2
The MySQL Installer for the Mac has started.

2. The next few screens contain general information regarding installation and the MySQL license. Read these screens and click Continue to move through them.

3. After stepping through the information and licensing screens, you must select an installation destination. Select the appropriate drive, as shown in Figure 2.3, and then click the Continue button.

FIGURE 2.3
Select an installation location.

4. The next screen verifies your installation location selection and requires you to click the Install button to continue. At this point, you might be prompted to

enter the administrator username and password before the installation process continues. When it continues, let the process run until you see that the installation is complete, as shown in Figure 2.4.

FIGURE 2.4
MySQL has
been installed.

Also included in the installation package is the MySQL Startup Item installer. If you want MySQL to start automatically at system startup, install this additional package. Installation of the MySQL Startup Item follows the standard installation method just described: Double-click the `*.pkg` file, select a destination disk, and allow the installation process to run to completion. After installing the MySQL Startup Item, use the following command in a terminal window to start MySQL:

```
# sudo /Library/StartupItems/MySQLCOM/MySQLCOM start
```

When attempting to start MySQL, you might be asked to enter your administrator password. After you do so, you can press Ctrl+D to exit the shell once MySQL has started.

After completing the installation steps in this section, you can skip to the "Basic Security Guidelines" section later in this chapter. If you experienced any issues with your installation, check the "Troubleshooting Your Installation" section.

Installing MySQL on Windows

The MySQL installation process on Windows uses a standard Microsoft Windows Installer (MSI) file to walk you through the installation and configuration of MySQL on your Windows XP, Windows Server 2003, Windows Vista, or Windows 7 machine.

Go to the MySQL downloads page at http://dev.mysql.com/downloads/mysql/5.5.html and select the Windows option from the drop-down menu. Download the

Windows MSI Installer file for your system, either 32- or 64-bit. When this file has been downloaded (or copied from the CD-ROM for this book), double-click it to begin the installation process.

The following steps detail the installation of MySQL 5.5.21 on Windows 7; the installation sequence follows the same steps regardless of your Windows environment.

A ZIP Archive version is also available for Windows users. If you want to install the ZIP Archive version, be sure to read the descriptions and instructions in the MySQL Manual at http://dev.mysql.com/doc/refman/5.5/en/windows-choosing-package.html.

NOTE

Jumping right into the installation sequence, just follow these steps:

1. Double-click the *.msi file to begin the installation sequence. You will see the first screen of the MySQL Setup Wizard, as shown in Figure 2.5. Click Next to continue.

FIGURE 2.5
The first step of the MySQL Setup Wizard for Windows.

2. After agreeing to the terms and conditions, you are asked to choose a setup type—Typical, Custom, or Complete (see Figure 2.6). The Custom option allows you to pick and choose elements of MySQL to install, whereas the Complete option installs all the components of MySQL, which range from documentation to benchmarking suites. The Typical installation method is suitable for most users because it includes the client, server, and numerous tools for general management of your MySQL installation. Select Typical as the installation method and click Next to continue.

FIGURE 2.6
Select an
installation
type.

3. Confirm your choice in the next screen and click the Install button to continue. The installation process takes over and installs files in their proper locations.

4. When the installation is complete, you have the option of continuing to the MySQL Instance Configuration Wizard. This wizard is highly recommended because it creates a custom my.ini file tailored to your particular needs. To continue to the MySQL Instance Configuration Wizard, check the Launch the MySQL Instance Configuration Wizard check box and click the Finish button, as shown in Figure 2.7.

FIGURE 2.7
MySQL has
been installed.
Now continue
to the MySQL
Instance
Configuration
Wizard.

5. When you see the MySQL Instance Configuration Wizard Welcome screen, click the Next button to go to the next step in the wizard. You will see two options for server configuration: Detailed and Standard. We use the Detailed

Configuration option so that you can see all the options available to you. If you decide to select the Standard Configuration option, you must manually modify the resulting my.ini file to achieve the configuration you want. Select the Detailed Configuration radio button, and then click Next to continue.

6. The next selection you must make is shown in Figure 2.8. In this step, you select the type of machine you are running: Developer Machine, Server Machine, or Dedicated MySQL Server Machine. Your selection on this screen determines the allotments for memory, disk, and processor usage. If you are using MySQL on your personal machine for testing purposes, select the Developer Machine option. If MySQL is running on a machine with other server software and can take up more system resources than if you were running it on your personal machine, select the Server Machine option. Select the Dedicated MySQL Server Machine option if MySQL is the primary service running on the machine and can take up the bulk of the system resources. After making your selection, click Next to continue.

FIGURE 2.8
Select your server type as part of the MySQL configuration.

7. The next configuration option pertains to database usage. The options are Multifunctional Database, for both InnoDB and MyISAM storage engines, with resources split evenly between the two; Transactional Database, which enables both InnoDB and MyISAM, but dedicates the most server resources to InnoDB; and Non-Transactional Database Only, which disables InnoDB and applies all resources to MyISAM. Unless you know exactly what your database will be used for, select the Multifunctional Database radio button and click Next to continue.

8. If you have selected a database usage option that includes the InnoDB storage engine, the next step in the configuration process enables you to configure the

disk location and storage thresholds. The defaults are shown in Figure 2.9, which you can simply confirm by clicking Next to continue, or you can change these settings and then click Next to continue with your custom settings in place.

FIGURE 2.9
Tune the disk usage options for the InnoDB storage engine.

9. The next configuration option determines the number of concurrent connections to your MySQL server. Your setting will depend on the amount of traffic and database usage by your website or application. The default setting is Decision Support (DSS)/OLAP, which has a maximum number of 100 concurrent connections with an average of 20 assumed. The Online Transaction Processing (OLTP) option has a maximum of 500 concurrent connections, and the Manual setting allows you to select a number from a drop-down list or enter your own. Make your selection and click Next to continue.

10. The Networking Options screen is next in the configuration sequence. Here you enable or disable TCP/IP networking and configure the port number used to connect to MySQL—the default is 3306, but you can use any unused port you choose. The other option on this screen is to enable or disable strict mode; enabling strict mode is recommended unless you know what you're changing. See http://dev.mysql.com/doc/refman/5.5/en/server-sql-mode.html for more information. Make your selections and click Next to continue.

NOTE

Remember to modify your firewall rules to allow traffic to flow on port 3306 or whichever port you decide to use for MySQL.

11. After the Networking Options screen come the character set options. The default option is Standard Character Set, which results in Latin1 being used

throughout your database. You can also select the Best Support for Multilingualism option, which results in UTF8 as the character set; UTF8 allows you to store multiple languages in a single character set. If you want to use a specific character set, select the Manual Selected Default Character Set radio button, and then select the appropriate character set from the drop-down list. After making your selection, click Next to continue.

12. It is recommended that MySQL be installed as a service. Check the Install as Windows Service check box and select a name for the service. Optionally, check the Launch the MySQL Server Automatically check box. You also have the option of adding the MySQL `bin` directory to your Windows PATH for easier invocation of MySQL from the `cmd` prompt; check the box if this is appropriate for you. When you have completed your selections, click Next to continue.

13. The Security Options configuration screen is the most important screen of all. As shown in Figure 2.10, use this configuration screen to set a root password. Enter the password twice to confirm it. Do *not* check the Enable Root Access from Remote Machines check box unless you really know what you're doing; typically, root connections are allowed only from `localhost`. In addition, you can create an anonymous account, but doing so is not recommended for security reasons. After completing the configuration options in this screen, click Next to continue.

FIGURE 2.10
Creating a password for root during MySQL configuration.

14. One step remains in the configuration sequence, and that is to click the Execute button to start the process. After the wizard has made it through the various configuration steps, you will see a confirmation screen, as shown in Figure 2.11, indicating the configuration file has been created and the MySQL service has been started. Click Finish to close the wizard.

FIGURE 2.11
The MySQL
Configuration
Wizard com-
pletes its tasks.

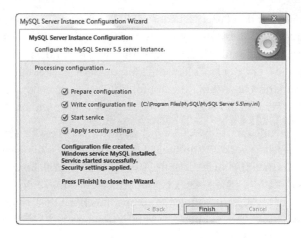

The completion of the installation and configuration wizards results in a running MySQL service and a custom my.ini file in the C:\Program Files\MySQL\MySQL Server 5.5\ directory.

TIP

You can manually edit the my.ini file with any text editor. After making changes, you must restart your MySQL server.

Now that MySQL has been started, skip to the "Basic Security Guidelines" section later in this chapter. If you experienced any issues with your installation, check the "Troubleshooting Your Installation" section.

Troubleshooting Your Installation

If you have any problems during the installation of MySQL, the first place you should look is Appendix A, "Problems and Common Errors," in the MySQL Manual, which is located at http://dev.mysql.com/doc/refman/5.5/en/problems.html.

The following are just a few of the common installation problems:

▶ On Linux/UNIX and Mac OS X, incorrect permissions do not allow you to start the MySQL daemon. If this is the case, be sure that you have changed owners and groups to match those indicated in the installation instructions.

▶ If you see the message Access denied when connecting to MySQL, be sure that you are using the correct username and password.

▶ If you see the message Can't connect to server, make sure that the MySQL daemon is running.

If you still have trouble after reading Appendix A in the MySQL Manual, sending an email to the MySQL mailing list (see http://lists.mysql.com/ for more information) will likely produce results. You can also purchase support contracts from MySQL AB.

Basic Security Guidelines

Regardless of whether you are running MySQL on Windows, Linux/UNIX, or Mac OS X, and no matter whether you administer your own server or use a system provided to you by your Internet service provider, you must understand basic security guidelines. If you are accessing MySQL through your Internet service provider, there are several aspects of server security that you, as a non-root user, should not be able to modify or circumvent. Unfortunately, many Internet service providers pay no mind to security guidelines, leaving their clients exposed—and for the most part, unaware of the risk.

Starting MySQL

Securing MySQL begins with the server startup procedure. If you are not the administrator of the server, you cannot change this, but you can certainly check it out and report vulnerabilities to your Internet service provider.

If your MySQL installation is on Linux/UNIX or Mac OS X, your primary concern should be the owner of the MySQL daemon—it should not be root. Running the daemon as a non-root user such as mysql or database limits the ability of malicious individuals to gain access to the server and overwrite files.

TIP

You can verify the owner of the process using the ps (process status) command on your Linux/UNIX or Mac OS X system.

If you see that MySQL is running as root on your system, immediately contact your Internet service provider and complain. If you are the server administrator, you should start the MySQL process as a non-root user or specify the preferred username in the startup command line:

```
# mysqld --user=non_root_user_name
```

For example, if you want to run MySQL as user mysql, use this command:

```
# mysqld --user=mysql
```

However, the recommended method for starting MySQL is through the `mysqld_safe` startup script in the `bin` directory of your MySQL installation:

```
# bin/mysqld_safe --user=mysql &
```

Securing Your MySQL Connection

You can connect to the MySQL monitor (command-line interface) or other MySQL applications in several different ways, each of which has its own security risks. If your MySQL installation is on your own workstation, you have less to worry about than users who have to use a network connection to reach their server.

If MySQL is installed on your workstation, your biggest security concern is leaving your workstation unattended with your MySQL monitor or MySQL GUI administration tool up and running. In this type of situation, anyone can walk over and delete data, insert bogus data, or shut down the server. Use a screensaver or lock-screen mechanism with a password if you must leave your workstation unattended in a public area.

If MySQL is installed on a server outside your network, the security of the connection should be of some concern. As with any transmission of data over the Internet, data can be intercepted. If the transmission is unencrypted, the person who intercepted the data can piece it together and use the information. Suppose that the unencrypted transmission is your MySQL login information; a rogue individual now has access to your database, masquerading as you.

One way to prevent this from happening is to connect to MySQL through a secure connection such as Secure Shell (SSH), through which all transmissions to and from the remote machine are encrypted. Similarly, if you use a web-based administration interface, such as the highly recommended phpMyAdmin (see http://www.phpmyadmin.net/ for more information, and note that phpMyAdmin is installed as part of the XAMPP-based quick-start installation in Chapter 1, "Installation QuickStart Guide with XAMPP") or another tool used by your Internet service provider, access that tool over a secure HTTP connection.

In the next section, you learn about the MySQL privilege system, which helps secure your database even further.

Introducing the MySQL Privilege System

The MySQL privilege system is always on. The first time you try to connect, and for each subsequent action, MySQL checks the following three things:

▶ Where you are accessing from (your host)

▶ Who you say you are (your username and password)

▶ What you're allowed to do (your command privileges)

All this information is stored in the database called mysql, which is automatically created when MySQL is installed. There are several privilege-related tables in the mysql database, such as the following:

▶ **columns_priv**—Defines user privileges for specific fields within a table

▶ **db**—Defines the permissions for all databases on the server

▶ **host**—Defines the acceptable hosts that can connect to a specific database

▶ **procs_priv**—Defines user privileges for stored routines

▶ **tables_priv**—Defines user privileges for specific tables within a database

▶ **user**—Defines the command privileges for a specific user

These tables will become more important to you later in this chapter as you add a few users to MySQL. For now, just remember that these tables exist and must have relevant data in them for users to complete actions.

Understanding the Two-Step Authentication Process

As you've learned, MySQL checks three things during the authentication process. The actions associated with these three things are performed in two steps:

1. MySQL looks at the host you are connecting from and the username and password pair you are using. If your host is allowed to connect, your password is correct for your username, and the username matches one assigned to the host, MySQL moves to the second step.

2. For whichever SQL command you are attempting to use, MySQL verifies that your user has permissions to perform that action for that database, table, and field.

If step 1 fails, you see an error about it and you cannot continue on to step 2. For example, suppose that you are connecting to MySQL with a username of joe and a password of abc123 and you want to access a database called myDB. You will receive an error message if any of those connection variables is incorrect for any of the following reasons:

▶ Your password is incorrect.

▶ Username joe doesn't exist.

▶ User joe can't connect from localhost.

▶ User joe can connect from localhost but cannot use the myDB database.

You may see an error like the following:

```
# mysql -h localhost -u joe -pabc123 test
Error 1045: Access denied for user: 'joe@localhost' (Using password: YES)
```

If user joe with a password of abc123 is allowed to connect from localhost to the myDB database, MySQL checks the actions that joe can perform in step 2 of the process. For our purposes, suppose that joe is allowed to select data but is not allowed to insert data. The sequence of events and errors would look like the following:

```
# mysql -h localhost -u joe -pabc123 test
Reading table information for completion of table and column names
You can turn off this feature to get a quicker startup with -A

Welcome to the MySQL monitor.  Commands end with ; or \g.
Your MySQL connection id is 12 to server version: 5.5.21-log
Type 'help;' or '\h' for help. Type '\c' to clear the buffer.

mysql> SELECT * FROM test_table;
+----+------------+
| id | test_field |
+----+------------+
|  1 | blah       |
|  2 | blah blah  |
+----+------------+
2 rows in set (0.0 sec)

mysql> INSERT INTO test_table VALUES ('', 'my text');
Error 1044: Access denied for user: 'joe@localhost' (Using password: YES)
```

Action-based permissions are common in applications with several levels of administration. For example, if you have created an application containing personal financial data, you might grant only SELECT privileges to entry-level staff members, but INSERT and DELETE privileges to executive-level staff with security clearances.

In most cases when you are accessing MySQL through an Internet service provider, you have only one user and one database available to you. By default, that user has access to all tables in that database and is allowed to perform all commands. In this case, the responsibility is yours as the developer to create a secure application through your programming.

However, if you are the administrator of your own server, or if your Internet service provider allows you to add as many databases and users as you want and to modify the access privileges of your users, you can do so as described in the following subsections.

Adding Users to MySQL

Administering your server through a third-party application might afford you a simple method for adding users by using a wizard-like process or a graphical interface. However, adding users through the MySQL monitor is not difficult, especially if you understand the security checkpoints used by MySQL, which you just learned.

The simplest method for adding new users is the GRANT command. By connecting to MySQL as the root user, you can issue one command to set up a new user. The other method is to issue INSERT statements into all the relevant tables in the mysql database, which requires you to know all the fields in the tables used to store permissions. This method works just as well but is more complicated than the simple GRANT command. The simple syntax of the GRANT command is shown here:

```
GRANT privileges
ON databasename.tablename
TO username@host
IDENTIFIED BY "password";
```

Following are some of the common privileges you can grant. (For a complete list, see the GRANT entry in the MySQL Manual at http://dev.mysql.com/doc/refman/5.5/en/grant.html.)

- **ALL**—Gives the user all common privileges.
- **ALTER**—User can alter (modify) tables, columns, and indexes.
- **CREATE**—User can create databases and tables.
- **DELETE**—User can delete records from tables.
- **DROP**—User can drop (delete) tables and databases.
- **FILE**—User can read and write files; this privilege is used to import or dump data.
- **INDEX**—User can add or delete indexes.
- **INSERT**—User can add records to tables.

▶ **PROCESS**—User can view and stop system processes; only trusted users should be able to do this.

▶ **RELOAD**—User can issue FLUSH statements; only trusted users should be able to do this.

▶ **SELECT**—User can select records from tables.

▶ **SHUTDOWN**—User can shut down the MySQL server; only trusted users should be able to do this.

▶ **UPDATE**—User can update (modify) records in tables.

If, for instance, you want to create a user called john with a password of 99hjc!5, with SELECT and INSERT privileges on all tables in the database called myDB, and you want this user to be able to connect from any host, use this command:

```
GRANT SELECT, INSERT
ON myDB.*
TO john@"%"
IDENTIFIED BY "99hjc!5";
```

Note the use of two wildcards: * and %. These wildcards replace values. In this example, * replaces the entire list of tables, and % replaces a list of all hosts in the known world—a very long list indeed.

Here's another example of adding a user with the GRANT command, this time to add a user called jane with a password of 45sdg11, with ALL privileges on a table called employees in the database called myCompany. This new user can connect only from a specific host:

```
GRANT ALL
ON myCompany.employees
TO jane@janescomputer.company.com
IDENTIFIED BY "45sdg11";
```

If you know that janescomputer.company.com has an IP address of 63.124.45.2, you can substitute that address in the hostname portion of the command, as follows:

```
GRANT ALL
ON myCompany.employees
TO jane@janescomputer.company.com
IDENTIFIED BY "45sdg11";
```

One note about adding users: Always use a password and make sure that the password is a good one!

If you use the GRANT command to add users, the changes take immediate effect. To make absolutely sure of this, you can issue the FLUSH PRIVILEGES command in the MySQL monitor to reload the privilege tables.

Removing User Privileges

Removing privileges is as simple as adding them; instead of the GRANT command, you use REVOKE. The REVOKE command syntax is as follows:

```
REVOKE privileges
ON databasename.tablename
FROM username@hostname;
```

In the same way that you can grant permissions using INSERT commands, you can also revoke permissions by issuing DELETE commands to remove records from tables in the mysql database. However, this requires that you be familiar with the fields and tables, and it is much easier and safer to use REVOKE.

To revoke the ability for user john to INSERT items in the myCompany database, you issue this REVOKE statement:

```
REVOKE privileges
ON databasename.tablename
FROM username@hostname;
```

Changes made to the data in the privilege tables happen immediately, but for the server to be aware of your changes, issue the FLUSH PRIVILEGES command in the MySQL monitor.

Summary

Thanks to a wizard-based installation method, installing MySQL on Windows and Mac OS X is a simple process. Linux/UNIX users do not have a wizard-based installation process, but it is not difficult to follow a simple set of commands to unpack the MySQL client and server binaries. Linux/UNIX users can also use RPMs for installation.

Security is always a priority, and you can take several steps to ensure a safe and secure installation of MySQL. Even if you are not the administrator of the server, you should be able to recognize security breaches and raise a ruckus with the server administrator.

The MySQL server should never run as the root user. In addition, named users within MySQL should always have a password, and their access privileges should be well defined.

MySQL uses the privilege tables in a two-step process for each request that is made. MySQL needs to know who you are and where you are connecting from, and each piece of this information must match an entry in its privilege tables. Also, the user whose identity you are using must have specific permission to perform the type of request you are making.

You can add user privileges using the GRANT command, which uses a simple syntax to add entries to the user table in the mysql database. The REVOKE command, which is equally simple, is used to remove those privileges.

Q&A

Q. *How do I completely remove a user? The REVOKE command just eliminates the privileges.*

A. To completely remove a user from the privilege table, you have to issue a specific DELETE query from the user table in the mysql database.

Q. *What if I tell my Internet service provider to stop running MySQL as root and it won't?*

A. Switch providers. If your Internet service provider doesn't recognize the risks of running something as important as your database as the root user and doesn't listen to your request, find another provider. There are providers with plans as low as $2.95/month (or even free) that do not run important processes as the root user.

Workshop

The workshop is designed to help you review what you've learned and begin putting your knowledge into practice.

Quiz

1. True or false: SSH is a perfectly acceptable method to securely connect to MySQL from a remote host.

2. Which three pieces of information does MySQL check each time a request is made?

3. What command would you use to grant SELECT, INSERT, and UPDATE privileges to a user named bill on localhost to all tables on the BillDB database? Also, what piece of information is missing from this statement that is recommended for security purposes?

Answers

1. True. SSH encrypts data between hosts and therefore enables you to securely connect to your server.

2. Who you are, where you are accessing from, and what actions you're allowed to perform.

3. The command is as follows:

```
GRANT SELECT, INSERT, UPDATE
ON BillDB.*
TO bill@localhost;
```

The important missing piece is a password for the user.

Activities

1. Think of situations in which you might want to restrict command access at the table level. For example, you wouldn't want the intern-level administrator to have shutdown privileges for the corporate database.

2. If you have administrative privileges in MySQL, issue several GRANT commands to create dummy users. It doesn't matter whether the tables and databases you name are actually present.

3. Use REVOKE to remove some of the privileges of the users you created in activity 2.

CHAPTER 3

Installing and Configuring Apache

In this chapter, you learn the following:

▶ How to install the Apache server
▶ How to make configuration changes to Apache
▶ Where Apache log and configuration files are stored

In this chapter, you install the Apache web server and familiarize yourself with its main components, including log and configuration files.

Current and Future Versions of Apache

The Apache HTTPD server website at http://httpd.apache.org shows announcements for releases of the Apache 2.0.x, Apache 2.2.x, and Apache 2.4.x versions. As you can understand by the version numbers, Apache 2.0.x is the oldest of the three versions. The Apache Software Foundation maintains all three versions, but the features in Apache 2.4.x include the latest and greatest; it is the version used in this chapter. However, if you choose to install (or already have installed either in a local or external development environment) Apache 2.2.x or even Apache 2.0.x, all the PHP and MySQL code in this book will still work as described. In fact, you will find a number of hosting providers still using Apache 2.0.x—not even Apache 2.2.x, let alone the newest Apache 2.4.x branch. If you experience any issues with installing Apache 2.4.x as described in this chapter, try an earlier version (for example, Apache 2.2.x); the installation instructions are remarkably similar. The installation instructions in this chapter refer to Apache HTTPD server version 2.4.1 except where noted, which is the best available version of the software at the time of this writing.

The Apache Software Foundation uses minor and revision numbers for updates containing security enhancements or bug fixes. Neither minor nor revision releases follow a set release schedule. When enhancements or fixes are added to the code and thoroughly tested, the Apache Software Foundation releases a new version.

By the time you purchase this book, the version number might have changed to 2.4.1 or later. If so, read the list of changes, which is linked from the download area at http://httpd.apache.org/download.cgi, for any installation/configuration process changes. These processes make up the bulk of this chapter.

Although it is unlikely that any installation instructions will change between version updates, always check the changelog of software that you install and maintain. If a minor or revision change does occur while you are reading this book but the changelog notes no installation changes, just make a mental note and substitute the new version number wherever it appears in the installation instructions and accompanying figures.

Choosing the Appropriate Installation Method

You have several options when it comes to getting a basic Apache installation in place. Apache is open source, meaning that you can have access to the full source code of the software, which in turn enables you to build your own custom server. In addition, prebuilt Apache binary distributions are available for most modern UNIX platforms. Finally, Apache comes already bundled with a variety of Linux distributions, and you can even purchase commercial versions with support packages from vendors. The examples in this chapter teach you how to build Apache from source if you are using Linux/UNIX, and how to use the installer if you plan to run Apache on a Windows system.

Building from Source

Building from source gives you the greatest flexibility because it enables you to build a custom server, remove modules you do not need, and extend the server with third-party modules. Building Apache from source code enables you to easily upgrade to the latest versions and quickly apply security patches, whereas updated versions from vendors can take days or weeks to appear. The process of building Apache from source is not especially difficult for simple installations, but can grow in complexity when third-party modules and libraries are involved.

Installing a Binary

Linux/UNIX binary installations are available from vendors or you can download them from the Apache Software Foundation website. Binary installations provide a convenient way to install Apache for users with limited system administration knowledge or with no special configuration needs. Third-party commercial vendors provide prepackaged Apache installations together with an application server, additional modules, support, and so on. The Apache Software Foundation provides an installer for Windows systems—a platform where a compiler is less commonly available than in Linux/UNIX systems.

Installing Apache on Linux/UNIX

This section explains how to install a fresh build of Apache 2.4.1 on Linux/UNIX. The general steps necessary to successfully install Apache from source are as follows:

1. Download the software.

2. Run the configuration script.

3. Compile the code and install it.

The following sections describe these steps in detail.

Downloading the Apache Source Code

The official Apache download site is located at http://httpd.apache.org/download.cgi. You can find several versions of the Apache source code, packaged with different compression methods. The distribution files are first packed with the tar utility and then compressed with either the gzip tool or the compress utility. Download the *.tar.gz version if you have the gunzip utility installed on your system. This utility comes installed by default in open source operating systems such as FreeBSD and Linux. Download the *.tar.Z file if gunzip is not present in your system. (It isn't included in the default installation of many commercial UNIX operating systems.)

The file you want to download will be named something similar to httpd-VERSION.tar.gz, where VERSION is the most recent release of Apache. For example, Apache version 2.4.1 is distributed as a file named httpd-2.4.1.tar.gz. Keep the downloaded file in a directory reserved for source files, such as /usr/src/ or /usr/local/src/.

Uncompressing the Source Code

If you downloaded the tarball compressed with gzip (it will have a tar.gz suffix), you can uncompress it using the gunzip utility (part of the gzip distribution).

NOTE

> *Tarball* is a commonly used nickname for software packed using the tar utility.

You can uncompress and unpack the software by typing the following command:

```
# gunzip < httpd-2.4*.tar.gz | tar xvf -
```

Uncompressing the tarball creates a structure of directories, with the top-level directory named httpd-*VERSION*. Change your current directory to this top-level directory to prepare for configuring the software.

Preparing to Build Apache

You can specify which features the resulting binary will have by using the configure script in the top-level distribution directory. By default, Apache is compiled with a set of standard modules compiled statically and is installed in the /usr/local/apache2 directory. If you are happy with these settings, you can issue the following command to configure Apache:

```
# ./configure
```

However, in preparation for the PHP installation in Chapter 4, "Installing and Configuring PHP," you need to make sure that mod_so is compiled into Apache. This module, named for the UNIX shared object (*.so) format, enables the use of dynamic modules such as PHP with Apache. To configure Apache to install itself in a specific location (in this case, /usr/local/apache2/) and to enable the use of mod_so, issue the following command:

```
# ./configure --prefix=/usr/local/apache2 --enable-so
```

The purpose of the configure script is to figure out everything related to finding libraries, compile-time options, platform-specific differences, and so on, and to create a set of special files called *makefiles*. Makefiles contain instructions to perform different tasks, called *targets*, such as building Apache. The make utility reads these files and carries out the targets' tasks. If everything goes well, after executing configure, you will see a set of messages related to the different checks just performed and will return to the prompt:

```
...
configure ok
```

```
creating test/Makefile
config.status: creating docs/conf/httpd.conf
...
config.status: executing default commands
#
```

If the `configure` script fails, warnings appear, alerting you to track down additional software that must be installed, such as compilers or libraries. After you install any missing software, you can try the `configure` command again, after deleting the `config.log` and `config.status` files from the top-level directory.

CAUTION

If the configuration process ends with a warning that you do not have APR installed, go to httpd://apr.apache.org/ and download both the APR and APR-util packages, and unpack them in the `srclib` subdirectory of your `httpd-VERSION` source directory. Once they are installed, rerun the `configure` command.

Similarly, if the configuration process ends with a warning that you do not have PCRE installed, go to http://www.pcre.org and download the files and install it on your system according to the instructions found at the website. Once installed, rerun the configure command.

Both of these requirements are changes in the requirements for the Apache 2.4.x installation process, different from the Apache 2.2.x process.

Building and Installing Apache

The make utility reads the information stored in the makefiles and builds the server and modules. Type **make** at the command line to build Apache. You will see several messages indicating the progress of the compilation, and you will end up back at the prompt. After compilation is finished, you can install Apache by typing **make install** at the prompt. The makefiles install files and directories and return you to the prompt:

```
...
Installing header files
Installing build system files
Installing man pages and online manual
...
make[1]: Leaving directory '/usr/local/bin/httpd-2.4.1'
#
```

The Apache distribution files should now be in the `/usr/local/apache2` directory, as specified by the `--prefix` switch in the `configure` command. To test that the `httpd` binary built correctly, type the following at the prompt:

```
# /usr/local/apache2/bin/httpd -v
```

You should see the following output (your version and build date will be different):

```
Server version: Apache/2.4.1 (Unix)
Server built:   March 12 2012 11:47:22
```

Unless you want to learn how to install Apache on Mac OS X or Windows, skip ahead to the "Apache Configuration File Structure" section to learn about the Apache configuration file.

Installing Apache on Mac OS X

Lucky you, Apache is already installed on Mac OS X! By default, the Apache server binary is located at /usr/sbin/httpd. Configuration files such as httpd.conf, the master configuration file for Apache, are in /etc/httpd. Because Apache is ready to go and fully prepared to use PHP, skip ahead to the "Apache Configuration File Structure" section to learn more about the Apache configuration file and how to use it.

NOTE

If you want to use an all-in-one package installer for Mac OS X, you can do so as shown with XAMPP in Chapter 1, "Installation QuickStart Guide with XAMPP," or you can install the MAMP package from http://www.mamp.info.

Installing Apache on Windows

CAUTION

At the time of this writing, Apache 2.4.x is not available for Windows. Therefore, the instructions that follow are for Apache 2.2.x. The installation process will be similar for Apache 2.4.x when it becomes available.

Apache 2.2 runs on most Windows platforms and offers increased performance and stability over earlier versions for Windows. You can build Apache from source, but because not many Windows users have compilers, this section deals with the MSI installer version.

Before installing Apache, make sure that you are not currently running a web server (for instance, a previous version of Apache or Microsoft Internet Information Services) on your machine. You might want to uninstall or otherwise disable existing servers. You can run several web servers, but they must run in different address and port combinations.

Before downloading the installer, take a moment—a very important moment—and look for a statement on the downloads page (found at http://httpd.apache.org/download.cgi) that says "If you are downloading the Win32 distribution, please read these important notes." The direct URL to these notes is http://www.apache.org/dist/httpd/binaries/win32/README.html.

The Apache Software Foundation maintains this page for the benefit of Windows users who want to run a version of the Apache server. On this page, there are notes for nearly every flavor of Windows still in use, and it is in your best interest to read the information presented. I guarantee that if you are running Apache as either a production or development server, you will find relevant information on the notes page.

When you're ready to begin the installation, look for the link labeled Win32 Binary including OpenSSL(MSI Installer). After you download the installer, double-click the file to start the installation process. You will get a welcome screen, as shown in Figure 3.1.

FIGURE 3.1
The Windows installer welcome screen.

Click Next to continue the installation process, and you will be prompted to accept the Apache license. Basically, the license says that you can do whatever you want with the software—including making proprietary modifications—except claim that you wrote it, but be sure to read the license so that you fully understand the terms.

After you accept the license, the installer presents you with a brief introduction to Apache. Following that, it asks you to provide basic information about your computer, as shown in Figure 3.2. This includes the full network address for the server (for instance, `mycomputer.mydomain.com`) and the administrator's email address.

The server name is the name your clients will use to access your server, and the administrator email address is added to error messages so that visitors know how to contact you when something goes wrong.

FIGURE 3.2
The basic information screen.

Also on this screen, you are prompted to select which installation shortcuts should be installed—those for starting Apache as a service or those for starting Apache manually. Installing Apache as a service causes it to run every time Windows starts, and you can control it through the standard Windows service administration tools. Installing Apache for the current user requires you to start Apache manually and set the default port on which Apache listens to requests to 8080 (instead of 80). Select the appropriate radio button and click Next to continue.

TIP

If your machine does not have a full network address, use `localhost` or `127.0.0.1` as the server name.

The next screen enables you to choose the type of installation: typical or custom. A *typical installation* means that Apache binaries and documentation are installed, but headers and libraries are not. This is the best option to choose unless you plan to compile your own modules.

A *custom installation* enables you to choose whether to install header files or documentation. After selecting the target installation directory, which defaults to `c:\Program Files (x86)\Apache Software Foundation\Apache 2.2`, the program proceeds with the installation process. If everything goes well, it presents you with the final screen, shown in Figure 3.3.

FIGURE 3.3
The successful
installation
screen.

In the next section, you learn about the Apache configuration file and eventually start up your new server.

Apache Configuration File Structure

Apache keeps all its configuration information in text files. The main file is httpd.conf. This file contains directives and containers that enable you to customize your Apache installation. *Directives* configure specific settings of Apache, such as authorization, performance, and network parameters. *Containers* specify the context to which those settings refer. For example, authorization configuration can refer to the server as a whole, to a directory, or to a single file.

Directives

The following rules apply for Apache directive syntax:

- The directive arguments follow the directive name.

- The directive arguments are separated by spaces.

- The number and type of arguments vary from directive to directive; some have no arguments.

- A directive occupies a single line, but you can continue it on a different line by ending the previous line with a backslash character (\).

- The pound sign (#) should precede the directive, and must appear on its own line.

The Apache server documentation offers a quick reference for directives at http://httpd.apache.org/docs/2.4/mod/quickreference.html. You'll soon learn about some of the basic directives, but you should supplement your knowledge using the online documentation.

The Apache documentation for directives typically follows this model:

▶ **Description**—This entry provides a brief description of the directive.

▶ **Syntax**—This entry explains the format of the directive options. Compulsory parameters appear in italics, and optional parameters appear in italics and brackets.

▶ **Default**—If the directive has a default value, it appears here.

▶ **Context**—This entry details the containers or sections in which the directive can appear. The next section explains containers. The possible values are server config, virtual host, directory, and .htaccess.

▶ **Override**—Apache directives belong to different categories. The Override field specifies which directive categories can appear in .htaccess per-directory configuration files.

▶ **Status**—This entry indicates whether the directive is built in Apache (core), belongs to one of the bundled modules (base or extension, depending on whether they are compiled by default), is part of a multiprocessing module (MPM), or is bundled with Apache but not ready for use in a production server (experimental).

▶ **Module**—This entry indicates the module to which the directive belongs.

▶ **Compatibility**—This entry contains information about which versions of Apache support the directive.

Further explanation of the directive follows these entries in the documentation, and a reference to related directives or documentation might appear at the end.

Containers

Directive containers, also called *sections*, limit the scope for which directives apply. If directives are not inside a container, they belong to the default server scope (server config) and apply to the server as a whole.

These are the default Apache directive containers:

▶ **<VirtualHost>**—A VirtualHost directive specifies a virtual server. Apache enables you to host different websites with a single Apache installation. Directives inside this container apply to a particular website. This directive accepts a domain name or IP address and an optional port as arguments. You learn more about virtual hosts in Chapter 29, "Apache Performance Tuning and Virtual Hosting."

▶ **<Directory>, <DirectoryMatch>**—These containers allow directives to apply to a certain directory or group of directories in the filesystem. Directory containers take a directory or directory pattern argument. Enclosed directives apply to the specified directories and their subdirectories. The DirectoryMatch container allows regular expression patterns to be specified as an argument. For example, the following allows a match of all second-level subdirectories of the www directory and made up of four numbers, such as a directory named after a year and month (0212 for February 2012):

```
<DirectoryMatch "^/www/.*/[0-9]{4}">
```

▶ **<Location>, <LocationMatch>**—These containers allow directives to apply to certain requested URLs or URL patterns. They are similar to their Directory counterparts. LocationMatch takes a regular expression as an argument. For example, the following matches directories containing either "/my/data" or "/your/data":

```
<LocationMatch "/(my|your)/data">
```

▶ **<Files>, <FilesMatch>**—Similar to the Directory and Location containers, Files sections allow directives to apply to certain files or file patterns.

Containers surround directives, as shown in Listing 3.1.

LISTING 3.1   Container Directives Example

```
 1: <Directory "/some/directory">
 2: SomeDirective1
 3: SomeDirective2
 4: </Directory>
 5: <Location "/downloads/*.html">
 6: SomeDirective3
 7: </Location>
 8: <Files "\.(gif|jpg)">
 9: SomeDirective4
10: </Files>
```

Directives *SomeDirective1* and *SomeDirective2* apply to the directory `/some/directory` and its subdirectories. *SomeDirective3* applies to URLs referring to pages with the `.html` extension under the `/downloads/` URL. *SomeDirective4* applies to all files with `.gif` or `.jpg` extensions.

Conditional Evaluation

Apache provides support for conditional containers. Directives enclosed in these containers are processed only if certain conditions are met:

▶ **`<IfDefine>`**—Directives in this container are processed if a specific command-line switch is passed to the Apache executable. The directive in Listing 3.2 is processed only if the `-DMyModule` switch is passed to the Apache binary being executed. You can pass this directly or by modifying the `apachectl` script, as described in the "Apache-Related Commands" section later in this chapter.

IfDefine containers also allow you to negate the argument. That is, directives inside a `<IfDefine !MyModule>` section—notice the exclamation point before the *MyModule* name—are processed only if no `-DMyModule` parameter is passed as a command-line argument.

▶ **`<IfModule>`**—Directives in an `IfModule` section are processed only if the module passed as an argument is present in the web server. For example, Apache ships with a default `httpd.conf` configuration file that provides support for different MPMs. Only the configuration belonging to the MPM compiled into Apache is processed, as you can see in Listing 3.3. The purpose of the example is to illustrate that only one of the directive groups will be evaluated.

LISTING 3.2   `IfDefine` **Example**

```
1: <IfDefine MyModule>
2: LoadModule my_module modules/libmymodule.so
3: </IfDefine>
```

LISTING 3.3   `IfModule` **Example**

```
 1: <IfModule prefork.c>
 2: StartServers          5
 3: MinSpareServers       5
 4: MaxSpareServers      10
 5: MaxClients           20
 6: MaxRequestsPerChild   0
 7: </IfModule>
 8:
 9: <IfModule worker.c>
10: StartServers          3
```

```
11: MaxClients            8
12: MinSpareThreads       5
13: MaxSpareThreads      10
14: ThreadsPerChild      25
15: MaxRequestsPerChild   0
16: </IfModule>
```

The ServerRoot Directive

The ServerRoot directive takes a single argument: a directory path pointing to the directory where the server lives. All relative path references in other directives are relative to the value of ServerRoot. If you compiled Apache from source on Linux/UNIX, as described earlier in this chapter, the default value of ServerRoot is /usr/local/apache2. The ServerRoot for Mac OS X users defaults to /Library/WebServer. If you used the Windows installer, the ServerRoot is C:\Program Files (x86)\Apache Software Foundation\Apache 2.2\.

Per-Directory Configuration Files

Apache uses per-directory configuration files to allow directives to exist outside the main configuration file, httpd.conf. These special files can be placed in the filesystem. Apache processes the content of these files if a document is requested in a directory containing one of these files or any subdirectories under it. The contents of all the applicable per-directory configuration files are merged and processed. For example, if Apache receives a request for the /usr/local/apache2/htdocs/index.html file, it looks for per-directory configuration files in the /, /usr, /usr/local, /usr/local/apache2, and /usr/local/apache2/htdocs directories, in that order.

CAUTION

Enabling per-directory configuration files has a performance penalty. Apache must perform expensive disk operations looking for these files in every request, even if the files do not exist.

Per-directory configuration files are called .htaccess by default. This is for historical reasons; they originally protected access to directories containing HTML files.

The AccessFileName directive enables you to change the name of the per-directory configuration files from .htaccess to something else. It accepts a list of filenames that Apache will use when looking for per-directory configuration files.

To determine whether you can override a directive in the per-directory configuration file, check whether the Context: field of the directive syntax definition contains

.htaccess. Apache directives belong to different groups, as specified in the Override field in the directive syntax description. Possible values for the Override field are as follows:

- ▶ **AuthConfig**—Directives controlling authorization

- ▶ **FileInfo**—Directives controlling document types

- ▶ **Indexes**—Directives controlling directory indexing

- ▶ **Limit**—Directives controlling host access

- ▶ **Options**—Directives controlling specific directory features

You can control which of these directive groups can appear in per-directory configuration files by using the AllowOverride directive. AllowOverride can also take an All or a None argument. All means that directives belonging to all groups can appear in the configuration file. None disables per-directory files in a directory and any of its subdirectories. Listing 3.4 shows how to disable per-directory configuration files for the server as a whole. This improves performance and is the default Apache configuration.

LISTING 3.4 Disabling Per-Directory Configuration Files

```
1: <Directory />
2: AllowOverride none
3: </Directory>
```

Apache Log Files

Apache includes two log files by default. The access_log file is for tracking client requests. The error_log file is for recording important events, such as errors or server restarts. These files don't exist until you start Apache the first time. The names of the files are access.log and error.log in Windows platforms.

The access_log File

When a client requests a file from the server, Apache records several parameters associated with the request, including the IP address of the client, the document requested, the HTTP status code, and the current time. Listing 3.5 shows an example of access_log entries. Chapter 26, "Logging and Monitoring Web Server Activity," shows you how to modify which parameters are logged.

LISTING 3.5 `access_log` **Entries**

```
1: 127.0.0.1 - - [12/Mar/202:08:33:25 -0700] "GET / HTTP/1.1" 200 44
2: 127.0.0.1 - - [12/Mar/2012:08:33:25 -0700] "GET /favicon.ico HTTP/1.1" 404 209
```

The `error_log` File

The `error_log` file includes error messages, startup messages, and any other significant events in the life cycle of the server. This is the first place to look when you have a problem with Apache. Listing 3.6 shows an example of `error_log` entries.

LISTING 3.6 `error_log` **Entries**

```
1: Starting the Apache2.4 service [The Apache2.4 service is running.]
2: Apache/2.4.1 (Unix) configured -- resuming normal operations
3: [Tue Mar 13 08:29:34 2012] [notice] Server built: Mar 12 2012 11:47:22
4: [Tue Mar 13 08:29:34 2012] [notice] Parent: Created child process 3504
5: [Tue Mar 13 08:29:35 2012] [notice] Child 3504: Child process is running
6: [Tue Mar 13 08:29:35 2012] [notice] Child 3504: Acquired the start mutex.
```

Additional Files

The `httpd.pid` file contains the process ID of the running Apache server. You can use this number to send signals to Apache manually, as described in the next section. The `scoreboard` file, the present on Linux/UNIX Apache, is used by the process-based MPMs to communicate with their children. In general, you do not need to worry about these files.

Apache-Related Commands

The Apache distribution includes several executables. This section covers only the server binary and related scripts. Chapter 25, "Restricting Access to Your Applications," and Chapter 29, "Apache Performance Tuning and Virtual Hosting," cover additional utilities included with the Apache distribution.

Apache Server Binary

The name of the Apache executable is `httpd` in Linux/UNIX and Mac OS X, and `httpd.exe` in Windows. It accepts several command-line options, some of which are described in Table 3.1. You can get a complete listing of options by typing **/usr/local/apache2/bin/httpd -h** on Linux/UNIX, by typing **/usr/sbin/httpd -h** on Mac OS X, or by typing **httpd.exe -h** from a command prompt on Windows.

TABLE 3.1 Some `httpd` Options

Option	Meaning
-D	Allows you to pass a parameter that can be used for <IfDefine> section processing
-l	Lists compiled-in modules
-v	Shows version number and server compilation time
-f	Allows you to pass the location of `httpd.conf` if it differs from the compile-time default

After Apache is running, you can use the `kill` command on Linux/UNIX and Mac OS X to send signals to the parent Apache process. Signals provide a mechanism to send commands to a process. To send a signal, execute the following command:

`# kill -SIGNAL pid`

In this syntax, *pid* is the process ID, and *SIGNAL* is one of the following:

▶ **HUP**—Stop the server

▶ **USR1** or **WINCH**—Graceful restart; which signal to use depends on the underlying operating system

▶ **SIGHUP**—Restart

If you make some changes to the configuration files and you want them to take effect, you must signal Apache that the configuration has changed. You can do this by stopping and starting the server or by sending a restart signal. This tells Apache to reread its configuration.

A normal restart can result in a momentary pause in service. A graceful restart takes a different approach: Each thread or process serving a client continues processing the current request, but when it finishes, it is killed and replaced by a new thread or process with the new configuration. This allows seamless operation of the web server with no downtime.

On Windows, you can signal Apache using the `httpd.exe` executable. Some commands are listed here:

▶ **httpd.exe -k restart**—Tells Apache to restart

▶ **httpd.exe -k graceful**—Tells Apache to do a graceful restart

▶ **httpd.exe -k stop**—Tells Apache to stop

You can access shortcuts to these commands in the Start menu entries that the Apache installer created. If you installed Apache as a service, you can start or stop Apache by using the Windows service interface: In Control Panel, select Administrative Tasks and then click the Services icon.

Apache Control Script

Although it is possible to control Apache on Linux/UNIX using the httpd binary, it is recommended that you use the apachectl tool. The apachectl support program wraps common functionality in an easy-to-use script. To use apachectl, type the following:

```
# /usr/local/apache2/bin/apachectl command
```

In this syntax, command can be stop, start, restart, or graceful. You can also edit the contents of the apachectl script to add extra command-line options. Some OS distributions provide you with additional scripts to control Apache; check the documentation included with your distribution.

Starting Apache for the First Time

Before you start Apache, verify that the minimal set of information is present in the Apache configuration file, httpd.conf. The following sections describe the basic information needed to configure Apache and to start the server.

Check Your Configuration File

You can edit the Apache httpd.conf file with your favorite text editor. In Linux/UNIX and Mac OS X, this probably means vi or emacs. In Windows, you can use Notepad or WordPad. You must remember to save the configuration file in plaintext, which is the only format Apache understands.

You might need to change just two parameters to enable you to start Apache for the first time: the name of the server and the address and port to which it is listening. The name of the server is the one Apache will use when it needs to refer to itself (for example, when redirecting requests).

Apache can usually figure out its server name from the IP address of the machine, but not always. If the server does not have a valid DNS (domain name service) entry, you might need to specify one of the IP addresses of the machine. If the server is not connected to a network (you might want to test Apache on a standalone machine), you can use the value 127.0.0.1, which is the loopback address. The default port value is 80. You might need to change this value if a server is already running in the machine at port 80 or if you do not have administrator permissions—on Linux/UNIX and Mac OS X systems, only the root user can bind to privileged ports (those with port numbers lower than 1024).

You can change both the listening address and the port values with the Listen directive. The Listen directive takes either a port number or an IP address and a port, separated by a colon. If you specify only the port, Apache listens on that port at all available IP addresses in the machine. If you provide an additional IP address, Apache listens at only that address and port combination. For example, Listen 80 tells Apache to listen for requests at all IP addresses on port 80. Listen 10.0.0.1:443 tells Apache to listen at only 10.0.0.1 on port 443.

The ServerName directive enables you to define the name the server will report in any self-referencing URLs. The directive accepts a DNS name and an optional port, separated by a colon. Make sure that ServerName has a valid value. Otherwise, the server will not function properly; for example, it will issue incorrect redirects.

On Linux/UNIX and Mac OS X platforms, you can use the User and Group directives to specify which user and group IDs the server will run as. The nobody user is a good choice for most platforms. However, there are problems in the HP-UX platform with this user ID, so you must create and use a different user ID, such as www.

Starting Apache

To start Apache on Linux/UNIX, change to the directory containing the apachectl script and execute the following command:

```
# /usr/local/apache2/bin/apachectl start
```

Mac OS X users can type the following at the prompt:

```
# /usr/sbin/httpd
```

To manually start Apache on Windows, click the Start link in the Control Apache Server section, within the Apache HTTP Server 2.2 program group in the Start menu. If you installed Apache as a service, you must start the Apache service instead.

If everything goes well, you can access Apache using a browser. A default installation page displays, such as the one shown in Figure 3.4. If you cannot start the web server or an error page appears instead, consult the "Troubleshooting" section that follows. Make sure that you are accessing Apache in one of the ports specified in the Listen directive—usually port 80 or 8080.

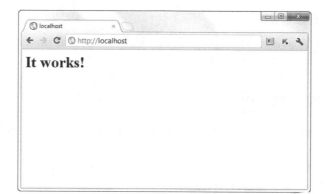

FIGURE 3.4
Apache has
been installed.

Troubleshooting

The following subsections describe several common problems that you might encounter the first time you start Apache.

Already an Existing Web Server

If a server is already running on the machine and is listening to the same IP address and port combination, Apache cannot start successfully. You will get an entry in the error log file indicating that Apache cannot bind to the port:

```
[crit] (48)Address already in use: make_sock: could not bind...[alert] no
  listening sockets available, shutting down
```

To solve this problem, you need to stop the running server or change the Apache configuration to listen on a different port.

No Permission to Bind to Port

You will get an error if you do not have administrator permissions and you try to bind to a privileged port (between 0 and 1024):

```
[crit] (13)Permission denied: make_sock: could not bind to address 10.0.0.2:80
[alert] no listening sockets available, shutting down
```

To solve this problem, you must either log on as the administrator before starting Apache or change the port number; 8080 is a commonly used nonprivileged port.

Access Denied

You might not be able to start Apache if you do not have permission to read the configuration files or to write to the log files. You will get an error similar to the following:

```
(13)Permission denied: httpd: could not open error log file
```

This problem can arise if the user who built and installed Apache is different from the user trying to run it.

Wrong Group Settings

You can configure Apache to run under a certain username and group. Apache has default values for the running server username and group. Sometimes the default value is not valid and you will get an error containing `setgid: unable to set group id`.

To solve this problem on Linux/UNIX and Mac OS X, you must change the value of the Group directive in the configuration file to a valid value. Check the `/etc/groups` file for existing groups.

Summary

This chapter explained different ways of getting an Apache web server installed and running on your Linux/UNIX, Mac OS X, or Windows machine. It covered both binary and source installation and explained the basic build-time options. In addition, you learned the location of the server configuration files and the syntax of the commands used to modify your Apache configuration. You learned about the two main log files: `access_log` and `error_log`. You also saw how to start and stop the server using the Apache control scripts or the Apache server binary on Linux/UNIX, Mac OS X, and Windows platforms.

Q&A

Q. *How can I start a clean build?*

A. If you need to build a new Apache from source and do not want the result of earlier builds to affect the new one, it is always a good idea to run the `make clean` command. Doing so takes care of cleaning up any existing binaries, intermediate object files, and so on.

Q. *Why are per-directory configuration files useful?*

A. Although per-directory configuration files have an effect on server perform-ance, they can be useful for delegated administration. Because per-directory configuration files are read every time a request is made, there is no need to restart the server when a change is made to the configuration.

You can allow users of your website to make configuration changes on their own without granting them administrator privileges. In this way, they can password-protect sections of their home pages, for example.

Q. *What do you mean by a valid ServerName directive?*

A. The DNS system associates IP addresses with domain names. The value of ServerName is returned when the server generates a URL. If you are using a certain domain name, you must make sure that it is included in your DNS sys-tem and will be available to clients visiting your site.

Workshop

The workshop is designed to help you review what you've learned and begin putting your knowledge into practice.

Quiz

1. How can you specify the location where you want to install Apache?

2. What is the main difference between the <Location> and <Directory> sec-tions?

3. What is the difference between a restart and a graceful restart?

Answers

1. Linux/UNIX users can use the --prefix option of the configure script. If an existing installation is present at that location, the configuration files are pre-served, but the binaries are replaced. On Windows, this location is set in the Installation Wizard.

2. Directory sections refer to filesystem objects; Location sections refer to ele-ments in the address bar of the web page.

3. During a normal restart, the server is stopped and then started, causing some requests to be lost. A graceful restart allows Apache children to continue to serve their current requests until they can be replaced with children running the new configuration.

Activities

1. Practice the various types of server shutdown and restart procedures.

2. Make some configuration changes, such as different port assignments and `ServerName` changes.

CHAPTER 4

Installing and Configuring PHP

In this chapter, you learn the following:

- ▶ How to install PHP
- ▶ How to test your PHP installation
- ▶ How to find help when things go wrong
- ▶ The basics of the PHP language

In this chapter, you acquire, install, and configure PHP and make some basic changes to your Apache installation.

Current and Future Versions of PHP

The installation instructions in this chapter refer to PHP version 5.4.0, which is the current version of the software.

The PHP Group uses revisions and minor releases for updates containing security enhancements or bug fixes. These releases do not follow a set release schedule; when enhancements or fixes are added to the code and are thoroughly tested, the PHP Group releases a new version with a new revision number.

It is possible that by the time you purchase this book the minor version number will have changed, to 5.4.1 or beyond. If that is the case, you should read the list of changes at http://www.php.net/ChangeLog-5.php for any installation/configuration process changes. These processes make up the bulk of this chapter.

Although it is unlikely that any installation instructions will change between minor version updates, always check the changelog of software that you install and maintain. If a revision does occur while you are reading this book but the changelog notes no installation changes, just make a mental note and substitute the new version number wherever it appears in the installation instructions and accompanying figures.

Building PHP on Linux/UNIX with Apache

This section examines one way of installing PHP with Apache on Linux/UNIX. The process is more or less the same for any UNIX-like operating system. Although you might be able to find prebuilt versions of PHP for your system, compiling PHP from source gives you greater control over the features built in to your binary.

To download the PHP distribution files, go to the home of PHP, http://www.php.net/, and follow the link to the Downloads section. Grab the latest version of the source code—for this example, we are using 5.4.0. Your distribution will be named something similar to php-*VERSION*.tar.gz, where *VERSION* is the most recent release number. This archive will be a compressed tar file, so you need to unpack it:

```
# gunzip < php-VERSION.tar.gz | tar xvf -
```

Keep the downloaded file in a directory reserved for source files, such as /usr/src/ or /usr/local/src/. After your distribution is unpacked, you should move to the PHP distribution directory:

```
# cd php-VERSION
```

In your distribution directory, you will find a script called configure. This script accepts additional information that is provided when the configure script is run from the command line. These command-line arguments control the features that PHP supports. This example includes the basic options you need to install PHP with Apache and MySQL support. We discuss some of the available configure options later in the chapter and throughout the book as they become relevant.

```
# ./configure  --prefix=/usr/local/php \
--with-mysqli=/usr/local/mysql/bin/mysql_config \
--with-apxs2=/usr/local/apache2/bin/apxs
```

CAUTION

> If you have installed MySQL or Apache in a different location than the paths indicated in the configuration shown here, ensure that you substitute the appropriate directory paths in the command.

After the `configure` script has run, you are returned to the prompt. For example:

```
...
Generating files
updating cache ./config.cache
creating ./config.status
creating php5.spec
creating main/build-defs.h
creating scripts/phpize
creating scripts/man1/phpize.1
creating scripts/php-config
creating scripts/man1/php-config.1
creating sapi/cli/php.1
creating main/php_config.h
creating main/internal_functions.c
creating main/internal_functions_cli.c
+--------------------------------------------------------------------+
| License:                                                           |
| This software is subject to the PHP License, available in this     |
| distribution in the file LICENSE.  By continuing this installation |
| process, you are bound by the terms of this license agreement.     |
| If you do not agree with the terms of this license, you must abort |
| the installation process at this point.                            |
+--------------------------------------------------------------------+

Thank you for using PHP.

#
```

From the prompt, issue the `make` command, followed by the `make install` command. These commands should end the process of PHP compilation and installation and return you to your prompt:

```
...
chmod 755 /usr/local/apache2/modules/libphp5.so
[activating module 'php5' in /usr/local/apache2/conf/httpd.conf]
Installing PHP CLI binary:        /usr/local/php/bin/
Installing PHP CLI man page:      /usr/local/php/php/man/man1/
Installing PHP CGI binary:        /usr/local/php/bin/
Installing build environment:     /usr/local/php/lib/php/build/
Installing header files:          /usr/local/php/include/php/
Installing helper programs:       /usr/local/php/bin/
  program: phpize
  program: php-config
Installing man pages:             /usr/local/php/php/man/man1/
  page: phpize.1
  page: php-config.1
...
#
```

You need to ensure that two very important files are copied to their correct locations. First, issue the following command to copy the development version of php.ini to its default location. You learn more about php.ini later in this chapter:

```
# cp php.ini-development /usr/local/lib/php.ini
```

Next, copy the PHP shared object file to its proper place in the Apache installation directory, if it has not already been placed there by the installation process; it usually will be, as you can see in the `make install` output, just shown:

```
# cp libs/libphp5.so /usr/local/apache2/modules/
```

You should now be able to configure and run Apache, but let's cover some additional configuration options before heading on to the "Integrating PHP with Apache on Linux/UNIX" section.

Additional Linux/UNIX Configuration Options

In the previous section, when we ran the PHP `configure` script, we included some command-line arguments that determined some features that the PHP engine will include. The `configure` script itself gives you a list of available options, including the ones we used. From the PHP distribution directory, type the following:

```
# ./configure --help
```

This command produces a long list, so you might want to add it to a file and read it at your leisure:

```
# ./configure --help > configoptions.txt
```

If you discover additional functionality you want to add to PHP after you install it, simply run the configuration and build process again. Doing so creates a new version of `libphp5.so` and places it in the Apache directory structure. All you have to do is restart Apache to load the new file.

Integrating PHP with Apache on Linux/UNIX

To ensure that PHP and Apache get along with one another, you need to check for—and potentially add—a few items to the `httpd.conf` configuration file. First, look for a line like the following:

```
LoadModule php5_module        modules/libphp5.so
```

If this line is not present or only appears with a pound sign (#) at the beginning of the line, you must add the line or remove the #. This line tells Apache to use the PHP shared object file created by the PHP build process (`libphp5.so`).

Next, look for this section:

```
#
# AddType allows you to add to or override the MIME configuration
# file mime.types for specific file types.
#
```

Add the following line to that section:

```
AddType application/x-httpd-php .php
```

This statement ensures that the PHP engine will parse files that end with the `.php` extension. Your selection of filenames might differ; you might want to parse all files ending with `*.html` as PHP, for example.

Save this file and then restart Apache. When you look in your `error_log`, you should see something like the following line:

```
[Tue Mar 13 10:42:47 2012] [notice] Apache/2.4.1 (Unix) PHP/5.4.0 configured
```

PHP is now part of the Apache web server. If you want to learn how to install PHP on a Mac OS X or Windows platforms, keep reading. Otherwise, you can skip ahead to the "Testing Your Installation" section.

Installing PHP on Mac OS X

There are a few different options for installing PHP with Apache on Mac OS X, including building from source as described in the previous section. Some users may find the simplest method is to install PHP from a precompiled binary package, such as those from MacPorts (at http://www.macports.org/) or as part of the all-in-one installation packages from XAMPP (as shown in Chapter 1, "Installation QuickStart Guide with XAMPP") or MAMP (at http://www.mamp.info). However, if you are comfortable with the command line, I recommend following the instructions in the previous section, "Building PHP on Linux/UNIX with Apache."

Installing PHP on Windows

Installing PHP on Windows requires nothing more than downloading the distribution file. To download the PHP distribution files, go to the home of PHP on Windows, http://windows.php.net/, and follow the link to the Downloads page. Grab the latest version of the thread-safe ZIP package—for this example, we are using 5.4.0. Your distribution will be named something similar to `php-VERSION.zip`, where `VERSION` is the most recent release number.

After the file downloads to your system, double-click it to launch your unzipping software. The distribution is packed up with relative pathnames already in place, so extract the files to a new directory called `C:\php\`, where it will place all the files and subdirectories under that new directory.

Next, go to the C:\php\ directory and copy the php.ini-development file to php.ini. Now, to get a basic version of PHP working with Apache, you need to make a few minor modifications to the Apache configuration file.

> On some Windows systems you might need to set an explicit environment variable in order for PHP to run correctly; setting it will not cause any harm so even if you are unsure if it is necessary, there's no reason not to. For information on adding the PHP directory to the PATH environment variable, see the entry in the PHP FAQ at http://www.php.net/manual/en/faq.installation.php#faq.installation.addtopath.

Integrating PHP with Apache on Windows

To ensure that PHP and Apache get along with one another, you need to add a few items to the httpd.conf configuration file. First, find a section that looks like this:

```
# Example:
# LoadModule foo_module modules/mod_foo.so
#
LoadModule access_module modules/mod_access.so
...
#LoadModule vhost_alias_module modules/mod_vhost_alias.so
```

At the end of this section, add the following:

```
LoadModule php5_module C:/php/php5apache2_2.dll
```

In addition, add the following to ensure Apache knows where php.ini resides:

```
PHPIniDir "C:/php/"
```

Next, look for this section:

```
#
# AddType allows you to add to or override the MIME configuration
# file mime.types for specific file types.
#
```

Add the following line:

```
AddType application/x-httpd-php .php
```

This statement ensures that the PHP engine will parse files that end with the .php extension. Your selection of filenames might differ; for example, you might want to parse all *.html files as PHP files.

Save the httpd.conf file and then restart Apache. The server should start without warning; PHP is now part of the Apache web server.

php.ini **Basics**

After you have compiled or installed PHP, you can still change its behavior
with the php.ini file. On Linux/UNIX systems, the default location for this file is
/usr/local/php/lib or the lib subdirectory of the PHP installation location you
used at configuration time. On a Windows system, this file should be in the PHP
directory or another directory as specified by the value of PHPIniDir in the Apache
httpd.conf file.

Directives in the php.ini file come in two forms: values and flags. *Value directives*
take the form of a directive name and a value separated by an equal sign. Possible
values vary from directive to directive. *Flag directives* take the form of a directive
name and a positive or negative term separated by an equal sign. Positive terms
include 1, On, Yes, and True. Negative terms include 0, Off, No, and False.
Whitespace is ignored.

On Windows systems, it is important to explicitly provide the value for the
extension_dir directive. If you installed PHP in C:\php then the value of
extension_dir should be "C:\php\ext".

NOTE

You can change your php.ini settings at any time, but after you do, you need to
restart the server for the changes to take effect. At some point, take time to read
through the php.ini file on your own to see the types of things that you can
configure.

Testing Your Installation

The simplest way to test your PHP installation is to create a small test script that
uses the phpinfo() function. This function produces a long list of configuration
information. Open a text editor and type the following line:

```
<?php phpinfo(); ?>
```

Save this file as phpinfo.php and place it in the document root of your web server—
the htdocs subdirectory of your Apache installation or the /Library/WebServer/
Documents directory on Mac OS X. Access this file using your web browser, and you
should see something like what is shown in Figure 4.1.

FIGURE 4.1
The results of
phpinfo().

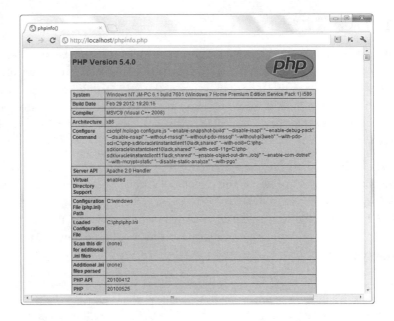

The exact output of phpinfo() depends on your operating system, PHP version, and configuration options.

Getting Installation Help

Help is always at hand on the Internet, particularly for problems concerning open source software. Wait a moment before you click the Send button, however. No matter how intractable your installation, configuration, or programming problem might seem, chances are you are not alone. Someone has probably already answered your question.

When you hit a brick wall, your first recourse should be to the official PHP site at http://www.php.net/ (particularly the annotated manual at http://www.php.net/manual/). If you still cannot find your answer, don't forget that the PHP site is searchable. The advice you are seeking may be lurking in a press release or a FAQ file. You can also search the mailing list archives at http://www.php.net/search.php. These archives represent a huge information resource with contributions from many of the great minds in the PHP community. Spend some time trying out a few keyword combinations.

If you are still convinced that your problem has not been addressed, you might well be doing the PHP community a service by exposing it. You can join the PHP mailing lists at http://www.php.net/mailing-lists.php. Although these lists often have high volume, you can learn a lot from them. If you are serious about PHP scripting, you should certainly subscribe to at least a digest list. After you've subscribed to the list that matches your concerns, consider posting your problem.

When you post a question, it is a good idea to include as much information as possible (without writing a novel). The following items are often pertinent:

- ▶ Your operating system

- ▶ The version of PHP you are running or installing

- ▶ The configuration options you chose

- ▶ Any output from the `configure` or `make` commands that preceded an installation failure

- ▶ A reasonably complete example of the code that is causing problems

Why all these cautions about posting a question to a mailing list? First, developing research skills will stand you in good stead. A good researcher can generally solve a problem quickly and efficiently. Posting a naive question to a technical list often results in a wait rewarded only by a message or two referring you to the archives where you should have begun your search for answers in the first place.

Second, remember that a mailing list is not analogous to a technical support call center. No one is paid to answer your questions. Despite this, you have access to an impressive pool of talent and knowledge, including that of some of the creators of PHP itself. A good question and its answer will be archived to help other coders. Asking a question that has already been answered several times just adds more noise.

Having said this, don't be afraid to post a problem to the list. PHP developers are a civilized and helpful breed, and by bringing a problem to the attention of the community, you might be helping others to solve the same problem.

The Basics of PHP Scripts

Let's jump straight in with a PHP script. To begin, open your favorite text editor. Like HTML documents, PHP files are made up of plain text. You can create them with any text editor, and most popular HTML editors and programming IDEs (integrated development environments) provide support for PHP.

TIP

A good website for finding PHP-friendly editors is at http://www.php-editors.com.

Type in the example in Listing 4.1 and save the file to the document root of your web server, using a name something like `first.php`.

Listing 4.1 A Simple PHP Script

```
1: <?php
2:     echo "<h1>Hello Web!</h1>";
3: ?>
```

If you are not working directly on the machine that will be serving your PHP script, you need to use a File Transfer Protocol (FTP) or Secure Copy (SCP) client to upload your saved document to the server. When the document is in place on the server, you should be able to access it using your browser. If all has gone well, you should see the script's output. Figure 4.2 shows the output from the `first.php` script.

FIGURE 4.2
Success: the output from `first.php`.

Beginning and Ending a Block of PHP Statements

When writing PHP, you need to inform the PHP engine that you want it to execute your commands. If you don't do this, the code you write will be mistaken for HTML and will be output to the browser. You can designate your code as PHP with special tags that mark the beginning and end of PHP code blocks. Table 4.1 shows four such PHP delimiter tags.

Table 4.1   PHP Start and End Tags

Tag Style	Start Tag	End Tag
Standard tags	`<?php`	`?>`
Short tags	`<?`	`?>`
ASP tags	`<%`	`%>`
Script tags	`<script language="php">`	`</script>`

Of the tags in Table 4.1, only the standard and script tags are guaranteed to work on any configuration. You must explicitly enable the short and ASP-style tags in your php.ini file.

To activate recognition for short tags, you must make sure that the short_open_tag switch is set to On in php.ini:

```
short_open_tag = On;
```

To activate recognition for the ASP-style tags, you must enable the asp_tags setting in php.ini:

```
asp_tags = On;
```

> To ensure portable, reusable code, it is best to use the standard tags rather than short tags or ASP-style tags for the simple reason that server configurations are unique—use the standard style because you know you can count on it as part of any configuration.

NOTE

After you have edited php.ini and restarted Apache, you should be able to use any of the four styles in your scripts. This is largely a matter of preference, although if you intend to include XML in your script, you should disable the short tags (`<? ?>`) and work with the standard tags (`<?php ?>`).

> The character sequence `<?` tells an XML parser to expect a processing instruction and is therefore often included in XML documents. If you include XML in your script and have short tags enabled, the PHP engine is likely to confuse XML processing instructions and PHP start tags. Disable short tags if you intend to incorporate XML in your document.

CAUTION

Let's run through some of the ways in which you can legally write the code in Listing 4.1. Given the configuration changes shown earlier, you can use any of the four PHP start and end tags that you have seen:

```
<?
echo "Hello Web!";
?>

<?php
echo "Hello Web!";
?>

<%
echo "Hello Web!";
%>

<script language="php">
echo "Hello Web!";
</script>
```

You can also put single lines of code in PHP on the same line as the PHP start and end tags:

```
<?php echo "Hello Web!"; ?>
```

Now that you know how to define a block of PHP code, let's take a closer look at the code in Listing 4.1 itself.

The `echo` and `print()` Statements

Simply put, you can use the `echo` statement to output data. In most cases, anything output by `echo` ends up viewable in the browser. Alternatively, you could have used the `print()` statement in place of the `echo` statement. Using `echo` or `print()` is a matter of taste; when you look at other people's scripts, you might see either used, which is why I included both here.

Referring back to the code you have seen so far, note the only line of code in Listing 4.1 ended with a semicolon. The semicolon informs the PHP engine that you have completed a statement, and is probably the most important bit of coding syntax you could learn at this stage.

A *statement* represents an instruction to the PHP engine. Broadly, it is to PHP what a sentence is to written or spoken English. A sentence should usually end with a period; a statement should usually end with a semicolon. Exceptions to this rule include statements that enclose other statements and statements that end a block of code. In most cases, however, failure to end a statement with a semicolon will confuse the PHP engine and result in an error.

Combining HTML and PHP

The script in Listing 4.1 is pure PHP. You can incorporate this into an HTML document by simply adding HTML outside the PHP start and end tags, as shown in Listing 4.2.

Listing 4.2 A PHP Script Incorporated into HTML

```
1: <!DOCTYPE html>
2: <html>
3: <head>
4: <title>A PHP script including HTML</title>
5: </head>
6: <body>
7: <h1><?php echo "hello world"; ?></h1>
8: </body>
9: </html>
```

As you can see, incorporating PHP code into a predominantly HTML document is simply a matter of typing in the code. The PHP engine ignores everything outside the PHP open and close tags. If you were to save the contents of Listing 4.2 as helloworld.php, place it in your document root, and then view it with a browser, as shown in Figure 4.3, you would see the string hello world in a bold heading. If you were to view the document source, as shown in Figure 4.4, the listing would look exactly like a normal HTML document.

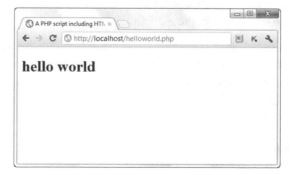

FIGURE 4.3
The output of helloworld.php as viewed in a browser.

FIGURE 4.4
The output of
helloworld.php
as HTML source
code.

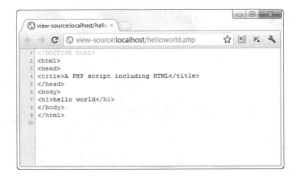

You can include as many blocks of PHP code as you need in a single document, interspersing them with HTML as required. Although you can have multiple blocks of code in a single document, they combine to form a single script. Any variables defined in the first block will usually be available to subsequent blocks.

Adding Comments to PHP Code

Code that seems clear at the time you write it can seem like a hopeless tangle when you try to amend it 6 months later. Adding comments to your code as you write can save you time later on and make it easier for other programmers to work with your code.

A *comment* is text in a script that is ignored by the PHP engine. Comments can make code more readable or annotate a script.

Single-line comments begin with two forward slashes (//)—the preferred style—or a single hash or pound sign (#). The PHP engine ignores all text between these marks and either the end of the line or the PHP close tag:

```
// this is a comment
#  this is another comment
```

Multiline comments begin with a forward slash followed by an asterisk (/*) and end with an asterisk followed by a forward slash (*/):

```
/*
this is a comment
none of this will
be parsed by the
PHP engine
*/
```

Summary

In this chapter, you learned how to install and configure PHP 5.4.0 for use with Apache on Linux/UNIX, Mac OS X, or Windows. You learned that various `config-ure` options in the Linux/UNIX build script can change the features that are supported. You learned about `php.ini` and how to change the values of its directives.

Using the `phpinfo()` function, you tested your installation and produced a list of its configuration values. You created a simple PHP script using a text editor. You examined four sets of tags that you can use to begin and end blocks of PHP code.

Finally, you learned how to use the `echo` and `print` statements to send data to the browser, and you brought HTML and PHP together into the same script. In the next chapter, you use these skills to test some of the fundamental building blocks of the PHP language, including variables, data types, and operators.

Q&A

Q. *This chapter covered an installation for Linux/UNIX, Mac OS X, or Windows, and the Apache web server. Does this mean that the material presented in this book will not apply to other servers and operating systems?*

A. No. One of PHP's great strengths is that it runs on multiple platforms. You can find installation instructions for different web servers and configuration directives for database support in the PHP Manual. Although the examples throughout this book are specifically geared toward the combination of PHP, MySQL, and Apache, only slight modifications are needed to work with the examples using different web servers or databases.

Q. *Which are the best start and end tags to use?*

A. It is largely a matter of preference. For the sake of portability, the standard tags (<?php ?>) are preferred.

Q. *What editors should I avoid when creating PHP code?*

A. Do not use word processors that format text for printing (Microsoft Word, for example). Even if you save files created using this type of editor in plaintext format, hidden characters are likely to creep into your code.

Q. *When should I comment my code?*

A. Again, this is a matter of preference. Some short scripts will be self-explanatory even after a long interval. For scripts of any length or complexity, you should comment your code. Comments in your code often save you time and frustration in the long run.

Workshop

The workshop is designed to help you review what you've learned and begin putting your knowledge into practice.

Quiz

1. From a Linux/UNIX operating system, how would you get help on configuration options (the options that you pass to the `configure` script in your PHP distribution)?

2. What line should you add to the Apache configuration file to ensure that the `.php` extension is recognized?

3. What is PHP's configuration file called?

4. Can a person browsing your website read the source code of PHP script you have successfully installed?

Answers

1. You can get help on configuration options by calling the `configure` script in the PHP distribution folder and passing it the `--help` argument:

```
./configure --help
```

2. This line ensures that Apache will treat files ending with the `.php` extension as PHP scripts:

```
AddType application/x-httpd-php .php
```

3. PHP's configuration file is called `php.ini`.

4. No, the user will see only the output of your script.

Activities

1. Install PHP on your system. If it is already in place, review your `php.ini` file and check your configuration.

2. Familiarize yourself with the process of creating, uploading, and running PHP scripts. In particular, create your own "Hello World" script. Add HTML code to it, and add additional blocks of PHP. Experiment with the different PHP delimiter tags. Which ones are enabled in your configuration? Take a look at your `php.ini` file to confirm your findings. Don't forget to add some comments to your code.

CHAPTER 5

The Building Blocks of PHP

In this chapter, you learn the following:

▶ About variables—what they are, why you need to use them, and how to use them

▶ How to define and access variables

▶ About data types

▶ About some of the more commonly used operators

▶ How to use operators to create expressions

▶ How to define and use constants

In this chapter, you get your hands dirty with some of the nuts and bolts of the PHP scripting language. Those of you new to programming might feel overwhelmed at times, but don't worry—you can always refer to this chapter later on. Concentrate on understanding the concepts, rather than memorizing the features covered, because these elements are repeated throughout the scripts in this book. Eventually you'll get it, if not the first time.

If you're already an experienced programmer, you should at least skim this chapter because it covers a few PHP-specific features with regard to global variables, data types, and changing types.

Variables

A *variable* is a special container that you can define, which then "holds" a value, such as a number, string, object, array, or a Boolean. Variables are fundamental to programming. Without variables, you would be forced to hard-code each specific value used in your scripts. The following hard-coded statement adds two numbers together and prints the result, which solves a simple mathematics problem:

```
echo (2 + 4);
```

However, this snippet of code is useful only for people who specifically want to know the sum of 2 and 4. To get past this limitation, you could write a script for finding the sum of another set of numbers, say 3 and 5. However, this approach to programming is clearly absurd, and this is where variables come into play.

With variables, you can create templates for operations, such as adding two numbers, without worrying about the specific values the variables represent. Values are given to the variables when the script is run, possibly through user input, through a database query, or from the result of another action earlier in the script. In other words, variables should be used whenever the data in your script is liable to change—either during the lifetime of the script or when it is passed to another script for later use.

A variable consists of a name of your choosing, preceded by a dollar sign ($). Variable names can include letters, numbers, and the underscore character (_), but they cannot include spaces. Names must begin with a letter or an underscore. The following list shows some legal variables:

```
$a;
$a_longish_variable_name;
$2453;
$sleepyZZZZ;
```

NOTE

> Your variable names should be meaningful as well as consistent in style. For example, if your script deals with name and password values, do not create a variable called $n for the name and $p for the password—those are not meaningful names for anyone other than you, at that particular moment. If you pick up that script weeks later, you might think that $n is the variable for *number* rather than *name* and that $p stands for *page* rather than *password*. And what if a co-worker has to modify your script? How will that person know what $n and $p stood for? You can use whatever naming convention you want for variables in your scripts, as long as the names are descriptive and follow some sort of pattern that others can understand.

A semicolon (;)—also known as the *instruction terminator*—is used to end a PHP statement. The semicolons in the previous fragment of code are not part of the variable names, but are used to end the statement that declares the variable as "alive and kicking," if you will. To declare a variable, you need only include it in your script. When you declare a variable, you usually assign a value to it in the same statement, as shown here:

```
$num1 = 8;

$num2 = 23;
```

The preceding lines declare two variables and use the assignment operator (=) to assign values to them. You learn about assignment in more detail in the "Operators and Expressions" section, later in this chapter. After you assign values to your variables, you can treat them exactly as if they were the values themselves. In other words

```
echo $num1;
```

is equivalent to

```
echo 8;
```

as long as $num1 is assigned a value of 8.

Global Variables

In addition to the rules for naming variables, there are rules regarding the availability of variables. In general, the assigned value of a variable is present only within the function or script where it resides. For example, if you have scriptA.php that holds a variable called $name with a value of joe, and you want to create scriptB.php that also uses a $name variable, you can assign to that second $name variable a value of jane without affecting the variable in scriptA.php. The value of the $name variable is *local* to each script, and the assigned values are independent of each other.

However, you can also define the $name variable as *global* within a script or function. If the $name variable is defined as a global variable in both scriptA.php and scriptB.php, and these scripts are connected to each other (that is, one script calls the other or includes the other), there will be just one value for the now-shared $name variable. Examples of global variable scope are explained in more detail in Chapter 7, "Working with Functions."

Superglobal Variables

In addition to global variables of your own creation, PHP has several predefined variables called *superglobals*. These variables are always present, and their values are available to all your scripts. Each of the following superglobals is actually an array of other variables:

- ▶ $_GET contains any variables provided to a script through the GET method.

- ▶ $_POST contains any variables provided to a script through the POST method.

- ▶ $_COOKIE contains any variables provided to a script through a cookie.

- ► `$_FILES` contains any variables provided to a script through file uploads.

- ► `$_SERVER` contains information such as headers, file paths, and script locations.

- ► `$_ENV` contains any variables provided to a script as part of the server environment.

- ► `$_REQUEST` contains any variables provided to a script via GET, POST, or COOKIE input mechanisms.

- ► `$_SESSION` contains any variables that are currently registered in a session.

The examples in this book use superglobals in all applicable situations. Using super-globals is crucial in creating secure applications because they reduce the likelihood of user-injected input to your scripts. By coding your scripts to accept only what you want, in the manner defined by you (from a form using the POST method, or from a session, for example), you can eliminate some of the problems created by loosely written scripts.

Data Types

Different types of data take up different amounts of memory and may be treated differently when they are manipulated by a script. Some programming languages therefore demand that the programmer declare in advance which type of data a variable will contain. By contrast, PHP is *loosely typed*, meaning that it automatically determines the data type at the time data is assigned to each variable.

This automatic typing is a mixed blessing. On the one hand, it means that variables can be used flexibly—in one instance, a variable can hold a string and then later in the script it can hold an integer or some other data type. On the other hand, this flexibility can lead to problems in larger scripts if you are specifically expecting a variable to hold one data type when in fact it holds something completely different. For example, suppose that you have created code to manipulate an array variable. If the variable in question instead contains a number value and no array structure is in place, errors will occur when the code attempts to perform array-specific operations on the variable.

Table 5.1 shows the eight standard data types available in PHP.

TABLE 5.1   Standard Data Types

Type	Example	Description
Boolean	true	One of the special values true or false
Integer	5	A whole number
Float or double	3.234	A floating-point number
String	"hello"	A collection of characters
Object		An instance of a class
Array		An ordered set of keys and values
Resource		Reference to a third-party resource (a database, for example)
NULL		An uninitialized variable

Resource types are often returned by functions that deal with external applications or files. For example, you will see references to "the MySQL resource ID" in Chapter 18, "Interacting with MySQL Using PHP." The NULL type is reserved for variables that have been declared but no value has been assigned to them.

PHP has several functions available to test the validity of a particular type of variable—one for each type, in fact. The is_* family of functions, such as is_bool(), tests whether a given value is a Boolean. Listing 5.1 assigns different data types to a single variable and then tests the variable with the appropriate is_* function. The comments in the code show you where the script is in the process.

> You can read more about calling functions in Chapter 7.   **NOTE**

LISTING 5.1   Testing the Type of a Variable

```
1:  <?php
2:  $testing; // declare without assigning
3:  echo "is null? ".is_null($testing); // checks if null
4:  echo "<br/>";
5:  $testing = 5;
6:  echo "is an integer? ".is_int($testing); // checks if integer
7:  echo "<br/>";
8:  $testing = "five";
9:  echo "is a string? ".is_string($testing); // checks if string
10: echo "<br/>";
11: $testing = 5.024;
12: echo "is a double? ".is_double($testing); // checks if double
13: echo "<br/>";
14: $testing = true;
15: echo "is boolean? ".is_bool($testing); // checks if boolean
16: echo "<br/>";
```

LISTING 5.1 Continued

```
17: $testing = array('apple', 'orange', 'pear');
18: echo "is an array? ".is_array($testing); // checks if array
19: echo "<br/>";
20: echo "is numeric? ".is_numeric($testing); // checks if is numeric
21: echo "<br/>";
22: echo "is a resource? ".is_resource($testing); // checks if is a resource
23: echo "<br/>";
24: echo "is an array? ".is_array($testing); // checks if is an array
25: echo "<br/>";
26: ?>
```

Put these lines into a text file called testtype.php, and place this file in your web server document root. When you access this script through your web browser, it produces the following output:

```
is null? 1
is an integer? 1
is a string? 1
is a double? 1
is boolean? 1
is an array? 1
is numeric?
is a resource?
is an array? 1
```

When the $testing variable is declared in line 2, no value is assigned to it, so when the variable is tested in line 3 to see whether it is NULL (using is_null()), the result is 1 (true).

NOTE

If you have configured PHP to show all notices, warnings, and errors, you will see a notice when you run this script:

Notice: Undefined variable: testing in **/path/to/testtype.php** on line **3**

Notices are turned on by default when you use the php-development.ini rather than php-production.ini, and can be very helpful when debugging scripts.

After the check to see whether $testing is NULL, values are assigned to $testing by using the = sign and then the variable istested with the appropriate is_* function. An integer, assigned to the $testing variable in line 5, is a whole or real number. In simple terms, you can think of a *whole number* as a number without a decimal point. A *string*, assigned to the $testing variable in line 8, is a collection of characters. When you work with strings in your scripts, they should always be surrounded by double or single quotation marks (" or '). A *double*, assigned to the $testing variable in line 11, is a floating-point number (that is, a number that includes a decimal point). A *Boolean*, assigned to the $testing variable in line 14, can have one of two special values: true or false. In line 17, an array is created using the array() function, which you learn more about in Chapter 8, "Working with Arrays." This particular array contains three items, and the script dutifully reports $testing to have a type of array.

From line 20 through the end of the script, no value is reassigned to $testing—only the type is tested. Lines 20 and 22 test whether $testing is a numeric or resource type, respectively, and because it is not, no value is displayed to the user. In line 24, the script tests again to see whether $testing is an array, and because it is, the value of 1 is displayed.

Changing Type with settype()

PHP also provides the function settype(), which is used to change the type of a variable. To use settype(), you place the variable to change and the type to change it to between the parentheses and separate the elements with a comma, like this:

```
settype($variabletochange, 'new type');
```

Listing 5.2 converts the value 3.14 (a float) to each of the four standard types examined in this chapter.

LISTING 5.2   Changing the Type of a Variable with settype()

```
1:  <?php
2:  $undecided = 3.14;
3:  echo "is ".$undecided." a double? ".is_double($undecided)."<br/>"; // double
4:  settype($undecided, 'string');
5:  echo "is ".$undecided." a string? ".is_string($undecided)."<br/>"; // string
6:  settype($undecided, 'integer');
7:  echo "is ".$undecided." an integer? ".is_integer($undecided)."<br/>"; //
    integer
8:  settype($undecided, 'double');
9:  echo "is ".$undecided." a double? ".is_double($undecided)."<br/>"; // double
10: settype($undecided, 'bool');
11: echo "is ".$undecided." a boolean? ".is_bool($undecided)."<br/>"; // boolean
12: ?>
```

> Per the PHP Manual, "double" is returned in case of a float, and not simply "float". Your eyes are not deceiving you.

NOTE

In each case, we use the appropriate is_* function to confirm the new data type and to print the value of the variable $undecided to the browser using echo. When we convert the string "3.14" to an integer in line 6, any information beyond the decimal point is lost forever. That's why $undecided contains 3 after we change it back to a double in line 8. Finally, in line 10, we convert $undecided to a Boolean. Any number other than 0 becomes true when converted to a Boolean. When printing a Boolean in PHP, true is represented as 1, and false is represented as an empty string; so in line 11, $undecided is printed as 1.

Put these lines into a text file called settype.php and place this file in your web server document root. When you access this script through your web browser, it produces the following output:

```
is 3.14 a double? 1
is 3.14 a string? 1
is 3 an integer? 1
is 3 a double? 1
is 1 a boolean? 1
```

NOTE

> You will not see a notice about an undefined variable like you did in the previous section, because the variable $undecided is defined and assigned a value at the beginning of this particular script.

Changing Type by Casting

The principal difference between using settype() to change the type of an existing variable and changing type by *casting* is the fact that casting produces a copy, leaving the original variable untouched. To change type through casting, you indicate the name of a data type, in parentheses, in front of the variable you are copying. For example, the following line creates a copy of the $originalvar variable, with a specific type (integer) and a new name $newvar. The $originalvar variable is still available, and is its original type; $newvar is a completely new variable.

```
$newvar = (integer) $originalvar
```

Listing 5.3 illustrates changing data types through casting.

LISTING 5.3   Casting a Variable

```
1:  <?php
2:  $undecided = 3.14;
3:  $holder = (double) $undecided;
4:  echo "is ".$holder." a double? ".is_double($holder)."<br/>"; // double
5:  $holder = (string) $undecided;
6:  echo "is ".$holder." a string? ".is_string($holder)."<br/>"; // string
7:  $holder = (integer) $undecided;
8:  echo "is ".$holder." an integer? ".is_integer($holder)."<br/>"; // integer
9:  $holder = (double) $undecided;
10: echo "is ".$holder." a double? ".is_double($holder)."<br/>"; // double
```

```
11: $holder = (boolean) $undecided;
12: echo "is ".$holder." a boolean? ".is_bool($holder)."<br/>"; // boolean
13: echo "<hr/>";
14: echo "original variable type of $undecided: ";
15: echo gettype($undecided); // double
16: ?>
```

Listing 5.3 never actually changes the type of the $undecided variable, which remains a double throughout this script, as illustrated on line 15, where the get-type() function is used to determine the type of $undecided.

> Despite its usage here, do not use gettype() to test for a certain type because it can be slow and is likely to be deprecated in future versions. Use the is_* family of functions to test type in production, as shown in Listing 5.1. This usage is simply for illustrative purposes.

NOTE

In fact, casting $undecided creates a copy that is then converted to the type specified at the time of the cast and stored in the variable $holder. This casting occurs first in line 3, and again in lines 5, 7, 9, and 11. Because the code is working with only a copy of $undecided and not the original variable, it never lost its original value, as the $undecided variable did in line 6 of Listing 5.2 when its type changed from a string to an integer.

Put the contents of Listing 5.3 into a text file called casttype.php and place this file in your web server document root. When you access this script through your web browser, it produces the following output:

```
is 3.14 a double? 1
is 3.14 a string? 1
is 3 an integer? 1
is 3.14 a double? 1
is 1 a boolean? 1
original variable type of 3.14: double
```

Now that you've seen how to change the contents of a variable from one type to another either by using settype() or by casting, consider why this might be useful. It is not a procedure that you will have to use often because PHP automatically casts your variables for you when the context of the script requires a change. However, such an automatic cast is temporary, and you might want to make a variable persistently hold a particular data type, which is why PHP gives you the ability to specifically change types.

For example, the numbers that a user types into an HTML form are made available to your script as the string type. If you try to add two strings together because they contain numbers, PHP helpfully converts these strings into numbers while the addition is taking place. So

```
"30cm" + "40cm"
```

results in an answer of 70.

NOTE

> The generic term *number* is used here to mean integers and floats. If the user input were in float form, and the strings added together were "3.14cm" and "4.12cm", the answer provided would be 7.26.

During the casting of a string into an integer or float, PHP ignores any non-numeric characters. The string is truncated, and any characters from the location of the first non-numeric character onward are ignored. So, whereas "30cm" is transformed into "30", the string "6ft2in" becomes just 6 because the rest of the string evaluates to 0.

You might want to clean up the user input yourself and use it in a particular way in your script. Imagine that the user has been asked to submit a number. We can simulate this by declaring a variable and assigning the user's input to it:

```
$test = "30cm";
```

As you can see, the user has added units to his number—instead of entering "30", the user has entered "30cm". You can make sure that the user input is clean by casting it as an integer:

```
$newtest = (integer) $test;
echo "Your imaginary box has a width of $newtest centimeters.";
```

The resulting output is as follows:

```
Your imaginary box has a width of 30 centimeters.
```

Had the the user input not been cast, and the value of the original variable, $test, been used in place of $newtest when printing the statement about the width of a box, the result would have been this:

```
Your imaginary box has a width of 30cm centimeters.
```

This output looks strange; in fact, it looks like parroted user input that has not been cleaned up (which is exactly what it is).

Why Test Type?

Why might it be useful to know the type of a variable? In programming, circumstances often arise when data is passed to you from another source, such as a function. In Chapter 7, you learn how to create functions; data is often passed between one or more functions because they can accept information as arguments from the code that calls them. For the function to work with the data it is given, it is a good idea to first verify that the function has been given values of the correct data type. For example, a function expecting data that has a type of resource will not work well when passed a string.

Operators and Expressions

With what you have learned so far, you can assign data to variables, and you can even investigate and change the data type of a variable. A programming language isn't very useful, though, unless you can manipulate the data you have stored. *Operators* are symbols used to manipulate data stored in variables, to make it possible to use one or more values to produce a new value, or to check the validity of data to determine the next step in a condition, and so forth. A value operated on by an operator is referred to as an *operand*.

An *operator* is a symbol or series of symbols that, when used in conjunction with values, performs an action, and usually produces a new value.

An *operand* is a value used in conjunction with an operator. There are usually two or more operands to one operator.

NOTE

In this simple example, two operands are combined with an operator to produce a new value:

(4 + 5)

The integers 4 and 5 are operands. The addition operator (+) operates on these operands to produce the integer 9. Operators almost always sit between two operands, although you will see a few exceptions later in this chapter.

The combination of operands with an operator to produce a result is called an *expression*. Although operators and their operands form the basis of expressions, an expression need not contain an operator. In fact, an expression in PHP is defined as anything that can be used as a value. This includes integer constants such as 654, variables such as $user, and function calls such as is_int(). The expression (4 + 5), for example, consists of two expressions (4 and 5) and an operator (+). When an expression produces a value, it is often said to *resolve to* that value. That is, when all subexpressions are taken into account, the expression can be treated as if it were a code for the value itself. In this case, the expression (4 + 5) resolves to 9.

NOTE

> An *expression* is any combination of functions, values, and operators that resolves to a value. As a rule of thumb, if you can use it as if it were a value, it is an expression.

Now that you have the principles out of the way, it's time to take a tour of the operators commonly used in PHP programming.

The Assignment Operator

You have seen the assignment operator in use each time a variable was declared in an example; the assignment operator consists of the single character: =. The assignment operator takes the value of the right-side operand and assigns it to the left-side operand:

```
$name = "Jimbo";
```

The variable $name now contains the string "Jimbo". This construct is also an expression. Although it might seem at first glance that the assignment operator simply changes the variable $name without producing a value, a statement that uses the assignment operator always resolves to a copy of the value of the right operand. Therefore

```
echo $name = "Jimbo";
```

prints the string "Jimbo" to the browser while it also assigns the value "Jimbo" to the $name variable.

Arithmetic Operators

The *arithmetic operators* do exactly what you would expect—they perform arithmetic operations. Table 5.2 lists these operators along with examples of their usage and results.

TABLE 5.2 Arithmetic Operators

Operator	Name	Example	Sample Result
+	Addition	10+3	13
-	Subtraction	10-3	7
/	Division	10/3	3.3333333333333
*	Multiplication	10*3	30
%	Modulus	10%3	1

The addition operator adds the right-side operand to the left-side operand. The subtraction operator subtracts the right-side operand from the left-side operand. The division operator divides the left-side operand by the right-side operand. The multiplication operator multiplies the left-side operand by the right-side operand. The modulus operator returns the remainder of the left-side operand divided by the right-side operand.

The Concatenation Operator

The concatenation operator is represented by a single period (.). Treating both operands as strings, this operator appends the right-side operand to the left-side operand. So

```
"hello"." world"
```

returns

```
"hello world"
```

Note that the resulting space between the words occurs because there is a leading space in the second operand (" world" rather than "world"). The concatenation operator literally smashes together two strings without adding any padding. So, if you try to concatenate two strings without leading or trailing spaces, such as

```
"hello"."world"
```

you will get this as your result:

```
"helloworld"
```

Regardless of the data types of the operands used with the concatenation operator, they are treated as strings, and the result is always of the string type. You will encounter concatenation frequently throughout this book when the results of an expression of some kind must be combined with a string, as in the following:

```
$cm = 212;
echo "the width is ".($cm/100)." meters";
```

Combined Assignment Operators

Although there is only one true assignment operator, PHP provides a number of combination operators that transform the left-side operand and return a result while also modifying the original value of the variable. As a rule, operators use operands but do not change their original values, but combined assignment operators break this rule. A combined assignment operator consists of a standard operator symbol followed by an equal sign. Combination assignment operators save you the trouble of using two operators in two different steps within your script. For example, if you have a variable with a value of 4, and you want to increase this value to 4 more, you might see this:

```
$x = 4;
$x = $x + 4; // $x now equals 8
```

However, you can also use a combination assignment operator (+=) to add and return the new value, as shown here:

```
$x = 4;
$x += 4; // $x now equals 8
```

Each arithmetic operator, as well as the concatenation operator, also has a corresponding combination assignment operator. Table 5.3 lists these new operators and shows an example of their usage.

TABLE 5.3   Some Combined Assignment Operators

Operator	Example	Equivalent To
+=	$x += 5	$x = $x + 5
-=	$x -= 5	$x = $x - 5
/=	$x /= 5	$x = $x / 5
*=	$x *= 5	$x = $x * 5
%=	$x %= 5	$x = $x % 5
.=	$x .= " test"	$x = $x." test"

Each of the examples in Table 5.3 transforms the value of $x using the value of the right-side operand. Subsequent uses of $x will refer to the new value. For example

```
$x = 4;
$x += 4; // $x now equals 8
$x += 4; // $x now equals 12
$x -= 3; // $x now equals 9
```

These operators are used throughout the scripts in the book. You will frequently see the combined concatenation assignment operator when you begin to create dynamic text. Looping through a script and adding content to a string, such as dynamically building the HTML markup to represent a table, is a prime example of the use of a combined assignment operator.

Automatically Incrementing and Decrementing an Integer Variable

When coding in PHP, you will often find it necessary to increment or decrement a variable that is an integer type. You usually need to do this when you are counting the iterations of a loop. You have already learned two ways of doing this—either by incrementing the value of $x using the addition operator

```
$x = $x + 1; // $x is incremented by 1
```

or by using a combined assignment operator

```
$x += 1; // $x is incremented by 1
```

In both cases, the new value is assigned to $x. Because expressions of this kind are common, PHP provides some special operators that allow you to add or subtract the integer constant 1 from an integer variable, assigning the result to the variable itself. These are known as the *post-increment* and *post-decrement* operators. The post-increment operator consists of two plus symbols appended to a variable name:

```
$x++; // $x is incremented by 1
```

This expression increments the value represented by the variable $x by 1. Using two minus symbols in the same way decrements the variable:

```
$x--; // $x is decremented by 1
```

If you use the post-increment or post-decrement operators in conjunction with a conditional operator, the operand is modified only after the first operation has finished:

```
$x = 3;
$y = $x++ + 3;
```

In this instance, $y first becomes 6 (the result of 3 + 3), and then $x is incremented.

In some circumstances, you might want to increment or decrement a variable in a test expression before the test is carried out. PHP provides the pre-increment and pre-decrement operators for this purpose. These operators behave in the same way as the post-increment and post-decrement operators, but they are written with the plus or minus symbols preceding the variable:

```
++$x; // $x is incremented by 1
--$x; // $x is decremented by 1
```

If these operators are used as part of a test expression, incrementing occurs before the test is carried out. For example, in the next fragment, $x is incremented before it is tested against 4:

```
$x = 3;
++$x < 4; // false
```

The test expression returns false because 4 is not smaller than 4.

Comparison Operators

Comparison operators perform comparative tests using their operands and return the Boolean value true if the test is successful or false if the test fails. This type of expression is useful when using control structures in your scripts, such as if and while statements. This book covers if and while statements in Chapter 6, "Flow Control Functions in PHP."

For example, to test whether the value contained in $x is smaller than 5, you can use the less-than operator as part of your expression:

```
$x < 5
```

If $x contains the value 3, this expression has the value true. If $x contains 7, the expression resolves to false.

Table 5.4 lists the comparison operators.

TABLE 5.4   Comparison Operators

Operator	Name	Returns True If...	Example ($x Is 4)	Result
==	Equivalence	Left is equivalent to right.	$x == 5	false
!=	Nonequivalence	Left is not equivalent to right.	$x != 5	true

TABLE 5.4   Continued

Operator	Name	Returns True If...	Example ($x Is 4)	Result
===	Identical	Left is equivalent to right, and they are the same type.	$x === 4	true
	Nonequivalence	Left is equivalent to right, but they are not the same type.	$x === "4"	false
>	Greater than	Left is greater than right.	$x > 4	false
>=	Greater than or equal to	Left is greater than or equal to right.	$x >= 4	true
<	Less than	Left is less than right.	$x < 4	false
<=	Less than or equal to	Left is less than or equal to right.	$x <= 4	true

These operators are most commonly used with integers or doubles, although the equivalence operator is also used to compare strings. Be very sure to understand the difference between the == and = operators. The == operator tests equivalence, whereas the = operator assigns value. Also, remember that === tests equivalence with regard to both value and type.

Creating Complex Test Expressions with the Logical Operators

Logical operators test combinations of Boolean values. For example, the or operator, which is indicated by two pipe characters (||) or simply the word or, returns the Boolean value true if either the left or the right operand is true:

```
true || false
```

This expression returns true.

The and operator, which is indicated by two ampersand characters (&&) or simply the word and, returns the Boolean value true only if both the left and right operands are true:

```
true && false
```

This expression returns the Boolean value `false`. It's unlikely that you will use a logical operator to test Boolean constants because it makes more sense to test two or more expressions that resolve to a Boolean. For example

```
($x > 2) && ($x < 15)
```

returns the Boolean value `true` if $x contains a value that is greater than 2 and smaller than 15. Parentheses are used when comparing expressions to make the code easier to read and to indicate the precedence of expression evaluation. Table 5.5 lists the logical operators.

TABLE 5.5   Logical Operators

Operator	Name	Returns True If...	Example	Result
`||`	Or	Left or right is true.	`true || false`	`true`
`or`	Or	Left or right is true.	`true or false`	`true`
`xor`	Xor	Left or right is true, but not both.	`true xor true`	`false`
`&&`	And	Left and right are true.	`true && false`	`false`
`and`	And	Left and right are true.	`true and false`	`false`
`!`	Not	The single operand is not true.	`! true`	`false`

You might wonder why are there two versions of both the or and the and operators, and that's a good question. The answer lies in operator precedence, which we examine next.

Operator Precedence

When you use an operator within an expression, the PHP engine usually reads your expression from left to right. For complex expressions that use more than one operator, though, the PHP engine could be led astray without some guidance. First, consider a simple case:

```
4 + 5
```

There's no room for confusion here; PHP simply adds 4 to 5. But what about the following fragment, with two operators:

```
4 + 5 * 2
```

This presents a problem. Should PHP find the sum of 4 and 5, and then multiply it by 2, providing the result 18? Or does it mean 4 plus the result of 5 multiplied by 2, resolving to 14? If you were simply to read from left to right, the former would be true. However, PHP attaches different precedence to different operators, and because the multiplication operator has higher precedence than the addition operator, the second solution to the problem is the correct one: 4 plus the result of 5 multiplied by 2.

However, you can override operator precedence by putting parentheses around your expressions. In the following fragment, the addition expression is evaluated before the multiplication expression:

```
(4 + 5) * 2
```

Whatever the precedence of the operators in a complex expression, it is a good idea to use parentheses to make your code clearer and to save you from bugs such as applying sales tax to the wrong subtotal in a shopping cart situation. The following is a list of the operators covered in this chapter in precedence order (those with the highest precedence listed first):

```
++, --, (cast)
/, *, %
+, -
<, <=, =>, >
==, ===, !=
&&
||
=, +=, -=, /=, *=, %=, .=
and
xor
or
```

As you can see, or has a lower precedence than ||, and and has a lower precedence than &&, so you can use the lower-precedence logical operators to change the way a complex test expression is read. In the following fragment, the two expressions are equivalent, but the second is much easier to read:

```
$x and $y || $z
```

```
$x && ($y || $z)
```

Taking it one step further, the following fragment is easier still:

```
$x and ($y or $z)
```

However, all three examples are equivalent.

The order of precedence is the only reason that both && and and are available in PHP. The same is true of || and or. In most circumstances, the use of parentheses makes for clearer code and fewer bugs than code that takes advantage of the difference in precedence of these operators. This book tends to use the more common || and && operators, and relies on parenthetical statements to set specific operator precedence.

Constants

Variables offer a flexible way of storing data because you can change their values and the type of data they store at any time during the execution of your scripts. However, if you want to work with a value that must remain unchanged throughout your script's execution, you can define and use a *constant*. You must use PHP's built-in define() function to create a constant, which subsequently cannot be changed unless you specifically define() it again. To use the define() function, place the name of the constant and the value you want to give it within parentheses and separated by a comma:

```
define("YOUR_CONSTANT_NAME", 42);
```

The value you want to set can be a number, a string, or a Boolean. By convention, the name of the constant should be in capital letters. Constants are accessed with the constant name only; no dollar symbol is required. Listing 5.4 shows you how to define and access a constant.

LISTING 5.4   Defining and Accessing a Constant

```
1: <?php
2: define("THE_YEAR", "2012");
3: echo "It is the year ".THE_YEAR;
4: ?>
```

TIP

Constants can be used anywhere in your scripts, including in functions stored in external files.

Notice that in line 3 the concatenation operator is used to append the value held by the constant to the string "It is the year " because PHP does not distinguish between a constant and a string within quotation marks.

Put these few lines into a text file called `constant.php` and place this file in your web server document root. When you access this script through your web browser, it produces the following output:

```
It is the year 2012
```

The `define()` function can also accept a third Boolean argument that determines whether the constant name should be case sensitive. By default, constant names are case sensitive. However, by passing `true` to the `define()` function, you can change this behavior. So, if you were to set up our `THE_YEAR` constant as

```
define("THE_YEAR", "2012", true);
```

you could access its value without worrying about case:

```
echo the_year;
echo ThE_YeAr;
echo THE_YEAR;
```

The preceding three expressions are equivalent, and all result in an output of 2012. This feature can make scripts a little friendlier for other programmers who work with our code because they will not need to consider case when accessing a constant we have already defined. However, given the fact that other constants *are* case sensitive, this might make for more, rather than less, confusion as programmers forget which constants to treat in which way. Unless you have a compelling reason to do otherwise, the safest course is to keep your constants case sensitive and define them using uppercase characters, which is an easy-to-remember (not to mention standard) convention.

Predefined Constants

PHP automatically provides some built-in constants for you. For example, the constant `__FILE__` returns the name of the file that the PHP engine is currently reading. The constant `__LINE__` returns the current line number of the file. These are but two examples of what are called "magic constants," because they are not statically predefined and instead change depending on the context in which they are used. For a complete list, see http://www.php.net/manual/en/language.constants.predefined.php.

You can also find out which version of PHP is interpreting the script with the `PHP_VERSION` constant. This constant can be useful if you need version information included in script output when sending a bug report. The `PHP_VERSION` constant *is* a predefined constant (and a reserved word). For a complete list of reserved constants, see http://www.php.net/manual/en/reserved.constants.php.

Summary

This chapter covered some of the basic features of the PHP language. You learned about variables and how to assign values to them using the assignment operator. You also learned about the scope of variables and built-in superglobals. This chapter also covered operators, and you learned how to combine some of the most common of these into expressions. Finally, you learned how to define and access constants.

Now that you have mastered some of the fundamentals of PHP, the next chapter really puts you in the driver's seat. You learn how to make scripts that can make decisions and repeat tasks, with help from variables, expressions, and operators.

Q&A

Q. *Why is it useful to know the type of data that a variable holds?*

A. Often the data type of a variable constrains what you can do with it. For example, you cannot perform array-related functions on simple strings. Similarly, you might want to make sure that a variable contains an integer or a float before using it in a mathematical calculation, even though PHP will often help you by changing data types for you in this situation.

Q. *Should I obey any conventions when naming variables?*

A. Your goal should always be to make your code easy to read and understand. A variable such as $ab123245 tells you nothing about its role in your script and invites typos. Keep your variable names short and descriptive.

A variable named $f is unlikely to mean much to you when you return to your code after a month or so. A variable named $filename, however, should make more sense.

Q. *Should I learn the operator precedence table?*

A. There is no reason you shouldn't, but I would save the effort for more useful tasks. By using parentheses in your expressions, you can make your code easy to read while defining your own order of precedence.

Workshop

The workshop is designed to help you review what you've learned and begin putting your knowledge into practice.

Quiz

1. Which of the following variable names are not valid?

```
$a_value_submitted_by_a_user
$666666xyz
$xyz666666
$____counter____
$the first
$file-name
```

2. What does the following code fragment output?

```
$num = 33;
(boolean) $num;
echo $num;
```

3. What does the following statement output?

```
echo gettype("4");
```

4. What is the output from the following code fragment?

```
$test_val = 5.5466;
settype($test_val, "integer");
echo $test_val;
```

5. Which of the following statements does not contain an expression?

```
4;
is_int(44);
5/12;
```

6. Which of the statements in question 5 contains an operator?

7. What value does the following expression return?

```
5 < 2
```

What data type will the returned value be?

Answers

1. The variable name $666666xyz is not valid because it does not begin with a letter or an underscore character. The variable name $the first is not valid because it contains a space. $file-name is also invalid because it contains a nonalphanumeric character (-).

2. The fragment prints the integer 33. The cast to Boolean produces a converted copy of the value stored in $num. It does not alter the value actually stored there.

3. The statement outputs the string `"string"`.

4. The code outputs the value 5. When a float is converted to an integer, any information beyond the decimal point is lost.

5. They are all expressions because they all resolve to values.

6. The statement `5/12;` contains a division operator.

7. The expression resolves to `false`, which is a Boolean value.

Activities

1. Create a script that contains at least five different variables. Populate them with values of different data types and use the `is_*` `family` of functions to test and print the type to the browser.

2. Assign values to two variables. Use comparison operators to test whether the first value is

   ▶ The same as the second

   ▶ Less than the second

   ▶ Greater than the second

   ▶ Less than or equal to the second

   Print the result of each test to the browser.

   Change the values assigned to your test variables and run the script again.

## CHAPTER 6

Flow Control Functions in PHP

In this chapter, you learn the following:

▶ How to use the `if` statement to execute code if a test expression evaluates to `true`

▶ How to execute alternative blocks of code when the test expression of an `if` statement evaluates to `false`

▶ How to use the `switch` statement to execute code based on the value returned by a test expression

▶ How to repeat execution of code using a `while` statement

▶ How to use `for` statements to make neater loops

▶ How to break out of loops

▶ How to nest one loop within another

▶ How to use PHP start and end tags within control structures

The scripts created in the previous chapter flow only in a single direction: forward. That is, the same statements execute in the same order every time a script is run. This does not allow for much flexibility because any sort of dynamic programming must, at the very least, have a loop or two, not to mention the ability to check for the validity of certain conditions before proceeding onward. You now learn about the programming structures that enable your scripts to adapt to circumstances.

Switching Flow

It is common for scripts to evaluate conditions and change their behavior accordingly. These decisions are what make your PHP pages dynamic—that is, able to change output according to circumstances. Like most programming languages, PHP enables you to do this with an `if` statement.

The if **Statement**

The if statement is a way of controlling the execution of a statement that follows it (that is, a single statement or a block of code inside braces). The if statement evaluates an expression found between parentheses. If this expression results in a true value, the statement is executed. Otherwise, the statement is skipped entirely. This functionality enables scripts to make decisions based on any number of factors:

```
if (expression) {
    // code to execute if the expression evaluates to true
}
```

Listing 6.1 executes a block of code only if a variable contains the string "happy".

LISTING 6.1   An if Statement

```
1: <?php
2: $mood = "happy";
3: if ($mood == "happy") {
4:     echo "Hooray! I'm in a good mood!";
5: }
6: ?>
```

In line 2, the value "happy" is assigned to the variable $mood. In line 3, the comparison operator == compares the value of the variable $mood with the string "happy". If they match, the expression evaluates to true, and the subsequent code is executed until the closing bracket is found (in this case, in line 5).

Put these lines into a text file called testif.php and place this file in your web server document root. When you access this script through your web browser, it produces the following output:

```
Hooray! I'm in a good mood!
```

If you change the assigned value of $mood to "sad" or any other string besides "happy", and then run the script again, the expression in the if statement evaluates to false, and the code block is skipped. The script remains silent, which leads to the else clause.

Using the else **Clause with the** if **Statement**

When working with an if statement, you might want to define an alternative block of code that should be executed if the expression you are testing evaluates to false. You can do this by adding else to the if statement followed by a further block of code:

```
if (expression) {
    // code to execute if the expression evaluates to true
} else {
    // code to execute in all other cases
}
```

Listing 6.2 amends the example in Listing 6.1 so that a default block of code is executed if the value of $mood is not equivalent to "happy".

LISTING 6.2   An `if` Statement That Uses `else`

```
1: <?php
2: $mood = "sad";
3: if ($mood == "happy") {
4:     echo "Hooray! I'm in a good mood!";
5: } else {
6:     echo "I'm in a $mood mood.";
7: }
8: ?>
```

Put these lines into a text file called `testifelse.php` and place this file in your web server document root. When you access this script through your web browser, it produces the following output:

```
I'm in a sad mood.
```

Notice in line 2 that the value of $mood is the string "sad", which obviously is not equal to "happy", so the expression in the if statement in line 3 evaluates to false. This results in the first block of code (line 4) being skipped. However, the block of code after else *is* executed, and the alternate message is printed: I'm in a sad mood. The string "sad" is the value assigned to the variable $mood.

Using an else clause in conjunction with an if statement allows scripts to make decisions about code execution. However, your options are limited to an either-or branch: either the code block following the if statement or the code block following the else statement. You'll now learn about additional options for the evaluation of multiple expressions, one after another.

Using the `elseif` Clause with the `if` Statement

You can use an if...elseif...else clause to test multiple expressions (the if...else portion) before offering a default block of code (the elseif portion):

```
if (expression) {
   // code to execute if the expression evaluates to true
} elseif (another expression) {
   // code to execute if the previous expression failed
   // and this one evaluates to true
} else {
   // code to execute in all other cases
}
```

If the initial if expression does not evaluate to true, the first block of code is ignored. The elseif clause presents another expression for evaluation. If it evaluates to true, its corresponding block of code is executed. Otherwise, the block of code associated with the else clause is executed. You can include as many elseif clauses as you want; and if you don't need a default action, you can omit the else clause.

NOTE

> The elseif clause can also be written as two words (else if). The syntax you use is a matter of taste, but coding standards employed by PEAR (the PHP Extension and Application Repository) and PECL (the PHP Extension Community Library) use elseif.

Listing 6.3 adds an elseif clause to the previous example.

LISTING 6.3 An if Statement That Uses else and elseif

```
1:  <?php
2:  $mood = "sad";
3:  if ($mood == "happy") {
4:      echo "Hooray! I'm in a good mood!";
5:  } elseif ($mood == "sad") {
6:      echo "Awww. Don't be down!";
7:  } else {
8:      echo "I'm neither happy nor sad, but $mood.";
9:  }
10: ?>
```

Once again, the $mood variable has a value of "sad", as shown in line 2. This value is not equal to "happy", so the code in line 4 is ignored. The elseif clause in line 5 tests for equivalence between the value of $mood and the value "sad", which in this case evaluates to true. The code in line 6 is therefore executed. In lines 7 through 9, a default behavior is provided, which would be invoked if the previous test conditions were all false. In that case, we would simply print a message including the actual value of the $mood variable.

Put these lines into a text file called testifelseif.php and place this file in your web server document root. When you access this script through your web browser, it produces the following output:

```
Awww. Don't be down!
```

Change the value of $mood to "iffy" and run the script. It produces the following output:

```
I'm neither happy nor sad, but iffy.
```

The `switch` **Statement**

The `switch` statement is an alternative way of changing flow, based on the evaluation of an expression. Using the `if` statement in conjunction with `elseif`, you can evaluate multiple expressions, as you've just seen. However, a `switch` statement evaluates only one expression in a list of expressions, selecting the correct one based on a specific bit of matching code. Whereas the result of an expression evaluated as part of an `if` statement is interpreted as either `true` or `false`, the expression portion of a `switch` statement is subsequently tested against any number of values, in hopes of finding a match:

```
switch (expression) {
        case result1:
                // execute this if expression results in result1
                break;
        case result2:
                // execute this if expression results in result2
                break;
        default:
                // execute this if no break statement
                // has been encountered hitherto
}
```

The expression used in a `switch` statement is often just a variable, such as `$mood`. Within the `switch` statement, you find a number of `case` statements. Each of these cases tests a value against the value of the `switch` expression. If the case value is equivalent to the expression value, the code within the `case` statement is executed. The `break` statement ends the execution of the `switch` statement altogether.

If the `break` statement is omitted, the next `case` statement is executed, regardless of whether a previous match has been found. If the optional `default` statement is reached without a previous matching value having been found, its code is executed.

CAUTION

It is important to include a `break` statement at the end of any code that will be executed as part of a `case` statement. Without a `break` statement, the program flow continues to the next `case` statement and ultimately to the `default` statement. In most cases, this results in unexpected behavior, likely incorrect!

Listing 6.4 re-creates the functionality of the `if` statement example using the `switch` statement.

LISTING 6.4   A switch **Statement**

```
 1: <?php
 2: $mood = "sad";
 3: switch ($mood) {
 4:     case "happy":
 5:         echo "Hooray! I'm in a good mood!";
 6:         break;
 7:     case "sad":
 8:         echo "Awww. Don't be down!";
 9:         break;
10:     default:
11:          echo "I'm neither happy nor sad, but $mood.";
12:          break;
13: }
14: ?>
```

Once again, in line 2 the $mood variable is initialized with a value of "sad". The switch statement in line 3 uses this variable as its expression. The first case statement in line 4 tests for equivalence between "happy" and the value of $mood. There is no match in this case, so script execution moves on to the second case statement in line 7. The string "sad" is equivalent to the value of $mood, so this block of code is executed. The break statement in line 9 ends the process. Lines 10 through 12 provide the default action, should neither of the previous cases evaluate as true.

Put these lines into a text file called testswitch.php and place this file in your web server document root. When you access this script through your web browser, it produces the following output:

```
Awww. Don't be down!
```

Change the value of $mood to "happy" and run the script. It produces the following output:

```
Hooray! I'm in a good mood!
```

To emphasize the caution about the importance of the break statement, try running this script without the second break statement. Be sure to change the value of $mood back to "sad" and then run the script. Your output will be as follows:

```
Awww. Don't be down!I'm neither happy nor sad, but sad.
```

This is definitely not the desired output, so be sure to include break statements where appropriate.

Using the ?: Operator

The ?: or *ternary* operator is similar to the if statement, except that it returns a value derived from one of two expressions separated by a colon. This construct provides you with three parts of the whole, hence the name *ternary*. The expression used to generate the returned value depends on the result of a test expression:

```
(expression) ? returned_if_expression_is_true : returned_if_expression_is_false;
```

If the test expression evaluates to true, the result of the second expression is returned; otherwise, the value of the third expression is returned. Listing 6.5 uses the ternary operator to set the value of a variable according to the value of $mood.

LISTING 6.5   Using the ?: Operator

```
1: <?php
2: $mood = "sad";
3: $text = ($mood == "happy") ? "I am in a good mood!" : "I am in a $mood
   mood.";
4: echo "$text";
5: ?>
```

In line 2, $mood is set to "sad". In line 3, $mood is tested for equivalence to the string "happy". Because this test returns false, the result of the third of the three expressions is returned.

Put these lines into a text file called testtern.php and place this file in your web server document root. When you access this script through your web browser, it produces the following output:

```
I am in a sad mood.
```

The ternary operator can be difficult to read, but is useful if you are dealing with only two alternatives and want to write compact code.

Loops

So far, you've looked at decisions that a script can make about what code to execute. Scripts can also decide how many times to execute a block of code. Loop statements are specifically designed to enable you to perform repetitive tasks because they continue to operate until a specified condition is achieved or until you explicitly choose to exit the loop.

The while **Statement**

The while statement looks similar in structure to a basic if statement, but has the ability to loop:

```
while (expression) {
     // do something
}
```

Unlike an if statement, a while statement executes for as long as the expression evaluates to true, over and over again if need be. Each execution of a code block within a loop is called an *iteration*. Within the block, you usually change something that affects the while statement's expression; otherwise, your loop continues indefinitely. For example, you might use a variable to count the number of iterations and act accordingly. Listing 6.6 creates a while loop that calculates and prints multiples of 2 up to 24.

LISTING 6.6   A while **Statement**

```
1: <?php
2: $counter = 1;
3: while ($counter <= 12) {
4:     echo $counter." times 2 is ".($counter * 2)."<br />";
5:     $counter++;
6: }
7: ?>
```

This example initializes the variable $counter in line 2 with a value of 1. The while statement in line 3 tests the $counter variable so that as long as the value of $counter is less than or equal to 12, the loop continues to run. Within the while statement's code block, the value of $counter is multiplied by 2, and the result is printed to the browser. In line 5, the value of $counter is incremented by 1. This step is extremely important because if you did not increment the value of the $counter variable, the while expression would never resolve to false and the loop would never end.

Put these lines into a text file called testwhile.php and place this file in your web server document root. When you access this script through your web browser, it produces the following output:

```
1 times 2 is 2
2 times 2 is 4
3 times 2 is 6
4 times 2 is 8
5 times 2 is 10
6 times 2 is 12
7 times 2 is 14
```

```
8 times 2 is 16
9 times 2 is 18
10 times 2 is 20
11 times 2 is 22
12 times 2 is 24
```

The do...while **Statement**

A do...while statement looks a little like a while statement turned on its head. The essential difference between the two is that the code block is executed *before* the truth test and not after it:

```
do  {
    // code to be executed
} while (expression);
```

CAUTION

> The test expression of a do...while statement should always end with a semicolon.

This type of statement is useful when you want the code block to be executed at least once, even if the while expression evaluates to false. Listing 6.7 creates a do...while statement. The code block is executed a minimum of one time.

LISTING 6.7   The do...while **Statement**

```
1: <?php
2: $num = 1;
3: do {
4:     echo "The number is: ".$num."<br />";
5:     $num++;
6: } while (($num > 200) && ($num < 400));
7: ?>
```

The do...while statement tests whether the variable $num contains a value that is greater than 200 and less than 400. Line 2 initializes $num to 1, so this expression returns false. Nonetheless, the code block is executed at least one time before the expression is evaluated, so the statement prints a single line to the browser.

Put these lines into a text file called testdowhile.php and place this file in your web server document root. When you access this script through your web browser, it produces the following output:

```
The number is: 1
```

If you change the value of $num in line 2 to 300 and then run the script, the loop displays

```
The number is: 300
```

and continues to print similar lines, with increasing numbers, through

```
The number is: 399
```

The for **Statement**

Anything you want to do with a for statement can also be done with a while statement, but a for statement is often a more efficient method of achieving the same effect. In Listing 6.6, you saw how a variable was initialized outside the while statement and then tested within its expression and incremented within the code block. With a for statement, you can achieve this same series of events, but in a single line of code. This allows for more compact code and makes it less likely that you might forget to increment a counter variable, thereby creating an infinite loop:

```
for (initialization expression; test expression; modification expression) {
    // code to be executed
}
```

NOTE

> *Infinite loops* are, as the name suggests, loops that run without bounds. If your loop is running infinitely, your script is running for an infinite amount of time. This behavior is very stressful on your web server and renders the web page unusable.

The expressions within the parentheses of the for statement are separated by semicolons. Usually, the first expression initializes a counter variable, the second expression is the test condition for the loop, and the third expression increments the counter. Listing 6.8 shows a for statement that re-creates the example in Listing 6.6, which multiplies 12 numbers by 2.

LISTING 6.8   Using the for **Statement**

```
1: <?php
2: for ($counter=1; $counter<=12; $counter++) {
3:     echo $counter." times 2 is ".($counter * 2)."<br />";
4: }
5: ?>
```

Put these lines into a text file called testfor.php and place this file in your web server document root. When you access this script through your web browser, it produces the following output:

```
1 times 2 is 2
2 times 2 is 4
3 times 2 is 6
4 times 2 is 8
5 times 2 is 10
6 times 2 is 12
7 times 2 is 14
8 times 2 is 16
9 times 2 is 18
10 times 2 is 20
11 times 2 is 22
12 times 2 is 24
```

The results of Listings 6.6 and 6.8 are the same, but the for statement makes the code in Listing 6.8 more compact. Because the $counter variable is initialized and incremented at the beginning of the statement, the logic of the loop is clear at a glance. That is, as shown in line 2, the first expression initializes the $counter variable and assigns a value of 1, the test expression verifies that $counter contains a value that is less than or equal to 12, and the final expression increments the $counter variable. Each of these items is found in the single line of code.

When the sequence of script execution reaches the for loop, the $counter variable is initialized and the test expression is evaluated. If the expression evaluates to true, the code block is executed. The $counter variable is then incremented and the test expression is evaluated again. This process continues until the test expression evaluates to false.

Breaking Out of Loops with the break Statement

Both while and for statements incorporate a built-in test expression with which you can end a loop. However, the break statement enables you to break out of a loop based on the results of additional tests. This can provide a safeguard against error. Listing 6.9 creates a simple for statement that divides a large number by a variable that is incremented, printing the result to the screen.

LISTING 6.9 A for Loop That Divides 4000 by 10 Incremental Numbers

```
1: <?php
2: for ($counter=1; $counter <= 10; $counter++) {
3:     $temp = 4000/$counter;
4:     echo "4000 divided by ".$counter." is...".$temp."<br />";
5: }
6: ?>
```

In line 2, this example initializes the variable $counter and assigns a value of 1. The test expression in the for statement verifies that the value of $counter is less than or equal to 10. Within the code block, 4000 is divided by $counter, printing the result to the browser.

Put these lines into a text file called testfor2.php and place this file in your web server document root. When you access this script through your web browser, it produces the following output:

```
4000 divided by 1 is... 4000
4000 divided by 2 is... 2000
4000 divided by 3 is... 1333.33333333
4000 divided by 4 is... 1000
4000 divided by 5 is... 800
4000 divided by 6 is... 666.666666667
4000 divided by 7 is... 571.428571429
4000 divided by 8 is... 500
4000 divided by 9 is... 444.444444444
4000 divided by 10 is... 400
```

This seems straightforward enough. But what if the value you place in $counter comes from user input? The value could be a negative number or even a string. Let's take the first instance, where the user input value is a negative number. Changing the initial value of $counter from 1 to -4 causes 4000 to be divided by 0 when the code block is executed for the fifth time. It is generally not a good idea for your code to divide by 0 because such an operation results in an answer of "undefined." Listing 6.10 guards against this occurrence by breaking out of the loop if the value of the $counter variable equals 0.

LISTING 6.10   Using the break Statement

```
1: <?php
2: $counter = -4;
3: for (; $counter <= 10; $counter++) {
4:     if ($counter == 0) {
5:         break;
6:     } else {
7:         $temp = 4000/$counter;
8:         echo "4000 divided by ".$counter." is...".$temp."<br />";
9:     }
10: }
11 ?>
```

NOTE

Dividing a number by 0 does not cause a fatal error in PHP. Instead, PHP generates a warning and execution continues.

Listing 6.10 uses an if statement, shown in line 4, to test the value of $counter before attempting mathematical operations using this value. If the value of $counter is equal to 0, the break statement immediately halts execution of the code block, and program flow continues after the for statement (line 11).

Put these lines into a text file called testfor3.php and place this file in your web server document root. When you access this script through your web browser, it produces the following output:

```
4000 divided by -4 is... -1000
4000 divided by -3 is... -1333.33333333
4000 divided by -2 is... -2000
4000 divided by -1 is... -4000
```

Notice that the $counter variable was initialized in line 2, outside the for statement's parentheses. This method was used to simulate a situation in which the value of $counter is set from outside the script.

TIP

You can omit any of the expressions from a for statement, but you must remember to retain the separation semicolons.

Skipping an Iteration with the continue Statement

The continue statement ends execution of the current iteration but doesn't cause the loop as a whole to end. Instead, the next iteration begins immediately. Using the break statement as in Listing 6.10 is a little drastic. With the continue statement in Listing 6.11, you can avoid a divide-by-0 error without ending the loop completely.

LISTING 6.11   Using the continue Statement

```
1:  <?php
2:  $counter = -4;
3:  for (; $counter <= 10; $counter++) {
4:      if ($counter == 0) {
5:          continue;
6:      }
7:      $temp = 4000/$counter;
8:      echo "4000 divided by ".$counter." is...".$temp."<br />";
9:  }
10: ?>
```

Line 5 swaps the break statement for a continue statement. If the value of the $counter variable is equivalent to 0, the iteration is skipped, and the next one starts immediately.

Put these lines into a text file called testcontinue.php and place this file in your web server document root. When you access this script through your web browser, it produces the following output:

```
4000 divided by -4 is... -1000
4000 divided by -3 is... -1333.33333333
4000 divided by -2 is... -2000
4000 divided by -1 is... -4000
4000 divided by 1 is... 4000
4000 divided by 2 is... 2000
4000 divided by 3 is... 1333.33333333
4000 divided by 4 is... 1000
4000 divided by 5 is... 800
4000 divided by 6 is... 666.666666667
4000 divided by 7 is... 571.428571429
4000 divided by 8 is... 500
4000 divided by 9 is... 444.44444444444
4000 divided by 10 is... 400
```

CAUTION

> Using the break and continue statements can make code more difficult to read because they often add layers of complexity to the logic of the loop statements that contain them. Use these statements with care, or comment your code to show other programmers (or yourself) exactly what you're trying to achieve with these statements.

Nesting Loops

Loops can contain other loop statements, as long as the logic is valid and the loops are tidy. The combination of such statements proves particularly useful when working with dynamically created HTML tables. Listing 6.12 uses two for statements to print a multiplication table to the browser.

LISTING 6.12   Nesting Two for Loops

```
1:  <?php
2:  echo "<table style=\"border: 1px solid #000;\"> \n";
3:  for ($y=1; $y<=12; $y++) {
4:      echo "<tr> \n";
5:      for ($x=1; $x<=12; $x++) {
6:          echo "<td style=\"border: 1px solid #000; width: 25px;
7:                  text-align:center;\">";
```

```
8:          echo ($x * $y);
9:          echo "</td> \n";
10:    }
11:    echo "</tr> \n";
12:    }
13:    echo "</table>";
14:    ?>
```

Before you examine the for loops, take a closer look at line 2 in Listing 6.12:

```
echo "<table style=\"border: 1px solid black;\"> \n";
```

Notice that Listing 6.12 uses the backslash character (\) before each of the quotation marks within the string containing the style information for the table. These back-slashes also appear in lines 6 and 7, in the style information for the table data cell. This is necessary because it tells the PHP engine that we want to use the quotation mark character, rather than have PHP interpret it as the beginning or end of a string. If you did not "escape" the quotation marks with the backslash character, the statement would not make sense to the engine; it would read it as a string followed by a number followed by another string. Such a construct would generate an error. This line also uses \n to represent a newline character, which makes the source easier to read when it is rendered by the browser, which is useful especially when looking at HTML for tables.

The outer for statement (line 3) initializes a variable called $y, assigning to it a starting value of 1. This for statement defines an expression that intends to verify that the value of $y is less than or equal to 12, and then defines the increment that will be used. In each iteration, the code block prints a tr (table row) HTML element (line 4) and begins another for statement (line 5). This inner loop initializes a variable called $x and defines expressions along the same lines as for the outer loop. For each iteration, the inner loop prints a td (table cell) element to the browser (lines 6 and 7), as well as the result of $x multiplied by $y (line 8). Line 9 closes the table cell. After the inner loop has finished, execution falls back through to the outer loop, where the table row closes on line 11, ready for the process to begin again. When the outer loop has finished, the result is a neatly formatted multiplication table. Listing 6.12 wraps things up by closing the table on line 13.

Put these lines into a text file called testnestfor.php and place this file in your web server document root. When you access this script through your web browser, it should look like Figure 6.1.

FIGURE 6.1
Output of
testnestfor.php.

Code Blocks and Browser Output

In Chapter 4, "Installing and Configuring PHP," you learned that you can slip in and out of HTML mode at will using the PHP start and end tags. In this chapter, you have discovered that you can present distinct output to the user according to a decision-making process you can control with `if` and `switch` statements. This section combines these two techniques.

Imagine a script that outputs a table of values only when a variable is set to the Boolean value `true`. Listing 6.13 shows a simplified HTML table constructed with the code block of an `if` statement.

LISTING 6.13   A Code Block Containing Multiple echo Statements

```
1: <?php
2: $display_prices = true;
3: if ($display_prices) {
4:       echo "<table border=\"1\">\n";
5:       echo "<tr><td colspan=\"3\">";
6:       echo "today's prices in dollars";
7:       echo "</td></tr>";
8:       echo "<tr><td>\$14.00</td><td>\$32.00</td><td>\$71.00</td></tr>\n";
9:       echo "</table>";
10: }
11: ?>
```

CAUTION

In line 8, note the dollar sign, which when meant literally and not as part of a variable declaration, must be escaped with a backslash for it to be interpreted as the dollar sign character.

If the value of $display_prices is set to true in line 2, the table is printed. For the sake of readability, we split the output into multiple echo() statements, and once again use the backslash to escape any quotation marks used in the HTML output.

Put these lines into a text file called testmultiecho.php and place this file in your web server document root. When you access this script through your web browser, it should look like Figure 6.2.

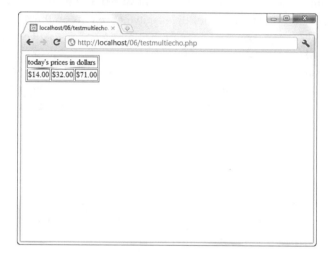

FIGURE 6.2
Output of test-multiecho.php.

There's nothing wrong with the way this is coded, but you can save yourself some typing by simply slipping back into HTML mode within the code block. Listing 6.14 does just that.

LISTING 6.14   Returning to HTML Mode Within a Code Block

```
1: <?php
2: $display_prices = true;
3: if ($display_prices) {
4: ?>
5: <table border="1">
6: <tr><td colspan="3">today's prices in dollars</td></tr>
7: <tr><td>$14.00</td><td>$32.00</td><td>$71.00</td></tr>
8: </table>
9: <?php
10: }
11: ?>
```

The important thing to note here is that the shift to HTML mode on line 4 occurs only if the condition of the if statement is fulfilled. This can save you the bother of escaping quotation marks and wrapping our output in echo() statements. This approach might, however, affect the readability of the code in the long run, especially if the script grows larger.

Summary

In this chapter, you learned about control structures and the ways in which they can help to make your scripts flexible and dynamic. Most of these structures reappear regularly throughout the rest of the book.

You learned how to define an `if` statement and how to provide for alternative actions with the `elseif` and `else` clauses. You learned how to use the `switch` statement to change flow according to multiple equivalence tests on the result of an expression. You learned about loops—in particular, the `while` and `for` statements—and you learned how to use `break` and `continue` to prematurely end the execution of a loop or to skip an iteration. You learned how to nest one loop within another and saw a typical use for this structure. You also looked at a technique for using PHP start and end tags in conjunction with conditional code blocks, to alleviate having to escape (use the backslash in front of) special characters such as the quotation mark and dollar sign.

You should now know enough of the basics to write scripts of your own that make decisions and perform repetitive tasks. In the next chapter, you learn how to add even more power to your applications. You learn how functions enable you to organize your code, preventing duplication and improving reusability.

Q&A

Q. *Must a control structure's test expression result in a Boolean value?*

A. Ultimately, yes. But in the context of a test expression, `0`, an undefined variable, or an empty string is converted to `false`. All other values evaluate to `true`.

Q. *Must I always surround a code block in a control statement with brackets?*

A. If the code you want executed as part of a control structure consists of only a single line, you can omit the brackets. However, the habit of always using opening and closing brackets, regardless of structure length, is a good one.

Workshop

The workshop is designed to help you review what you've learned and begin putting your knowledge into practice.

Quiz

1. How do you use an `if` statement to print the string `"Youth message"` to the browser if an integer variable, $age, is between 18 and 35? If $age contains any other value, the string `"Generic message"` should be printed to the browser.

2. How do you extend your code in question 1 to print the string `"Child message"` if the $age variable is between 1 and 17?

3. How do you create a `while` statement that increments through and prints every odd number between 1 and 49?

4. How do you convert the `while` statement you created in question 3 into a `for` statement?

Answers

1.

```
$age = 22;

if (($age >= 18) && ($age <= 35)) {
    echo "Youth message";
} else {
    echo "Generic message";
}
```

2.

```
$age = 12;

if (($age >= 18) && ($age <= 35)) {
    echo "Youth message";
} elseif (($age >= 1) && ($age <= 17)) {
    echo "Child message";
} else {
    echo "Generic message";
}
```

3.

```
$num = 1;

while ($num <= 49) {
    echo $num."<br />";
    $num += 2;
}
```

4.

```php
for ($num = 1; $num <= 49; $num += 2) {
    echo $num."<br />";
}
```

Activities

1. Review the syntax for control structures. Think about how the techniques you've learned will help you in your scripting. Perhaps some of the script ideas you develop will be able to behave in different ways according to user input or will loop to display an HTML table.

2. Start to build the control structures you will be using. Use temporary variables to mimic user input or database queries for the time being.

## CHAPTER 7

Working with Functions

In this chapter, you learn the following:

- ▶ How to define and call functions from within your scripts
- ▶ How to pass values to functions and receive values in return
- ▶ How to call a function dynamically using a string stored in a variable
- ▶ How to access global variables from within a function
- ▶ How to give a function a "memory"
- ▶ How to pass data to functions by reference
- ▶ How to verify that a function exists before calling it

Functions are at the heart of a well-organized script and make your code easy to read and reuse. No large project would be manageable without them because the problem of repetitive code would bog down the development process. Throughout this chapter, you investigate functions and learn some of the ways functions can save you from repetitive work.

What Is a Function?

You can think of a function as an input/output machine. This machine takes the raw materials you feed it (input) and works with them to produce a product (output). A function accepts values, processes them, and then performs an action (printing to the browser, for example), returns a new value, or both.

If you needed to bake a single cake, you would probably do it yourself, in your own kitchen with your standard oven. But if you needed to bake thousands of cakes, you would probably build or acquire a special cake-baking machine, built for baking cakes in massive quantities. Similarly, when deciding whether to create a function for reuse, the most important factor to consider is the extent to which it can save you from writing repetitive code.

A *function* is a self-contained block of code that can be called by your scripts. When called, the function's code is executed and performs a particular task. You can pass values to a function, which then uses the values appropriately—storing them, transforming them, displaying them, whatever the function is told to do. When finished, a function can also pass a value back to the original code that called it into action.

Calling Functions

Functions come in two flavors: those built in to the language and those you define yourself. PHP has hundreds of built-in functions. Look at the following snippet for an example of a function in use:

```
strtoupper("Hello Web!");
```

This example calls the `strtoupper()` function, passing it the string `"Hello Web!"`. The function then goes about its business of changing the contents of the string to uppercase letters. A function call consists of the function name (`strtoupper` in this case) followed by parentheses. If you want to pass information to the function, you place it between these parentheses. A piece of information passed to a function in this way is called an *argument*. Some functions require that more than one argument be passed to them, separated by commas:

```
some_function($an_argument, $another_argument);
```

`strtoupper()` is typical for a function in that it returns a value. Most functions return some information back after they've completed their task; they usually at least tell whether their mission was successful. `strtoupper()` returns a string value, so its usage requires the presence of a variable to accept the new string, such as the following:

```
$new_string = strtoupper("Hello Web!");
```

You may now use $new_string in your code, such as to print it to the screen:

```
echo $new_string;
```

This code results in the following text on the screen:

```
HELLO WEB!
```

NOTE

> The `print()` and `echo()` functions are not actually functions, they're language constructs designed to output strings to the browser. However, you will find them in the PHP function list, at http://www.php.net/print and http://www.php.net/echo, respectively. These constructs are similar in functionality and can be used interchangably. Whichever one you use is a matter of taste.

The abs() function, for example, requires a signed numeric value and returns the absolute value of that number. Let's try it out in Listing 7.1.

LISTING 7.1   Calling the Built-In abs() Function

```
1: <?php
2: $num = -321;
3: $newnum = abs($num);
4: echo $newnum;
5: //prints "321"
6: ?>
```

This example assigns the value -321 to a variable $num. It then passes that variable to the abs() function, which makes the necessary calculation and returns a new value. The code assigns this to the variable $newnum and displays the result.

Put these lines into a text file called abs.php and place this file in your web server document root. When you access this script through your web browser, it produces the following:

321

In fact, Listing 7.1 could have dispensed with temporary variables altogether, passing the number straight to the abs() function and directly printing the result:

```
echo abs(-321);
```

This example uses the temporary variables $num and $newnum, though, to make each step of the process as clear as possible. Sometimes you can make your code more readable by breaking it up into a greater number of simple expressions.

You can call user-defined functions in exactly the same way that we have been calling built-in functions.

Defining a Function

You can define your own functions using the function statement:

```
function some_function($argument1, $argument2)
{
    //function code here
}
```

The name of the function follows the function statement and precedes a set of parentheses. If your function requires arguments, you must place comma-separated variable names within the parentheses. These variables are filled by the values passed to your function. Even if your function doesn't require arguments, you must nevertheless supply the parentheses.

NOTE The naming rules for functions are similar to the naming rules for variables, which you learned in Chapter 5, "The Building Blocks of PHP." Names cannot include spaces, and they must begin with a letter or an underscore. As with variables, your function names should be meaningful and consistent in style. The capitalization of function names is one such stylistic touch you can add to your code; using mixed case in names, such as `MyFunction()` or `handleSomeDifficultTask()`, makes your code much easier to read. You may hear this naming convention referred to as CamelCase or lower CamelCase, depending on whether the first character is capitalized.

Listing 7.2 declares and calls a function.

LISTING 7.2   Declaring and Calling a Function

```
1: <?php
2: function bighello()
3: {
4:      echo "<h1>HELLO!</h1>";
5: }
6: bighello();
7: ?>
```

The script in Listing 7.2 simply outputs the string "HELLO!" wrapped in an HTML h1 element.

Put these lines into a text file called `bighello.php` and place this file in your web server document root. When you access this script through your web browser, it should look like Figure 7.1.

FIGURE 7.1
Output of
`bighello.php`.

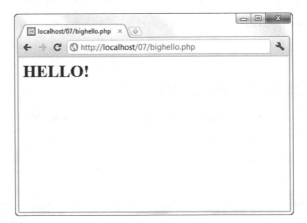

Listing 7.2 declares a function, `bighello()`, that requires no arguments. Because of this, the parentheses are left empty. Although `bighello()` is a working function, it is not terribly useful. Listing 7.3 creates a function that requires an argument and actually does something with it.

LISTING 7.3   Declaring a Function That Requires an Argument

```
1: <?php
2: function printBR($txt)
3: {
4:     echo $txt."<br/>";
5: }
6: printBR("This is a line.");
7: printBR("This is a new line.");
8: printBR("This is yet another line.");
9: ?>
```

> **NOTE**
>
> Unlike variable names, function names are not case sensitive. In Listing 7.3, the `printBR()` function could have been called as `printbr()`, `PRINTBR()`, or any combination thereof, with success.

Put these lines into a text file called `printbr.php` and place this file in your web server document root. When you access this script through your web browser, it should look like Figure 7.2.

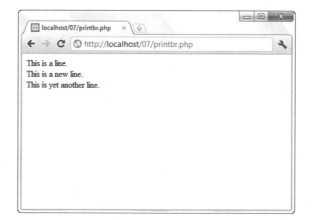

FIGURE 7.2
A function that prints a string with an appended `<br/>` tag.

In line 2, the `printBR()` function expects a string, so the variable name $txt is placed between the parentheses when the function is declared. Whatever is passed to `printBR()` is stored in this $txt variable. Within the body of the function, line 3 prints the $txt variable, appending a `<br/>` element to it.

When you want to print a line to the browser, such as in line 6, 7, or 8, you can call printBR() instead of the built-in print(), saving you the bother of typing the <br/> element.

Returning Values from User-Defined Functions

The previous example output an amended string to the browser within the printBR() function. Sometimes, however, you will want a function to provide a value that you can work with yourself. If your function has transformed a string that you have provided, you might want to get the amended string back so that you can pass it to other functions. A function can return a value using the return statement in conjunction with a value. The return statement stops the execution of the function and sends the value back to the calling code.

Listing 7.4 creates a function that returns the sum of two numbers.

LISTING 7.4   A Function That Returns a Value

```
1: <?php
2: function addNums($firstnum, $secondnum)
3: {
4:     $result = $firstnum + $secondnum;
5:     return $result;
6: }
7: echo addNums(3,5);
8: //will print "8"
9: ?>
```

Put these lines into a text file called addnums.php and place this file in your web server document root. When you access this script through your web browser, it produces the following:

8

Notice in line 2 that addNums() should be called with two numeric arguments (line 7 shows those to be 3 and 5 in this case). These values are stored in the variables $firstnum and $secondnum. Predictably, addNums() adds the numbers contained in these variables and stores the result in a variable called $result.

The return statement can return a value or nothing at all. How you arrive at a value passed by return can vary. The value can be hard-coded:

return 4;

It can be the result of an expression:

```
return $a/$b;
```

It can be the value returned by yet another function call:

```
return another_function($an_argument);
```

Variable Scope

A variable declared within a function remains local to that function. In other words, it is not available outside the function or within other functions. In larger projects, this can save you from accidentally overwriting the contents of a variable when you declare two variables with the same name in separate functions.

Listing 7.5 creates a variable within a function and then attempts to print it outside the function.

LISTING 7.5 Variable Scope: A Variable Declared Within a Function Is Unavailable Outside the Function

```
1: <?php
2: function test()
3: {
4:     $testvariable = "this is a test variable";
5: }
6: echo "test variable: ".$testvariable."<br/>";
7: ?>
```

Put these lines into a text file called scopetest.php and place this file in your web server document root. When you access this script through your web browser, it should look like Figure 7.3.

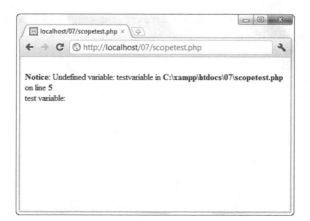

FIGURE 7.3
Output of
scopetest.php.

NOTE

> The exact output you see depends on your PHP error settings. That is, it might or might not produce a "notice" as shown in Figure 7.3, but it will show the lack of an additional string after "test variable".

The value of the variable $testvariable is not printed because no such variable exists outside the test() function. Remember that the attempt in line 6 to access a nonexistent variable produces a notice such as the one displayed only if your PHP settings are set to display all errors, notices, and warnings. If your error settings are not strictly set, only the string "test variable:" is shown.

Similarly, a variable declared outside a function is not automatically available within it.

Accessing Variables with the global Statement

From within one function, you cannot (by default) access a variable defined in another function or elsewhere in the script. Within a function, if you attempt to use a variable with the same name, you will only set or access a local variable. Let's put this to the test in Listing 7.6.

LISTING 7.6   Variables Defined Outside Functions Are Inaccessible from Within a Function by Default

```
1: <?php
2: $life = 42;
3: function meaningOfLife()
4: {
5:      echo "The meaning of life is ".$life";
6: }
7: meaningOfLife();
8: ?>
```

Put these lines into a text file called scopetest2.php and place this file in your web server document root. When you access this script through your web browser, it should look like Figure 7.4.

As you might expect, the meaningOfLife() function does not have access to the $life variable in line 2; $life is empty when the function attempts to print it. On the whole, this is a good thing because it saves you from potential clashes between identically named variables, and a function can always demand an argument if it needs information about the outside world. Occasionally, you might want to access an important variable from within a function without passing it in as an argument. This is where the global statement comes into play. Listing 7.7 uses global to restore order to the universe.

LISTING 7.7   Accessing Global Variables with the global Statement

```
1: <?php
2: $life=42;
3: function meaningOfLife()
4: {
5:     global $life;
6:     echo "The meaning of life is ".$life";
7: }
8: meaningOfLife();
9: ?>
```

Put these lines into a text file called scopetest3.php and place this file in your web server document root. When you access this script through your web browser, it should look like Figure 7.5.

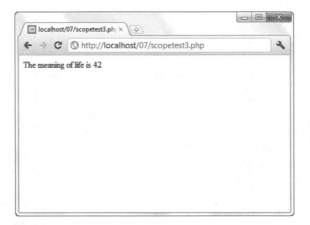

When you place the `global` statement in front of the `$life` variable when it is declared in the `meaningOfLife()` function (line 5), it refers to the `$life` variable declared outside the function (line 2).

You need to use the `global` statement within every function that needs to access a particular named global variable. Be careful, though: If you manipulate the contents of the variable within the function, the value of the variable changes for the script as a whole.

You can declare more than one variable at a time with the `global` statement by simply separating each of the variables you want to access with commas:

```
global $var1, $var2, $var3;
```

CAUTION

Usually, an argument is a copy of whatever value is passed by the calling code; changing it in a function has no effect beyond the function block. Changing a global variable within a function, however, changes the original and not a copy. Use the `global` statement carefully.

Saving State Between Function Calls with the `static` Statement

Local variables within functions have a short but happy life—they come into being when the function is called and die when execution is finished, as they should. Occasionally, however, you might want to give a function a rudimentary memory.

Assume that you want a function to keep track of the number of times it has been called so that numbered headings can be created by a script. You could, of course, use the global statement to do this, as shown in Listing 7.8.

LISTING 7.8 Using the `global` Statement to Remember the Value of a Variable Between Function Calls

```
1:  <?php
2:  $num_of_calls = 0;
3:  function numberedHeading($txt)
4:  {
5:      global $num_of_calls;
6:      $num_of_calls++;
7:      echo "<h1>".$num_of_calls." ".$txt."</h1>";
8:  }
9:  numberedHeading("Widgets");
10: echo "<p>We build a fine range of widgets.</p>";
11: numberedHeading("Doodads");
12: echo "<p>Finest in the world.</p>";
13: ?>
```

Put these lines into a text file called numberedheading.php and place this file in your web server document root. When you access this script through your web browser, it should look like Figure 7.6.

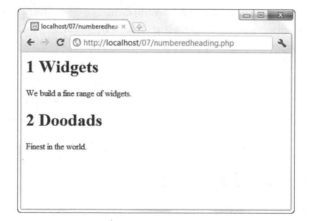

FIGURE 7.6
Using the global statement to keep track of the number of times a function has been called.

This does the job. Listing 7.8 declares a variable, $num_of_calls, in line 2, outside the function numberedHeading(). Line 5 makes this variable available to the function by using the global statement.

Every time numberedHeading() is called, the value of $num_of_calls is incremented (line 6). You can then print out the heading complete with the properly incremented heading number.

This is not the most elegant solution, however. Functions that use the global statement cannot be read as standalone blocks of code. In reading or reusing them, we need to look out for the global variables that they manipulate.

This is where the static statement can be useful. If you declare a variable within a function in conjunction with the static statement, the variable remains local to the function, and the function "remembers" the value of the variable from execution to execution. Listing 7.9 adapts the code from Listing 7.8 to use the static statement.

LISTING 7.9   Using the static **Statement to Remember the Value of a Variable Between Function Calls**

```
 1:  <?php
 2:  function numberedHeading($txt)
 3:  {
 4:      static $num_of_calls = 0;
 5:      $num_of_calls++;
 6:      echo "<h1>".$num_of_calls." ". $txt."</h1>";
 7:  }
 8:  numberedHeading("Widgets");
 9:  echo "<p>We build a fine range of widgets.</p>";
10:  numberedHeading("Doodads");
11:  echo "<p>Finest in the world.</p>";
12:  ?>
```

The numberedHeading() function has become entirely self-contained. When the $num_of_calls variable is declared on line 4, an initial value is assigned to it. This assignment is made when the function is first called on line 8. This initial assignment is ignored when the function is called a second time on line 10. Instead, the code remembers the previous value of $num_of_calls. You can now paste the numberedHeading() function into other scripts without worrying about global variables. Although the output of Listing 7.9 is the same as that of Listing 7.8, the code is a bit more elegant.

More About Arguments

You've already seen how to pass arguments to functions, but there's plenty more to cover. This section covers a technique for giving your arguments default values and explores a method of passing variables by reference rather than by value. This means that the function is given an alias of the original value rather than a copy of it.

Setting Default Values for Arguments

PHP provides a nifty feature to help build flexible functions. Until now, you've heard that some functions require one or more arguments. By making some arguments optional, you can render your functions a little less autocratic.

Listing 7.10 creates a useful little function that wraps a string in an HTML span element. To give the user of the function the chance to change the font-size style, you
can demand a $fontsize argument in addition to the string (line 2).

LISTING 7.10   A Function Requiring Two Arguments

```
1:  <?php
2:  function fontWrap($txt, $fontsize)
3:  {
4:      echo "<span style=\"font-size:$fontsize\">".$txt."</span>";
5:  }
6:  fontWrap("A Heading<br/>","24pt");
7:  fontWrap("some body text<br/>","16pt");
8:  fontWrap("smaller body text<br/>","12pt");
9:  fontWrap("even smaller body text<br/>","10pt");
10: ?>
```

Put these lines into a text file called fontwrap.php and place this file in your web
server document root. When you access this script through your web browser, it
should look like Figure 7.7.

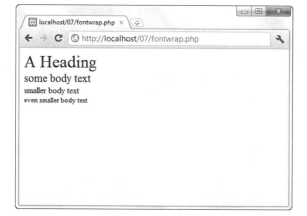

FIGURE 7.7
A function that
formats and
outputs strings.

By assigning a value to an argument variable within the function definition's parentheses, you can make the $fontsize argument optional. If the function call doesn't
define an argument for this argument, the value you have assigned to the argument
is used instead. Listing 7.11 uses this technique to make the $fontsize argument
optional.

LISTING 7.11   A Function with an Optional Argument

```
1:  <?php
2:  function fontWrap($txt, $fontsize = "12pt")
3:  {
4:      echo "<span style=\"font-size:$fontsize\">".$txt."</span>";
```

LISTING 7.11   Continued

```
5:  }
6:  fontWrap("A Heading<br/>","24pt");
7:  fontWrap("some body text<br/>");
8:  fontWrap("smaller body text<br/>");
9:  fontWrap("even smaller body text<br/>");
10: ?>
```

When the fontWrap() function is called with a second argument, as in line 6, this value is used to set the font-size attribute of the span element. When this argument is omitted, as in lines 7, 8, and 9, the default value of "12pt" is used instead. You can create as many optional arguments as you want, but when you've given an argument a default value, all subsequent arguments should also be given defaults.

Passing Variable References to Functions

When you pass arguments to functions, they are stored as copies in parameter variables. Any changes made to these variables in the body of the function are local to that function and are not reflected beyond it, as illustrated in Listing 7.12.

LISTING 7.12   Passing an Argument to a Function by Value

```
1: <?php
2: function addFive($num)
3: {
4:     $num += 5;
5: }
6: $orignum = 10;
7: addFive($orignum);
8: echo $orignum;
9: ?>
```

Put these lines into a text file called addfive.php and place this file in your web server document root. When you access this script through your web browser, it produces the following:

```
10
```

The addFive() function accepts a single numeric value and adds 5 to it, but it returns nothing. A value is assigned to a variable $orignum in line 6 and then this variable is passed to addFive() in line 7. A copy of the contents of $orignum is stored in the variable $num. Although $num is incremented by 5, this has no effect on the value of $orignum. When $orignum is printed, you find that its value is still 10. By default, variables passed to functions are passed by value. In other words, local copies of the values of the variables are made.

You can change this behavior by creating a reference to your original variable. You can think of a reference as a signpost that points to a variable. In working with the reference, you are manipulating the value to which it points.

Listing 7.13 shows this technique in action. When you pass an argument to a function by reference, as in line 7, the contents of the variable you pass ($orignum) are accessed by the argument variable and manipulated within the function, rather than just a copy of the variable's value (10). Any changes made to an argument in these cases change the value of the original variable. You can pass an argument by reference by adding an ampersand to the argument name in the function definition, as shown in line 2.

LISTING 7.13   Using a Function Definition to Pass an Argument to a Function by Reference

```
1: <?php
2: function addFive(&$num)
3: {
4:      $num += 5;
5: }
6: $orignum = 10;
7: addFive($orignum);
8: echo $orignum;
9: ?>
```

Put these lines into a text file called addfive2.php and place this file in your web server document root. When you access this script through your web browser, it produces the following:

15

Testing for the Existence of a Function

You do not always know that a function exists before you try to invoke it. Different builds of the PHP engine might include different functionality, and if you are writing a script that may be run on multiple servers, you might want to verify that key features are available. For instance, you might want to write code that uses MySQL if MySQL-related functions are available but simply log data to a text file otherwise.

You can use function_exists() to check for the availability of a function. function_exists() requires a string representing a function name. It returns true if the function can be located, and false otherwise.

Listing 7.14 shows function_exists() in action and illustrates some of the other topics we have covered in this chapter.

LISTING 7.14   Testing for a Function's Existence

```php
1:  <?php
2:  function tagWrap($tag, $txt, $func = "")
3:  {
4:      if ((!empty($txt)) && (function_exists($func))) {
5:          $txt = $func($txt);
6:          return "<".$tag.">".$txt."</".$tag."><br/>";
7:      } else {
8:          return "<strong>".$txt."</strong><br/>";
9:      }
10: }
11:
12: function underline($txt)
13: {
14:     return "<span style=\"text-decoration:underline;\">".$txt."</span>";
15: }
16: echo tagWrap('strong', 'make me bold');
17: echo tagWrap('em', 'underline and italicize me', "underline");
18: echo tagWrap('em', 'make me italic and quote me',
19: create_function('$txt', 'return "&quot;$txt&quot;";'));
20: ?>
```

Listing 7.14 defines two functions, `tagWrap()` (line 2) and `underline()` (line 12). The `tagWrap()` function accepts three strings: a tag, the text to format, and an optional function name. It returns a formatted string. The `underline()` function requires a single argument—the text to be formatted—and returns the text wrapped in `<span>` tags with appropriate style attributes.

When you first call `tagWrap()` on line 16, you pass it the string `strong` and the string `"make me bold"`. Because you haven't passed a value for the function argument, the default value (an empty string) is used. Line 4 checks whether the `$func` variable contains characters, and, if it is not empty, `function_exists()` is called to check for a function by that name. Of course, in this case, the `$func` variable is empty, so the `$txt` variable is wrapped in `<strong>` tags in the `else` clause on lines 7 and 8 and the result is returned.

The code calls `tagWrap()` on line 17 with the string `'em'`, some text, and a third argument: `"underline"`. `function_exists()` finds a function called `underline()` (line 12), so it calls this function and passes the `$txt` argument variable to it before any further formatting is done. The result is an italicized, underlined string.

Finally, on line 18, the code calls `tagWrap()`, which wraps text in quotation entities. It is quicker to simply add the entities to the text to be transformed ourselves, but this example serves to illustrate the point that `function_exists()` works as well on anonymous functions as it does on strings representing function names.

Put these lines into a text file called `exists.php` and place this file in your web server document root. When you access this script through your web browser, it should look like Figure 7.8.

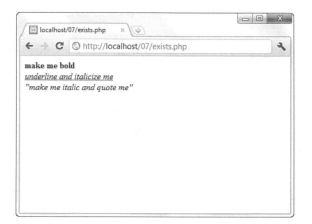

FIGURE 7.8
Output of
exists.php.

Summary

This chapter taught you about functions and how to deploy them. You learned how to define and pass arguments to a function, how to use the global and static statements, how to pass references to functions, and how to create default values for function arguments. You also learned to test for the existence of functions.

Q&A

Q. *Can I include a function call within a double- or single-quoted string, as I can with a variable?*

A. No. You must call functions outside quotation marks. However, you can break the string apart and place the function call between the parts of the string, using the concatenation operator to tie them together, as follows:

```
$newstring = "I purchased".numPurchase($somenum)." items.";
```

Q. *What happens if I call a function that does not exist, or if I declare a function with a name already in use?*

A. Calling a function that does not exist or declaring a function with the same name as another existing function causes the script to stop execution. Whether an error message displays in the browser depends on the error settings in your php.ini file.

Workshop

The workshop is designed to help you review what you've learned and begin putting your knowledge into practice.

Quiz

1. True or false: If a function doesn't require an argument, you can omit the parentheses in the function call.

2. How do you return a value from a function?

3. What does the following code fragment print to the browser?

```
$number = 50;

function tenTimes() {
    $number = $number * 10;
}

tenTimes();
echo $number;
```

4. What does the following code fragment print to the browser?

```
$number = 50;

function tenTimes() {
    global $number;
    $number = $number * 10;
}

tenTimes();
echo $number;
```

5. What does the following code fragment print to the browser?

```
$number = 50;

function tenTimes( &$n ) {
    $n = $n * 10;
}

tenTimes( $number );
echo $number;
```

Answers

1. The statement is false. You must always include the parentheses in your function calls, whether or not you are passing arguments to the function.

2. You must use the `return` keyword.

3. It prints 50. The `tenTimes()` function has no access to the global `$number` variable. When it is called, it manipulates its own local `$number` variable.

4. It prints 500. This example uses the `global` statement, which gives the `tenTimes()` function access to the `$number` variable.

5. It prints 500. By adding the ampersand to the parameter variable `$n`, you ensure that this argument is passed by reference. `$n` and `$number` point to the same value, so any changes to `$n` are reflected when you access `$number`.

Activities

1. Review the syntax for creating a function that accepts arguments, manipulates those values, and returns a string.

2. Create a function that accepts four string variables and returns a string that contains an HTML table element, enclosing each of the variables in its own cell.

CHAPTER 8

Working with Arrays

In this chapter, you learn the following:

▶ How to create associative and multidimensional arrays
▶ How to use the myriad array-related functions built in to PHP

Arrays are used to store and organize data. PHP includes many functions that enable you to create, modify, and manipulate arrays, which you use often throughout the procedural programming method described in this book.

What Are Arrays?

You've already learned about and used scalar variables in the earlier chapters in this book, and therefore you know that these variables are used to store values. But scalar variables can store only one value at a time—the $color variable can hold only a value of red or blue, and so forth, but it cannot be used to hold a list of colors in the rainbow. But arrays are special types of variables that enable you to store as many values as you want, including all seven of those rainbow colors.

CAUTION
Although you can store as many values as you want in an array, some array functions have an upper limit of 100,000 values. If you are storing large amounts of data in your arrays, be sure to read the PHP Manual entry for array functions you want to use and find out whether the function has an upper limit for working with data.

Arrays are indexed, which means that each entry is made up of a *key* and a *value*. The key is the index position, beginning with 0 and increasing incrementally by 1 with each new element in the array. The value is whatever value you associate with that position—a string, an integer, or whatever you want. Think of an array as a filing cabinet and each key/value pair as a file folder. The key is the label written on the top of the folder, and the value is what is inside. You'll see this type of structure in action as you create arrays in the next section.

Creating Arrays

You can create an array using either the array() function or the array operator []. The array() function is usually used when you want to create a new array and populate it with more than one element, all in one fell swoop. The array operator is often used when you want to create a new array with just one element at the outset, or when you want to add to an existing array element.

The following code snippet shows how to create an array called $rainbow using the array() function, containing all its various colors:

```
$rainbow = array("red", "orange", "yellow", "green", "blue", "indigo",
    "violet");
```

The following snippet shows the same array being created incrementally using the array operator:

```
$rainbow[] = "red";
$rainbow[] = "orange";
$rainbow[] = "yellow";
$rainbow[] = "green";
$rainbow[] = "blue";
$rainbow[] = "indigo";
$rainbow[] = "violet";
```

Both snippets create a seven-element array called $rainbow, with values starting at index position 0 and ending at index position 6. If you want to be literal about it, you can specify the index positions, such as in this code:

```
$rainbow[0] = "red";
$rainbow[1] = "orange";
$rainbow[2] = "yellow";
```

```
$rainbow[3] = "green";
$rainbow[4] = "blue";
$rainbow[5] = "indigo";
$rainbow[6] = "violet";
```

However, PHP handles this numbering for you when positions are not specified, and that eliminates the possibility that you might misnumber your elements when order is important, as in this example:

```
$rainbow[0] = "red";
$rainbow[1] = "orange";
$rainbow[2] = "yellow";
$rainbow[5] = "green";
$rainbow[6] = "blue";
$rainbow[7] = "indigo";
$rainbow[8] = "violet";
```

Regardless of whether you initially create your array using the array() function or the array operator, you can still add to it using the array operator. In the first line of the following snippet, six elements are added to the array, and one more element is added to the end of the array in the second line:

```
$rainbow = array("red", "orange", "yellow", "green", "blue", "indigo");
$rainbow[] = "violet";
```

The examples used in this section are of numerically indexed arrays, arguably the most common type you'll see. In the next two sections, you learn about two other types of arrays: associative and multidimensional.

Creating Associative Arrays

Whereas numerically indexed arrays use an index position as the key—0, 1, 2, and so forth—associative arrays use actual named keys. The following example demonstrates this by creating an array called $character with four elements:

```
$character = array(
          "name" => "Bob",
          "occupation" => "superhero",
          "age" => 30,
          "special power" => "x-ray vision"
          );
```

The four keys in the $character array are name, occupation, age, and special power. The associated values are Bob, superhero, 30, and x-ray vision, respectively. You can reference specific elements of an associative array using the specific key, such as in this example:

```
echo $character['occupation'];
```

The output of this snippet is this:

```
superhero
```

As with numerically indexed arrays, you can use the array operator to add to an associative array:

```
$character['supername'] = "Mega X-Ray Guy";
```

This example adds a key called supername with a value of Mega X-Ray Guy.

The only difference between an associative array and a numerically indexed array is the key name. In a numerically indexed array, the key name is a number. In an associative array, the key name is a meaningful word.

Creating Multidimensional Arrays

The first two types of arrays hold strings and integers, whereas this third type holds other arrays. If each set of key/value pairs constitutes a dimension, a multidimensional array holds more than one series of these key/value pairs. For example, Listing 8.1 defines a multidimensional array called $characters, each element of which contains an associative array. This might sound confusing, but it's really only an array that contains another array.

LISTING 8.1   Defining a Multidimensional Array

```
1:  <?php
2:  $characters = array(
3:              array(
4:                "name" => "Bob",
5:                "occupation" => "superhero",
6:                "age" => 30,
7:                "special power" => "x-ray vision"
8:                ),
9:              array(
10:               "name" => "Sally",
11:               "occupation" => "superhero",
12:               "age" => 24,
13:               "special power" => "superhuman strength"
14:               ),
15:              array(
16:               "name" => "Jane",
17:               "occupation" => "arch villain",
18:               "age" => 45,
19:               "special power" => "nanotechnology"
20:               )
21:              );
22: ?>
```

In line 2, the $characters array is initialized using the array() function. Lines 3–8 represent the first element, lines 9–14 represent the second element, and lines 15–20 represent the third element. These elements can be referenced as $characters[0], $characters[1], and $characters[2].

Each element consists of an associative array, itself containing four elements: name, occupation, age, and special_power.

However, if you attempt to print the master elements like so

```
echo $characters[1];
```

the output will be

```
Array
```

because the master element indeed holds an array as its content. To really get to the content you want (that is, the specific information found within the inner array element), you need to access the master element index position plus the associative name of the value you want to view.

Take a look at this example:

```
echo $characters[1]['occupation'];
```

It prints this:

```
superhero
```

If you add the following lines to the end of the code in Listing 8.1, it prints the information stored in each element, with an added line displayed in the browser for good measure:

```
foreach ($characters as $c) {
        while (list($k, $v) = each ($c)) {
                echo "$k ... $v <br/>";
        }
        echo "<hr/>";
}
```

The foreach loop is concerned with the master array element, $characters. It loops through this array and assigns the temporary name $c to the element contained within each position. Next, the code begins a while loop. This loop uses two functions to extract the contents of the inner array. First, the list() function names placeholder variables, $k and $v, which will be populated with the keys and values gathered from the each() function. The each() function looks at each element of the $c array and extracts the information accordingly.

The echo statement simply prints each key and value ($k and $v) extracted from the $c array using the each() function and adds a line break for display purposes. Figure 8.1 shows the result of this file, called mdarray.php.

FIGURE 8.1
Looping through a multidimensional array.

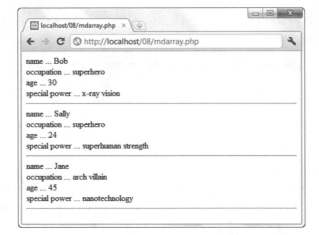

Some Array-Related Constructs and Functions

More than 70 array-related functions are built in to PHP, which you can read about in detail at http://www.php.net/array. Some of the more common (and useful) functions are described briefly in this section:

▶ **count() and sizeof()**—Each of these functions counts the number of elements in an array; they are aliases of each other. Given the following array

```
$colors = array("blue", "black", "red", "green");
```

both count($colors); and sizeof($colors); return a value of 4.

▶ **each() and list()**—These functions (well, list() is a language construct that *looks* like a function) usually appear together, in the context of stepping through an array and returning its keys and values. You saw an example of this previously, where we stepped through the $c array and printed its contents.

▶ **foreach()**—This control structure (that looks like a function) is used to step through an array, assigning the value of an element to a given variable, as you saw in the previous section.

▶ **reset()**—This function rewinds the pointer to the beginning of an array, as in this example:

```
reset($character);
```

This function proves useful when you are performing multiple manipulations on an array, such as sorting, extracting values, and so forth.

▶ **array_push()**—This function adds one or more elements to the end of an existing array, as in this example:

```
array_push($existingArray, "element 1", "element 2", "element 3");
```

▶ **array_pop()**—This function removes (and returns) the last element of an existing array, as in this example:

```
$last_element = array_pop($existingArray);
```

▶ **array_unshift()**—This function adds one or more elements to the beginning of an existing array, as in this example:

```
array_unshift($existingArray, "element 1", "element 2", "element 3");
```

▶ **array_shift()**—This function removes (and returns) the first element of an existing array, as in this example, where the value of the element in the first position of $existingArray is assigned to the variable $first_element:

```
$first_element = array_shift($existingArray);
```

▶ **array_merge()**—This function combines two or more existing arrays, as in this example:

```
$newArray = array_merge($array1, $array2);
```

▶ **array_keys()**—This function returns an array containing all the key names within a given array, as in this example:

```
$keysArray = array_keys($existingArray);
```

▶ **array_values()**—This function returns an array containing all the values within a given array, as in this example:

```
$valuesArray = array_values($existingArray);
```

▶ **shuffle()**—This function randomizes the elements of a given array. The syntax of this function is simply as follows:

```
shuffle($existingArray);
```

This brief rundown of array-related functions only scratches the surface of using arrays. However, arrays and array-related functions are used in the code examples throughout this book, so you will get your fill soon enough. If you don't, there's always the array section of the PHP Manual at http://www.php.net/array that discusses all array-related functions in great detail, including more than 10 different methods just for sorting your arrays.

Summary

This chapter introduced you to the concepts of arrays, including how they are created and referenced. The three array types are the numerically indexed array, associative array, and multidimensional array. In addition, you saw examples of some of the numerous array-related functions already built in to PHP. You can use these functions to manipulate and modify existing arrays, sometimes even creating entirely new ones.

Q&A

Q. *How many dimensions can multidimensional arrays have?*

A. You can create as many dimensions in your multidimensional array as you can manage, but remember the more dimensions you have, the more you have to manage. If you have data with more than a few dimensions, it might be wise to ask yourself whether that data should be stored differently, such as in a database and accessed that way.

Q. *If all I'm doing is creating a contact form, why would I care about arrays?*

A. Arrays are useful in even the most basic client-server interactions, such as a contact form in a website. You will learn more about forms in Chapter 11, "Working with Forms," but here's something to keep in mind before you work with the information in that chapter: If your form contains any series of checkboxes or lists from which a user can select more than one option, that data will be sent to your form as an array. You'll need to get that data out of the array if you want to work with it, and this chapter shows a few basic examples of doing just that.

Workshop

The workshop is designed to help you review what you've learned and begin putting your knowledge into practice.

Quiz

1. What construct can you use to define an array?

2. What function would you use to join two arrays?

Answers

1. `array()`

2. `array_merge()`

Activities

1. Review the process of defining a multidimensional array and referencing its items.

2. Create a multidimensional array of movies organized by genre. This should take the form of an associative array with genres as keys, such as `Science Fiction`, `Action`, `Adventure`, and so forth. Each of the array's elements should be an array containing movie names, such as *Alien*, *Terminator 3*, *Star Wars*, and so on. After creating your arrays, loop through them, printing the name of each genre and its associated movies.

CHAPTER 9

Working with Objects

In this chapter, you learn the following:

▶ The basic structure of an object

▶ How to create and manipulate objects and the data they contain

Programmers use objects to store and organize data. Object-oriented programming is a type of programming in which the structure of the program (or application) is designed around these objects and their relationships and interactions. Object-oriented programming structures are found in many programming languages, and are also evident in PHP. In fact, many PHP programmers—especially those coming from a highly object-oriented programming background—choose to develop PHP applications in an object-oriented way.

However, in PHP, it is not required that you write your scripts in an object-oriented manner. Many PHP scripts, and in fact most of the ones in this book, are procedural and functional rather than object-oriented. That is to say, the emphasis is on stepping through the use of variables, data and control structures, and subroutines and functions in the course of creating a program. The reason for this is simply that if you are altogether new to programming it's important to gain experience in procedural programming and the fundamentals of the language before you tackle a programming paradigm that itself has many books written about it. This chapter gives you a brief glimpse into the world of objects, because it is an important data type and concept to be familiar with as you move on to gather even more skills and experience.

NOTE ───

If you are coming to PHP with a background in object-oriented programming, this chapter will help you to understand the object model in PHP.

Creating an Object

Explaining the concept of an object is a little difficult if you've never encountered the concept before, because it is inherently abstract: It's a sort of theoretical box of things—variables, functions, and so forth—that exists in a templated structure called a *class*. Although it's easy to visualize a scalar variable, such as $color, with a value of red, or an array called $character with three or four different elements inside it, some people have a difficult time visualizing objects.

For now, try to think of an object as a little box with inputs and outputs on either side of it. The input mechanisms are *methods*, and methods have properties. Throughout this section, we look at how classes, methods, and properties work together to produce various outputs.

NOTE ───

If the concept of classes is completely foreign to you, you can supplement your knowledge by reading the "Classes and Objects" chapter in the PHP Manual. You can find it at http://www.php.net/manual/en/language.oop5.php.

As mentioned previously, an object exists in a structure called a *class*. In each class, you define a set of characteristics. For example, suppose you have created an automobile class. In the automobile class, you might have color, make, and model characteristics. Each automobile object uses all the characteristics, but each object initializes the characteristics to different values, such as silver, Mazda, and Protege5, or red, Porsche, and Boxter.

The whole purpose of using objects is to create reusable code. Because classes are so tightly structured but self-contained and independent of one another, you can reuse them from one application to another. For example, suppose that you write a text-formatting class for one project and decide you can use that class in another project. Because a class is just a set of characteristics, you can pick up the code and use it in the second project, reaching into it with methods specific to the second application but using the inner workings of the existing code to achieve new results.

Creating an object is simple; you just declare it to be in existence:

```
class myClass {
    //code will go here
}
```

Now that you have a class, you can create a new instance of an object:

```
$object1 = new myClass();
```

In Listing 9.1, you have proof that your object exists, even though there's nothing in it—it's just been named.

LISTING 9.1   Proof That Your Object Exists

```
1:  <?php
2:  class myClass {
3:      //code will go here
4:  }
5:  $object1 = new myClass();
6:  echo "\$object1 is an ".gettype($object1)."<br/>";
7:
8:  if (is_object($object1)) {
9:      echo "Really! I swear \$object1 is an object!";
10: }
11: ?>
```

If you save this code as proofofclass.php, place it in your document root, and access it with your web browser, you will see the following on your screen:

```
$object1 is an object.
Really! I swear $object1 is an object!
```

This is not a particularly useful class because it does absolutely nothing, but it is valid and shows you how the class template works in lines 2–5. Lines 8–10 use the is_object() function to test whether something is an object; in this case, the *something* is $object1. Because the test of is_object() evaluates to true, the string within the if statement is printed to the screen.

Next, you learn about using object properties and methods within the class template.

Properties of Objects

The variables declared inside an object are called *properties*. It is standard practice to declare your variables at the top of the class. These properties can be values, arrays, or even other objects. The following snippet uses simple scalar variables inside the class, prefaced with the public keyword:

```
class myCar {
    public$color = "silver";
    public$make = "Mazda";
    public$model = "Protege5";
}
```

NOTE

If you use the keyword public, protected, or private before the variable name, you can indicate if the class member (the variable) can be accessed everywhere (public), within the class itself or a parent class or an inherited class (protected), or only by the class itself (private).

Now when you create a myCar object, it will always have those three properties. Listing 9.2 shows you how to access properties after they have been declared and values have been assigned to them.

LISTING 9.2   Showing Object Properties

```
1:  <?php
2:  class myCar {
3:      public$color = "silver";
4:      public$make = "Mazda";
5:      public$model = "Protege5";
6:  }
7:  $car = new myCar();
8:  echo "I drive a: ".$car -> color." ".$car -> make." ".$car -> model;
9:  ?>
```

If you save this code as objproperties.php, place it in your document root, and access it with your web browser, you will see the following on your screen:

```
I drive a: silver Mazda Protege5
```

Because the odds are low that you also drive a silver Mazda Protege5, you'll want to change the properties of the myCar object. Listing 9.3 shows you how to do just that.

LISTING 9.3   Changing Object Properties

```
1:  <?php
2:  class myCar {
3:      public$color = "silver";
4:      public$make = "Mazda";
5:      public$model = "Protege5";
6:  }
7:  $car = new myCar();
8:  $car -> color = "red";
9:  $car -> make = "Porsche";
10: $car -> model = "Boxter";
11: echo "I drive a: ".$car -> color." ".$car -> make." ".$car -> model;
12: ?>
```

If you save this code as objproperties2.php, place it in your document root, and access it with your web browser, you will see the following on your screen:

```
I drive a: red Porsche Boxter
```

NOTE

In this instance, even if the $color, $make, and $model properties had no initial values when declared, lines 8–10 would assign a value to them. As long as the properties are declared, you can use them later (initial values or not).

The purpose of Listing 9.3 is to show that as long as you have a well-defined class with properties, you can still easily change the values of the properties to fit your needs.

Object Methods

Methods add functionality to your objects. No longer will your objects just sit there, holding on to their properties for dear life—they'll actually do something! Listing 9.4 shows just that.

LISTING 9.4 A Class with a Method

```
1: <?php
2: class myClass {
3:     function sayHello() {
4:         echo "HELLO!";
5:     }
6: }
7: $object1 = new myClass();
8: $object1 -> sayHello();
9: ?>
```

Although it is not the most thrilling example of action, if you save this code as helloclass.php, place it in your document root, and access it with your web browser, you will see the following on your screen:

HELLO!

A method looks and acts like a normal function but is defined within the framework of a class. The -> operator is used to call the object method in the context of your script. Had there been any variables stored in the object, the method would have been capable of accessing them for its own purposes, as illustrated in Listing 9.5.

LISTING 9.5 Accessing Class Properties Within a Method

```
1: <?php
2: class myClass {
3:     public$name = "Jimbo";
4:     function sayHello() {
5:         echo "HELLO! My name is ".$this->name;
6:     }
7: }
8: $object1 = new myClass();
9: $object1 -> sayHello();
10: ?>
```

If you save this code as `helloclass2.php`, place it in your document root, and access it with your web browser, you will see the following on your screen:

HELLO! My name is Jimbo

The special variable `$this` is used to refer to the currently instantiated object as you see on line 5. Anytime an object refers to itself, you must use the `$this` variable. Using the `$this` variable in conjunction with the `->` operator enables you to access any property or method in a class, within the class itself.

One final tidbit regarding the basics of working with an object's properties is how to change a property from within a method. Previously, a property's value changed outside the method in which it was contained. Listing 9.6 shows how to make the change from inside a method.

LISTING 9.6   Changing the Value of a Property from Within a Method

```php
1: <?php
2: class myClass {
3:     public$name = "Jimbo";
4:     function setName($n) {
5:         $this->name = $n;
6:     }
7:     function sayHello() {
8:         echo "HELLO! My name is ".$this->name;
9:     }
10: }
11: $object1 = new myClass();
12: $object1 -> setName("Julie");
13: $object1 -> sayHello();
14: ?>
```

If you save this code as `helloclass3.php`, place it in your document root, and access it with your web browser, you will see the following on your screen:

HELLO! My name is Julie

Why? Because in lines 4–6 a new function called `setName()` was created. When it is called in line 12, it changes the value of $name to `Julie`. Therefore, when the `sayHello()` function is called in line 13 and it looks for `$this->name`, it uses `Julie`, which is the new value that was just set by the `setName()` function. In other words, an object can modify its own property—in this case, the $name variable.

Constructors

A *constructor* is a function that lives within a class and, given the same name as the class, is automatically called when a new instance of the class is created using `new classname`. Using constructors enables you to provide arguments to your class, which will then be processed immediately when the class is called. You see constructors in action in the next section.

Object Inheritance

Having learned the absolute basics of objects, properties, and methods, you can start to look at object inheritance. Inheritance with regard to classes is just what it sounds like: One class inherits functionality from its parent class. Listing 9.7 shows an example.

LISTING 9.7   A Class Inheriting from Its Parent

```
1:   <?php
2:   class myClass {
3:       public$name = "Matt";
4:       function myClass($n) {
5:             $this->name = $n;
6:       }
7:       function sayHello() {
8:             echo "HELLO! My name is ".$this->name;
9.       }
10: }
11: class childClass extends myClass {
12: //code goes here
13: }
14: $object1 = new childClass("Baby Matt");
15: $object1 -> sayHello();
16: ?>
```

If you save this code as inheritance.php, place it in your document root, and access it with your web browser, you will see the following on your screen:

```
HELLO! My name is Baby Matt
```

Lines 4–6 make up a constructor. Notice that the name of this function is the same as the class in which it is contained: myClass. Lines 11–13 define a second class, childClass, that contains no code. That's fine because, in this example, the class exists only to demonstrate inheritance from the parent class. The inheritance occurs through the extends clause shown in line 11. The second class inherits the elements of the first class because this clause is used.

Listing 9.8 shows you one last example of how a child class can override the methods of the parent class.

LISTING 9.8   The Method of a Child Class Overriding That of Its Parent

```
1:   <?php
2:   class myClass {
```

LISTING 9.8   Continued

```
3:      public$name = "Matt";
4:      function myClass($n) {
5:          $this->name = $n;
6:      }
7:      function sayHello() {
8:          echo "HELLO! My name is ".$this->name;
9:      }
10: }
11: class childClass extends myClass {
12:     function sayHello() {
13:         echo "I will not tell you my name.";
14:     }
15: }
16: $object1 = new childClass("Baby Matt");
17: $object1 -> sayHello();
18: ?>
```

The only changes in this code from Listing 9.7 are the new lines 12–14. In these lines, a function is created called sayHello() that, instead of printing HELLO! My name is..., prints the message I will not tell you my name. Because the sayHello() function now exists in childClass, and childClass is the class called in line 16, its version of sayHello() is the one used.

If you save this code as inheritance2.php, place it in your document root, and access it with your web browser, you will see the following on your screen:

```
I will not tell you my name
```

Like most elements of object-oriented programming, inheritance is useful when attempting to make your code flexible. Suppose that you create a text-formatting class that organizes and stores data, format it in HTML, and output the result to a browser—your own personal masterpiece. Now suppose that you have a client who wants to use that concept, but instead of formatting the content into HTML and sending it to a browser, he wants to format it for plaintext and save it to a text file. No problem; you just add a few methods and properties, and away you go. Finally, the client comes back and says that he really wants the data to be formatted and sent as an email—and then, what the heck, why not create XML-formatted files, as well?

Although you might want to pull your hair out in frustration, you're really not in a bad situation. If you separate the compilation and storage classes from the formatting classes—one for each of the various delivery methods (HTML, text, email, XML)—you essentially have a parent-child relationship. Consider the parent class as the one that holds the compilation and storage methods. The formatting classes are the children: They inherit the information from the parent and output the result based on their own functionality. Everybody wins.

Summary

This chapter provided a foundation for working with object-oriented code. In no way does this content cover all the aspects of object-oriented programming. Universities teach entire series of classes (no pun intended) devoted to this topic, so you can imagine that these pages are a little light. However, you did learn to create classes and instantiate objects from them. You learned how to create and access the properties and methods of a class, how to build new classes, and how to inherit features from parent classes. That's not too shabby!

Q&A

Q. *Why have I seen `var` instead of `public`, `private`, or `protected` in property declarations?*

A. In earlier versions of PHP, `var` was used to declare properties in classes. For backward compatibility, if you use code that still says `var` in it, it will be treated as public and not cause an error (unless you want it to be a private or protected property).

Q. *Do I have to understand object-oriented programming to become a good PHP programmer or even to finish this book?*

A. Not at all. In fact, the projects in this book are procedural or functional in nature and do *not* contain object-oriented programming. Object-oriented programming is an organizational approach intended to improve the reusability and extensibility of the code that makes up a given application. You might not know enough about your project in the beginning stages of development to fully plan for an object-oriented design. When it is complete—or, at least, approaching a solid state—you might start to see areas in which an object-oriented approach can be taken, and you might start to combine your code into classes, properties, and methods. But for the most part, you won't write simple scripts performing particular duties in object-oriented fashion unless it is your background and comes naturally to you. For a great deal more information on the object model in PHP, see the appropriate section of the PHP Manual, at http://www.php.net/manual/en/language.oop5.php.

Workshop

The workshop is designed to help you review what you've learned and begin putting your knowledge into practice.

Quiz

1. How can you declare a class called `emptyClass` that has no methods or properties?

2. How do you choose a name for a constructor method?

3. If a variable is declared `private`, where can it be used?

Answers

1. Use the `class` keyword:

```
class emptyClass {
}
```

2. You don't—a constructor is named for the class in which it resides.

3. Variables declared `private` can only be used in the class itself.

Activities

1. Create a class called `baseCalc()` that stores two numbers as properties. Next, create a `calculate()` method that prints the numbers to the browser.

2. Now create classes called `addCalc()`, `subCalc()`, `mulCalc()`, and `divCalc()` that inherit functionality from `baseCalc()` but override the `calculate()` method and print appropriate totals to the browser.

CHAPTER 10

Working with Strings, Dates, and Time

In this chapter, you learn the following:

▶ How to format strings

▶ How to determine the length of a string

▶ How to find a substring within a string

▶ How to break a string down into component parts

▶ How to remove whitespace from the beginning or end of a string

▶ How to replace substrings

▶ How to change the case of a string

▶ How to acquire the current date and time

▶ How to get information about a date and time

▶ How to format date and time information

▶ How to test dates for validity

▶ How to set dates and times

No matter how rich your web content might be, at the heart of it is just HTML that tells the browser how to render string-based content. It is no accident, then, that PHP provides many functions with which you can format and manipulate strings. Similarly, dates and times are so much a part of everyday life that it becomes easy to use them without thinking. However, because the quirks of the Gregorian calendar can be difficult to work with, PHP provides powerful tools that make date manipulation an easy task.

Numerous PHP functions are available to you when it comes to the manipulations of strings, dates, and times, and this chapter does not even begin to cover all of them. However, this chapter does provide a foundation for using some of the basic string, date, and time functions, and an idea of how to begin thinking about using these types of functions in your code. The rule of thumb is this: If you want to transform, manipulate, or display a string, date, or time, don't build your own custom solution without first visiting the PHP Manual, because chances are good that a function already exists for your desired task.

Formatting Strings with PHP

Until now, you have simply printed any strings you want to display directly to the browser in their original state. PHP provides two functions that enable you first to apply formatting, whether to round doubles to a given number of decimal places, define alignment within a field, or display data according to different number systems. In this section, you learn a few of the formatting options provided by `printf()` and `sprintf()`.

Working with `printf()`

If you have any experience with a C-like programming language, you are probably familiar with the concept of the `printf()` function. The `printf()` function requires a string argument, known as a *format control string*. It also accepts additional arguments of different types, which you learn about in a moment. The format control string contains instructions regarding the display of these additional arguments. The following fragment, for example, uses `printf()` to output an integer as an octal (or base-8) number:

```
<?php
printf("This is my number: %o", 55);
// prints "This is my number: 67"
?>
```

Included within the format control string (the first argument) is a special code, known as a *conversion specification*. A conversion specification begins with a percent (%) symbol and defines how to treat the corresponding argument to `printf()`. You can include as many conversion specifications as you want within the format control string, as long as you send an equivalent number of arguments to `printf()`.

The following fragment outputs two floating-point numbers using `printf()`:

```
<?php
printf("First number: %f<br/>Second number: %f<br/>", 55, 66);
// Prints:
// First number: 55.000000
// Second number: 66.000000
?>
```

The first conversion specification corresponds to the first of the additional arguments to `printf()`, or 55. The second conversion specification corresponds to 66. The f following the percent symbol requires that the data be treated as a floating-point number. This part of the conversion specification is the *type specifier*.

`printf()` **and Type Specifiers**

You have already come across two type specifiers, o, which displays integers as octals, and f, which displays integers as floating-point numbers. Table 10.1 lists the other type specifiers available.

TABLE 10.1 Type Specifiers

Specifier	Description
d	Display argument as a decimal number
b	Display an integer as a binary number
c	Display an integer as ASCII equivalent
f	Display an integer as a floating-point number (double)
o	Display an integer as an octal number (base 8)
s	Display argument as a string
x	Display an integer as a lowercase hexadecimal number (base 16)
X	Display an integer as an uppercase hexadecimal number (base 16)

Listing 10.1 uses `printf()` to display a single number according to some of the type specifiers listed in Table 10.1. Notice that the listing does not only add conversion specifications to the format control string. Any additional text included is also printed.

LISTING 10.1 Demonstrating Some Type Specifiers

```
1:  <?php
2:  $number = 543;
3:  printf("Decimal: %d<br/>", $number);
4:  printf("Binary: %b<br/>", $number);
5:  printf("Double: %f<br/>", $number);
6:  printf("Octal: %o<br/>", $number);
7:  printf("String: %s<br/>", $number);
8:  printf("Hex (lower): %x<br/>", $number);
9:  printf("Hex (upper): %X<br/>", $number);
10: ?>
```

Put these lines into a text file named printftest.php and place this file in your web server document root. When you access this script through your web browser, it should look something like Figure 10.1. As you can see, printf() is a quick way of converting data from one number system to another and outputting the result.

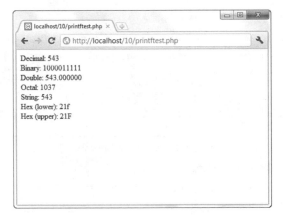

When specifying a color in HTML, you combine three hexadecimal numbers between 00 and FF, representing the values for red, green, and blue. You can use printf() to convert three decimal numbers between 0 and 255 to their hexadecimal equivalents:

```php
<?php
$red = 204;
$green = 204;
$blue = 204;
printf("#%X%X%X", $red, $green, $blue);
// prints "#CCCCCC"
?>
```

Although you can use the type specifier to convert from decimal to hexadecimal numbers, you cannot use it to determine how many characters the output for each argument should occupy. Within an HTML color code, each hexadecimal number should be padded to two characters, which would become a problem if you changed the $red, $green, and $blue variables in the previous fragment to contain 1, for example. You would end up with the output #111. You can force the output of leading zeros by using a *padding specifier*.

Padding Output with a Padding Specifier

You can require that output be padded by leading characters. The padding specifier should directly follow the percent sign that begins a conversion specification. To pad output with leading zeros, the padding specifier should consist of a zero followed by the number of characters you want the output to take up. If the output occupies fewer characters than this total, zeros fill the difference:

```php
<?php
printf("%04d", 36);
// prints "0036"
?>
```

To pad output with leading spaces, the padding specifier should consist of a space character followed by the number of characters that the output should occupy:

```php
<?php
printf("% 4d", 36)
// prints "  36"
?>
```

> **TIP**
>
> A browser will not display multiple spaces in an HTML document. You can force the display of spaces and newlines by placing <pre> tags around your output:
>
> ```
> <pre>
> <?php
> echo "The        spaces      will be visible";
> ?>
> </pre>
> ```
>
> If you want to format an entire document as text, you can use the header() function to change the Content-Type header:
>
> ```
> header("Content-Type: text/plain");
> ```
>
> Remember that your script must not have sent any output to the browser for the header() function to work as desired.

You can specify any character other than a space or a zero in your padding specifier with a single quotation mark followed by the character you want to use:

```php
<?php
printf ("%'x4d", 36);
// prints "xx36"
?>
```

You now have the tools you need to complete your HTML code example. Until now, you could convert three numbers to hexadecimal, but could not pad the hexadecimal values with leading zeros:

```php
<?php
$red = 1;
$green = 1;
$blue = 1;
printf("#%02X%02X%02X", $red, $green, $blue);
// prints "#010101"
?>
```

Each variable is output as a hexadecimal number. If the output occupies fewer than two spaces, leading zeros are added.

Specifying a Field Width

You can specify the number of spaces within which your output should sit. A *field width specifier* is an integer that should be placed after the percent sign that begins a conversion specification (assuming that no padding specifier is defined). The following fragment outputs a list of four items, all of which sit within a field of 20 spaces. To make the spaces visible on the browser, place all the output within a pre element:

```php
<?php
echo "<pre>";
printf("%20s\n", "Books");
printf("%20s\n", "CDs");
printf("%20s\n", "DVDs");
printf("%20s\n", "Games");
printf("%20s\n", "Magazines");
echo "</pre>";
?>
```

Figure 10.2 shows the output of this fragment.

FIGURE 10.2
Aligning with field width specifiers.

By default, output is right-aligned within the field you specify. You can make it left-aligned by prepending a minus (dash) to the field width specifier:

```php
printf("%-20s\n", "Left aligned");
```

Note that alignment applies to the decimal portion of any number that you output. In other words, only the portion before the decimal point of a double will sit flush to the end of the field width when right-aligned.

Specifying Precision

If you want to output data in floating-point format, you can specify the precision to which you want to round your data. This proves particularly useful when dealing with currency. The precision identifier should be placed directly before the type specifier. It consists of a dot followed by the number of decimal places to which you want to round. This specifier has an effect only on data that is output with the f type specifier:

```php
<?php
printf("%.2f", 5.333333);
// prints "5.33"
?>
```

NOTE

> In the C language, it is possible to use a precision specifier with printf() to specify padding for decimal output. The precision specifier has no effect on decimal output in PHP. Use the padding specifier to add leading zeros to integers.

Conversion Specifications: A Recap

Table 10.2 lists the specifiers that can make up a conversion specification in the order that they would be included. Note that it is difficult to use both a padding specifier and a field width specifier. You should choose to use one or the other, but not both.

TABLE 10.2 Components of Conversion Specification

Name	Description	Example
Padding specifier	Determines the number of characters that output should occupy, and the characters to add otherwise	' 4'
Field width specifier	Determines the space within which output should be formatted	'20'
Precision specifier	Determines the number of decimal places to which a double should be rounded	'.4'
Type specifier	Determines the data type that should be output	'd'

Listing 10.2 uses `printf()` to output a list of products

LISTING 10.2   Using `printf()` to Format a List of Product Prices

```
1:  <?php
2:  $products = array("Green armchair" => "222.4",
3:                      "Candlestick"=> "4",
4:                      "Coffee table"=> "80.6");
5:  echo "<pre>";
6:  printf("%-20s%20s\n", "Name", "Price");
7:  printf("%'-40s\n", "");
8:  foreach ($products as $key=>$val) {
9:      printf( "%-20s%20.2f\n", $key, $val );
10: }
11: echo "</pre>";
12: ?>
```

The listing first defines an associative array containing product names and prices in lines 2 through 4. It prints the opening tag of the `pre` element, in line 5, so that the browser will recognize the spaces and newlines. The first `printf()` call on line 6 uses the following format control string:

`"%-20s%20s\n"`

The first conversion specification in the format control string (`"%-20s"`) defines a width specifier of 20 characters, with the output to be left-justified. The string type specifier is also used. The second conversion specification (`"%20s"`) sets up a right-aligned field width. This `printf()` call outputs our field headers.

The second `printf()` function call on line 7 draws a line containing - characters, 40 characters wide. You achieve this with a padding specifier, which adds padding to an empty string.

The final `printf()` call on line 9 is part of a `foreach` statement that loops through the product array. The code uses two conversion specifications here—the first (`"%-20s"`) prints the product name as a string left-justified within a 20-character field, and the second (`"%20.2f"`) uses a field width specifier to ensure that output will be right-aligned within a 20-character field. It also uses a precision specifier to ensure that the output is rounded to two decimal places.

Put these lines into a text file named **printftest2.php** and place this file in your web server document root. When you access this script through your web browser, it should look like Figure 10.3.

FIGURE 10.3
Products and
prices formatted
with printf().

Argument Swapping

Suppose that you are printing dates to the browser. As shown in the following snippet, assume the dates are in a multidimensional array and you are using printf() to format the output:

```php
<?php
$dates = array(
        array('mon'=> 12, 'mday'=>25, 'year'=>2011),
        array('mon'=>  1, 'mday'=>23, 'year'=>2012),
        array('mon'=> 10, 'mday'=>29, 'year'=>2011)
        );
$format = include("local_format.php");
foreach($dates as $date) {
    printf("$format", $date['mon'], $date['mday'], $date['year']);
}
?>
```

In the preceding snippet, the format control string comes from an include file named local_format.php. Assuming that this file contains only

```php
<?php
return "%02d/%02d/%d<br/>";
?>
```

the output will be in the format mm/dd/yyyy:

```
12/25/2011
01/23/2012
10/29/2011
```

Imagine now that you are installing your script for a European site, where dates are commonly presented with days before months (dd/mm/yyyy). Assume that the core code is written in stone and cannot be changed. What should you do? Luckily, you can now alter the order in which the arguments are presented from within the format control code by changing the `return` statement to the following:

```
return "%2\$02d/%1\$02d/%3\$d<br/>";
```

You can insert the argument number you are interested in after the initial percentage character that marks each conversion specification, followed by an escaped dollar ($) character. So, in the fragment, you are demanding that the second argument be presented

```
%2\$02d
```

followed by the first argument:

```
%1\$02d
```

and concluded with the third argument:

```
%3\$d
```

The result of the new code is a list of dates in British format:

```
25/12/2011
23/01/2012
29/10/2011
```

Storing a Formatted String

The `printf()` function outputs data to the browser, which means that the results are not available to your scripts. You can, however, use the function `sprintf()`, which is used just like `printf()` except that it returns a string that can be stored in a variable for later use. The following fragment uses `sprintf()` to round a double to two decimal places, storing the result in $cash:

```php
<?php
$cash = sprintf("%.2f", 21.334454);
echo "You have \$$cash to spend.";
// Prints "You have $21.33 to spend."
?>
```

One particular use of `sprintf()` is to write formatted data to a file—you can call `sprintf()` and assign its return value to a variable that can then be printed to a file with `fputs()`.

Investigating Strings in PHP

You do not always know everything about the data you are working with. Strings can arrive from many sources, including user input, databases, files, and web pages. Before you begin to work with data from an external source, you often need to find out more about the data. PHP provides many functions that enable you to acquire information about strings.

A Note About Indexing Strings

This book frequently uses the word *index* in relation to strings. You have come across this word in the context of arrays, such as in Chapter 8, "Working with Arrays." In fact, strings and arrays are not as different as you might imagine. You can think of a string as an array of characters, and thus you can access the individual characters of a string as if they were elements of an array:

```php
<?php
$test = "phpcoder";
echo $test[0]; // prints "p"
echo $test[4]; // prints "o"
?>
```

It is important to remember that when this book discusses the position or index of a character within a string, the characters, just like array elements, have a starting index value of 0, not 1.

Finding the Length of a String with `strlen()`

You can use the built-in `strlen()` function to determine the length of a string. This function requires a string as its argument and returns an integer representing the number of characters in the string you passed to it. `strlen()` might be used to check the length of user input, as in the following fragment, which tests a membership code to ensure that it is exactly four characters long:

```php
<?php
$membership = "pAB7";
if (strlen($membership) == 4) {
    echo "<p>Thank you!</p>";
} else {
    echo "<p>Your membership number must be four characters long.</p>";
}
?>
```

The user is thanked for his input only if the $membership variable holds a string that is exactly four characters long. Otherwise, an error message is presented.

Finding a Substring Within a String with `strstr()`

You can use the `strstr()` function to test whether a string exists within another string. This function requires two arguments: the source string and the substring you want to find within it. The function returns `false` if it cannot find the substring; otherwise, it returns the portion of the source string, beginning with the substring. For the following example, imagine that you want to treat membership codes that contain the string AB differently from those that do not:

```php
<?php
$membership = "pAB7";
if (strstr($membership, "AB")) {
    echo "<p>Your membership expires soon!</p>";
} else {
    echo "<p>Thank you!</p>";
}
?>
```

Because the value of the $membership variable contains the substring AB, the `strstr()` function returns the string AB7. The function resolves to `true` when tested, so the code prints the appropriate message, `"Your membership expires soon!"`. But what happens if you search for `"pab7"`? Because `strstr()` is case sensitive, AB will not be found. The `if` statement's original test will fail, and the default message (`"Thank you!"`) will be printed to the browser. If you want to search for either AB or ab within the string, you must use `strstr()` in place of `substr()`; the function is used in exactly the same way, but its search is not case sensitive.

Finding the Position of a Substring with `strpos()`

The `strpos()` function tells you whether a string exists within a larger string as well as where it is found. The `strpos()` function requires two arguments: the source string and the substring you are seeking. The function also accepts an optional third argument, an integer representing the index from which you want to start searching. If the substring does not exist, `strpos()` returns `false`; otherwise, it returns the index at which the substring begins. The following fragment uses `strpos()` to ensure that a string begins with the string mz:

```php
<?php
$membership = "mz00xyz";
if (strpos($membership, "mz") === 0) {
    echo "Hello mz!";
}
?>
```

Notice the trick that had to be played to get the expected results. Although the `strpos()` function finds mz in the string, it finds it at the first element—the 0 position. Returning zero will resolve to `false` in the `if` condition test. To work around this, the code uses the equivalence operator ===, which returns true if the left and right operands are equivalent and of the same type, as they are in this case.

This is just one of several variations on string-related functions meant to find needles in haystacks. Visit the PHP Manual page for this function for links to many other related functions.

Extracting Part of a String with substr()

The substr() function returns a string based on the start index and length of the characters you are looking for. This function requires two arguments: a source string and the starting index. Using these arguments, the function returns all the characters from the starting index to the end of the string you are searching. You can also (optionally) provide a third argument—an integer representing the length of the string you want returned. If this third argument is present, substr() returns only that number of characters, from the start index onward:

```
<?php
$test = "phpcoder";
echo substr($test,3)."<br/>";  // prints "coder"
echo substr($test,3,2)."<br/>"; // prints "co"
?>
```

If you pass substr() a negative number as its second (starting index) argument, it will count from the end rather than the beginning of the string. The following fragment writes a specific message to people who have submitted an email address ending in .fr:

```
<?php
$test = "pierre@wanadoo.fr";
if ($test = substr($test, -3) == ".fr") {
    echo "<p>Bonjour! Nous avons des prix spéciaux de vous.</p>";
} else {
    echo "<p>Welcome to our store.</p>";
}
?>
```

Tokenizing a String with strtok()

You can parse a string word by word using the strtok() function. This function requires two arguments: the string to tokenize and the delimiters by which to split the string. The delimiter string can include as many characters as you want, and the function will return the first token found. After strtok() has been called for the first time, the source string is cached—for subsequent calls, you should pass only the delimiter string to the strtok() function. The function returns the next found token every time it is called, returning false when the end of the string is reached. The strtok() function is usually called repeatedly within a loop. Listing 10.3 uses strtok() to tokenize a URL, splitting the host and path from the query string and further dividing the name/value pairs of the query string.

LISTING 10.3   Dividing a String into Tokens with strtok()

```php
1: <?php
2: $test  = "http://www.google.com/search?";
3: $test .= "hl=en&ie=UTF-8&q=php+development+books&btnG=Google+Search";
4: $delims = "?&";
5: $word = strtok($test, $delims);
6: while (is_string($word)) {
7:    if ($word) {
8:       echo $word."<br/>";
9:    }
10:    $word = strtok($delims);
11: }
12: ?>
```

Put these lines into a text file named **teststrtotok.php** and place this file in your web server document root. When you access this script through your web browser, it should look like Figure 10.4.

FIGURE 10.4
Output of test-strtotok.php, a tokenized string.

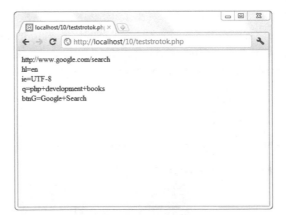

The strtok() function is something of a blunt instrument, and a few tricks are required to work with it. The code first stores the delimiters to work with in a variable, $delims, on line 4. It calls strtok() on line 5, passing it the URL to tokenize and the $delims string, and stores the first result in $word. Within the conditional expression of the while loop on line 6, the code tests that $word is a string. If it isn't, the end of the string has been reached and no further action is required.

Listing 10.3 tests the return type because a string containing two delimiters in a row would cause `strtok()` to return an empty string when it reaches the first of these delimiters. So, a more conventional test such as

```
while ($word) {
      $word = strtok($delims);
}
```

would fail if $word is an empty string, even if the end of the source string has not yet been reached.

Having established that $word contains a string, the code can go on to work with it. If $word does not contain an empty string, print it to the browser on line 8. The code must then call `strtok()` again on line 10 to repopulate the $word variable for the next test. Notice that the source string to `strtok()` is not passed a second time. (If were to do this, the first word of the source string would be returned once again, and you would find yourself in an infinite loop.)

Manipulating Strings with PHP

PHP provides many functions that transform a string argument, subtly or radically, as you'll soon see.

Cleaning Up a String with `trim()`, `ltrim()`, and `strip_tags()`

When you acquire text from user input or an external file, you cannot always be sure that you haven't also picked up whitespace at the beginning and end of your data. The `trim()` function shaves any whitespace characters, including newlines, tabs, and spaces, from both the start and end of a string. It accepts the string to modify, returning the cleaned-up version. For example:

```
<?php
$text = "\t\tlots of room to breathe        ";
echo "<pre>$text</pre>";
// prints "         lots of room to breathe        ";
$text = trim($text);
echo "<pre>$text</pre>";
// prints "lots of room to breathe";
?>
```

Of course, this might be more work than you require. You might want to keep whitespace at the beginning of a string but remove it from the end. You can use PHP's `rtrim()` function exactly as you would use `trim()`. However, `rtrim()` removes whitespace at only the end of the string argument:

```php
<?php
$text = "\t\tlots of room to breathe        ";
echo "<pre>$text</pre>";
// prints "        lots of room to breathe        ";
$text = rtrim($text);
echo "<pre>$text</pre>";
// prints "        lots of room to breathe";
?>
```

PHP provides the ltrim() function to strip whitespace from only the beginning of a string. Once again, you call this function with the string you want to transform and it returns a new string, shorn of tabs, newlines, and spaces:

```php
<?php
$text = "\t\tlots of room to breathe        ";
echo "<pre>$text</pre>";
// prints "        lots of room to breathe        ";
$text = ltrim($text);
echo "<pre>$text</pre>";
// prints "lots of room to breathe        ";
?>
```

It is not unusual to have to remove tags from a block of text to display it without any HTML formatting. PHP provides the strip_tags() function for this purpose. The strip_tags() function accepts two arguments: the text to transform and an optional set of HTML tags that strip_tags() can leave in place. The tags in this list should not be separated by any characters:

```php
<?php
$string = "<p>\"I <em>simply</em> will not have it,\" <br/>said Mr Dean.</p>
<p><strong>The end.</strong></p>";
echo strip_tags($string, "<br/><p>");
?>
```

The previous code fragment creates an HTML-formatted string. When you call strip_tags(), you pass it the $string variable and a list of exceptions. The result is that the <br/> and <p> tags are left in place and all other tags are stripped out. In addition, the matching tag for <p>—</p>—is also removed.

The output of this snippet is as follows:

```
"I simply will not have it,"
said Mr Dean.

The end.
```

Note that the emphasis and strong formatting are gone, but the paragraphs and line breaks remain.

Replacing a Portion of a String Using `substr_replace()`

The `substr_replace()` function works similarly to the `substr()` function, except it enables you to replace the portion of the string that you extract. The function requires three arguments: the string to transform, the text to add to it, and the starting index; it also accepts an optional length argument. The `substr_replace()` function finds the portion of a string specified by the starting index and length arguments, replaces this portion with the string provided, and returns the entire transformed string.

The following code fragment for renewing a user's membership number changes its second two characters:

```php
<?php
$membership = "mz11xyz";
$membership = substr_replace($membership, "12", 2, 2);
echo "New membership number: $membership";
// prints "New membership number: mz12xyz"
?>
```

The result of this code is that the old membership number, "mz11xyz", is transformed into the new membership number, "mz12xyz".

Replacing Substrings Using `str_replace`

The `str_replace()` function is used to replace all instances of a given string within another string. It requires three arguments: the search string, the replacement string, and the master string. The function returns the transformed string.

The following example uses `str_replace()` to change all references to 2010 to 2012 within a master string:

```php
<?php
$string = "<h1>The 2010 Guide to All Things Good in the World</h1>";
$string .= "<p>Site contents copyright 2010.</p>";
echo str_replace("2010","2012",$string);
?>
```

The `str_replace()` function accepts arrays as well as strings for all its arguments. This enables you to perform multiple search and replace operations on a subject string, and even on more than one subject string. Take the following snippet, for instance:

```php
<?php
$source = array(
    "The package which is at version 4.2 was released in 2005.",
    "The year 2005 was an excellent time for PointyThing 4.2!");
$search  = array("4.2", "2005");
```

```
$replace = array("6.3", "2012");
$source = str_replace($search, $replace, $source);
foreach($source as $str) {
    echo "$str<br>";
}
?>
```

The output is of this snippet is as follows:

```
The package which is at version 6.3 was released in 2012.
The year 2012 was an excellent time for PointyThing 6.3!
```

When an array of strings is passed to str_replace() for its first and second arguments, it attempts to switch each search string with its corresponding replace string in the text to be transformed. When the third argument is an array, the str_replace() function returns an array of strings. The search and replace operation will have been executed on each string in the array.

Converting Case

PHP provides several functions that allow you to convert the case of a string. Changing case is often useful for string comparisons. To get an uppercase version of a string, use the strtoupper() function. This function requires only the string that you want to convert and returns the converted string:

```php
<?php
$membership = "mz11xyz";
$membership = strtoupper($membership);
echo "$membership"; // prints "MZ11XYZ"
?>
```

To convert a string to lowercase characters, use the strtolower() function. Once again, this function requires the string you want to convert and returns the converted version:

```php
<?php
$membership = "MZ11XYZ";
$membership = strtolower($membership);
echo "$membership"; // prints "mz11xyz"
?>
```

PHP also provides a case function that has a useful cosmetic purpose. The ucwords() function makes the first letter of every word in a string uppercase. The following fragment makes the first letter of every word in a user-submitted string uppercase:

```php
<?php
$full_name = "violet elizabeth bott";
$full_name = ucwords($full_name);
```

```php
echo $full_name; // prints "Violet Elizabeth Bott"
?>
```

Although this function makes the first letter of each word uppercase, it does not touch any other letters. So, if the user had had problems with her Shift key in the previous example and submitted VIolEt eLIZaBeTH bOTt, the preceding approach would not have done much to fix the string. The output would have been VIolEt ELIZaBeTH BOTt, which isn't much of an improvement. You can deal with this by making the submitted string lowercase with the strtolower() function before invoking ucwords():

```php
<?php
$full_name = "VIolEt eLIZaBeTH bOTt";
$full_name = ucwords(strtolower($full_name));
echo $full_name; // prints "Violet Elizabeth Bott"
?>
```

Finally, the ucfirst() function capitalizes only the first letter in a string. The following fragment capitalizes the first letter in a user-submitted string:

```php
<?php
$myString = "this is my string.";
$myString = ucfirst($myString);
echo $myString; // prints "This is my string."
?>
```

Working with case-related string functions can prove useful when attempting to authenticate passwords that are not case sensitive, for example. If the user inputs MyPass and the stored password is mypass but you do not want the match to be case sensitive, you can attempt to match a lowercase (or uppercase) version of the user input with the lowercase (or uppercase) version of the stored password. If they match in their similarly cased format, the user can be authenticated even if he typed something different from what was actually stored.

Wrapping Text with wordwrap() and nl2br()

When you present plaintext within a web page, you are often faced with a problem in which new lines are not displayed and your text runs together into one big mess. The nl2br() function conveniently converts every new line into an HTML break. So

```php
<?php
$string  = "one line\n";
$string .= "another line\n";
$string .= "a third for luck\n";
echo nl2br($string);
?>
```

outputs

```
one line<br />
another line<br />
a third for luck<br />
```

The nl2br() function is great for maintaining newlines that are already in the text you are converting. Occasionally, you might want to add arbitrary line breaks to format a column of text. The wordwrap() function is perfect for this. wordwrap() requires one argument: the string to transform. By default, wordwrap() wraps lines every 75 characters and uses \n as its line break character. So, the code fragment

```php
<?php
$string  = "Given a long line, wordwrap() is useful as a means of ";
$string .= "breaking it into a column and thereby making it easier to read";
echo wordwrap($string);
?>
```

outputs the following:

```
Given a long line, wordwrap() is useful as a means of breaking it into a
column and thereby making it easier to read
```

Because the lines are broken with the character \n, the formatting does not show up in HTML code, of course—the output here is what you see if you view the source in your browser. The wordwrap() function has two more optional arguments: a number representing the maximum number of characters per line and a string representing the end of line string you want to use. So, applying the function call

```php
echo wordwrap($string, 24, "<br/>\n");
```

to the $string variable used earlier, the output is this:

```
Given a long line,<br/>
wordwrap() is useful as<br/>
a means of breaking it<br/>
into a column and<br/>
thereby making it easier<br/>
to read
```

The wordwrap() function does not automatically break at your line limit if a word has more characters than the limit. You can, however, use an optional fourth argument to enforce this. The argument should be a positive integer. So, using word-wrap() in conjunction with the fourth argument, you can wrap a string even when it contains words that extend beyond the limit you are setting. This fragment

```php
<?php
$string  = "As usual you will find me at http://www.witteringonaboutit.com/";
$string .= "chat/eating_green_cheese/forum.php. Hope to see you there!";
echo wordwrap($string, 24, "<br/>\n", 1);
?>
```

outputs

```
As usual you will find<br/>
me at<br/>
http://www.witteringonab<br/>
outit.com/chat/eating_gr<br/>
een_cheese/forum.php.<br/>
Hope to see you there!
```

instead of

```
As usual you will find<br/>
me at<br/>
http://www.witteringonaboutit.com/chat/eating_green_cheese/forum.php. <br/>
Hope to see you there!
```

Breaking Strings into Arrays with explode()

The delightfully named explode() function is similar in some ways to strtok(). But explode() breaks up a string into an array, which you can then store, sort, or examine as you want. The explode() function requires two arguments: the delimiter string that you want to use to break up the source string and the source string itself. The function optionally accepts a third argument that determines the maximum number of pieces the string can be broken into. The delimiter string can include more than one character, all of which form a single delimiter (unlike multiple delimiter characters passed to strtok(), each of which will be a delimiter in its own right). The following fragment breaks up a date and stores the result in an array:

```php
<?php
$start_date = "2012-02-19";
$date_array = explode("-", $start_date);
// $date_array[0] == "2012"
// $date_array[1] == "02"
// $date_array[2] == "19"
echo $date_array[0]."-".$date_array[1]."-".$date_array[2];
//prints 2012-02-19
?>
```

Now that your head is full with some common PHP string functions, let's move on to date and time functions.

Using Date and Time Functions in PHP

The following sections introduce you to the date- and time-related functions specifically in PHP. Try out each listing for yourself to see how simple and powerful these functions can be.

Getting the Date with `time()`

PHP's `time()` function gives you all the information you need about the current date and time. It requires no arguments and returns an integer. For us humans, the returned number is a little hard on the eyes, but it's extremely useful nonetheless:

```
echo time();
// sample output: 1326853185
// this represents January 17, 2012 at 09:19PM
```

The integer returned by `time()` represents the number of seconds elapsed since midnight GMT on January 1, 1970. This moment is known as the *UNIX epoch*, and the number of seconds that have elapsed since then is referred to as a *timestamp*. PHP offers excellent tools to convert a timestamp into a form that humans are comfortable with. Even so, you might think, "Isn't a timestamp a needlessly convoluted way of storing a date?" In fact, the opposite is true. From just one number, you can extract enormous amounts of information. Even better, a timestamp can make date arithmetic much easier than you might imagine.

Think of a homegrown date system in which you record days of the month as well as months and years. Now imagine a script that must add one day to a given date. If this date happened to be 31 December 1999, rather than adding 1 to the date, you'd have to write code to set the day of the month to 1, the month to January, and the year to 2000. Using a timestamp, you need add only a day's worth of seconds (60 * 60 * 24, or 86,400) to your current figure and you're done. You can convert this new figure into something friendlier, at your leisure.

Converting a Timestamp with `getdate()`

Now that you have a timestamp to work with, you must convert it before you present it to the user. `getdate()` optionally accepts a timestamp and returns an associative array containing information about the date. If you omit the timestamp, `getdate()` works with the current timestamp as returned by `time()`. Table 10.3 lists the elements contained in the array returned by `getdate()`.

TABLE 10.3 The Associative Array Returned by getdate()

Key	Description	Example
seconds	Seconds past the minute (0–59)	53
minutes	Minutes past the hour (0–59)	44
hours	Hours of the day (0–23)	17
mday	Day of the month (1–31)	3
wday	Day of the week (0–6)	0
mon	Month of the year (1–12)	2
year	Year (four digits)	2008
yday	Day of year (0–365)	33
weekday	Day of the week (name)	Sunday
month	Month of the year (name)	February
0	Timestamp	1202082293

Listing 10.4 uses getdate() in line 2 to extract information from a timestamp, employing a foreach statement to print each element (line 3). You can see typical output of this script, called getdate.php, in Figure 10.5.

LISTING 10.4 Acquiring Date Information with getdate()

```
1: <?php
2: $date_array = getdate(); // no argument passed so today's date will be used
3: foreach ($date_array as $key => $val) {
4:     echo "$key = $val<br>";
5: }
6: ?>
7: <hr/>
8: <?php
9: echo "<p>Today's date: ".$date_array['mon']."/".$date_array['mday']."/".
10:     $date_array['year']."</p>";
11: ?>
```

FIGURE 10.5
Using getdate().

```
seconds = 11
minutes = 21
hours = 21
mday = 17
wday = 2
mon = 1
year = 2012
yday = 16
weekday = Tuesday
month = January
0 = 1326853271

Today's date: 1/17/2012
```

CAUTION

If running this code results in a warning such as

```
Warning: getdate(): It is not safe to rely on the system's timezone settings.
  You are *required* to use the date.timezone setting or the
  date_default_timezone_set() function.
```

you need to make a modification to your php.ini file. Specifically, look for lines like this:

```
; Defines the default timezone used by the date functions
; http://php.net/date.timezone
;date.timezone =
```

Change the value of date.timezone to your time zone. (See http://php.net/date.timezone for a valid list.) For example:

```
; Defines the default timezone used by the date functions
; http://php.net/date.timezone
date.timezone = America/New_York
```

Be sure to restart Apache after making changes to php.ini.

Converting a Timestamp with date()

You can use getdate() when you want to work with the elements that it outputs. Sometimes, though, you want to display the date as a string. The date() function returns a formatted string that represents a date. You can exercise an enormous amount of control over the format that date() returns with a string argument that you must pass to it. In addition to the format string, date() optionally accepts a timestamp. Table 10.4 lists some of the codes that a format string can contain. You can find the complete list at http://www.php.net/date. Any other data you include in the format string passed to date() is included in the return value.

TABLE 10.4 Some Format Codes for Use with `date()`

Format	Description	Example
a	am or pm (lowercase)	`am`
A	AM or PM (uppercase)	`AM`
d	Day of month (number with leading zeros)	`01`
D	Day of week (three letters)	`Tue`
e	Timezone identifier	`America/New_York`
F	Month name	`January`
h	Hour (12-hour format—leading zeros)	`09`
H	Hour (24-hour format—leading zeros)	`21`
g	Hour (12-hour format—no leading zeros)	`9`
G	Hour (24-hour format—no leading zeros)	`21`
i	Minutes	`21`
j	Day of the month (no leading zeros)	`17`
l	Day of the week (name)	`Tuesday`
L	Leap year (1 for yes, 0 for no)	`1`
m	Month of year (number—leading zeros)	`01`
M	Month of year (three letters)	`Jan`
n	Month of year (number—no leading zeros)	`1`
s	Seconds of hour	`11`
S	Ordinal suffix for the day of the month	`th`
r	Full date standardized to RFC 822 (http://www.faqs.org/rfcs/rfc822.html)	`Tue, 17 Jan 2012 09:21:11 -0500`
U	Timestamp	`1326853271`
y	Year (two digits)	`12`
Y	Year (four digits)	`2012`
z	Day of year (0–365)	`17`
Z	Offset in seconds from GMT	`-18000`

Listing 10.5 puts a few of these formats to the test.

LISTING 10.5 Formatting a Date with `date()`

```
1: <?php
2: $time = time(); //stores the exact timestamp to use in this script
3: echo date("m/d/y G:i:s e", $time);
4: echo "<br/>";
```

LISTING 10.5   Continued

```
5: echo "Today is ";
6: echo date("jS \of F Y, \a\\t g:ia \i\\n e", $time);
7: ?>
```

Listing 10.5 calls date() twice: the first time on line 3 to output an abbreviated date format, and the second time on line 6 for a longer format. Save the text of this listing in a file named datetest.php and open it in your web browser. Your date will differ from the following, obviously, but here's some sample output:

```
01/17/12 21:29:31 America/New_York
Today is 17th of January 2012, at 9:29pm in America/New_York
```

Although the format string looks arcane, it's easy to build. If you want to add a string that contains letters that are also format codes to the format, you can escape them by placing a backslash (\) in front of them. For characters that become control characters when escaped, you must escape the backslash that precedes them. For example, \t is a format code for a tab. So to ensure that the tab prints, use \\t as in the example in Listing 10.5.

Another example is in the context of a word you are adding to a string (for example, *the*). The word *the* is made up of three format codes, so all must be escaped:

```
<?php
echo date('l \t\h\e jS');
//prints Tuesday the 3rd
?>
```

Also note that the date() function returns information according to your local time zone. If you want to format a date in GMT, you use the gmdate() function, which works in exactly the same way.

Creating Timestamps with mktime()

You can already get information about the current time, but you cannot yet work with arbitrary dates. mktime() returns a timestamp that you can then use with date() or getdate(). mktime() accepts up to six integer arguments in the following order:

Hour

Minute

Second

Month

Day of month

Year

Listing 10.6 uses `mktime()` to get a timestamp it then uses with the `date()` function.

LISTING 10.6   Creating a Timestamp with `mktime()`

```
1: <?php
2: // make a timestamp for Jan 17 2012 at 9:34 pm
3: $ts = mktime(21, 34, 0, 1, 17, 2012);
4: echo date("m/d/y G:i:s e", $ts);
5: echo "<br/>";
6: echo "The date is ";
7: echo date("jS \of F Y, \a\\t g:ia \i\\n e", $ts );
8: ?>
```

This code calls `mktime()` on line 3 and assigns the returned timestamp to the `$ts` variable. It then uses the `date()` function on lines 4 and 7 to output formatted versions of the date using `$ts`. You can choose to omit some of or all the arguments to `mktime()`, and the value appropriate to the current time is used instead. `mktime()` also adjusts for values that go beyond the relevant range, so an hour argument of 25 translates to 1:00 a.m. on the day after that specified in the month, day, and year arguments.

Save the text of this listing in a file named `mktimetest.php` and open it in your web browser. You should see the following

```
01/17/12 21:34:00 America/New_York
The date is 17th of January 2012, at 9:34pm in America/New_York
```

Testing a Date with `checkdate()`

You might need to accept date information from user input. Before you work with a user-entered date or store it in a database, make sure that the date is valid. `check-date()` accepts three integers: month, day, and year. `checkdate()` returns `true` if the month is between 1 and 12, the day is acceptable for the given month and year (accounting for leap years), and the year is between 0 and 32767. Be careful, though: A date might be valid but not acceptable to other date functions. For example, the following line returns `true`:

```
checkdate(4, 4, 1066)
```

If you were to attempt to build a date with `mktime()` using these values, you'd end up with a timestamp of -1. As a rule of thumb, don't use `mktime()` with years before 1902, and be cautious of using date functions with any date before 1970, because negative numbers are not valid dates. Because the UNIX epoch began January 1, 1970, anything before that is an invalid (negative) timestamp.

Other String, Date, and Time Functions

PHP does not lack for functions, especially for common items such as strings and dates. It is worth your while to bookmark the following chapters in the PHP Manual:

▶ "Strings" at http://www.php.net/manual/en/ref.strings.php

▶ "Date/Time" at http://www.php.net/manual/en/ref.datetime.php

In addition to keeping up with functions as they are added to PHP, the user-contributed notes for each function often offer solutions to various programming tasks that you might find useful as you build your own applications.

Summary

In this chapter, you learned about some of the functions that enable you to take control of the strings in your PHP scripts. You learned how to format strings with `printf()` and `sprint()`. You should be able to use these functions to create strings that both transform and format data. You learned about functions that investigate strings. You should be able to discover the length of a string with `strlen()`, determine the presence of a substring with `strpos()`, and extract a substring with `substr()`. You should be able to tokenize a string with `strtok()`.

You also learned about functions that transform strings. You can now remove whitespace from the beginning or end of a string with `trim()`, `ltrim()`, or `rtrim()`. You can change the case of characters in a string with `strtoupper()`, `strtolower()`, or `ucwords()`. You can replace all instances of a string with `str_replace()`.

You also learned how to use various PHP functions to perform date- and time-related actions. The `time()` function gets a date stamp for the current date and time, and you can use `getdate()` to extract date information from a timestamp and `date()` to convert a timestamp into a formatted string. You learned how to create a timestamp using `mktime()`, and how to test a date for validity with `checkdate()`. You learn many more powerful date-related functions in Chapter 16, "Learning Basic SQL Commands," so much so that you might find yourself using MySQL and not PHP for many of your date-related needs.

Workshop

The workshop is designed to help you review what you've learned and begin putting your knowledge into practice.

Q&A

Q. *Can I combine multiple string functions?*

A. Yes. You can nest any function, not just string functions. Just remember to count your opening and closing parentheses to ensure that you've nested your functions appropriately.

Q. *What do I do with dates and times stored in my database, not just in my scripts?*

A. You will learn about MySQL date and time functions in Chapter 16, "Learning Basic SQL Commands," but in general a good rule of thumb is that if you are extracting dates and times from a database and you want to perform date and time-related operations (such as calculating time or converting time from one type to another), you make your database do the work for you. But there's nothing stopping you from using PHP date and time functions on data extracted out of the database.

Quiz

1. What conversion specifier would you use with `printf()` to format an integer as a double? Indicate the full syntax required to convert the integer 33.

2. How would you pad the conversion you effected in question 1 with zeros so that the part before the decimal point is four characters long?

3. How would you specify a precision of two decimal places for the floating-point number you have been formatting in the previous questions?

4. What function would you use to extract a substring from a string?

5. How might you remove whitespace from the beginning of a string?

6. How would you break up a delimited string into an array of substrings?

7. Using PHP, how do you acquire a UNIX timestamp that represents the current date and time?

8. Which PHP function accepts a timestamp and returns an associative array that represents the given date?

9. Which PHP function do you use to format date information?

10. Which PHP function could you use to check the validity of a date?

Answers

1. The conversion specifier f is used to format an integer as a double:

```
printf("%f", 33);
```

2. You can pad the output from `printf()` with the padding specifier—that is, a space or a zero followed by a number representing the number of characters you want to pad by:

```
printf("%04f", 33);
```

3. The precision specifier consists of a dot (.) followed by a number representing the precision you want to apply. You should place the precision specifier before the conversion specifier:

```
printf("%04.2f", 33);
```

4. The `substr()` function extracts and returns a substring.

5. The `ltrim()` function removes whitespace from the start of a string.

6. The `explode()` function splits up a string into an array.

7. Use `time()`.

8. The `getdate()` function returns an associative array whose elements contain aspects of the given date.

9. Use `date()`.

10. You can check a date with the `checkdate()` function.

Activities

1. Create a feedback form that accepts a user's full name and an email address. Use case-conversion functions to capitalize the first letter of each name the user submits and print the result back to the browser. Check that the user's email address contains the @ symbol and print a warning otherwise.

2. Create an array of doubles and integers. Loop through the array, converting each element to a floating-point number with a precision of 2. Right-align the output within a field of 20 characters.

3. Create a birthday countdown script. Given form input of month, day, and year, output a message that tells the user how many days, hours, minutes, and seconds until the big day.

CHAPTER 11

Working with Forms

In this chapter, you learn the following:

▶ How to access information from form fields

▶ How to work with form elements that allow multiple selections

▶ How to create a single document that contains both an HTML form and the PHP code that handles its submission

▶ How to save state with hidden fields

▶ How to redirect the user to a new page

▶ How to build HTML forms and PHP code that send mail

▶ How to build HTML forms that upload files and write the PHP code to handle the uploads

Until now, the PHP examples in this book have been missing a crucial dimension. Sure, you know the basics, can set variables and arrays, create and call functions, and work with strings. But that's all meaningless if users cannot interact in a meaningful way with your website. HTML forms are the principal means by which substantial amounts of information pass from the user to the server, so this chapter moves into this dimension and looks at strategies for acquiring and working with user input.

Creating a Simple Input Form

For now, let's keep the HTML separate from the PHP code. Listing 11.1 builds a simple HTML form.

LISTING 11.1 A Simple HTML Form

```
1:  <!DOCTYPE html>
2:  <html>
3:  <head>
4:  <title>A simple HTML form</title>
```

LISTING 11.1   Continued

```
5:  </head>
6:  <body>
7:  <form method="post" action="send_simpleform.php">
8:  <p><label for="user">Name:</label><br/>
9:  <input type="text" id="user" name="user"></p>
10: <p><label for="message">Message:</label><br/>
11: <textarea id="message" name="message" rows="5" cols="40"></textarea></p>
12: <button type="submit" name="submit" value="send">Send Message</button>
13: </form>
14: </body>
15: </html>
```

Put these lines into a text file called `simpleform.html` and place that file in your web server document root. This listing defines a form that contains a text field with the name `"user"` on line 9, a text area with the name `"message"` on line 11, and a submit button on line 12. The `FORM` element's `ACTION` argument points to a file called `send_simpleform.php`, which processes the form information. The method of this form is `POST`, so the variables are stored in the `$_POST` superglobal.

Listing 11.2 creates the code that receives user input and displays it within the context of an HTML page.

LISTING 11.2   Reading Input from a Form

```
1:  <!DOCTYPE html>
2:  <html>
3:  <head>
4:  <title>A simple response</title>
5:  </head>
6:  <body>
7:  <p>Welcome, <strong><?php echo $_POST['user']; ?></strong>!</p>
8:  <p>Your message is:
9:  <strong><?php echo $_POST['message']; ?></strong></p>
10: </body>
11: </html>
```

Put these lines into a text file called `send_simpleform.php` and place that file in your web server document root. Now access the form itself (`simpleform.html`) with your web browser, and you should see something like Figure 11.1.

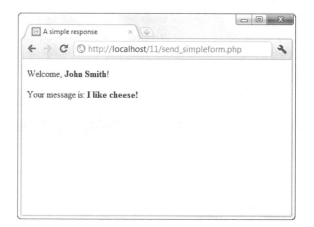

FIGURE 11.1
The form creat-
ed by `simple-
form.html`.

The script in Listing 11.2 is called when the user submits the form created in Listing 11.1. The code in Listing 11.2 accesses two variables: `$_POST['user']` and `$_POST['message']`. These are references to the variables in the `$_POST` superglobal, which contain the values that the user entered in the user text field and the message text area. Forms in PHP really *are* as simple as that.

Enter some information in the form fields and click the Send Message button. You should see your input echoed to the screen.

You could also use the GET method in this form (and others). POST can handle more data than GET and does not pass the data in the query string. If you use the GET method, be sure to change your superglobal to `$_GET` and not `$_POST`.

NOTE

Accessing Form Input with User-Defined Arrays

The previous example showed how to gather information from HTML elements that submit a single value per element name, such as text fields, text areas, and radio buttons. This leaves you with a problem when working with elements such as checkboxes because it is possible for the user to choose one or more items. If you name the checkbox INPUT element with a plain name, like so

```
<input type="checkbox" id="products" name="products">
```

the script that receives this data has access to only a single value corresponding to this name ($_POST['products']) (and therefore only the first checkbox in the list that the user selected). You can change this behavior by renaming an element of this kind so that its name ends with an empty set of square brackets. Listing 11.3 does this.

LISTING 11.3   An HTML Form Including Multiple Check Boxes

```
 1: <!DOCTYPE html>
 2: <html>
 3: <head>
 4: <title>An HTML form with checkboxes</title>
 5: </head>
 6: <body>
 7: <form action="send_formwithcb.php" method="POST">
 8: <p><label>Name:</label><br/>
 9: <input type="text" name="user" /></p>
10: <fieldset>
11: <legend>Select Some Products:</legend><br/>
12: <input type="checkbox" id="tricorder"
13:        name="products[]" value="Tricorder">
14:        <label for="tricorder">Tricorder</label><br/>
15:
16: <input type="checkbox" id="ORAC_AI"
17:        name="products[]" value="ORAC AI">
18:        <label for="ORAC_AI">ORAC AI</label><br/>
19:
20: <input type="checkbox" id="HAL_2000"
21:        name="products[]" value="HAL 2000">
22:        <label for="HAL_2000">HAL 2000</label>
23: </fieldset>
24: <button type="submit" name="submit" value="submit">Submit Form</button>
25: </form>
26: </body>
27: </html>
```

Put these lines into a text file called formwithcb.html and place that file in your web server document root. Next, in the script that processes the form input, you find that the value of all checked checkboxes with the "products[]" name are available in an array called $_POST['products']. Each checkbox is indicated in lines 12 through 22. That the user's choices are made available is demonstrated in an array in Listing 11.4.

LISTING 11.4   Reading Input from the Form in Listing 11.3

```
 1: <!DOCTYPE html>
 2: <html>
 3: <head>
 4: <title>Reading checkboxes</title>
```

```
 5:  </head>
 6:  <body>
 7:  <p>Welcome, <strong><?php echo $_POST['user']; ?></strong>!</p>
 8:  <p>Your product choices are:
 9:  <?php
10:  if (!empty($_POST['products'])) {
11:      echo "<ul>";
12:      foreach ($_POST['products'] as $value) {
13:          echo "<li>$value</li>";
14:      }
15:      echo "</ul>";
16:  } else {
17:      echo "None";
18:  }
19:  ?>
20:  </body>
21:  </html>
```

Put these lines into a text file called send_formwithcb.php and place that file in your web server document root. Now access the form (formwithcb.html) with your web browser and check some checkboxes. Figure 11.2 shows an example.

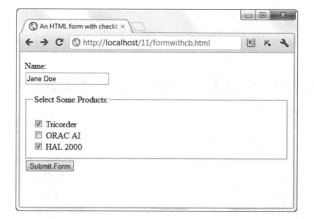

FIGURE 11.2
The form created in Listing 11.3.

Line 7 of the script in Listing 11.4 accesses the $_POST['user'] variable, which is derived from the user INPUT field in the form. On line 10, the code tests for the $_POST['products'] variable. If $_POST['products'] is present and is not empty, execution loops through it on line 12, and outputs each choice to the browser on line 13. The text within the value attribute of the selected checkbox becomes one of the stored values in the array.

Submit the form, and you might see something like that shown in Figure 11.3.

FIGURE 11.3
Sample output of
`send_formwithcb.php`.

Although the looping technique is particularly useful with checkboxes, it can also work with other types of form elements. For example, if you use a SELECT element that allows for multiple selections, you are also enabling a user to choose many values within a single field name.

As long as the name you choose ends with empty square brackets, PHP compiles the user input for this field into an array.

Combining HTML and PHP Code on a Single Page

In some circumstances, you might want to include the form-parsing PHP code on the same page as a hard-coded HTML form. Such a combination can prove useful if you need to present the same form to the user more than once. You would have more flexibility if you were to write the entire page dynamically, of course, but you would miss out on one of the great strengths of PHP, which is that it mingles well with standard HTML. The more standard HTML you can include in your pages, the easier they are for designers and page builders to amend without asking you, the programmer, for help.

For the following examples, imagine that you're creating a site that teaches basic math to preschool children and have been asked to create a script that takes a number from form input and tells the user whether it's larger or smaller than a predefined integer.

Listing 11.5 creates the HTML. For this example, you need only a single text field, but even so, the code listing includes a little PHP.

LISTING 11.5 An HTML Form That Calls Itself

```
1: <!DOCTYPE html>
2: <html>
3: <head>
4: <title>An HTML form that calls itself</title>
5: </head>
6: <body>
7: <form action="<?php echo $_SERVER['PHP_SELF']; ?>" method="POST">
8: <p><label for="guess">Type your guess here:</label> <br/>
9: <input type="text" id="guess" name="guess" /></p>
10: <button type="submit" name="submit" value="submit">Submit</button>
11: </form>
12: </body>
13: </html>
```

The action of this script is $_SERVER['PHP_SELF'], as shown in line 7. This global variable represents the name of the current script. In other words, the action tells the script to reload itself. The script in Listing 11.5 does not produce any output, but if you upload the script to your web server, access the page, and view the source of the page, you will notice that the form action now contains the name of the script itself.

In Listing 11.6, you begin to build up the PHP element of the page.

LISTING 11.6 A PHP Number-Guessing Script

```
1:  <?php
2:  $num_to_guess = 42;
3:  if (!isset($_POST['guess'])) {
4:      $message = "Welcome to the guessing machine!";
5:  } elseif (!is_numeric($_POST['guess'])) { // is not numeric
6:      $message = "I don't understand that response.";
7:  } elseif ($_POST['guess'] == $num_to_guess) { // matches!
8:      $message = "Well done!";
9:  } elseif ($_POST['guess'] > $num_to_guess) {
10:     $message = $_POST['guess']." is too big! Try a smaller number.";
11: } elseif ($_POST['guess'] < $num_to_guess) {
12:     $message = $_POST['guess']." is too small! Try a larger number.";
13: } else  { // some other condition
14:     $message = "I am terribly confused.";
15: }
16: ?>
```

First, you must define the number that the user guesses, and this is done in line 2 when 42 is assigned to the $num_to_guess variable. Next, you must determine whether the form has been submitted. You can test for submission by looking for the existence of the variable $_POST['guess'], which is available only if the form script has been submitted (with or without a value in the field). If a value for $_POST['guess'] isn't present, you can safely assume that the user arrived at the page without submitting a form. If the value *is* present, you can test the value it contains. The test for the presence of the `$_POST['guess']` variable takes place on line 3.

Lines 3 through 15 represent an `if...elseif...else` control structure. Only one of these conditions will be true at any given time, depending on what (if anything) was submitted from the form. Depending on the condition, a different value is assigned to the `$message` variable. That variable is then printed to the screen in line 23 in Listing 11.6, which is part of the HTML portion of the script.

LISTING 11.6   A PHP Number-Guessing Script (Continued)

```
17: <!DOCTYPE html>
18: <html>
19: <head>
20: <title>A PHP number guessing script</title>
21: </head>
22: <body>
23: <h1><?php echo $message; ?></h1>
24: <form action="<?php echo $_SERVER['PHP_SELF']; ?>" method="POST">
25: <p><label for="guess">Type your guess here:</label><br/>
26: <input type="text" is="guess" name="guess" /></p>
27: <button type="submit" name="submit" value="submit">Submit</button>
28: </form>
29: </body>
30: </html>
```

Place the PHP anfd HTML code (all the lines in Listing 11.6) into a text file called `numguess.php` and put this file in your web server document root. Now access the script with your web browser, and you should see something like Figure 11.4.

FIGURE 11.4
The form created in Listing 11.6.

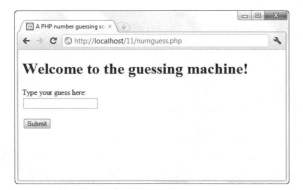

You could still make a few more additions, but you can probably see how simple it would be to hand the code to a designer for aesthetic treatment. The designer can do her part without having to disturb the programming in any way—the PHP code is at the top, and the rest is almost entirely HTML.

Using Hidden Fields to Save State

The script in Listing 11.6 has no way of knowing how many guesses a user has made, but you can use a hidden field to keep track of this value. A hidden field behaves the same as a text field, except that the user cannot see it unless he views the HTML source of the document that contains it.

Take the original numguess.php script and save a copy as numguess2.php. In the new version, add a line after the initial assignment of the $num_to_guess variable:

```
$num_tries = (isset($_POST['num_tries'])) ? $num_tries + 1 : 1;
```

This line initializes a variable called $num_tries and assigns a value to it. If the form has not yet been submitted (if $_POST['num_tries'] is empty), the value of the $num_tries variable is 1 because you are on your first attempt at guessing the number. If the form has already been sent, the new value is the value of $_POST['num_tries'] plus 1.

The next change comes after the HTML level H1 heading:

```
<p><strong>Guess number:</strong> <?php echo $num_tries; ?></p>
```

This new line simply prints the current value of $num_tries to the screen.

Finally, before the HTML code for the form submission button, add the hidden field. This field saves the incremented value of $num_tries:

```
<input type="hidden" name="num_tries" value="<?php echo $num_tries; ?>"/>
```

Listing 11.7 shows the new script in its entirety.

LISTING 11.7 Saving State with a Hidden Field

```
1:  <?php
2:  $num_to_guess = 42;
3:  $num_tries = (isset($_POST['num_tries'])) ? $num_tries + 1 : 1;
4:  if (!isset($_POST['guess'])) {
5:    $message = "Welcome to the guessing machine!";
6:  } elseif (!is_numeric($_POST['guess'])) { // is not numeric
7:      $message = "I don't understand that response.";
8:  } elseif ($_POST['guess'] == $num_to_guess) { // matches!
9:      $message = "Well done!";
10: } elseif ($_POST['guess'] > $num_to_guess) {
11:     $message = $_POST['guess']." is too big! Try a smaller number.";
12: } elseif ($_POST['guess'] < $num_to_guess) {
13:     $message = $_POST['guess']." is too small! Try a larger number.";
14: } else  { // some other condition
15:     $message = "I am terribly confused.";
16: }
17: ?>
18: <!DOCTYPE html>
```

LISTING 11.7   Continued

```
19: <html>
20: <head>
21: <title>A PHP number guessing script</title>
22: </head>
23: <body>
24: <h1><?php echo $message; ?></h1>
25: <p><strong>Guess number:</strong> <?php echo $num_tries; ?></p>
26: <form action="<?php echo $_SERVER['PHP_SELF']; ?>" method="POST">
27: <p><label for="guess">Type your guess here:</label><br/>
28: <input type="text" id="guess" name="guess" /></p>
29: <input type="hidden" name="num_tries" value="<?php echo $num_tries; ?>"/>
30: <button type="submit" name="submit" value="submit">Submit</button>
31: </form>
32: </body>
33: </html>
```

Save the numguess2.php file and place it in your web server document root. Access the form a few times with your web browser and try to guess the number (pretending you don't already know it). The counter should increment by 1 each time you access the form.

Redirecting the User

Our simple script still has one major drawback: The form is reloaded whether or not the user guesses correctly. The fact that the HTML is hard-coded makes it difficult to avoid writing the entire page. You can, however, redirect the user to a congratulations page, thereby sidestepping the issue altogether.

When a server script communicates with a client, it must first send some headers that provide information about the document to follow. PHP usually handles this for you automatically, but you can choose to send your own header lines with PHP's header() function.

To call the header() function, you must be absolutely sure that no output has been sent to the browser. The first time content is sent to the browser, PHP sends out headers of its own, and it's too late for you to send any more. Any output from your document, even a line break or a space outside your script tags, causes headers to be sent. If you intend to use the header() function in a script, you must make certain that nothing precedes the PHP code that contains the function call. You should also check any libraries that you might be using.

Listing 11.8 shows typical headers sent to the browser by PHP, beginning with line 3, in response to the request in line 1.

LISTING 11.8 Typical Server Headers Sent from a PHP Script

```
1: HTTP/1.1 200 OK
2: Date: Sun,  29 Jan 2012 15:50:28 PST
3: Server: Apache/2.2.21 (Win32) PHP/5.4.0
4: X-Powered-By: PHP/5.4.0
5: Connection: close
6: Content-Type: text/html
```

By sending a `Location` header rather than PHP's default header, you can cause the browser to be redirected to a new page, such as the following:

```
header("Location: http://www.samspublishing.com");
```

Assuming that you've created a suitably upbeat page called `congrats.html`, we can amend the number-guessing script to redirect the user if she guesses correctly, as shown in Listing 11.9. The only change between this and Listing 11.7 comes after the `elseif` clause on line 8.

LISTING 11.9 Using `header()` to Redirect User

```
1:  <?php
2:  $num_to_guess = 42;
3:  $num_tries = (isset($_POST['num_tries'])) ? $num_tries + 1 : 1;
4:  if (!isset($_POST['guess'])) {
5:    $message = "Welcome to the guessing machine!";
6:  } elseif (!is_numeric($_POST['guess'])) { // is not numeric
7:      $message = "I don't understand that response.";
8:  } elseif ($_POST['guess'] == $num_to_guess) { // matches!
9:      header("Location: congrats.html");
10:     exit;
11: } elseif ($_POST['guess'] > $num_to_guess) {
12:     $message = $_POST['guess']." is too big! Try a smaller number.";
13: } elseif ($_POST['guess'] < $num_to_guess) {
14:     $message = $_POST['guess']." is too small! Try a larger number.";
15: } else  { // some other condition
16:     $message = "I am terribly confused.";
17: }
18: ?>
19:
20: <!DOCTYPE html>
21: <html>
22: <head>
23: <title>A PHP number guessing script</title>
24: </head>
25: <body>
26: <h1><?php echo $message; ?></h1>
27: <p><strong>Guess number:</strong> <?php echo $num_tries; ?></p>
28: <form action="<?php echo $_SERVER['PHP_SELF']; ?>" method="POST">
29: <p><label for="guess">Type your guess here:</label><br/>
30: <input type="text" id="guess" name="guess" /></p>
31: <input type="hidden" name="num_tries" value="<?php echo $num_tries; ?>"/>
32: <button type="submit" name="submit" value="submit">Submit</button>
33: </form>
34: </body>
35: </html>
```

The `elseif` clause of the `if` statement on line 8 now causes the browser to send the user away to a page called `congrats.html`. The `exit` statement on line 10 immediately ends execution and output of this script, which ensures that all output from the current page is aborted.

Sending Mail on Form Submission

You've already seen how to take form responses and print the results to the screen, so you're only one step away from sending those responses in an email message. Before learning about sending mail, however, read through the next section to make sure that your system is properly configured.

System Configuration for the `mail()` Function

Before you can use the `mail()` function to send mail, you need to set up a few directives in the `php.ini` file so that the function works properly. Open `php.ini` with a text editor and look for these lines:

```
[mail function]
; For Win32 only.
; http://php.net/smtp
SMTP = localhost
; http://php.net/smtp-port
smtp_port = 25

; For Win32 only.
; http://php.net/sendmail-from
;sendmail_from = me@example.com

; For Unix only.  You may supply arguments as well (default: "sendmail -t -i").
; http://php.net/sendmail-path
;sendmail_path =
```

If you're using Windows as your web server platform, the first two directives apply to you. For the `mail()` function to send mail, it must be able to access a valid outgoing mail server. If you plan to use the outgoing mail server of your choosing, the entry in `php.ini` could look like this:

```
SMTP = smtp.yourisp.net
```

The second configuration directive is `sendmail_from`, which is the email address used in the `From` header of the outgoing email. It can be overwritten in the mail script itself but normally operates as the default value, as in this example:

```
sendmail_from = youraddress@yourdomain.com
```

A good rule of thumb for Windows users is that whatever outgoing mail server you've set up in your email client on that machine, you should also use as the value of SMTP in php.ini.

If your web server is running on a Linux/UNIX platform, you use the sendmail functionality of that particular machine. In this case, only the last directive applies to you: sendmail_path. The default is sendmail -t -i, but if sendmail is in an odd place or if you need to specify different arguments, feel free to do so, as in the following example, which does not use real values:

```
sendmail_path = /opt/sendmail -odd -arguments
```

After making any changes to php.ini on any platform, you must restart the web server process for the changes to take effect.

Creating the Form

In Listing 11.10, you see the basic HTML for creating a simple feedback form named feedback.html. This form has an action of sendmail.php, which you create in the next section. The fields in feedback.html are simple: Lines 8 and 9 create a name field and label, lines 10 and 11 create the return email address field and label, and lines 12 and 13 contain the text area and label for the user's message.

LISTING 11.10   Creating a Simple Feedback Form

```
1:  <!DOCTYPE html>
2:  <html>
3:  <head>
4:  <title>E-Mail Form</title>
5:  </head>
6:  <body>
7:  <form action="sendmail.php" method="POST">
8:  <p><label for="name">Name:</label><br/>
9:  <input type="text" size="25" id="name" name="name"/></p>
10: <p><label for="email">E-Mail Address:</label><br/>
11: <input type="text" size="25" id="email" name="email"/></p>
12: <p><label for="msg">Message:</label><br/>
13: <textarea id="msg" name="msg" cols="30" rows="5"></textarea></p>
14: <button type="submit" name="submit" value="send">Send Message</button>
15: </form>
16: </body>
17: </html>
```

Put all the lines shown in Listing 11.10 into a text file called feedback.html and place this file in your web server document root. Now access the script with your web browser, and you should see something like Figure 11.5.

FIGURE 11.5
The form created in Listing 11.10.

In the next section, you create the script that sends this form to a recipient.

Creating the Script to Send the Mail

This script differs only slightly in concept from the script in Listing 11.4, which simply printed form responses to the screen. In the script shown in Listing 11.11, in addition to printing the responses to the screen, you send them to an email address.

LISTING 11.11 Sending the Simple Feedback Form

```
1:  <?php
2:  //start building the mail string
3:  $msg  = "Name:    ".$_POST['name']."\n";
4:  $msg .= "E-Mail: ".$_POST['email']."\n";
5:  $msg .= "Message: ".$_POST['message']."\n";
6:
7:  //set up the mail
8:  $recipient = "you@yourdomain.com";
9:  $subject = "Form Submission Results";
10: $mailheaders  = "From: My Web Site <defaultaddress@yourdomain.com> \n";
11: $mailheaders .= "Reply-To: ".$_POST['email'];
12:
13: //send the mail
14: mail($recipient, $subject, $msg, $mailheaders);
15: ?>
16: <!DOCTYPE html>
17: <html>
18: <head>
19: <title>Sending mail from the form in Listing 11.10</title>
20: </head>
21: <body>
22: <p>Thanks, <strong><?php echo $_POST['name']; ?></strong>,
23:    for your message.</p>
```

```
24: <p>Your e-mail address:
25:   <strong><?php echo $_POST['email']; ?></strong></p>
26: <p>Your message: <br/> <?php echo $_POST['message']; ?> </p>
27: </body>
28: </html>
```

The variables printed to the screen in lines 22–26 are `$_POST['name']`, `$_POST['email']`, and `$_POST['message']`—the names of the fields in the form, their values saved as part of the `$_POST` superglobal. That's all well and good for printing the information to the screen, but in this script, you also want to create a string that's sent in email. For this task, you essentially build the email by concatenating strings to form one long message string, using the newline (\n) character to add line breaks where appropriate.

Lines 3 through 5 create the `$msg` variable, a string containing the values typed by the user in the form fields (and some label text for good measure). This string forms the body of the email. Note the use of the concatenation operator (.=) when adding to the `$msg` variable in lines 4 and 5.

Lines 8 and 9 are hard-coded variables for the email recipient and the subject of the email message. Replace you@yourdomain.com with your own email address, obviously. If you want to change the subject, feel free to do that, too!

Lines 10 and 11 set up some mail headers, namely the `From:` and `Reply-to:` headers. You could put any value in the `From:` header; this is the information that displays in the From or Sender column of your email application when you receive this mail.

> If your outbound mail server is a Windows machine, you should replace the \n newline character with \r\n.

The `mail()` function uses five parameters: the recipient, the subject, the message, any additional mail headers, and any additional sendmail parameters. In our example, we use only the first four parameters. The order of these parameters is shown in line 14.

Put these lines into a text file called sendmail.php and place that file in your web server document root. Use your web browser and go back to the form, enter some information, and click the submission button. You should see something like Figure 11.6 in your browser.

FIGURE 11.6
Sample results from
`sendmail.php`.

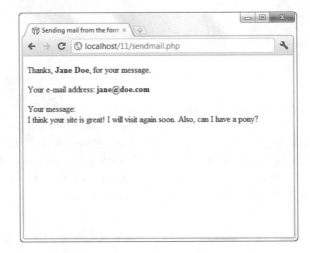

If you then check your email, you should have a message waiting for you. It might look something like Figure 11.7.

FIGURE 11.7
Email sent from
`sendmail.php`.

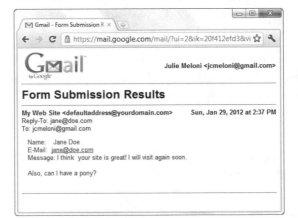

NOTE

This example does not include any server-side validation of form elements and just assumes that the user has entered values into the form. In a real-life situation, you would check for the presence and validity of the values entered in the form before doing anything with the mail, either through JavaScript or HTML5 form validation.

Formatting Your Mail with HTML

The "trick" to sending HTML-formatted email is not a trick at all. In fact, it only involves writing the actual HTML and modifying the headers sent by the mail() function. In Listing 11.12, a variation of Listing 11.11, changes were made in lines 12–14 and lines 18–19.

LISTING 11.12 Sending the Simple Feedback Form: HTML Version

```
1:  <?php
2:  //start building the mail string
3:  $msg  = "<p><strong>Name:</strong>     ".$_POST['name']."</p>";
4:  $msg .= "<p><strong>E-Mail:</strong>   ".$_POST['email']."</p>";
5:  $msg .= "<p><strong>Message:</strong> ".$_POST['message']."</p>";
6:
7:  //set up the mail
8:  $recipient = "you@yourdomain.com";
9:  $subject = "Form Submission Results";
10: $mailheaders  = "MIME-Version: 1.0\r\n";
11: $mailheaders .= "Content-type: text/html; charset=ISO-8859-1\r\n";
12: $mailheaders  = "From: My Web Site <defaultaddress@yourdomain.com> \n";
13: $mailheaders .= "Reply-To: ".$_POST['email'];
14:
15: //send the mail
16: mail($recipient, $subject, $msg, $mailheaders);
17: ?>
18: <!DOCTYPE html>
19: <html>
20: <head>
21: <title>Sending the Simple Feedback Form - HTML Version</title>
22: </head>
23: <body>
24: <p>Thanks, <strong><?php echo $_POST['name']; ?></strong>,
25:    for your message.</p>
26: <p>Your e-mail address:
27:    <strong><?php echo $_POST['email']; ?></strong></p>
28: <p>Your message: <br/> <?php echo $_POST['message']; ?> </p>
29: </body>
30: </html>
```

In lines 3–5, the message string now contains HTML code. Additional headers are created in lines 10–11, which set the Mime Version header to 1.0 and the Content-type header to text/html with a character set of ISO-8859-1. When opened in an HTML-enabled mail client, the HTML in the message string appears as intended, as shown in Figure 11.8.

FIGURE 11.8
Email sent from
Listing 11.12.

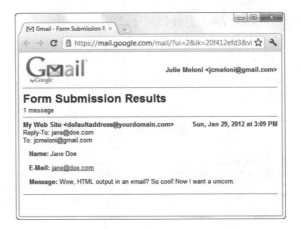

Working with File Uploads

So far, you've looked at simple form input. However, web browsers support file uploads, and so, of course, does PHP. In this section, you examine the features that PHP makes available to deal with this kind of input.

Information about the uploaded file becomes available to you in the $_FILES super-global, which is indexed by the name of the upload field (or fields) in the form. The corresponding value for each of these keys is an associative array. These fields are described in Table 11.1, using fileupload as the name of the form field used for the upload.

TABLE 11.1   File Upload Global Variables

Element	Contains	Example
$_FILES['fileupload']['name']	Original name of uploaded	file test.gif
$_FILES['fileupload']	Path to temporary file	/tmp/phprDfZvN ['tmp_name']
$_FILES['fileupload']['size']	Size (in bytes) of uploaded file	6835
$_FILES['fileupload']['type']	MIME type of uploaded file (where given by client)	image/gif

Keep these elements in the back of your mind for a moment while you create the upload form in the next section.

Creating the File Upload Form

First, you must create the HTML form to handle the upload. HTML forms that include file upload fields must include an ENCTYPE argument:

```
enctype="multipart/form-data"
```

PHP also works with an optional hidden field that can be inserted before the file upload field. This field must be called MAX_FILE_SIZE and should have a value representing the maximum size in bytes of the file that you're willing to accept. The MAX_FILE_SIZE field is obeyed at the browser's discretion, so you should rely on the php.ini setting, upload_max_filesize, to cap unreasonably large uploads. After the MAX_FILE_SIZE field has been entered, you are ready to add the upload field itself. This is simply an INPUT element with a TYPE argument of "file". You can give it any name you want. Listing 11.13 brings all this together into an HTML upload form.

LISTING 11.13   A Simple File Upload Form

```
 1: <!DOCTYPE html>
 2: <html>
 3: <head>
 4: <title>A simple file upload form</title>
 5: </head>
 6: <body>
 7: <form action="do_upload.php" enctype="multipart/form-data" method="POST">
 8: <input type="hidden" name="MAX_FILE_SIZE" value="1048576" />
 9: <p><label for="fileupload">File to Upload:</label>
10: <input type="file" id="fileupload" name="fileupload" /></p>
11: <button type="submit" name="submit" value="send">Upload File</button>
12: </form>
13: </body>
14: </html>
```

As you can see, file uploads are limited to 1MB (or 1048576 bytes) on line 8, and the name of the file upload field is fileupload, as shown on line 8. Save this listing in a text file called fileupload.html and place that file in your web server document root. Use your web browser to access this form and you should see something like Figure 11.9.

FIGURE 11.9
The form creat-
ed by Listing
11.13.

This form calls the do_upload.php script, which you create next.

Creating the File Upload Script

If you remember the information regarding the $_FILES superglobal, you have all the information you need to write a simple file upload script. This script is the back-end for the form created in Listing 11.14.

LISTING 11.14   A File Upload Script

```
1:   <?php
2:   $file_dir = "/path/to/upload/directory";
3:
4:   foreach($_FILES as $file_name => $file_array) {
5:       echo "path: ".$file_array['tmp_name']."<br/>\n";
6:       echo "name: ".$file_array['name']."<br/>\n";
7:       echo "type: ".$file_array['type']."<br/>\n";
8:       echo "size: ".$file_array['size']."<br/>\n";
9:
10:      if (is_uploaded_file($file_array['tmp_name'])) {
11:          move_uploaded_file($file_array['tmp_name'],
12:            "$file_dir/".$file_array['name'])
13:            or die ("Couldn't move file");
14:            echo "File was moved!";
15:      } else {
16:          echo "No file found.";
17:      }
18: }
19: ?>
```

In Listing 11.14, you first create the $file_dir variable on line 2 to store path information. This path should be one that exists on your system, and the web server user (for example, httpd, www, nobody) must have write permissions for it.

NOTE

> The path used in line 2 is a Linux/UNIX path. Windows users would use a path including the drive letter, such as the following:
>
> `$file_dir = "C:\Users\You\Desktop";`

Line 4 begins a foreach statement that loops through every element in the $_FILES array. A foreach loop is used rather than an if statement to make the script capable of scaling to deal with multiple uploads on the same page. The foreach loop beginning on line 4 stores the upload file's name in the $file_name variable and the file information in the $file_array variable. You can then output the information you have about the upload.

Before moving the uploaded file from its temporary position to the location specified in line 2, first check that the file exists (has been uploaded). The code does so on line 10, using the is_uploaded_file() function. This function accepts a path to an uploaded file and returns true only if the file in question is a valid upload file. This function therefore enhances the security of your scripts.

Assuming that all is well, the file is copied from its temporary home to a new directory on lines 11 to 13. Another function, move_uploaded_file(), is used for this purpose. This function copies a file from one place to another, first performing the same security checks as those performed by is_uploaded_file(). The move_uploaded_file() function requires a path to the source file and a path to the destination. It returns true if the move is successful and false if the file isn't a valid upload file or if the file couldn't be found.

CAUTION

> Beware of the names of uploaded files. Operating systems such as Mac OS and Windows are pretty relaxed when it comes to file naming, so expect uploaded files to come complete with spaces, quotation marks, and all manner of other unexpected characters. Therefore, it's a good idea to filter filenames.

Put all the code in Listing 11.14 into a text file called do_upload.php and place that file in your web server document root. Use your web browser to go back to the form and then try to upload a file. If successful, you should see something like Figure 11.10 in your browser.

FIGURE 11.10
Sample results
from Listing
11.14.

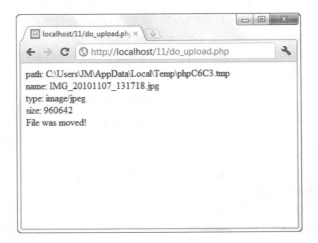

Summary

Things are really getting exciting now. A few items are still missing, of course, but there's plenty of book left. Now that you can get information from the user, it would be nice to be able to do something with it—write it to a file, perhaps? That's the subject of an upcoming chapter.

In this chapter, you learned how to work with various superglobals and form input. You also learned how to send raw headers to the client to redirect a browser. You learned how to acquire list information from form submissions and how to pass information from script call to script call using hidden fields. You also learned how to send your form results in email, and how to upload files through your web browser using a PHP script.

Q&A

Q. *When I submit other forms online, sometimes I see all the values I entered in the URL leading to the next page. Why is that?*

A. If you submit a form, such as a Google search, and the next URL you see includes the values that you entered, such as a search for "cheese" that might produce a URL like this:

```
https://www.google.com/#hl=en&output=search&q=cheese
```

Then what you are seeing is the output of a form that uses a GET action instead of a POST action. In this case, there are at least two fields—one hidden, called "output," and one that you see, called "q" (for query, presumably). The value of "cheese" is the value you typed in the INPUT field.

Q. *Why would I need to limit the upload size on a form?*

A. Without restricting the size of an upload in a form designed to upload files, you can run into the situation of leading users toward an action they can never complete, which could freeze up their system and yours. Think about the situation when you are looking to accept file uploads of digital images, and a user has created a very large image—let's say 10 megabytes. If the intention was to accept only thumbnails of images—something on the order of 350 kilobytes—simply telling the user to adhere to that limit isn't enough. With a combination of MAX_FILE_SIZE in the form and php.ini settings for upload_max_filesize (among others), you can ensure that a single user's action won't clog up the pipes.

Workshop

The workshop is designed to help you review what you've learned and begin putting your knowledge into practice.

Quiz

1. Which predefined variable do you use to find the name of the script?

2. Which built-in associative array contains all values submitted as part of a POST request?

3. Which built-in associative array contains all values submitted as part of a file upload?

4. What function do you use to redirect the browser to a new page?

5. What are the five arguments used by the mail() function?

6. On the client side, how do you limit the size of a file that a user can submit via a particular upload form?

Answers

1. The variable $_SERVER['PHP_SELF'] holds the name of the script.

2. The $_POST superglobal.

3. The $_FILES superglobal.

4. The header() function, along with a location.

5. The recipient, the subject, the message string, additional headers, and additional parameters.

6. Use a hidden field called MAX_FILE_SIZE in your form.

Activities

1. Create a calculator script that enables the user to submit two numbers and choose an operation (addition, multiplication, division, or subtraction) to perform on them.

2. Use hidden fields with the script you created in activity 1 to store and display the number of requests that the user submitted.

CHAPTER 12

Working with Cookies and User Sessions

In this chapter, you learn the following:

▶ How to store and retrieve cookie information

▶ What session variables are and how they work

▶ How to start or resume a session

▶ How to store variables in a session

▶ How to destroy a session

▶ How to unset session variables

PHP contains numerous functions for managing and keeping track of user information, including both simple cookies and all-encompassing user sessions. Sessions use techniques built in to the PHP language, making the act of saving state as easy as referencing a superglobal variable.

Introducing Cookies

You can use cookies within your PHP scripts to store small bits of information about a user. A *cookie* is a small amount of data stored by the user's browser in compliance with a request from a server or script. A single host can request that up to 20 cookies be stored by a user's browser. Each cookie consists of a name, value, and expiration date, as well as host and path information. The size of an individual cookie is limited to 4KB.

After a cookie is set, only the originating host can read the data, ensuring that the user's privacy is respected. Furthermore, users can configure their browser to notify them upon receipt of all cookies, or even to refuse all cookie requests. For this reason, cookies should be used in moderation and should not be relied on as an essential element of an environment design without first warning users.

The Anatomy of a Cookie

A PHP script that sets a cookie might send headers that look something like this:

```
HTTP/1.1 200 OK
Date: Wed, 18 Jan 2012 10:50:58 GMT
Server: Apache/2.2.21 (Unix) PHP/5.4.0
X-Powered-By: PHP/5.4.0
Set-Cookie: vegetable=artichoke; path=/; domain=yourdomain.com
Connection: close
Content-Type: text/html
```

As you can see, this `Set-Cookie` header contains a name/value pair, a path, and a domain. If set, the `expiration` field provides the date at which the browser should "forget" the value of the cookie. If no expiration date is set, the cookie expires when the user's session expires—that is, when he closes his browser.

The `path` and `domain` fields work together: The `path` is a directory found on the domain, below which the cookie should be sent back to the server. If the path is `"/"`, which is common, that means the cookie can be read by any files below the document root. If the path is "`/products/`", the cookie can be read only by files within the `/products` directory of the website.

The `domain` field represents the Internet domain from which cookie-based communication is allowed. For example, if your domain is www.yourdomain.com and you use www.yourdomain.com as the domain value for the cookie, the cookie will be valid only when browsing the www.domain.com website. This could pose a problem if you send the user to some domain like www2.domain.com or billing.domain.com within the course of his browsing experience, because the original cookie will no longer work. Therefore, it is common simply to begin the value of the domain slot in cookie definitions with a dot, leaving off the host (for example, .domain.com). In this manner, the cookie is valid for all hosts on the domain. The domain cannot be different from the domain from which the cookie was sent; otherwise, the cookie will not function properly, if at all, or the web browser will refuse the cookie in its entirety.

Accessing Cookies

If your web browser is configured to store cookies, it keeps the cookie-based information until the expiration date. If the user points the browser at any page that matches the path and domain of the cookie, it resends the cookie to the server. The browser's headers might look something like this:

```
GET / HTTP/1.0
Connection: Keep-Alive
User-Agent: Mozilla/5.0 (Windows NT 6.1; WOW64) AppleWebKit/535.7 (KHTML, like
  Gecko) Chrome/16.0.912.75 Safari/535.7
```

```
Host: www.yourdomain.com
Accept: image/gif, image/x-xbitmap, image/jpeg, image/pjpeg, image/png, */*
Accept-Encoding: gzip
Accept-Language: en,pdf
Accept-Charset: iso-8859-1,*,utf-8
Cookie: vegetable=artichoke
```

A PHP script then has access to the cookie in the environment variable HTTP_COOKIE or as part of the $_COOKIE superglobal variable, which you may access three different ways:

```
echo $_SERVER['HTTP_COOKIE'];    // will print "vegetable=artichoke"
echo getenv('HTTP_COOKIE');  // will print "vegetable=artichoke"
echo $_COOKIE['vegetable'];  // will print "artichoke"
```

Setting a Cookie with PHP

You can set a cookie in a PHP script in two ways. First, you can use the header() function to set the Set-Cookie header. The header() function requires a string that is then included in the header section of the server response. Because headers are sent automatically for you, header() must be called before any output at all is sent to the browser:

```
header("Set-Cookie: vegetable=artichoke; expires=Thu, 19-Jan-12 14:39:58 GMT;
path=/; domain=yourdomain.com");
```

Although not difficult, this method of setting a cookie requires you to build a function to construct the header string. Although formatting the date as in this example and URL-encoding the name/value pair is not a particularly arduous task, it is a repetitive one because PHP provides a function that does just that: setcookie().

The setcookie() function does what its name suggests—it outputs a Set-Cookie header. For this reason, it should be called before any other content is sent to the browser. The function accepts the cookie name, cookie value, expiration date in UNIX epoch format, path, domain, and integer that should be set to 1 if the cookie is to be sent only over a secure connection. All arguments to this function are optional apart from the first (cookie name) parameter.

Listing 12.1 uses setcookie() to set a cookie.

LISTING 12.1   Setting and Printing a Cookie Value

```
1: <?php
2: setcookie("vegetable", "artichoke", time()+3600, "/", ".yourdomain.com", 0);
3:
4: if (isset($_COOKIE['vegetable'])) {
5:   echo "<p>Hello again! You have chosen:  ".$_COOKIE['vegetable'].".</p>";
6: } else {
```

LISTING 12.1 Continued

```
7:   echo "<p>Hello, you. This may be your first visit.</p>";
8:  }
9:  ?>
```

Even though the listing sets the cookie (line 2) when the script is run for the first time, the $_COOKIE['vegetable'] variable is not created at this point. Because a cookie is read only when the browser sends it to the server, you cannot read it until the user revisits a page within this domain.

The cookie name is set to "vegetable" on line 2, and the cookie value to "artichoke". The time() function gets the current timestamp and adds 3600 to it (3,600 seconds in an hour). This total represents the expiration date. The code defines a path of "/", which means that a cookie should be sent for any page within this server environment. The domain argument is set to ".yourdomain.com" (you should make the change relevant to your own domain or leave it blank if you are working on localhost), which means that a cookie will be sent to any server in that group. Finally, the code passes 0 to setcookie(), signaling that cookies can be sent in an unsecure environment.

Passing setcookie() an empty string ("") for string arguments or 0 for integer fields causes these arguments to be skipped.

NOTE

With using a dynamically created expiration time in a cookie, as in Listing 12.1, note the expiration time is created by adding a certain number of seconds to the current system time of the machine running Apache and PHP. If this system clock is not accurate, the machine may send the cookie at an expiration time that has already passed.

You can view your cookies in most modern web browsers. Figure 12.1 shows the cookie information stored for Listing 12.1. The cookie name, content, and expiration date appear as expected; the domain name will differ when you run this script on your own domain.

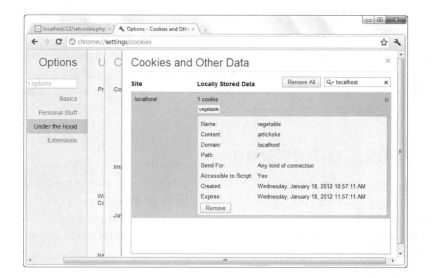

FIGURE 12.1
Viewing a
stored cookie in
a web browser.

For more information on using cookies, and the `setcookie()` function in particular, see the PHP Manual entry at http://www.php.net/setcookie.

Deleting a Cookie with PHP

Officially, to delete a cookie, you call `setcookie()` with the name argument only:

```
setcookie("vegetable");
```

This approach does not always work well, however, and you should not rely on it. Instead, to delete a cookie, it is safest to set the cookie with a date that you are sure has already expired:

```
setcookie("vegetable", "", time()-60, "/", ".yourdomain.com", 0);
```

Also make sure that you pass `setcookie()` the same path, domain, and secure parameters as you did when originally setting the cookie.

Session Function Overview

Session functions provide a unique identifier to a user, which can then be used to store and acquire information linked to that ID. When a visitor accesses a session-enabled page, either a new identifier is allocated or the user is reassociated with one that was already established in a previous visit. Any variables that have been associated with the session become available to your code through the `$_SESSION` superglobal.

Session state is usually stored in a temporary file, although you can implement database storage or other server-side storage methods using a function called `session_set_save_handler()`. The use of `session_set_save_handler()` and a discussion about other advanced session functionality are beyond the scope of this book, but you can find more information in the PHP Manual section for sessions for all items not discussed here.

Starting a Session

To work with a session, you need to explicitly start or resume that session *unless* you have changed your `php.ini` configuration file. By default, sessions do not start automatically. If you want to start a session this way, you must find the following line in your `php.ini` file and change the value from 0 to 1 (and restart the web server):

```
session.auto_start = 0
```

By changing the value of `session.auto_start` to 1, you ensure that a session initiates for every PHP document. If you don't change this setting, you need to call the `session_start()` function in each script.

After a session is started, you instantly have access to the user's session ID via the `session_id()` function. The `session_id()` function enables you to either set or retrieve a session ID. Listing 12.2 starts a session and prints the session ID to the browser.

LISTING 12.2   Starting or Resuming a Session

```
1: <?php
2: session_start();
3: echo "<p>Your session ID is ".session_id().".</p>";
4: ?>
```

When this script (let's call it `session_checkid.php`) is run for the first time from a browser, a session ID is generated by the `session_start()` function call on line 2. If the script is later reloaded or revisited, the same session ID is allocated to the user. This action assumes that the user has cookies enabled. For example, when I run this script the first time, the output is as follows:

```
Your session ID is 8jou17in51d08e5onsjkbles16.
```

When I reload the page, the output is still

```
Your session ID is 8jou17in51d08e5onsjkbles16.
```

because I have cookies enabled and the session ID still exists.

Because `start_session()` attempts to set a cookie when initiating a session for the first time, it is imperative that you call this function before you output anything else at all to the browser. If you do not follow this rule, your session will not be set, and you will likely see warnings on your page.

Sessions remain current as long as the web browser is active. When the user restarts the browser, the cookie is no longer stored. You can change this behavior by altering the `session.cookie_lifetime` setting in your `php.ini` file. The default value is 0, but you can set an expiry period in seconds.

Working with Session Variables

Accessing a unique session identifier in each of your PHP documents is only the start of session functionality. When a session is started, you can store any number of variables in the `$_SESSION` superglobal and then access them on any session-enabled page.

Listing 12.3 adds two variables into the `$_SESSION` superglobal: `product1` and `product2` (lines 3 and 4).

LISTING 12.3   Storing Variables in a Session

```
1: <?php
2: session_start();
3: $_SESSION['product1'] = "Sonic Screwdriver";
4: $_SESSION['product2'] = "HAL 2000";
5: echo "The products have been registered.";
6: ?>
```

The magic in Listing 12.3 will not become apparent until the user moves to a new page. Listing 12.4 creates a separate PHP script that accesses the variables stored in the `$_SESSION` superglobal.

LISTING 12.4   Accessing Stored Session Variables

```
1: <?php
2: session_start();
3: ?>
4: <p>Your chosen products are:</p>
5: <ul>
6: <li><?php echo $_SESSION['product1']; ?></li>
7: <li><?php echo $_SESSION['product2']; ?></li>
8: </ul>
```

Figure 12.2 shows the output from Listing 12.4. As you can see, you have access to the `$_SESSION['product1']` and `$_SESSION['product2']` variables in an entirely new page.

FIGURE 12.2
Accessing
stored session
variables.

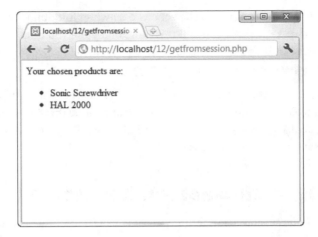

Although not a terribly interesting or useful example, the script does show how to access stored session variables. Behind the scenes, PHP writes information to a temporary file. You can find out where this file is being written on your system by using the `session_save_path()` function. This function optionally accepts a path to a directory and then writes all session files to it. If you pass it no arguments, it returns a string representing the current directory to which it saves session files. On my system, the following prints `/tmp`:

```
echo session_save_path();
```

A glance at my `/tmp` directory reveals a number of files with names like the following:

```
sess_fa963e3e49186764b0218e82d050de7b
sess_76cae8ac1231b11afa2c69935c11dd95
sess_bb50771a769c605ab77424d59c784ea0
```

Opening the file that matches the session ID I was allocated when I first ran Listing 12.2, I can see how the registered variables have been stored:

```
product1|s:17:"Sonic Screwdriver";product2|s:8:"HAL 2000";
```

When a value is placed in the `$_SESSION` superglobal, PHP writes the variable name and value to a file. This information can be read and the variables resurrected later—as you have already seen. After you add a variable to the `$_SESSION` superglobal, you can still change its value at any time during the execution of your script, but the altered value is not reflected in the global setting until you reassign the variable to the `$_SESSION` superglobal.

The example in Listing 12.3 demonstrates the process of adding variables to the $_SESSION superglobal. This example is not very flexible, however. Ideally, you should be able to register a varying number of values. You might want to let users pick products from a list, for example. In this case, you can use the serialize() function to store an array in your session.

Listing 12.5 creates a form that allows a user to choose multiple products. You use the session variables to create a rudimentary shopping cart.

LISTING 12.5   Adding an Array Variable to a Session Variable

```
 1: <?php
 2: session_start();
 3: ?>
 4: <!DOCTYPE html>
 5: <html>
 6: <head>
 7: <title>Storing an array with a session</title>
 8: </head>
 9: <body>
10: <h1>Product Choice Page</h1>
11: <?php
12: if (isset($_POST['form_products'])) {
13:     if (!empty($_SESSION['products'])) {
14:         $products = array_unique(
15:         array_merge(unserialize($_SESSION['products']),
16:         $_POST['form_products']));
17:         $_SESSION['products'] = serialize($products);
18:     } else {
19:         $_SESSION['products'] = serialize($_POST['form_products']);
20:     }
21:     echo "<p>Your products have been registered!</p>";
22: }
23: ?>
24: <form method="post" action="<?php echo $_SERVER['PHP_SELF']; ?>">
25: <p><label for="form_products">Select some products:</label><br />
26: <select id="form_products" name="form_products[]" multiple="multiple"
    size="3">
27: <option value="Sonic Screwdriver">Sonic Screwdriver</option>
28: <option value="Hal 2000">Hal 2000</option>
29: <option value="Tardis">Tardis</option>
30: <option value="ORAC">ORAC</option>
31: <option value="Transporter bracelet">Transporter bracelet</option>
32: </select></p>
33: <button type="submit" name="submit" value="choose">Submit Form</button>
34: </form>
35: <p><a href="session1.php">go to content page</a></p>
36: </body>
37: </html>
```

The listing starts or resumes a session by calling session_start() on line 2. This call gives access to any previously set session variables. An HTML form begins on line 24 and, on line 26, creates a SELECT element named form_products[], which contains OPTION elements for a number of products.

NOTE

Remember that HTML form elements that allow multiple selections, such as check boxes and multiple select lists, should have square brackets appended to the value of their NAME attributes. This makes the user's choices available to PHP in an array.

The block of PHP code beginning on line 11 tests for the presence of the $_POST['form_products'] array (line 12). If the variable is present, you can assume that the form has been submitted and information has already been stored in the $_SESSION superglobal.

Line 12 tests for an array called $_SESSION['products']. If the array exists, it was populated on a previous visit to this script, so the code merges it with the $_POST['form_products'] array, extracts the unique elements, and assigns the result back to the $products array (lines 14–16). Then the $products array is added to the $_SESSION superglobal on line 17.

Line 35 contains a link to another script, which will demonstrate access to the products the user has chosen. This new script is created in Listing 12.6, but in the meantime you can save the code in Listing 12.5 as **arraysession.php**.

Moving on to Listing 12.6, you see how to access the items stored in the session created in arraysession.php.

LISTING 12.6   Accessing Session Variables

```
1: <?php
2: session_start();
3: ?>
4: <!DOCTYPE html>
5: <html>
6: <head>
7: <title>Accessing session variables</title>
8: </head>
9: <body>
10: <h1>Content Page</h1>
11: <?php
12: if (isset($_SESSION['products'])) {
13:     echo "<strong>Your cart:</strong><ol>";
14:     foreach (unserialize($_SESSION['products']) as $p) {
15:         echo "<li>".$p."</li>";
16:     }
17:     echo "</ol>";
18: }
19: ?>
20: <p><a href="arraysession.php">return to product choice page</a></p>
```

```
21: </body>
22: </html>
```

Once again, `session_start()` resumes the session on line 2. Line 12 tests for the presence of the `$_SESSION['products']` variable. If it exists, the variable is unserialized and looped through on lines 14–16, printing each of the user's chosen items to the browser. Figure 12.3 shows an example of the output.

FIGURE 12.3
Accessing an array of session variables.

For a real shopping cart program, of course, you would keep product details in a database and test user input, rather than blindly store and present it, but Listings 12.5 and 12.6 demonstrate the ease with which you can use session functions to access array variables set in other pages.

Destroying Sessions and Unsetting Variables

You can use `session_destroy()` to end a session, erasing all session variables. The `session_destroy()` function requires no arguments. You should have an established session for this function to work as expected. The following code fragment resumes a session and abruptly destroys it:

```
session_start();
session_destroy();
```

When you move on to other pages that work with a session, the session you have destroyed will not be available to them, forcing them to initiate new sessions of their own. Any registered variables will be lost.

The session_destroy() function does not instantly destroy registered variables, however. They remain accessible to the script in which session_destroy() is called (until it is reloaded). The following code fragment resumes or initiates a session and registers a variable called test, set to 5. Destroying the session does not destroy the registered variable:

```
session_start();
$_SESSION['test'] = 5;
session_destroy();
echo $_SESSION['test']; // prints 5
```

To remove all registered variables from a session, you simply unset the variable:

```
session_start();
$_SESSION['test'] = 5;
session_destroy();
unset($_SESSION['test']);
echo $_SESSION['test']; // prints nothing (or a notice about an undefined index)
```

Using Sessions in an Environment with Registered Users

The examples you've seen so far have gotten your feet wet with sessions, but perhaps additional explanation is warranted for using sessions "in the wild," so to speak. The following two sections outline some examples of common session usage. In later chapters of this book, sessions are used in the sample applications you build.

Working with Registered Users

Suppose that you've created an online community, or a portal, or some other type of application that users can "join." The process usually involves a registration form, where the user creates a username and password and completes an identification profile. From that point forward, each time a registered user logs in to the system, you can grab the user's identification information and store it in the user's session.

The items you decide to store in the user's session should be those items you can imagine using quite a bit—and that would be inefficient to continually extract from the database. For example, suppose that you have created a portal in which users are assigned a certain level, such as administrator, registered user, anonymous guest, and so forth. Within your display modules, you would always want to check to verify that the user accessing the module has the proper permissions to do so. Thus, "user level" is an example of a value stored in the user's session, so that the authentication script used in the display of the requested module only has to check a session variable—there is no need to connect to, select, and query the database.

Working with User Preferences

If you are feeling adventurous in the design phase of a user-based application, you might build a system in which registered users can set specific preferences that affect the way they view your site. For example, you might allow your users to select from a predetermined color scheme, font type and size, and so forth. Or, you might allow users to turn "off" (or "on") the visibility of certain content groupings.

You can store each of those functional elements in a session. When the user logs in, the application loads all relevant values into the user's session and reacts accordingly for each subsequently requested page. Should the user decide to change her preferences, she could do so while logged in—you could even prepopulate a "preferences" form based on the items stored in the session instead of going back to the database to retrieve them. If the user changes any preferences while she is logged in, simply replace the value stored in the $_SESSION superglobal with the new selection—no need to force the user to log out and then log back in again.

Summary

In this chapter, you looked at different ways of saving state in a stateless protocol, including setting a cookie and starting a session. All methods of saving state use some manner of cookies or query strings, sometimes combined with the use of files or databases. These approaches all have their benefits and problems.

You learned that a cookie alone is not intrinsically reliable and cannot store much information. However, it can persist over a long period. Approaches that write information to a file or database involve some cost to speed and might become a problem on a popular site; this is a matter to explore with your systems administrators.

About sessions themselves, you learned how to initiate or resume a session with session_start(). When in a session, you learned how to add variables to the $_SESSION superglobal, check that they exist, unset them if you want, and destroy the entire session.

Q&A

Q. *What will happen to my application if users disable cookies?*

A. Simply put, if your application relies heavily on cookies and users have cookies disabled, your application won't work. However, you can do your part to warn users that cookies are coming by announcing your intention to use cookies, and also by checking that cookies are enabled before doing anything "important" with your application. The idea being, of course, that even if users ignore your note that cookies must be turned on in order to use your application, specifically disallowing users to perform an action if your cookie test fails will get their attention!

Q. *Should I be aware of any pitfalls with session functions?*

A. The session functions are generally reliable. However, remember that cookies cannot be read across multiple domains. So, if your project uses more than one domain name on the same server (perhaps as part of an e-commerce environment), you might need to consider disabling cookies for sessions by setting the

```
session.use_cookies
```

directive to 0 in the `php.ini` file.

Workshop

The workshop is designed to help you review what you've learned and begin putting your knowledge into practice.

Quiz

1. Which function would you use to start or resume a session within a PHP script?

2. Which function can return the current session's ID?

3. How can you end a session and erase all traces of it for future visits?

Answers

1. You can start a session by using the `session_start()` function within your script.

2. You can access the session's ID by using the `session_id()` function.

3. The `session_destroy()` function removes all traces of a session for future requests.

Activities

▶ Create a script that uses session functions to track which pages in your environment the user has visited.

▶ Create a new script that will list for the user all the pages she has visited within your environment, and when.

CHAPTER 13

Working with Files and Directories

In this chapter, you learn the following:

- ▶ How to include other files in your documents
- ▶ How to test for the existence of files and directories
- ▶ How to open a file before working with it
- ▶ How to read data from files
- ▶ How to write or append to a file
- ▶ How to lock a file
- ▶ How to work with directories
- ▶ How to pipe data to and from external applications
- ▶ How to send shell commands and display results in the browser

Testing for the existence of files, reading from them, and writing to them are important features of any rich programming language. PHP is no exception, in that it provides functions that make these processes straightforward. In addition, because PHP, Apache, and MySQL are not the only applications on your machine, you might sometimes need to access those other applications from within your PHP code, something you are shown how to do in this chapter.

Including Files

The include statement enables you to incorporate other files (usually other PHP scripts) into your PHP documents. PHP code in these included files will then be executed as if it were part of the main document. This is useful for including code libraries within multiple pages.

Suppose, for instance, you create a really useful function. Without the `include` statement, your only option is to paste your new function into every document that needs to use it. Of course, if you discover a bug or want to add a feature, you have to find every page you pasted the function into and make the change—over and over again. The `include` statement saves you from such a chore. You can add your newly created function to a single document, such as `myinclude.php` and, at run-time, read it into any page that needs it.

The `include` statement requires a single argument: a relative path to the file to include. Listing 13.1 creates a simple PHP script that uses `include` to incorporate and output the contents of a file.

LISTING 13.1   Using `include()`

```
1: <?php
2: include 'myinclude.php';
3: ?>
```

The `include` statement in Listing 13.1 incorporates the document `myinclude.php`, the contents of which you can see in Listing 13.2.

LISTING 13.2   The File Included in Listing 13.1

```
1: I have been included!!
```

Put the contents of Listing 13.1 in a file named **test_include.php**, and the contents of Listing 13.2 in a file named **myinclude.php**. Place both files in your web server document root. When you access `test_include.php` through your web browser, the output on the screen is as follows:

```
I have been included!!
```

This might seem strange to you, given that you're including plaintext within a block of PHP code. In fact, the contents of an included file display as text by default. *If you want to execute PHP code in an included file, you must enclose it in PHP start and end tags.* Listing 13.3 amends the contents of `myinclude.php` so that code is executed in the included file.

LISTING 13.3   An Include File Containing PHP Code

```
1: <?php
2: echo "I have been included!!<br/>";
3: echo "But now I can add up...  4 + 4 = ".(4 + 4);
4: ?>
```

Put the contents of Listing 13.3 in a file named **myinclude2.php** and change the value of the included file in test_include.php to point to this new file. Place both these files in your web server document root. Now, when you access test_include.php through your web browser, the output on the screen is as follows:

```
I have been included!!
But now I can add up... 4 + 4 = 8
```

The only way you would see the number 8 is if the code for adding 4 and 4 were executed as PHP, and it was.

Returning a Value from an Included Document

Included files in PHP can return a value in the same way that functions do. As in a function, using the return statement ends the execution of code within the included file. In addition, no further HTML is included. Listings 13.4 and 13.5 include a file and assign its return value to a variable.

LISTING 13.4 Using include to Execute PHP and Assign the Return Value

```
1: <?php
2: $addResult = include 'returnvalue.php';
3: echo "The include file returned ".$addResult;
4: ?>
```

LISTING 13.5 An Include File That Returns a Value

```
1: <?php
2: $retval = ( 4 + 4 );
3: return $retval;
4: ?>
5: This HTML will never be displayed because it comes after a return statement!
```

Put the contents of Listing 13.4 in a file named **test_returnvalue.php**; put the contents of Listing 13.5 in a file named **returnvalue.php**. Place both of these files in your web server document root. When you access test_returnvalue.php through your web browser, the output is this:

```
The include file returned 8.
```

Just as the string suggests on line 5 of Listing 13.5, anything outside the PHP block will not be displayed if there *is* a PHP block present in the included file.

Using include **Within Control Structures**

If you use an include statement within a conditional statement, it is treated like any other code—the file is included only if the condition is met. For example, the include statement in the following fragment will never be called:

```
$test = "1";
if ($test == "2") {
   include 'file.txt'; // won't be included
}
```

If you use an include statement within a loop, the file will literally be included each time the loop iterates. Listing 13.6 illustrates this concept by using an include statement in a for loop. The include statement references a different file for each iteration.

LISTING 13.6   Using include Within a Loop

```
1: <?php
2: for ($x = 1; $x<=3; $x++) {
3:    $incfile = "incfile".$x.".txt";
4:    echo "Attempting to include ".$incfile."<br/>";
5:    include $incfile;
6:    echo "<hr/>";
7: }
8: ?>
```

Save the contents of Listing 13.6 in a file named loopy_include.php and place it in the document root of the web server, along with three different files: incfile1.txt, incfile2.txt, and incfile3.txt. If we assume that each of these files simply contains a confirmation of its own name, the output should look like Figure 13.1.

FIGURE 13.1
Output of
loopy_
include.php.

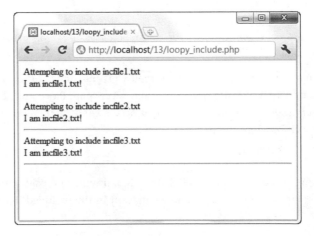

Although this code worked fine, using the include function in this manner is sometimes not such a great idea, as discussed in the next subsection.

Using `include_once`

One problem caused by using several different libraries of code within your code is
the danger of calling include twice on the same file. This sometimes happens in
larger projects when different library files call include on a common file. Including
the same file twice often results in repeated declarations of functions and classes,
thereby causing the PHP engine great unhappiness.

This situation is remedied by using the include_once statement in place of the
include statement. The include_once statement requires the path to an include
file and otherwise behaves the same way as the include statement the first time it
is called. However, if include_once is called again for the same file during script
execution, the file will *not* be included again. This makes include_once an excellent tool for the creation of reusable code libraries!

The `include_path` Directive

Using include and include_once to access your code libraries can increase the
flexibility and reusability of your projects. However, there are still headaches
to overcome. Portability, in particular, can suffer if you hard-code the paths to
included files. Imagine that you create a lib directory and reference it throughout
your project:

```
include_once '/home/user/bob/htdocs/project4/lib/mylib.inc.php';
```

When you move your project to a new server, you might find that you have to
change a hundred or more include paths, if this is hard-coded in a hundred or
more files. You can escape this fate by setting the include_path directive in your
php.ini file:

```
include_path   .:/home/user/bob/htdocs/project4/lib/
```

The include_path value can include as many directories as you want, separated by
colons (semicolons in Windows). The order of the items in the include_path directive determines the order in which the directories are searched for the named file.
The first dot (.) before the first colon indicates "current directory," and should be
present. Now any path used in include or include_once can be relative to the
value of include_path:

```
include_once 'mylib.inc.php';
```

When you move your project, you need to change only the include_path directive.

> PHP also has a require statement, which performs a similar function to include, and a require_once statement that works similarly to include_once.
>
> Anything pulled into your code by require is executed regardless of a script's flow, and therefore shouldn't be used as part of conditional or loop structures.
>
> Also, be aware that a file included as the result of a require statement cannot return a value.

Validating Files

Before you work with a file or directory within your code, it is often a good idea to learn more about it, and determining whether it actually exists is a pretty good start! PHP provides many functions to help you to discover information about files on your system. This section briefly covers some of the most useful functions.

Checking for Existence with file_exists()

You can test for the existence of a file with the file_exists() function. This function requires a string representation of an absolute or relative path to a file, which might or might not be present. If the file is found, the file_exists() function returns true; otherwise, it returns false:

```
if (file_exists('test.txt')) {
        echo "The file exists!";
}
```

This is all well and good, but what if you're unsure whether something is a file or a directory, and you really need to know? Read on.

A File or a Directory?

You can confirm that the entity you're testing is a file, as opposed to a directory, using the is_file() function. The is_file() function requires the file path and returns a Boolean value:

```
if (is_file('test.txt')) {
        echo "test.txt is a file!";
}
```

Conversely, you might want to check that the entity you're testing is a directory. You can do this with the is_dir() function. is_dir() requires the path to the directory and returns a Boolean value:

```
if (is_dir('/tmp')) {
        echo "/tmp is a directory";
}
```

After you know a file or directory exists, you might need to test its permissions. You learn about this in the next section.

Checking the Status of a File

When you know that a particular entity exists, and it's what you expect it to be (either a directory or a file), you need to know what you can do with it. Typically, you might want to read, write to, or execute a file. PHP can help you determine whether you can perform these operations.

The is_readable() function tells you whether you can read a file. On UNIX systems, you might be able to see a file but still be barred from reading its contents because of its user permissions. The is_readable() function accepts the file path as a string and returns a Boolean value:

```
if (is_readable('test.txt')) {
        echo "test.txt is readable";
}
```

The is_writable() function tells you whether you have the proper permission to write to a file. As with is_readable(), the is_writable() function requires the file path and returns a Boolean value.

```
if (is_writable('test.txt')) {
        echo "test.txt is writable";
}
```

The is_executable() function tells you whether you can execute the given file, relying on either the file's permissions or its extension, depending on your platform. The function accepts the file path and returns a Boolean value.

```
if (is_executable('test.txt')) {
        echo "test.txt is executable";
}
```

Permission-related information isn't all you might need to know about a file. The next section shows how to determine the file size.

Determining File Size with filesize()

Given the path to a file, the filesize() function attempts to determine and return its size in bytes. It returns false if it encounters problems:

```
echo "The size of test.txt is ".filesize('test.txt');
```

Finding the specific file size is important in situations where you want to attach a file to an email or stream a file to the user—you need to know the size so as to properly create the headers (in the case of the email) or know when to stop sending bytes to the user (in the case of the stream). For more general purposes, you might want to get the file size so that you can display it to the user before she attempts to download some monstrous application or high-resolution photograph from your site.

Getting Date Information About a File

Sometimes you need to know when a file was last written to or accessed. PHP provides several functions that can provide this information.

You can find out the last-accessed time of a file using the `fileatime()` function. This function requires the file path and returns the date that the file was last accessed. To *access* a file means either to read or write to it. Dates are returned from all the date information functions in timestamp—that is, the number of seconds since January 1, 1970. The examples in this book use the `date()` function to translate this value into human-readable form:

```
$atime = fileatime("test.txt");
echo "test.txt was last accessed on ".date("D d M Y g:i A", $atime);
// Sample output: test.txt was last changed on Sat 26 Apr 2008 12:52 PM
```

You can discover the modification date of a file with the function `filemtime()`, which requires the file path and returns the date in UNIX epoch format. To *modify* a file means to change its contents in some way:

```
$mtime = filemtime("test.txt");
echo "test.txt was last modified on ".date("D d M Y g:i A", $mtime);
// Sample output: test.txt was last modified on Wed 18 Jan 2012 7:11 PM
```

PHP also enables you to test the change time of a document with the `filectime()` function. On UNIX systems, the change time is set when a file's contents are modified or when changes are made to its permissions or ownership. On other platforms, the `filectime()` returns the creation date:

```
mtime = filemtime("test.txt");
echo "test.txt was last modified on ".date("D d M Y g:i A", $mtime);
// Sample output: test.txt was last modified on Wed 18 Jan 2012 7:11 PM
```

Creating a Function That Performs Multiple File Tests

Listing 13.7 creates a function that brings together the file-related functions just discussed into one script.

LISTING 13.7 A Function to Output the Results of Multiple File Tests

```php
1:  <?php
2:  function outputFileTestInfo($f) {
3:      if (!file_exists($f)) {
4:          echo "<p>$f does not exist</p>";
5:          return;
6:      }
7:      echo "<p>$f is ".(is_file($f) ? "" : "not ")."a file</p>";
8:      echo "<p>$f is ".(is_dir($f) ? "" : "not ")."a directory</p>";
9:      echo "<p>$f is ".(is_readable($f) ? "": "not ")."readable</p>";
10:     echo "<p>$f is ".(is_writable($f) ? "": "not ")."writable</p>";
11:     echo "<p>$f is ".(is_executable($f) ? "": "not ")."executable</p>";
12:     echo "<p>$f is ".(filesize($f))." bytes</p>";
13:     echo "<p>$f was accessed on ".date( "D d M Y g:i A",fileatime($f))."</p>";
14:     echo "<p>$f was modified on ".date( "D d M Y g:i A",filemtime($f))."</p>";
15:     echo "<p>$f was changed on ".date( "D d M Y g:i A",filectime($f) )."</p>";
16: }
17: $file = "test.txt";
18: outputFileTestInfo($file);
19: ?>
```

If you save this code to the document root of your web server as `filetests.php` and run through your web browser, the output would look something like Figure 13.2 (provided you have a file named `test.txt` also in the document root).

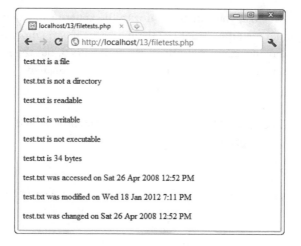

FIGURE 13.2
Output of
`filetests.php`.

Notice that the ternary operator is used as a compact way of working with some of these tests. Let's look at one such test, found in line 7, in more detail:

```php
echo "<p>$f is ".(is_file($f) ? "" : "not ")."a file</p>";
```

The is_file() function is used as the left-side expression of the ternary operator. If it returns true, an empty string is returned. Otherwise, the string "not " is returned. The return value of the ternary expression is added to the string to be printed with concatenation operators. This statement could be made clearer, but less compact, as follows:

```
$is_it = is_file($f) ? "" : "not ";
echo "<p>".$f." is ".$is_it." a file</p>";
```

You could, of course, be even clearer with an if statement, but imagine how large the function would become if you used the following:

```
if (is_file($f)) {
        echo "<p>$f is a file</p>";
} else {
        echo "<p>$f is not a file</p>";
}
```

Because the result of these three approaches is the same, the approach you take becomes a matter of preference.

Creating and Deleting Files

If a file does not yet exist, you can create it with the touch() function. Given a string representing a file path, touch() attempts to create an empty file of that name. If the file already exists, its contents is not disturbed, but the modification date is updated to reflect the time at which the function executed:

```
touch('myfile.txt');
```

You can remove an existing file with the unlink() function. As did the touch() function, unlink() accepts a file path:

```
unlink('myfile.txt');
```

All functions that create, delete, read, write, and modify files on UNIX systems require the correct file or directory permissions to be set.

Opening a File for Writing, Reading, or Appending

Before you can work with a file, you must first open it for reading or writing, or for performing both tasks. PHP provides the fopen() function for doing so, and this function requires a string that contains the file path, followed by a string that contains the mode in which the file is to be opened. The most common modes are read (r), write (w), and append (a).

The fopen() function returns a file resource you use later to work with the open file. To open a file for reading, you use the following:

```
$fp = fopen("test.txt", "r");
```

You use the following to open a file for writing:

```
$fp = fopen("test.txt", "w");
```

To open a file for *appending* (that is, to add data to the end of a file), you use this:

```
$fp = fopen("test.txt", "a");
```

The fopen() function returns false if the file cannot be opened for any reason. Therefore, it's a good idea to test the function's return value before proceeding to work with it. You can do so with an if statement:

```
if ($fp = fopen("test.txt", "w")) {
    // do something with the $fp resource
}
```

Or, you can use a logical operator to end execution if an essential file can't be opened:

```
($fp = fopen("test.txt", "w")) or die("Couldn't open file, sorry");
```

If the fopen() function returns true, the rest of the expression is not parsed, and the die() function (which writes a message to the browser and ends the script) is never reached. Otherwise, the right side of the or operator is parsed, and the die() function is called.

Assuming that all is well and you go on to work with your open file, you should remember to close it when you finish. You can do so by calling fclose(), which requires the file resource returned from a successful fopen() call as its argument:

```
fclose($fp);
```

The resource that became available ($fp) is now unavailable to you.

Reading from Files

PHP provides a number of functions for reading data from files. These functions enable you to read by the byte, by the whole line, and even by the single character.

Reading Lines from a File with `fgets()` and `feof()`

When you open a file for reading, you might want to access it line by line. To read a line from an open file, you can use the `fgets()` function, which requires the file resource returned from `fopen()` as its argument. You must also pass `fgets()` an integer as a second argument, which specifies the number of bytes that the function should read if it doesn't first encounter a line end or the end of the file. The `fgets()` function reads the file until it reaches a newline character (`"\n"`), the number of bytes specified in the length argument, or the end of the file—whichever comes first:

```
$line = fgets($fp, 1024); // where $fp is the file resource returned by fopen()
```

Although you can read lines with `fgets()`, you need some way to tell when you reach the end of the file. The `feof()` function does this by returning `true` when the end of the file has been reached and `false` otherwise. The `feof()` function requires a file resource as its argument:

```
feof($fp); // where $fp is the file resource returned by fopen()
```

You now have enough information to read a file line by line, as shown in Listing 13.8.

LISTING 13.8   Opening and Reading a File Line by Line

```
1: <?php
2: $filename = "test.txt";
3: $fp = fopen($filename, "r") or die("Couldn't open $filename");
4: while (!feof($fp)) {
5:     $line = fgets($fp, 1024);
6:     echo $line."<br/>";
7: }
8: ?>
```

If this code were saved to the document root of your web server as `readlines.php` and run through your web browser, the output would look something like Figure 13.3 (although the contents of your text file might differ).

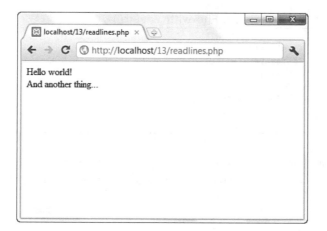

FIGURE 13.3
Output of
readlines.php.

The code calls fopen() on line 3, using the name of the file that you want to read as its argument. The or die() construct is used to ensure that script execution ends if the file cannot be read. This usually occurs if the file does not exist or if the file's permissions do not allow read access to the file.

The actual reading of the file contents takes place in the while statement on line 4. The while statement's test expression calls feof() for each iteration, ending the loop when it returns true. In other words, the loop continues until it reaches the end of the file. Within the code block, fgets() on line 5 extracts a line (or 1024 bytes, whichever comes first) from the file. The result is assigned to $line and printed to the browser on line 6, appending a <br/> tag for the sake of readability.

Reading Arbitrary Amounts of Data from a File with fread()

Rather than reading text by the line, you can choose to read a file in arbitrarily defined chunks. The fread() function accepts a file resource as an argument, as well as the number of bytes you want to read. The fread() function returns the amount of data you requested, unless the end of the file is reached first:

```
$chunk = fread($fp, 16);
```

Listing 13.9 amends the previous example so that it reads data in chunks of 8 bytes rather than by the line.

LISTING 13.9   Reading a File with `fread()`

```
1: <?php
2: $filename = "test.txt";
3: $fp = fopen($filename, "r") or die("Couldn't open $filename");
4: while (!feof($fp)) {
5:     $chunk = fread($fp, 8);
6:     echo $chunk."<br/>";
7: }
8: ?>
```

If this code were saved to the document root of your web server as `readlines2.php` and run through your web browser, the output would look something like Figure 13.4.

FIGURE 13.4
Output of
`readlines2.php`.

Although the `fread()` function enables you to define the amount of data acquired from a file, it doesn't let you decide the position from which the acquisition begins. You can set this manually with the `fseek()` function.

The `fseek()` function lets you to change your current position within a file. It requires a file resource and an integer that represents the offset from the start of the file (in bytes) to which you want to jump:

```
fseek($fp, 64);
```

Listing 13.10 uses `fseek()` and `fread()` to output the second half of a file to the browser.

LISTING 13.10   Moving Around a File with `fseek()`

```
 1: <?php
 2: $filename = "test.txt";
 3: $fp = fopen($filename, "r") or die("Couldn't open $filename");
 4: $fsize = filesize($filename);
 5: $halfway = (int)($fsize / 2);
 6: echo "Halfway point: ".$halfway." <br/>\n";
 7: fseek($fp, $halfway);
 8: $chunk = fread($fp, ($fsize - $halfway));
 9: echo $chunk;
10: ?>
```

If this code were saved to the document root of your web server as `readseek.php` and run through your web browser, the output would look something like Figure 13.5.

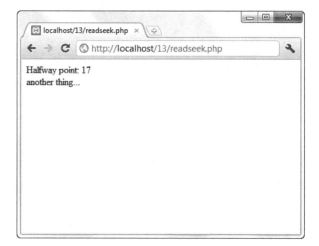

FIGURE 13.5
Output of `readseek.php`.

The code calculates the halfway point of our file on line 5, by dividing the return value of `filesize()` by 2. It uses this as the second argument to `fseek()` on line 7, jumping to the halfway point of the text file. Finally, on line 8, `fread()` is called to extract the second half of the file and then the result is printed to the browser.

Reading Characters from a File with `fgetc()`

The `fgetc()` function is similar to `fgets()` except that it returns only a single character from a file every time it is called. Because a character is always 1 byte in size, `fgetc()` doesn't require a length argument. You must simply pass it a file resource:

```
$char = fgetc($fp);
```

Listing 13.11 creates a loop that reads the file `test.txt` one character at a time, outputting each character to the browser on its own line.

LISTING 13.11   Moving Around a File with `fgetc()`

```
1: <?php
2: $filename = "test.txt";
3: $fp = fopen($filename, "r") or die("Couldn't open $filename");
4: while (!feof($fp)) {
5:     $char = fgetc($fp);
6:     echo $char."<br/>";
7: }
8: ?>
```

If this code were saved to the document root of your web server as `readchars.php` and run through your web browser, the output would look something like Figure 13.6.

FIGURE 13.6
Output of
`readchars.php`.

Reading File Contents with `file_get_contents()`

Now that you get the point of creating a file resource with `fopen()` and performing one or more actions on that resource, you can dispense with those pleasantries and get right to the point by using `file_get_contents()` to read an entire file into a string. For example, the following single line of code reads the contents of a file called `test.txt` into a variable called $contents:

```
$contents = file_get_contents("test.txt");
```

This function affords you some other possibilities as well; the following shows allowable options when calling `file_get_contents()`:

```
file_get_contents ($filename [$use_include_path [, $context [, $offset [,
  $maxlen ]]]]);
```

These additional options are described as such:

- ▶ **use_include_path**—a Boolean value that indicates whether or not the function should search the entire `include_path` for the filename.

- ▶ **context**—a context resource created by `stream_context_create()`; use NULL if not needed.

- ▶ **offset**—the point at which reading should start, such as 5 for the fifth character in the file. Note that while you can use `file_get_contents()` with non-local files (such as URLs), `offset` cannot be used in those situations.

- ▶ **maxlen**—the maximum length of data to read, in bytes. The default is to read all of the data.

If the fine-grained controls of the previous functions are not necessary in your scripts, then `file_get_contents()` will serve many of your basic file reading purposes quite well.

Writing or Appending to a File

The processes for writing to and appending to a file are the same—the difference lies in the mode with which you call the `fopen()` function. When you write to a file, you use the mode argument `"w"` when you call `fopen()`:

```
$fp = fopen("test.txt", "w");
```

All subsequent writing occurs from the start of the file. If the file doesn't already exist, it is created. If the file already exists, any prior content is destroyed and replaced by the data you write.

When you append to a file, you use the mode argument `"a"` in your `fopen()` call:

```
$fp = fopen("test.txt", "a");
```

Any subsequent writes to your file are added to the end of your existing content, but if you attempt to append content to a nonexistent file, the file is created first.

Writing to a File with `fwrite()` or `fputs()`

The `fwrite()` function accepts a file resource and a string, and then writes the string to the file. The `fputs()` function works in exactly the same way:

```
fwrite($fp, "hello world");
fputs($fp, "hello world");
```

Writing to files is as straightforward as that. Listing 13.12 uses `fwrite()` to print to a file. It then appends an additional string to the same file using `fputs()`.

LISTING 13.12   Writing and Appending to a File

```
 1: <?php
 2: $filename = "test.txt";
 3: echo "<p>Writing to ".$filename." ... </p>";
 4: $fp = fopen($filename, "w") or die("Couldn't open $filename");
 5: fwrite($fp, "Hello world\n");
 6: fclose($fp);
 7: echo "<p>Appending to ".$filename." ...</p>";
 8: $fp = fopen($filename, "a") or die("Couldn't open $filename");
 9: fputs($fp, "And another thing\n");
10: fclose($fp);
11: ?>
```

The screen output of this script, when run from your web browser, is as follows:

```
Writing to test.txt ...
Appending to test.txt ...
```

If you open the `test.txt` file or use `readlines.php` to read its contents, you find the file now contains the following:

```
Hello world
And another thing
```

Writing File Contents with `file_put_contents()`

Much like the `file_get_contents()` function discussed previously, the `file_put_contents()` function is a more streamlined approach to file operations. Specifically, `file_put_contents()` directly mimics the process of calling `fopen()`, `fwrite()`, and `fclose()` in succession, to write data to a file.

The following shows allowable parameters when calling `file_put_contents()`:

```
file_put_contents ($filename, $data [, $flags [, $context]]);
```

These additional options are described as such:

- ▶ **data**—a string or array that will contain the written data.

- ▶ **flags**—one or more of FILE_USE_INCLUDE_PATH (whether or not to look for the target file in the include_path), FILE_APPEND (whether or not to append data to a file if the file already exists), and LOCK_EX (whether or not to acquire an exclusive lock on writing to the target file), which can be combined with the | operator.

- ▶ **context**— a context resource created by stream_context_create(); use NULL if not needed.

If you were to rewrite Listing 13.12 using file_put_contents(), it would look like Listing 13.13:

LISTING 13.13   Writing and Appending to a File

```
1: <?php
2: $filename = "test.txt";
3: echo "<p>Writing to ".$filename." ... </p>";
4: file_put_contents ($filename, "Hello world\n");
5: echo "<p>Appending to ".$filename." ...</p>";
6: file_put_contents ($filename, "And another thing\n", FILE_APPEND);
7: ?>
```

Locking Files with flock()

The techniques you just learned for reading and amending files work fine if only a single user is accessing your script. In the real world, however, you would expect many users to access your website, and the scripts within it, at more or less the same time. Imagine what would happen if two users were to execute a script that writes to one file at the same moment: The file would quickly become corrupt.

PHP provides the flock() function to forestall this eventuality. The flock() function locks a file to warn other processes against writing to or reading from that file while the current process is working with it. The flock() function requires a valid file resource from an open file and an integer representing the kind of lock you want to set. PHP provides predefined constants for each of the integers you're likely to need. Table 13.1 lists three kinds of locks you can apply to a file.

TABLE 13.1　Integer Arguments to the `flock()` Function

Constant	Integer	Lock Type	Description
LOCK_SH	1	Shared	Allows other processes to read the file but prevents writing (used when reading a file)
LOCK_EX	2	Exclusive	Prevents other processes from either reading from or writing to a file (used when writing to a file)
LOCK_UN	3	Release	Releases a shared or exclusive lock

You should call `flock()` directly after calling `fopen()`, and then call it again to release the lock before closing the file. If the lock is not released, you cannot to read from or write to the file. Here is an example of this sequence of events:

```
$fp = fopen("test.txt", "a") or die("Couldn't open file.");
flock($fp, LOCK_EX); // create exclusive lock
// write to the file
flock($fp, LOCK_UN); // release the lock
fclose($fp);
```

TIP ———

> For more information on file locking, see the PHP Manual entry for the `flock()` function at http://www.php.net/flock.

Working with Directories

Now that you can test, read, and write to files, let's turn our attention to directories. PHP provides many functions for working with directories. Let's look at how to create, remove, and read from them.

Creating Directories with `mkdir()`

The `mkdir()` function enables you to create a directory. The `mkdir()` function requires a string that represents the path to the directory you want to create and an octal number integer that represents the mode you want to set for the directory. Remember, you specify an octal (base 8) number using a leading 0; for example, 0777 or 0400.

The mode argument has an effect only on UNIX systems. The mode should consist of three numbers between 0 and 7, representing permissions for the directory owner, group, and everyone, respectively. The `mkdir()` function returns true if it successfully creates a directory or `false` if it doesn't. If `mkdir()` fails, it is usually because the containing directory has permissions that preclude processes with the script's user ID from writing.

If you're not comfortable setting UNIX directory permissions, you should find that one of the following examples fits your needs. Unless you really need your directory to be world-writable, you should probably use 0755, which allows the world to read your directory but not to write to it:

```
mkdir("testdir", 0777); // global read/write/execute permissions
mkdir("testdir", 0755); // world/group: read/execute; owner: read/write/execute
```

Removing a Directory with `rmdir()`

The `rmdir()` function enables you to remove a directory from the filesystem if the process running your script has the right to do so, and if the directory is empty. The `rmdir()` function requires only a string representing the path to the directory you want to delete.

```
rmdir("testdir");
```

Opening a Directory for Reading with `opendir()`

Before you can read the contents of a directory, you must first obtain a directory resource. You can do so with the `opendir()` function. The `opendir()` function requires a string that represents the path to the directory you want to open. The `opendir()` function returns a directory handle unless the directory isn't present or readable; in that case, it returns `false`:

```
$dh = opendir("testdir");
```

In this case, $dh is the directory handle of the open directory.

Reading the Contents of a Directory with `readdir()`

Just as you use the `fgets()` function to read a line from a file, you can use `readdir()` to read a file or directory name from a directory. The `readdir()` function requires a directory handle and returns a string containing the item name. If the end of the directory is reached, `readdir()` returns `false`. Note that `readdir()` returns only the names of its items, rather than full paths. Listing 13.14 shows the contents of a directory.

LISTING 13.14 Listing the Contents of a Directory with `readdir()`

```
 1: <?php
 2: $dirname = ".";
 3 : $dh = opendir($dirname) or die("Couldn't open directory");
 4:
 5: while (!(($file = readdir($dh)) === false ) ) {
 6:     if (is_dir("$dirname/$file")) {
 7:             echo "(D) ";
 8:     }
 9:     echo $file."<br/>";
10: }
11: closedir($dh);
12: ?>
```

If this code were saved to the document root of your web server as `readdir.php` and run through your web browser, the output would look something like Figure 13.7.

FIGURE 13.7
Output of
readdir.php.

Listing 13.14 opens the directory for reading with the `opendir()` function on line 3 and uses a `while` statement to loop through each of its elements, beginning on line 5. It calls `readdir()` as part of the `while` statement's test expression and assigns the result to the `$file` variable.

Within the body of the `while` statement, the `$dirname` variable is used in conjunction with the `$file` variable to create a full file path, which is then tested on line 6. If the path represents a directory, the code prints D to the browser on line 7. Finally, the filename (or directory name) is printed on line 9.

Listing 13.14 uses a cautious construction in the test of the while statement. Most PHP programmers (myself included) would use something like the following:

```
while ($file = readdir($dh)) {
    echo $file."<br/>";
}
```

In this case, the value returned by readdir() is tested and, because any string other than "0" resolves to true, there should be no problem. Imagine, however, a directory that contains four files: 0, 1, 2, and 3. On my system, the output from the preceding code is as follows:

```
.
..
```

When the loop reaches the file named 0, the string returned by readdir() resolves to false, which causes the loop to end. The approach in Listing 13.14 uses === to check that the return value returned by readdir() is not *exactly* equivalent to false. The result 0 only *resolves* to false in the test, so the problem is circumvented.

NOTE

If you find the ordering of items in a directory listing to be arbitrary, it's because the filesystem determines the order. If you want the items ordered in a specific fashion, you must read the contents into an array, which can then be sorted to your liking and subsequently displayed.

Opening Pipes to and from Processes Using popen()

Earlier in this chapter, you learned how to open a file for reading and writing using the fopen() function. Now, you see that you can open a pipe to a process using the popen() function.

The popen() function is used like this:

```
$file_pointer = popen("some command", mode)
```

The *mode* is either r (read) or w (write).

Listing 13.15 is designed to produce an error—it attempts to open a nonexistent file for reading.

LISTING 13.15 Using popen() to Read a File

```
1: <?php
2: $file_handle = popen("/path/to/fakefile 2>&1", "r");
3: $read = fread($file_handle, 2096);
```

LISTING 13.15   Continued

```
4: echo $read;
5: pclose($file_handle);
6: ?>
```

Listing 13.15 first calls the popen() function in line 2, attempting to open a file for reading. In line 3, any error message stored in the $file_handle pointer is read and printed to the screen in line 4. Finally, line 5 closes the file pointer opened in line 2.

If you save this code as test_popen.php, place it in your document root, and access it with your web browser, you will see an error message such as this one:

```
The system cannot find the path specified.
```

Listing 13.16 also uses popen() to read the output of a process; in this case, the output of the UNIX who command.

LISTING 13.16   Using popen() to Read the Output of the UNIX who Command (UNIX Only)

```
1:  <?php
2:  $handle = popen("who", "r");
3:  while (!feof($handle)) {
4:     $line = fgets($handle,1024);
5:     if (strlen($line) >= 1) {
6:         echo $line."<br/>";
7:     }
8:  }
9:  pclose($handle);
10: ?>
```

In line 2, a file pointer is returned when popen() is used for reading. Line 3 begins a while loop that reads each line of output from the process and eventually prints the line—if it contains information—in line 6. The connection is closed in line 9.

If you save this code as popen_who.php, place it in your document root, and access it with your web browser, you will see something like the following (with your actual information, not mine, of course):

```
julie pts/0 Mar 14 06:19 (adsl-63-206-120-158.dsl.snfc21.pacbell.net)
```

Listing 13.17 shows how to use popen() in write mode to pass data to an external application. The external application in this case is called column. The goal of the script is to take the elements of a multidimensional array and output them in table format, in an ASCII file.

LISTING 13.17 Using popen() to Pass Data to the UNIX column Command (UNIX Only)

```
1:  <?php
2:  $products = array(
3:              array("HAL 2000", 2, "red"),
4:              array("Tricorder", 3, "blue"),
5:              array("ORAC AI", 1, "pink"),
6:              array("Sonic Screwdriver", 1, "orange")
7:              );
8:
9:  $handle = popen("column -tc 3 -s / > /somepath/purchases.txt", "w");
10: foreach ($products as $p) {
11:     fputs($handle, join('/',$p)."\n");
12: }
13: pclose($handle);
14: echo "done";
15: ?>
```

Lines 2–7 define a multidimensional array called $products and in it place four entries representing products with names, quantities, and colors. In line 9, popen() is used in write format to send a command to the column application. This command sends parameters to the column application telling it to format the input as a three-column table, using / as a field delimiter. The output is sent to a file named purchases.txt. (Be sure to change the pathname to one that exists on your system.)

Lines 10–12 use foreach to loop through the $products array and send each element to the open file pointer. The join() function is then used to convert the arrays to a string, with the specified delimiter appended to it. The code closes the open file pointer in line 13, and in line 14 prints a status message to the screen.

If you save this code as popen_column.php, place it in your document root, and access it with your web browser, it should create a file in the specified location. Looking at the file created on my machine, I see the following text:

```
HAL 2000          2  red
Tricorder         3  blue
ORAC AI           1  pink
Sonic Screwdriver 1  orange
```

You may or may not have the column program on your system, but this section illustrated the logic and syntax for opening a pipe to an application. Feel free to try out this logic with other programs available to you.

Running Commands with exec()

The exec() function is one of several functions you can use to pass commands to the shell. The exec() function requires a string representing the path to the command you want to run, and optionally accepts an array variable that will contain the output of the command and a scalar variable that will contain the return value (1 or 0). For example:

```
exec("/path/to/somecommand", $output_array, $return_val);
```

Listing 13.18 uses the exec() function to produce a directory listing with the shell-based ls command.

LISTING 13.18   Using exec() and ls to Produce a Directory Listing (UNIX Only)

```
1: <?php
2: exec("ls -al .", $output_array, $return_val);
3: echo "Returned ".$return_val."<br/><pre>";
4: foreach ($output_array as $o) {
5:    echo $o."\n";
6: }
7: echo "</pre>";
8: ?>
```

Line 2 issues the ls command using the exec() function. The output of the command is placed into the $output_array array and the return value in the $return_val variable. Line 3 simply prints the return value, whereas the foreach loop in lines 4–6 prints out each element in $output_array.

NOTE

> The string in line 3 includes an opening <pre> tag, and line 7 provides a closing tag. This simply ensures that your directory listing will be readable, using HTML preformatted text.

If you save this code as exec_ls.php, place it in your document root, and access it with your web browser, you will see something like Figure 13.8 (with your actual information, not mine, of course).

FIGURE 13.8
Output of
`exec_ls.php`.

As wonderful as PHP is, you might sometime want to integrate some sort of functionality within your PHP-based application but someone else has already written code in Perl that does the same thing. In cases like this, there's no need to reinvent the wheel; you can simply use `exec()` to access the existing script and utilize its functionality. However, remember that calling an external process always adds some amount of additional overhead to your script, in terms of both time and memory usage.

Running Commands with `system()` or `passthru()`

The `system()` function is similar to the `exec()` function in that it launches an external application, and it utilizes a scalar variable for storing a return value:

```
system("/path/to/somecommand", $return_val);
```

The `system()` function differs from `exec()` in that it outputs information directly to the browser, without programmatic intervention. The following snippet of code uses `system()` to print a man page for the man command, formatted with the `<pre></pre>` tag pair:

```
<?php
echo "<pre>";
system("man man | col -b", $return_val);
echo "</pre>";
?>
```

Similarly, the passthru() function follows the syntax of the system() function, but it behaves differently. When you are using passthru(), any output from the shell command is not buffered on its way back to you; this is suitable for running commands that produce binary data rather than simple text data. An example of this is to use shell tools to locate an image and send it back to the browser, as shown in Listing 13.19.

LISTING 13.19   Using passthru() to Output Binary Data

```
1: <?php
2: if ((isset($_GET['imagename'])) && (file_exists($_GET['imagename']))) {
3:    header("Content-type: image/gif");
4:    passthru("giftopnm ".$_GET['imagename']." |
5:        pnmscale -xscale .5 -yscale .5 | ppmtogif");
6: } else {
7:    echo "The image ".$_GET['imagename']." could not be found";
8: }
9: ?>
```

NOTE

The shell utilities used in this script—giftopnm, pnmscale, and ppmtogif—might or might not be installed on your system. If they are not, you can probably install them from your OS distribution CD, but don't worry about it just for this example. The point is just to use this listing to understand the concept of using the passthru() function.

If this file is named getbinary.php, it is called from HTML like this:

```
<img src="getbinary.php?imagename=<?php echo urlencode("test.gif") ?>">
```

In line 2 of Listing 13.19, the user input is tested to ensure that the file in question (test.gif, according to the HTML snippet) exists. Because the script outputs GIF data to the browser, the appropriate header is set on line 3.

On lines 4 and 5, the passthru() function consecutively executes three different commands (giftopnm, pnmscale, and ppmtogif), thus scaling the image to 50% of its original height and width. The output of the passthru() function—that is, the new image data—is sent to the browser.

NOTE

In this and other system-related examples, you could use escapeshellcmd() or escapeshellarg() function to escape elements in the user input. Doing so ensures that the user cannot trick the system into executing arbitrary commands such as deleting important system files or resetting passwords. These functions go around the first instance of the user input, such as the following:

```
$new_input = escapeshellcmd($_GET['someinput']);
```

NOTE

You then reference $new_input throughout the remainder of your script, instead of $_GET['someinput']. Using these two commands, plus ensuring that your script is written so as to only perform tasks *you* want it to do, and not commands from your users, is a way to keep your system secure.

Summary

In this chapter, you learned how to use the `include` family of statements (`include_once`, `require`, and `require_once` thrown in for good measure) to incorporate files into your documents and to execute any PHP code contained in include files. You learned how to use some of PHP's file-testing functions and explored functions for reading files by the line, by the character, and in arbitrary chunks. You learned how to write to files, by either replacing or appending to existing content, and you learned how to create, remove, and read directories.

You were also introduced to various methods of communicating with your system and its external applications. Although PHP is a fast and robust language, you might find it more cost- and time-effective to simply utilize preexisting scripts in other languages such as C or Perl. You can access these external applications using the `popen()`, `exec()`, `system()`, and `passthru()` functions.

You learned how to pipe data to a command using `popen()`, which is useful for applications that accept data from standard input and when you want to parse data as it is sent to you by an application. You also learned to use `exec()` and `system()` to pass commands to the shell and acquire user input. You also learned to use the `passthru()` function to accept binary data that is the result of a shell command.

Now that you can work with the filesystem a little more, you can save and access substantial amounts of data. If you need to look up data from large files, however, such scripts begin to slow down considerably. When that occurs, you should look into a database system, which will be coming your way shortly.

Q&A

Q. *Does the `include` statement slow down my scripts?*

A. Because an included file must be opened and parsed by the engine, it adds some overhead. However, the benefits of reusable code libraries often outweigh the relatively low performance overhead.

Q. *Should I always end script execution if a file cannot be opened for writing or reading?*

A. You should always allow for this possibility. If your script absolutely depends on the file you want to work with, you might want to use the die() function, writing an informative error message to the browser. In less-critical situations, you still need to allow for the failure, perhaps by adding it to a log file.

Q. *Where can I get more information about security on the web?*

A. One authoritative introduction to web security is "The World Wide Web Security FAQ" document written by Lincoln Stein, which you can find at http://www.w3.org/Security/Faq/.

Workshop

The workshop is designed to help you review what you've learned and begin putting your knowledge into practice.

Quiz

1. What functions do you use to add library code to the currently running script?

2. What function do you use to find out whether a file is present on your file-system?

3. How do you determine the size of a file?

4. What function do you use to open a file for reading or writing?

5. What function do you use to read a line of data from a file?

6. How can you tell when you've reached the end of a file?

7. What function do you use to write a line of data to a file?

8. How do you open a directory for reading?

9. What function do you use to read the name of a directory item after you've opened a directory for reading?

10. Which function do you use to open a pipe to a process?

11. How can you read data from a process after you have opened a connection? What about writing data?

12. How can you escape user input to make it a little safer before passing it to a shell command?

Answers

1. You can use the `require` or `include` statement to incorporate PHP files into the current document. You could also use `include_once` or `require_once`.

2. You can test for the existence of a file with the `file_exists()` function.

3. The `filesize()` function returns a file's size in bytes.

4. The `fopen()` function opens a file. It accepts the path to a file and a character representing the mode. It returns a file resource.

5. The `fgets()` function reads data up to the buffer size you pass it, the end of the line, or the end of the document, whichever comes first.

6. The `feof()` function returns `true` when the file resource it has passed reaches the end of the file.

7. You can write data to a file with the `fputs()` function.

8. The `opendir()` function enables you to open a directory for reading.

9. The `readdir()` function returns the name of a directory item from an opened directory.

10. The `popen()` function is used to open a pipe to a process.

11. You can read and write to and from a process just as you can with an open file, namely with `feof()` and `fgets()` for reading and `fputs()` for writing.

12. If user input is part of your shell command, you can use the `escapeshellcmd()` or `escapeshellarg()` function to properly escape it.

Activities

1. Create a form that accepts a user's first and second name. Create a script that saves this data to a file.

2. Create a script that reads the data file you created in the first activity. In addition to writing its contents to the browser (adding a `<br/>` tag to each line), print a summary that includes the number of lines in the file and the file's size.

CHAPTER 14

Working with Images

In this chapter, you learn the following:

▶ How to modify PHP to increase image-related functionality
▶ How to create a new image
▶ How to modify existing images

A standard installation of PHP has many built-in functions for dynamically creating and manipulating images. Popular uses include the creation of charts and graphs and the modifications of existing images to display watermarks. With a few adjustments, you can expand the functionality even more.

This chapter covers the basics of creating and manipulating images using PHP functions.

Understanding the Image-Creation Process

Creating an image with PHP is not like creating an image with a drawing program (for example, Sumo Paint, Corel DRAW, or Windows Draw): There's no pointing and clicking or dragging buckets of color into a predefined space to fill your image. Similarly, there's no Save As functionality, in which your drawing program automatically creates a GIF, JPEG, PNG, and so on, just because you ask it to do so.

Instead, *you* have to become the drawing application. As the programmer, you must tell the PHP engine what to do at each step along the way. You are responsible for using the individual PHP functions to define colors, draw and fill shapes, size and resize the image, and save the image as a specific file type. It's not as difficult as it might seem, however, if you understand each step along the way and complete the tasks in order.

<u>NOTE</u>

> The examples in this chapter are not the most exciting examples ever, but only so much can be printed in the pages of a book (especially when that book is printed in black and white). Rest assured that these examples cover the fundamental knowledge required to work with the image-related functions in PHP.

A Word About Color

When defining colors in your image-related scripts, you use the RGB color system. Using decimal values from 0 to 255 for each of the red, green, and blue (R, G, and B) entries, you can define a specific color. A value of 0 indicates no amount of that specific color, and a value of 255 indicates the highest amount of that color.

For example, the RGB value for pure red is (255,0,0) or the entire allocation of red values, no green, and no blue. Similarly, pure green has a value of (0,255,0), and pure blue has a value of (0,0,255). White has an RGB value of (255,255,255), and black has an RGB value of (0,0,0). A nice shade of purple has an RGB value of (153,51,153), and a light gray has an RGB value of (204,204,204). For reference, you can see a list of colors and their RGB values at http://en.wikipedia.org/wiki/Web_colors.

Necessary Modifications to PHP

Current versions of the PHP distribution include a bundled version of Thomas Boutell's GD graphics library. The inclusion of this library eliminates the need to download and install several third-party libraries, but this library needs to be activated at installation time.

To enable the use of the GD library at installation time, Linux/UNIX users must add the following to the `configure` parameters when preparing to build PHP:

`--with-gd`

After running the PHP `configure` program again, you must go through the `make` and `make install` process as you did in Chapter 4, "Installing and Configuring PHP." Windows users who want to enable GD simply have to activate `php_gd2.dll` as an extension in the `php.ini` file, as you learned in Chapter 4.

When using the GD library, you are limited to working with GIF files. Working with GIF files might suit your needs perfectly, but if you want to create JPEG or PNG files on Linux/UNIX, you must download and install the few libraries listed here and make some modifications to your PHP installation. (These libraries are included and enabled in a Windows installation.)

▶ JPEG libraries, from http://www.ijg.org/.

▶ PNG libraries, from http://www.libpng.org/pub/png/libpng.html.

▶ If you are working with PNG files, you should also install the zlib library, from http://www.zlib.net/.

Follow the instructions at these sites to install the libraries. After installation, Linux/UNIX users must again reconfigure and rebuild PHP by first adding the following to the PHP configure parameters (assuming that you want to use all three; if not, just add the applicable ones):

```
--with-jpeg-dir=[path to jpeg directory]
--with-png-dir=[path to PNG directory]
--with-zlib=[path to zlib directory]
```

After running the PHP configure program again, you need to go through the make and make install process as you did in Chapter 4. Your libraries should then be activated and ready for use.

Drawing a New Image

The basic PHP function used to create a new image is called ImageCreate(), but creating an image is not as simple as just calling the function. Creating an image is a stepwise process and includes the use of several different PHP functions.

Creating an image begins with the ImageCreate() function, but all this function does is set aside a canvas area for your new image. The following line creates a drawing area that is 300 pixels wide by 300 pixels high:

```
$myImage = ImageCreate(300,300);
```

With a canvas now defined, you should next define a few colors for use in that new image. The following examples define five such colors (black, white, red, green, and blue, respectively), using the ImageColorAllocate() function and RGB values:

```
$black = ImageColorAllocate($myImage, 0, 0, 0);
$white = ImageColorAllocate($myImage, 255, 255, 255);
$red   = ImageColorAllocate($myImage, 255, 0, 0);
$green = ImageColorAllocate($myImage, 0, 255, 0);
$blue  = ImageColorAllocate($myImage, 0, 0, 255);
```

> **NOTE**
>
> In your script, the first color you allocate is used as the background color of the image. In this case, the background color will be black. You could also have named the variable $background_color or some other contextually meaningful name.

Now that you know the basics of setting up your drawing canvas and allocated colors, you can move on to learning to draw shapes and actually output the image to a web browser.

Drawing Shapes and Lines

Several PHP functions can assist you in drawing shapes and lines on your canvas:

▶ `ImageEllipse()` is used to draw an ellipse.

▶ `ImageArc()` is used to draw a partial ellipse.

▶ `ImagePolygon()` is used to draw a polygon.

▶ `ImageRectangle()` is used to draw a rectangle.

▶ `ImageLine()` is used to draw a line.

Using these functions requires thinking ahead because you must set up the points where you want to start and stop the drawing that occurs. Each of these functions uses x-axis and y-axis coordinates as indicators of where to start drawing on the canvas. You must also define how far along the x-axis and y-axis you want the drawing to occur.

For example, the following line draws a rectangle on the canvas beginning at point (15,15) and continuing on for 80 pixels horizontally and 140 pixels vertically, so that the lines end at point (95,155). In addition, the lines will be drawn with the color red, which has already been defined in the variable $red.

```
ImageRectangle($myImage, 15, 15, 95, 155, $red);
```

If you want to draw another rectangle of the same size but with white lines, beginning at the point where the previous rectangle stopped, you would use this code:

```
ImageRectangle($myImage, 95, 155, 175, 295, $white);
```

Finally, to add another red rectangle aligned with the first, but beginning at the rightmost point of the white rectangle, use the following:

```
ImageRectangle($myImage, 175, 15, 255, 155, $red);
```

Listing 14.1 shows the image-creation script so far, with a few more lines added to output the image to the web browser.

LISTING 14.1   Creating a New Image

```
1:   <?php
2:   //create the canvas
```

```
3:  $myImage = ImageCreate(300,300);
4:
5:  //set up some colors for use on the canvas
6:  $black = ImageColorAllocate($myImage, 0, 0, 0);
7:  $white = ImageColorAllocate($myImage, 255, 255, 255);
8:  $red   = ImageColorAllocate($myImage, 255, 0, 0);
9:  $green = ImageColorAllocate($myImage, 0, 255, 0);
10: $blue = ImageColorAllocate($myImage, 0, 0, 255);
11:
12: //draw some rectangles
13: ImageRectangle($myImage, 15, 15, 95, 155, $red);
14: ImageRectangle($myImage, 95, 155, 175, 295, $white);
15: ImageRectangle($myImage, 175, 15, 255, 155, $red);
16:
17: //output the image to the browser
18: header ("Content-type: image/png");
19: ImagePng($myImage);
20:
21: //clean up after yourself
22: ImageDestroy($myImage);
23: ?>
```

Lines 18–19 output the stream of image data to the web browser by first sending the appropriate header() function, using the MIME type of the image being created. Then you use the ImageGif(), ImageJpeg(), or ImagePng() function as appropriate to output the data stream; this example outputs a PNG file. In line 22, you use the ImageDestroy() function to clear up the memory used by the ImageCreate() function at the beginning of the script.

Save this listing as imagecreate.php and place it in the document root of your web server. When accessed, it should look something like Figure 14.1, only in color.

FIGURE 14.1
A canvas with three drawn rectangles.

Using a Color Fill

The output of Listing 14.1 produced only outlines of rectangles. PHP has image functions designed to fill areas as well:

▶ `ImageFilledEllipse()` is used to fill an ellipse.

▶ `ImageFilledArc()` is used to fill a partial ellipse.

▶ `ImageFilledPolygon()` is used to fill a polygon.

▶ `ImageFilledRectangle()` is used to fill a rectangle.

You use these functions just like their nonfill counterparts. In Listing 14.2, the nonfill functions are replaced with functions designed to fill an area. In other words, only lines 13–15 have changed.

LISTING 14.2   Creating a New Image with Color Fills

```
1:  <?php
2:  //create the canvas
3:  $myImage = ImageCreate(300,300);
4:
5:  //set up some colors for use on the canvas
6:  $black = ImageColorAllocate($myImage, 0, 0, 0);
7:  $white = ImageColorAllocate($myImage, 255, 255, 255);
8:  $red   = ImageColorAllocate($myImage, 255, 0, 0);
9:  $green = ImageColorAllocate($myImage, 0, 255, 0);
10: $blue = ImageColorAllocate($myImage, 0, 0, 255);
11:
12: //draw some rectangles
13: ImageFilledRectangle($myImage, 15, 15, 95, 155, $red);
14: ImageFilledRectangle($myImage, 95, 155, 175, 295, $white);
15: ImageFilledRectangle($myImage, 175, 15, 255, 155, $red);
16:
17: //output the image to the browser
18: header ("Content-type: image/png");
19: ImagePng($myImage);
20:
21: //clean up after yourself
22: ImageDestroy($myImage);
23: ?>
```

Save this listing as `imagecreatefill.php` and place it in the document root of your web server. When accessed, it should look something like Figure 14.2, but again, in color.

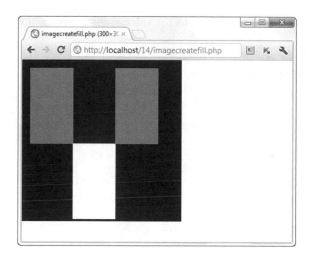

FIGURE 14.2
A canvas with
three drawn
and filled
rectangles.

Getting Fancy with Pie Charts

The previous examples were a little boring, but they introduced you to the basic process of creating images: defining the canvas, defining the colors, and then drawing and filling. You can use this same sequence of events to expand your scripts to create charts and graphs, using either static or dynamic data for the data points. Listing 14.3 draws a basic pie chart. Lines 1–10 look similar to the previous listings because they just set up the canvas size and colors to be used.

LISTING 14.3   A Basic Pie Chart

```
1:  <?php
2:  //create the canvas
3:  $myImage = ImageCreate(300,300);
4:
5:  //set up some colors for use on the canvas
6:  $white = ImageColorAllocate($myImage, 255, 255, 255);
7:  $red   = ImageColorAllocate($myImage, 255, 0, 0);
8:  $green = ImageColorAllocate($myImage, 0, 255, 0);
9:  $blue = ImageColorAllocate($myImage, 0, 0, 255);
10:
11: //draw a pie
12: ImageFilledArc($myImage, 100, 100, 200, 150, 0, 90, $red, IMG_ARC_PIE);
13: ImageFilledArc($myImage, 100, 100, 200, 150, 90, 180 , $green,
        IMG_ARC_PIE);
14: ImageFilledArc($myImage, 100, 100, 200, 150, 180, 360 , $blue,
        IMG_ARC_PIE);
15:
16: //output the image to the browser
17: header ("Content-type: image/png");
18: ImagePng($myImage);
19:
20: //clean up after yourself
21: ImageDestroy($myImage);
22: ?>
```

Because the first defined color is white, the color of the canvas will be white.

Lines 12–14 use the `ImageFilledArc()` function, which has several attributes:

- The image identifier
- The partial ellipse centered at x
- The partial ellipse centered at y
- The partial ellipse width
- The partial ellipse height
- The partial ellipse start point
- The partial ellipse end point
- Color
- Style

Look at line 14 from Listing 14.3:

```
14:   ImageFilledArc($myImage, 100, 100, 200, 150, 180, 360 , $blue,
          IMG_ARC_PIE);
```

The arc should be filled with the defined color `$blue` and should use the `IMG_ARC_PIE` style. The `IMG_ARC_PIE` style is one of several built-in styles (actually, defined constants) used in the display; this one says to create a rounded edge.

NOTE

> You can learn about all the predefined image-related constants in the PHP Manual, at http://us2.php.net/manual/en/image.constants.php.

Save this listing as `imagecreatepie.php` and place it in the document root of your web server. When accessed, it should look something like Figure 14.3, but in color.

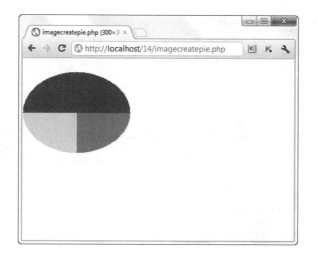

FIGURE 14.3
A simple pie
with slices.

You can extend the code in Listing 14.3 and give your pie a 3D appearance. To do so, define three more colors for the edge. These colors can be either lighter or darker than the base colors, as long as they provide some contrast. The following examples define lighter colors:

```
$lt_red = ImageColorAllocate($myImage, 255, 150, 150);
$lt_green = ImageColorAllocate($myImage, 150, 255, 150);
$lt_blue = ImageColorAllocate($myImage, 150, 150, 255);
```

To create the shading effect, you use a for loop to add a series of small arcs at the points (100,110) to (100,101), using the lighter colors as fill colors:

```
for ($i = 110;$i > 100;$i--) {
    ImageFilledArc ($myImage, 100, $i, 200, 150, 0, 90, $lt_red, IMG_ARC_PIE);
    ImageFilledArc ($myImage, 100, $i, 200, 150, 90, 180, $lt_green,
      IMG_ARC_PIE);
    ImageFilledArc ($myImage, 100, $i, 200, 150, 180, 360, $lt_blue,
      IMG_ARC_PIE);
}
```

Listing 14.4 shows the code used for a 3D pie.

LISTING 14.4 A 3D Pie Chart

```
1:  <?php
2:  //create the canvas
3:  $myImage = ImageCreate(300,300);
4:
5:  //set up some colors for use on the canvas
6:  $white = ImageColorAllocate($myImage, 255, 255, 255);
7:  $red  = ImageColorAllocate($myImage, 255, 0, 0);
```

LISTING 14.4   Continued

```
 8: $green = ImageColorAllocate($myImage, 0, 255, 0);
 9: $blue = ImageColorAllocate($myImage, 0, 0, 255);
10: $lt_red = ImageColorAllocate($myImage, 255, 150, 150);
11: $lt_green = ImageColorAllocate($myImage, 150, 255, 150);
12: $lt_blue = ImageColorAllocate($myImage, 150, 150, 255);
13:
14: //draw the shaded area
15: for ($i = 110;$i > 100;$i--) {
16:     ImageFilledArc ($myImage,100,$i,200,150,0,90,$lt_red,IMG_ARC_PIE);
17:     ImageFilledArc ($myImage,100,$i,200,150,90,180,$lt_green,IMG_ARC_PIE);
18:     ImageFilledArc ($myImage,100,$i,200,150,180,360,$lt_blue,IMG_ARC_PIE);
19: }
20:
21: //draw a pie
22: ImageFilledArc($myImage, 100, 100, 200, 150, 0, 90, $red, IMG_ARC_PIE);
23: ImageFilledArc($myImage, 100, 100, 200, 150, 90, 180 , $green, IMG_ARC_PIE);
24: ImageFilledArc($myImage, 100, 100, 200, 150, 180, 360 , $blue, IMG_ARC_PIE);
25:
26: //output the image to the browser
27: header ("Content-type: image/png");
28: ImagePng($myImage);
29:
30: //clean up after yourself
31: ImageDestroy($myImage);
32: ?>
```

Save this listing as imagecreate3dpie.php and place it in the document root of your web server. When accessed, it should look something like Figure 14.4, but in color.

FIGURE 14.4
A 3D pie, with slices.

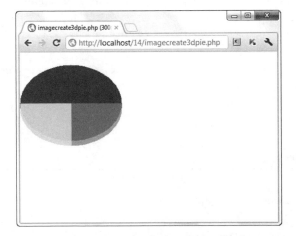

These are just basic examples that show the power of some of the image-drawing and filling functions. In the next section, you learn how to manipulate existing images.

Modifying Existing Images

The process of creating images from other images follows the same essential steps as creating a new image—the difference lies in what acts as the image canvas. Previously, you created a new canvas using the ImageCreate() function. When creating an image from a new image, you use the ImageCreateFrom*() family of functions.

You can create images from existing GIFs, JPEGs, PNGs, and plenty of other image types. The functions used to create images from these formats are called ImageCreateFromGif(), ImageCreateFromJpg(), ImageCreateFromPng(), and so forth. In the next example, you can see how easy it is to create a new image from an existing one. Figure 14.5 shows the base image.

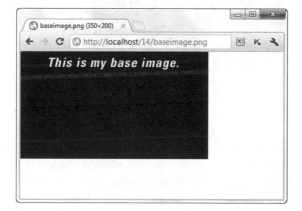

FIGURE 14.5
The base image.

Listing 14.5 shows how to use an existing image as the canvas, which then has filled ellipses drawn on it.

LISTING 14.5   Creating a New Image from an Existing Image

```
1:  <?php
2:  //use existing image as a canvas
3:  $myImage = ImageCreateFromPng("baseimage.png");
4:
5:  //allocate the color white
6:  $white = ImageColorAllocate($myImage, 255, 255, 255);
7:
8:  //draw on the new canvas
9:  ImageFilledEllipse($myImage, 100, 70, 20, 20, $white);
10: ImageFilledEllipse($myImage, 175, 70, 20, 20, $white);
11: ImageFilledEllipse($myImage, 250, 70, 20, 20, $white);
12:
13: //output the image to the browser
14: header ("Content-type: image/png");
15: ImagePng($myImage);
```

LISTING 14.5   Continued

```
16:
17: //clean up after yourself
18: ImageDestroy($myImage);
19: ?>
```

Save this listing as `imagefrombase.php` and place it in the document root of your web server. When accessed, it should look something like Figure 14.6.

FIGURE 14.6
Drawing on an existing image.

The next example takes this process a few steps forward and uses some different image-modification functions. In this case, the existing images are four PNG images, each with a differently colored triangular slice on a gray background. In Listing 14.6, you stack these images on top of each other and blend them together at each step so that the gray background becomes transparent and the image beneath it shows through.

LISTING 14.6   Stacking Images and Making Them Transparent

```
1:  <?php
2:  //select an image to start with
3:  $baseimage = ImageCreateFromPng("img1.png");
4:
5:  //loop through images #2 through the end
6:  for($i=2; $i <5; $i++) {
7:    //allocate the transparent color, and stack
8:    $myImage = ImageCreateFromPng("img".$i.".png");
9:    $gray = ImageColorAllocate($myImage, 185, 185, 185);
10:   ImageColorTransparent($myImage, $gray);
11:   ImageCopyMerge($baseimage,$myImage,0,0,0,0,150,150,100);
12: }
13:
14: //output the image to the browser
15: header ("Content-type: image/png");
16: ImagePng($baseimage);
17:
```

```
18: //clean up after yourself
19: ImageDestroy($baseimage);
20: ?>
```

In line 3, one of the images is selected to be the base image. In this case, it's img1.png. The for loop in lines 8–11 handles the bulk of the work. Knowing that you have four images and that you are already using the first one as the base, that leaves three more images to be stacked and made transparent.

After the new layer is created on line 8, its gray areas are indicated as transparent, and it is merged on top of the base image. As the layers are stacked, the base image contains an increasing number of layers until the total number of four layers is reached. At that point, the image is sent to the browser in lines 15–16.

Save this listing as imagestacker.php and place it in the document root of your web server. When accessed, it should look something like Figure 14.7.

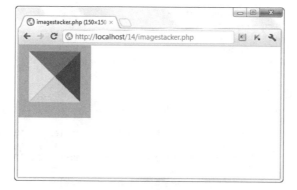

FIGURE 14.7
Stacked transparent images produce a composite.

Image Creation from User Input

In addition to creating images from other images and drawing images on your own, you can create images based on user input. No fundamental difference exists in how the scripts are created except for the fact that you gather values from a form instead of hard-coding them into your script.

Listing 14.7 creates an all-in-one form and script that asks for user input for a variety of attributes ranging from image size to text and background colors, as well as a message string. You are introduced to the imagestring() function, which is used to "write" a string onto an image.

Let's get into the script, where lines 2–38 represent the user input form, and the remaining lines handle the image created according to user specifications.

LISTING 14.7   Creating an Image from User Input

```
 1: <?php
 2: if (!$_POST) {
 3:     //show form
 4: ?>
 5: <!DOCTYPE html>
 6: <html>
 7: <head>
 8: <title>Image Creation Form</title>
 9:
10: <style type="text/css">
11: fieldset{border: 0; padding: 0px 0px 12px 0px;}
12: fieldset label   {margin-left: 24px;}
13: legend, label    {font-weight:bold;}
14: </style>
15:
16: </head>
17: <body>
18: <h1>Create an Image</h1>
19: <form method="POST" action="<?php echo $_SERVER['PHP_SELF']; ?>">
20:
21: <fieldset>
22: <legend>Image Size:</legend><br/>
23: <label for="w">W:</label>
24: <input type="text" id="w" name="w" size="5" maxlength="5" />
25: <label for="h">H:</label>
26: <input type="text" id="h" name="h" size="5" maxlength="5" />
27: </fieldset>
28:
29: <fieldset>
30: <legend>Background Color:</legend><br/>
31: <label for="b_r">R:</label>
32: <input type="text" id="b_r" name="b_r" size="3" maxlength="3" />
33: <label for="b_g">G:</label>
34: <input type="text" id="b_g" name="b_g" size="3" maxlength="3" />
35: <label for="b_b">B:</label>
36: <input type="text" id="b_b" name="b_b" size="3" maxlength="3" />
37: </fieldset>
38:
39: <fieldset>
40: <legend>Text Color:</legend><br/>
41: <label for="t_r">R:</label>
42: <input type="text" id="t_r" name="t_r" size="3" maxlength="3" />
43: <label for="t_g">G:</label>
44: <input type="text" id="t_g" name="t_g" size="3" maxlength="3" />
45: <label for="t_b">B:</label>
46: <input type="text" id="t_b" name="t_b" size="3" maxlength="3" />
47: </fieldset>
48:
49: <p><label for="string">Text String:</label>
50: <input type="text" id="string" name="string" size="35" /></p>
51:
52: <p><label for="font_size">Font Size:</label>
53: <select id="font_size" name="font_size">
54: <option value="1">1</option>
55: <option value="2">2</option>
56: <option value="3">3</option>
57: <option value="4">4</option>
```

```
58: <option value="5">5</option>
59: </select></p>
60:
61: <fieldset>
62: <legend>Text Starting Position:</legend><br/>
63: <label for="x">X:</label>
64: <input type="text" id="x" name="x" size="3" maxlength="3" />
65: <label for="y">Y:</label>
66: <input type="text" id="y" name="y" size="3" maxlength="3" />
67: </fieldset>
68:
69: <button type="submit" name="submit" value="create">Create Image</button>
70: </form>
71: </body>
72: </html>
```

The bulk of this code listing so far is just an HTML form that defines several fields to obtain the image specifications. You can see that lines 1–4 are the only PHP code in this listing so far, and those lines check to see whether the form has been submitted (if the $_POST superglobal exists). After that check has happened, we break out of PHP and just provide the code for the form, which is shown only if the form has not been submitted; you could have put this HTML in an echo statement within PHP, but there's no reason to make the PHP compiler do the work if it doesn't have to.

The form fields in lines 24 and 26 define the width and the height of the image you want to draw. Next, the code sets up form fields to obtain the RGB values for a background color (lines 32, 34, and 36) and a text color (lines 42, 44, and 46).

TIP

> You could create drop-down list boxes containing values 0 through 255 for the red, green, and blue values. This would ensure that the user input was within the required range.

Line 50 contains a form field for the input string. This string will be drawn onto the background of the image in the text color specified. Lines 53–59 represent a drop-down list for the selection of the font size. The function used to draw text on a string uses five sizes, 1 through 5 (the higher the number, the larger the font), for the default fixed-width font installed on the server.

NOTE

> You can specify fonts using the imageloadfont() and imagettftext() functions. Learn more at http://www.php.net/image.

Finally, lines 64 and 66 allow you to define the text starting position. The upper-left corner of the image area would be X position 0, Y position 0; 10 increments downward would be Y position 10, 10 increments to the right would be X position 10, and so forth.

If you stop the script here and close up the if...else statement and PHP block, you will see a form like Figure 14.8 when it's loaded in your web browser.

FIGURE 14.8
User input form for image creation.

In only 23 more lines, you can finish this script and generate images with text strings, so take a look at the remainder of Listing 14.7.

LISTING 14.7   (continued)

```
73: <?php
74: } else {
75:     //create image
76:     //create the canvas
77:     $myImage = ImageCreate($_POST['w'], $_POST['h']);
78:
79:     //set up some colors
80:     $background = ImageColorAllocate ($myImage, $_POST['b_r'],
81:         $_POST['b_g'], $_POST['b_b']);
82:     $text = ImageColorAllocate ($myImage, $_POST['t_r'],
83:         $_POST['t_g'], $_POST['t_b']);
84:
85:     // write the string at the top left
86:     ImageString($myImage, $_POST['font_size'], $_POST['x'],
87:         $_POST['y'], $_POST['string'], $text);
88:
89:     //output the image to the browser
90:     header ("Content-type: image/png");
91:     ImagePNG($myImage);
92:
93:     //clean up after yourself
```

```
94:     ImageDestroy($myImage);
95: }
96: ?>
```

The majority of lines 73–96 you've already seen, only this time it uses extracted elements from the $_POST superglobal to take the place of hard-coded values. Line 77 uses the width and height values from the form to set up the initial image. Lines 80–83 define two colors, $background and $text, using the appropriate RGB values provided by the form.

NOTE

Lines 86–87 represent the only new item in this script: the use of the ImageString() function. The six parameters for this function are the image stream ($myImage), the font size ($_POST['font_size']), the starting X and Y positions ($_POST['x'] and $_POST['y']), the string to be drawn ($_POST['string']), and the color in which to draw it ($text). Lines 90–91 output the image to the browser, and line 94 destroys and cleans up the image creation process.

If you save this file as imagestring.php, place it in the document root of the web server, and fill out the form, the output could look something like Figure 14.9. But quite likely your results will differ because there are many variables to play with.

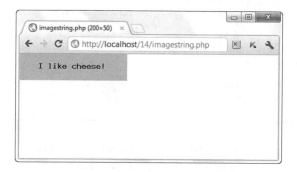

FIGURE 14.9
Sample output from image creation form.

Try it yourself, using various sizes, colors, and text strings.

Using Images Created by Scripts

All the earlier scripts produce image output, but you call them as standalone scripts. Using the results of an image created by a script, within your HTML, is as simple as using the name of the script—not an image—in the src attribute of the img tag. For example:

```
<img src="NameOfScript.php" />
```

In Listing 14.8, you create a simple script to produce an image. An img tag then calls this image and the browser displays it.

To add some new functionality to the mix, this basic script loads and uses a custom font to display a text string as a graphic—much like the user-generated text in the previous section, except the font is fancier. The reasons for this will soon become clear.

First, create the image-generating script. Listing 14.8 shows an example.

LISTING 14.8   Creating an Image with Custom Font and Text

```
1:  <?php
2:  //create the canvas
3:  $myImage = ImageCreate(150,25);
4:
5:  //set up some colors for use on the canvas
6:  $white = ImageColorAllocate($myImage, 255, 255, 255);
7:  $black = ImageColorAllocate($myImage, 0, 0, 0);
8:
9:  //load a font
10: $font = imageloadfont("hootie.gdf");
11:
12: // write the string
13: ImageString($myImage, $font, 0, 0, "CAPTCHA!", $black);
14:
15: //output the image to the browser
16: header ("Content-type: image/png");
17: ImagePng($myImage);
18:
19: //clean up after yourself
20: ImageDestroy($myImage);
21: ?>
```

Line 3 creates a canvas that is 150 pixels wide and 25 pixels high. This size is something commonly seen in a CAPTCHA. In fact, that's part of what you're creating here.

TIP

A *CAPTCHA* is a graphical challenge-response test to determine whether a user is a human. You might have encountered a CAPTCHA when completing a form to leave a comment on a website or to participate in a discussion forum, or when creating a user account. The idea is that only a human can read alphanumeric text in an image. You can read more about CAPTCHAs at http://en.wikipedia.org/wiki/Captcha.

Lines 5–7 set up the colors available to this script: white as the background and black as another color. Line 10 loads a font, using the `imageloadfont()` function. You could also use the `imagettftext()` function if you want to use TrueType fonts. In this example, the `hootie.gdf` font is a freely available font that comes in a single file placed on the filesystem and then loaded by the function calling it.

NOTE

You can find the font used in this example, as well as several other free fonts, just by searching "free GDF font" or "free TrueType font" in Google or your search engine of choice.

Line 13 uses the font loaded in line 10 as part of the `ImageString()` function call. In this example, `$font` is in the second parameter, meaning that the font and font size of the included font package are used in this instance of the function. The starting X and Y positions are hard-coded as 0 in the third and fourth parameters, and the string to be drawn—`"CAPTCHA!"`—is also hard-coded. The color in which to draw this string is `$black`, the value in the final parameter.

Lines 16–17 output the stream of image data to the web browser by first sending the appropriate `header()` function and then using `ImagePng()` to output the data stream; this example outputs a PNG file. Line 20 uses the `ImageDestroy()` function to clear up the memory used by the `ImageCreate()` function at the beginning of the script.

If you stop at this point, send the script to your web server, and simply load it in your browser window, it will display the CAPTCHA! in a custom font. But the purpose of this section is to show how to load this image with the img tag, and to do that you need a little HTML file. Listing 14.9 contains an img tag that does just that.

LISTING 14.9   Using Images Created by Scripts

```
1:  <!DOCTYPE html>
2:  <html>
3:  <head>
4:  <title>Using Images Created by Scripts</title>
5:  </head>
```

LISTING 14.9   Continued

```
 6:   </body>
 7:   <h1>Generated Image Below...</h1>
 8:   <img src="imagecustomfont.php" alt="generated image" />
 9:   </body>
10:   </html>
```

This little HTML file contains one line of interest: line 7. In line 7, you can see that the value of the src attribute of the img tag is the name of the script created in Listing 14.8: imagecustomfont.php. Name the HTML file something like useim-age.html, and send both the HTML and the PHP script to your web server.

Open useimage.html in your web browser and you will see something like Figure 14.10—namely, CAPTCHA! in a custom font, which is actually displayed in a graphic.

FIGURE 14.10
Using images
created by
scripts.

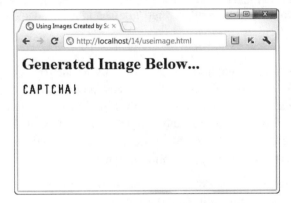

If you were really using this script as part of a CAPTCHA system, you would make at least two additions to it: randomizing the string instead of hard-coding it, and saving the randomized string in a database table so that the input matching process can occur.

Summary

This chapter briefly introduced you to what you can do with images and PHP. Reading the "Image Functions" section of the PHP Manual, at http://www.php.net/image, is highly recommended, not only for a complete list of image-related functions, but also for examples and discussion about their use in your applications.

In this chapter, you learned about installing and using additional libraries for working with images. (The examples used PNGs, but you were given instructions for using GIFs and JPGs, as well.) You learned the basic steps for creating an image canvas and allocating color and for drawing and filling shapes. You learned that your drawing canvas can consist of an existing image and that you can merge layers so that a final image is a composite of the merged layers. In addition, you saw how simple it is to use input from users (in this case, from an HTML form) in your image-creation scripts and how to use scripts as image sources in HTML code.

Q&A

Q. *How do I use dynamic data to create the slices of a pie chart?*

A. When creating any image, the start points and drawing lengths do not need to be statically indicated—they can be variables whose values are determined by a database, user input, or calculations within the script. For example, this code creates a red, filled arc of 90°:

```
ImageFilledArc($myImage,50,50,100,50,0,90,$red,IMG_ARC_PIE);
```

You could set this up so that the red-filled arc at the top of the pie holds the percentage of the total for May Sales in a variable called $may_sales_pct. The line then becomes something like this:

```
ImageFilledArc($myImage,50,50,100,50,0,$may_sales_pct,$red,IMG_ARC_PIE);
```

The number then is filled in from the calculations or database queries in your script. Be sure to add code to verify that all your arcs add up to 360.

Workshop

The workshop is designed to help you review what you've learned and begin putting your knowledge into practice.

Quiz

1. What RGB values would you use for pure black and pure white?

2. How do you create a new, blank canvas that is 300 pixels wide and 200 pixels tall?

3. What function is used to draw a polygon? A filled polygon?

Answers

1. (0,0,0) is pure black, and (255,255,255) is pure white.

2. To create a new, blank canvas that is 300 pixels wide and 200 pixels tall, use the following:

```
$new_image = ImageCreate(300,200);
```

3. `ImagePolygon()` and `ImageFilledPolygon()`

Activities

1. Instead of creating a pie chart, use your drawing skills to create a bar chart with either vertical or horizontal bars, each 30 pixels wide and filled with the same color, but of different lengths. Make sure that there are 10 pixels of space between each bar.

2. Extend the functionality from the first step by adding a form front end to it, and allow users to enter numbers of their choice. Generate your bar chart from those numbers.

## CHAPTER 15

Understanding the Database Design Process

In this chapter, you learn the following:

▶ Some advantages to good database design

▶ Three types of table relationships

▶ How to normalize your database

▶ How to implement a good database design process

In this chapter, you learn the reasoning behind designing a relational database. After this concept-focused chapter, you jump headlong into learning the basic MySQL commands in preparation for integrating MySQL in your own applications.

The Importance of Good Database Design

A good database design is crucial for a high-performance application, just as an aerodynamic body is important to a race car. If a car does not have smooth lines, it produces drag and goes slower. Without optimized relationships, your database will not perform as efficiently as possible. Thinking about relationships and database efficiency—which includes ease of maintenance, minimizing duplications, and avoiding inconsistencies—is part of *normalization*.

> Specifically, *normalization* refers to the process of structuring data to minimize duplication and inconsistencies.

Beyond the issue of performance is the issue of maintenance—your database should be easy to maintain. This includes storing only a limited amount (if any) of repetitive data. If you have a lot of repetitive data and one instance of that data undergoes a change (such as a name change), that change has to be made for all occurrences of the data. To eliminate duplication and enhance your ability to maintain the data, you might create a table of possible values and use a key to refer to the value. That way, if the value changes names, the change occurs only once—in the master table. The reference remains the same throughout other tables.

For example, suppose that you are responsible for maintaining a database of students and the classes in which they are enrolled. If 35 of these students are in the same class, let's call it Advanced Math, this class name would appear 35 times in the table. Now, if the instructor decides to change the name of the class to Mathematics IV, you must change 35 records to reflect the new name of the class. If the database were designed so that class names appeared in one table and just the class ID number was stored with the student record, you would have to change only 1 record—not 35—to update the name change.

The benefits of a well-planned and designed database are numerous, and it stands to reason that the more work you do up front, the less you have to do later. A really bad time for a database redesign is after the public launch of the application using it—although it does happen, and the results are costly.

So, before you even start coding an application, spend a lot of time designing your database. Throughout the rest of this chapter, you learn more about relationships and normalization, two important pieces to the design puzzle.

Types of Table Relationships

Table relationships come in several forms:

- ▶ One-to-one relationships
- ▶ One-to-many relationships
- ▶ Many-to-many relationships

For example, suppose that you have a table called `employees` that contains each person's Social Security number, name, and the department in which he or she works. Suppose that you also have a separate table called `departments`, containing the list of all available departments, made up of a Department ID and a name. In the `employees` table, the Department ID field matches an ID found in the `departments` table. You can see this type of relationship in Figure 15.1. The PK next to the field name indicates the primary key for the table.

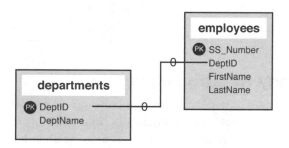

FIGURE 15.1
The `employees` and `departments` tables are related through the DeptID key.

In the following sections, you take a closer look at each of the relationship types.

One-to-One Relationships

In a one-to-one relationship, a key appears only once in a related table. The `employees` and `departments` tables do not have a one-to-one relationship because many employees undoubtedly belong to the same department. A one-to-one relationship exists, for example, if each employee is assigned one computer within a company. Figure 15.2 shows the one-to-one relationship of employees to computers.

FIGURE 15.2
One computer is assigned to each employee.

The `employees` and `computers` tables in your database would look something like Figure 15.3, which represents a one-to-one relationship.

FIGURE 15.3
One-to-one relationship in the data model.

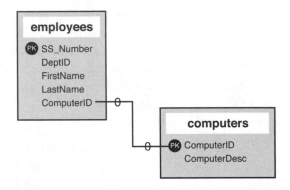

One-to-Many Relationships

In a one-to-many relationship, keys from one table appear multiple times in a related table. The example shown in Figure 15.1, indicating a connection between employees and departments, illustrates a one-to-many relationship. A real-world example is an organizational chart of the department, as shown in Figure 15.4.

FIGURE 15.4
One department contains many employees.

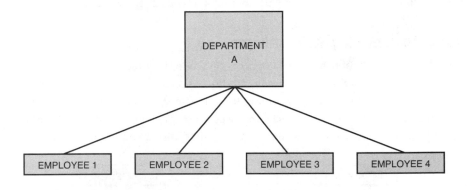

The one-to-many relationship is the most common type of relationship. Another practical example is the use of a state abbreviation in an address database; each state has a unique identifier (CA for California, PA for Pennsylvania, and so on), and each address in the United States has a state associated with it.

If you have eight friends in California and five in Pennsylvania, you use only two distinct abbreviations in your table. One abbreviation (CA) represents a one-to-eight relationship, and the other (PA) represents a one-to-five relationship.

Many-to-Many Relationships

The many-to-many relationship often causes problems in practical examples of normalized databases, so much so that it is common to simply break many-to-many relationships into a series of one-to-many relationships. In a many-to-many relationship, the key value of one table can appear many times in a related table. So far, it sounds like a one-to-many relationship, but here's the curveball: The opposite is also true, meaning that the primary key from that second table can also appear many times in the first table.

Think of such a relationship this way, using the example of students and classes: A student has an ID and a name. A class has an ID and a name. A student usually takes more than one class at a time, and a class always contains more than one student, as you can see in Figure 15.5.

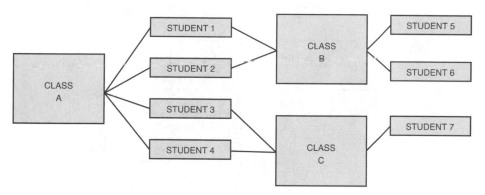

FIGURE 15.5
Students take classes, and classes contain students.

As you can see, this sort of relationship does not present an easy method for relating tables. Your tables could look like Figure 15.6, seemingly unrelated.

FIGURE 15.6
The students table and the classes table, unrelated.

To make the theoretical many-to-many relationship, you create an intermediate table, one that sits between the two tables and essentially maps them together. You might build such a table similar to the one in Figure 15.7.

FIGURE 15.7
The students_classes_map table acts as an intermediary.

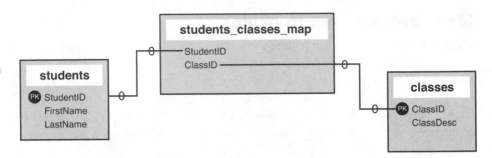

If you take the information in Figure 15.5 and put it into the intermediate table, you can create something like Figure 15.8.

FIGURE 15.8
The students_classes_map table populated with data.

STUDENTID	CLASSID
STUDENT 1	CLASS A
STUDENT 2	CLASS A
STUDENT 3	CLASS A
STUDENT 4	CLASS A
STUDENT 5	CLASS B
STUDENT 6	CLASS B
STUDENT 7	CLASS C
STUDENT 1	CLASS B
STUDENT 2	CLASS B
STUDENT 3	CLASS C
STUDENT 4	CLASS C

As you can see, many students and many classes happily coexist within the students_classes_map table.

With this introduction to the types of relationships, learning about normalization should be a snap.

Understanding Normalization

Normalization is simply a set of rules that will ultimately make your life easier when you are acting as a database administrator. It is the art of organizing your database in such a way that your tables relate where appropriate and are flexible for future growth.

The sets of rules used in normalization are called *normal forms*. If your database design follows the first set of rules, it is considered in the *first normal form*. If the first three sets of rules of normalization are followed, your database is said to be in the *third normal form*.

Throughout this chapter, you learn about each rule in the first, second, and third normal forms—the most foundational of the nine different normalizations—and, I hope, will follow them as you create your own applications. In the chapter, you use a sample set of tables for a students-and-courses database and take it to the third normal form.

Problems with the Flat Table

Before launching into the first normal form, you have to start with something that needs to be fixed. In the case of a database, it's the *flat table*. A flat table is like a spreadsheet—it has many, many columns. There are no relationships between multiple tables; all the data you could possibly want is right there in that flat table. This scenario is inefficient and consumes more physical space on your hard drive than a normalized database.

In your students-and-courses database, assume that you have the following fields in your flat table:

- **StudentName**—The name of the student.
- **CourseID1**—The ID of the first course taken by the student.
- **CourseDescription1**—The description of the first course taken by the student.
- **CourseInstructor1**—The instructor of the first course taken by the student.
- **CourseID2**—The ID of the second course taken by the student.
- **CourseDescription2**—The description of the second course taken by the student.

▶ `CourseInstructor2`—The instructor of the second course taken by the student.

▶ Repeat `CourseID`, `CourseDescription`, and `CourseInstructor` columns many more times to account for all the classes students can take during their academic career.

With what you've learned so far, you should be able to identify the first problem area: `CourseID`, `CourseDescription`, and `CourseInstructor` columns are repeated groups.

Eliminating redundancy is the first step in normalization, so next you take this flat table to first normal form. If your table remained in its flat format, you could have a lot of unclaimed space and a lot of space being used unnecessarily—not an efficient table design.

First Normal Form

The rules for the first normal form are as follows:

▶ Eliminate repeating information.

▶ Create separate tables for related data.

If you think about the flat table design with many repeated sets of fields for the students-and-courses database, you can identify two distinct topics: students and courses. Taking your students-and-courses database to the first normal form means that you create two tables: one for students and one for courses, as shown in Figure 15.9.

FIGURE 15.9
Breaking the
flat table into
two tables.

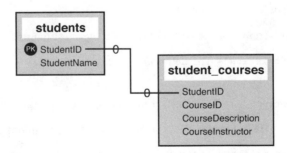

Your two tables now represent a one-to-many relationship of one student to many courses. Students can take as many courses as they want and are not limited to the number of `CourseID`/`CourseDescription`/`CourseInstructor` groupings that existed in the flat table.

The next step is to put the tables into second normal form.

Second Normal Form

The rule for the second normal form is as follows:

▶ No nonkey attributes depend on a portion of the primary key.

In plain English, this means that if fields in your table are not entirely related to a primary key, you have more work to do. In the students-and-courses example, you need to break out the courses into their own table and modify the students_courses table.

CourseID, CourseDescription, and CourseInstructor can become a table called courses with a primary key of CourseID. The students_courses table should then just contain two fields: StudentID and CourseID. You can see this new design in Figure 15.10.

FIGURE 15.10
Taking your tables to second normal form.

This structure should look familiar to you as a many-to-many relationship using an intermediary mapping table. The third normal form is the last form you look at here, and you should find that it is just as simple to understand as the first two.

Third Normal Form

The rule for the third normal form is as follows:

▶ No attributes depend on other nonkey attributes.

This rule simply means that you need to look at your tables and see whether you have more fields that can be broken down further and that are not dependent on a key. Think about removing repeated data and you'll find your answer: instructors. Inevitably, an instructor teaches more than one class. However, CourseInstructor is not a key of any sort. So, if you break out this information and create a separate table purely for the sake of efficiency and maintenance (as shown in Figure 15.11), that is the third normal form.

FIGURE 15.11
Taking your tables to third normal form.

Third normal form is usually adequate for removing redundancy and allowing for flexibility and growth. The next section gives you some pointers for the thought process involved in database design and where it fits in the overall design process of your application.

Following the Design Process

The greatest problem in application design is a lack of forethought. As it applies to database-driven applications, the design process must include a thorough evaluation of your database—what it should hold, how data relates to each other, and most important, whether it is scalable.

The general steps in the design process are as follow:

▶ Define the objective.

▶ Design the data structures (tables, fields).

▶ Discern relationships.

▶ Define and implement business rules.

▶ Create the application.

Creating the application is the last step, not the first. Many developers take an idea for an application, build it, and then go back and try to make a set of database tables fit into it. This approach is completely backward, inefficient, and will cost a lot of time and money.

Before you start any application design process, sit down and talk it out. If you cannot describe your application—including the objectives, audience, and target market—you are not ready to build it, let alone model the database.

After you can describe the actions and nuances of your application to other people and have it make sense to them, you can start thinking about the tables you want to create. Start with big flat tables because after you write them down, your newfound normalization skills will take over. You will be able to find your redundancies and visualize your relationships. As you become more experienced, you will be able to minimize the steps in this process, but there's nothing wrong with stepping through them carefully and explicitly.

The next step is to do the normalization. Go from a flat table to the first normal form and so on up to the third normal form if possible. Use paper, pencils, sticky notes, or whatever helps you to visualize the tables and relationships. There's no shame in data modeling on sticky notes until you are ready to create the tables themselves. Plus, using sticky notes is a lot cheaper than buying software to do it for you; modeling software ranges from one hundred to several thousands of dollars.

After you have a preliminary data model, look at it from the application's point of view. Or look at it from the point of view of the person using the application you are building. This is the point where you define business rules and see whether your data model breaks. An example of a business rule for an online registration application is, "Each user must have one email address, and it must not belong to any other user." If `EmailAddress` is not a unique field in your data model, your model will break based on the business rule.

After your business rules have been applied to your data model, only then can application programming begin. You can rest assured that your data model is solid and you will not be programming yourself into a brick wall. The latter event is all too common.

Summary

Following proper database design is the only way your application will be efficient, flexible, and easy to manage and maintain. An important aspect of database design is to use relationships between tables instead of throwing all your data into one long flat file. Types of relationships include one-to-one, one-to-many, and many-to-many.

Using relationships to properly organize your data is called normalization. There are many levels of normalization, but the primary levels are the first, second, and third normal forms. Each level has a rule or two that you must follow. Following all the rules helps ensure that your database is well organized and flexible.

To take an idea from inception through to fruition, you should follow a design process. This process essentially says, "Think before you act." Discuss rules, requirements, and objectives, and only then create the final version of your normalized tables.

Q&A

Q. *Are there only three normal forms?*

A. No, there are more than three normal forms. Additional forms are the Boyce-Codd normal form, fourth normal form, and fifth normal form/Join-Projection normal form. These forms are not often followed in practical application development because the benefits of doing so are outweighed by the cost in man-hours and database efficiency (but it is certainly fine if you implement them). For more information, please see http://en.wikipedia.org/wiki/Database_normalization#Normal_forms.

Workshop

The workshop is designed to help you review what you have learned and begin putting your knowledge into practice.

Quiz

1. Name three types of data relationships.

2. Because many-to-many relationships are difficult to represent in an efficient database design, what should you do?

3. Name a few ways you can create visualizations of data relationships.

Answers

1. One-to-one, one-to-many, many-to-many.

2. Create a series of one-to-many relationships using intermediary mapping tables.

3. You can use a range of tools, from sticky notes and string (where notes are the tables and string shows the relationships between tables) to software used to draw diagrams, to software programs that interpret your SQL statements and produce visualizations.

Activity

Explain each of the three normal forms to a person who works with spreadsheets and flat tables.

CHAPTER 16

Learning Basic SQL Commands

In this chapter, you learn the following:

▶ The basic MySQL data types

▶ How to use the CREATE TABLE command to create a table

▶ How to use the INSERT command to enter records

▶ How to use the SELECT command to retrieve records

▶ How to use basic functions, the WHERE clause, and the GROUP BY clause in SELECT expressions

▶ How to select from multiple tables, using JOIN or subselects

▶ How to use the UPDATE and REPLACE commands to modify existing records

▶ How to use the DELETE command to remove records

▶ How to use string functions built in to MySQL

▶ How to use date and time functions built in to MySQL

The preceding chapter explained the basics of the database design process, and this chapter provides a primer on the core SQL syntax, which you use to create and manipulate your MySQL database tables. This is a hands-on chapter, and it assumes that you can issue queries directly to MySQL, either through the MySQL command-line interface or through another management interface such as phpMyAdmin, which is included in the XAMPP installation provided through the Quick Start process in Chapter 1, "Installation QuickStart Guide with XAMPP."

Note that although this might not be the most exciting chapter in the book, it does show you many basic and functional examples of elements you'll use throughout the rest of your work.

Learning the MySQL Data Types

Properly defining the fields in a table is important to the overall optimization of your database. You should use only the type and size of field you really need to use; do not define a field as 10 characters wide if you know you're only going to use 2 characters—that's 8 extra characters the database has to account for, even if they are unused. These field types are also referred to as *data types*, as in the "type of data" you will be storing in those fields.

MySQL uses many different data types, broken into three categories: numeric, date and time, and string types. Pay close attention because properly defining the data type is more important than any other part of the table-creation process.

Numeric Data Types

MySQL uses all the standard ANSI SQL numeric data types. So if you're coming to MySQL from a different database system, these definitions will look familiar to you. The following list shows the common numeric data types and their descriptions:

NOTE

> The terms *signed* and *unsigned* are used in the list of numeric data types. If you remember your basic algebra, you'll recall that a signed integer can be a positive or negative integer, whereas an unsigned integer is always a non-negative integer.

- ▶ **INT**—A normal-sized integer that can be signed or unsigned. If signed, the allowable range is from –2147483648 to 2147483647. If unsigned, the allowable range is from 0 to 4294967295. You can specify a width of up to 11 digits.

- ▶ **TINYINT**—A small integer that can be signed or unsigned. If signed, the allowable range is from –128 to 127. If unsigned, the allowable range is from 0 to 255. You can specify a width of up to 4 digits.

- ▶ **SMALLINT**—A small integer that can be signed or unsigned. If signed, the allowable range is from –32768 to 32767. If unsigned, the allowable range is from 0 to 65535. You can specify a width of up to 5 digits.

- ▶ **MEDIUMINT**—A medium-sized integer that can be signed or unsigned. If signed, the allowable range is from –8388608 to 8388607. If unsigned, the allowable range is from 0 to 16777215. You can specify a width of up to 9 digits.

- ▶ **BIGINT**—A large integer that can be signed or unsigned. If signed, the allowable range is from –9223372036854775808 to 9223372036854775807. If unsigned, the allowable range is from 0 to 18446744073709551615. You can specify a width of up to 11 digits.

▶ **FLOAT(M,D)**—A floating-point number that cannot be unsigned. You can define the display length (M) and the number of decimals (D). This is not required and defaults to 10,2, where 2 is the number of decimals and 10 is the total number of digits (including decimals). Decimal precision can go to 24 places for a FLOAT.

▶ **DOUBLE(M,D)**—A double-precision floating-point number that cannot be unsigned. You can define the display length (M) and the number of decimals (D). This is not required and will default to 16,4, where 4 is the number of decimals. Decimal precision can go to 53 places for a DOUBLE. REAL is a synonym for DOUBLE.

▶ **DECIMAL(M,D)**—An unpacked floating-point number that cannot be unsigned. In unpacked decimals, each decimal corresponds to 1 byte. Defining the display length (M) and the number of decimals (D) is required. NUMERIC is a synonym for DECIMAL.

Of all the MySQL numeric data types, you will likely use INT most often. You can run into problems if you define your fields to be smaller than you actually need; for example, if you define an ID field as an unsigned TINYINT, you cannot successfully insert that 256th record if ID is a primary key (and thus required).

Date and Time Types

MySQL has several data types available for storing dates and times, and these data types are flexible in their input. In other words, you can enter dates that are not really days, such as February 30—February has only 28 or 29 days, never 30. Also, you can store dates with missing information. For example, if you know that someone was born sometime in November 1980, you can use 1980-11-00, where 00 would have been for the day, if you knew it.

The flexibility of MySQL's date and time types also means that the responsibility for date checking falls on the application developer (that would be you). MySQL checks only two elements for validity: that the month is between 0 and 12 and that the day is between 0 and 31. MySQL does not automatically verify that the thirtieth day of the second month (February 30) is a valid date. Therefore, any date validation you want to include in your application should happen in your PHP code before you even attempt to add a record with a bogus date into your database table.

The MySQL date and time data types are as follows:

▶ **DATE**—A date in YYYY-MM-DD format, between 1000-01-01 and 9999-12-31. For example, December 30, 1973, is stored as 1973-12-30.

▶ **DATETIME**—A date and time combination in YYYY-MM-DD HH:MM:SS format, between 1000-01-01 00:00:00 and 9999-12-31 23:59:59. For example, 3:30 in the afternoon on December 30, 1973, is stored as 1973-12-30 15:30:00.

▶ **TIMESTAMP**—A timestamp between midnight, January 1, 1970, and sometime in 2037. You can define multiple lengths to the TIMESTAMP field, which directly correlates to what is stored in it. The default length for TIMESTAMP is 14, which stores YYYYMMDDHHMMSS. This looks like the previous DATETIME format, only without the hyphens between numbers; 3:30 in the afternoon on December 30, 1973, is stored as 19731230153000. Other definitions of TIME-STAMP are 12 (YYMMDDHHMMSS), 8 (YYYYMMDD), and 6 (YYMMDD).

▶ **TIME**—Stores the time in HH:MM:SS format.

▶ **YEAR(M)**—Stores a year in two-digit or four-digit format. If the length is specified as 2 (for example, YEAR(2)), YEAR can be 1970 to 2069 (70 to 69). If the length is specified as 4, YEAR can be 1901 to 2155. The default length is 4.

You will likely use DATETIME or DATE more often than any other date- or time-related data type.

String Types

Although numeric and date types are fun, most data you'll store will be in string format. This list describes the common string data types in MySQL:

▶ **CHAR(M)**—A fixed-length string between 1 and 255 characters in length (for example, CHAR(5)), right-padded with spaces to the specified length when stored. Defining a length is not required, but the default is 1.

▶ **VARCHAR(M)**—A variable-length string between 1 and 255 characters in length; for example, VARCHAR(25). You must define a length when creating a VARCHAR field.

▶ **BLOB** or **TEXT**—A field with a maximum length of 65,535 characters. BLOBs are *Binary Large Objects* and are used to store large amounts of binary data, such as images or other types of files. Fields defined as TEXT also hold large amounts of data; the difference between the two is that sorts and comparisons on stored data are case sensitive on BLOBs and are not case sensitive in TEXT fields. You do not specify a length with BLOB or TEXT.

▶ **TINYBLOB** or **TINYTEXT**—A BLOB or TEXT column with a maximum length of 255 characters. You do not specify a length with TINYBLOB or TINYTEXT.

▶ **MEDIUMBLOB** or **MEDIUMTEXT**—A BLOB or TEXT column with a maximum length of 16,777,215 characters. You do not specify a length with MEDIUMBLOB or MEDIUMTEXT.

▶ **LONGBLOB** or **LONGTEXT**—A BLOB or TEXT column with a maximum length of 4,294,967,295 characters. You do not specify a length with LONGBLOB or LONG-TEXT.

▶ **ENUM**—An enumeration, which is a fancy term for *list*. When defining an ENUM, you are creating a list of items from which the value must be selected (or it can be NULL). For example, if you want your field to contain A or B or C, you would define your ENUM as ENUM ('A', 'B', 'C'), and only those values (or NULL) could ever populate that field. ENUMs can have 65,535 different values. ENUMs use an index for storing items.

<table>
<tr><td>The SET type is similar to ENUM in that it is defined as a list. However, the SET type is stored as a full value rather than an index of a value, as with ENUMs.</td><td>NOTE</td></tr>
</table>

You will probably use VARCHAR and TEXT fields more often than other field types, and ENUMs are useful as well.

Learning the Table-Creation Syntax

The table-creation command requires

▶ Name of the table

▶ Names of fields

▶ Definitions for each field

The generic table-creation syntax is

```
CREATE TABLE table_name (column_name column_type);
```

The table name is up to you, of course, but should be a name that reflects the usage of the table. For example, if you have a table that holds the inventory of a grocery store, you would not name the table s. You would probably name it something like grocery_inventory. Similarly, the field names you select should be as concise as possible and relevant to the function they serve and the data they hold. For example, you might call a field holding the name of an item item_name, not n.

The following table-creation example creates a generic `grocery_inventory` table with fields for ID, item name, item description, item price, and quantity. Each of the fields are a different type; the ID and quantity fields hold integers, the item name field holds up to 50 characters, the item description field holds up to 65,535 characters of text, and the item price field contains a float:

```
CREATE TABLE grocery_inventory (
    id INT NOT NULL PRIMARY KEY AUTO_INCREMENT,
    item_name VARCHAR (50) NOT NULL,
    item_desc TEXT,
    item_price FLOAT NOT NULL,
    curr_qty INT NOT NULL
);
```

NOTE

> The `id` field is defined as a *primary key*. You learn more about keys in later chapters, in the context of creating specific tables as parts of sample applications. In addition, by using `auto_increment` as an attribute of the field in the example here, you are telling MySQL to go ahead and add the next available number to the `id` field for you when a record is inserted.

The MySQL server responds with `Query OK` each time a command, regardless of type, is successful. Otherwise, an error message displays, telling you where your query went awry. Depending on the interface you are using, you may or may not see this specific response. However, regardless of the interface, it should provide you with some indication of the status of the query.

Using the INSERT Command

After you have created some tables, you use the SQL command `INSERT` for adding new records to these tables. The basic syntax of `INSERT` is

```
INSERT INTO table_name (column list) VALUES (column values);
```

Within the parenthetical list of values, you must enclose strings within quotation marks. The SQL standard is single quotes, but MySQL enables the usage of either single or double quotes. So, if you are used to working in Oracle, which forces single-quoted strings, there's no need to change your behavior. Remember to escape the type of quotation mark used, if it is within the string itself.

NOTE

> Integers do not require quotation marks around them.

Here is an example of a string where escaping is necessary:

```
O'Connor said "Boo"
```

If you enclose your strings in double quotes, the INSERT statement looks like this:

```
INSERT INTO table_name (column_name) VALUES ("O'Connor said \"Boo\"");
```

If you enclose your strings in single quotes instead, the INSERT statement looks like this:

```
INSERT INTO table_name (column_name) VALUES ('O\'Connor said "Boo"');
```

A Closer Look at INSERT

Besides the table name, the INSERT statement consists of two main parts: the column list and the value list. Only the value list is actually required, but if you omit the column list, you must specifically provide for each column in your value list—in the exact order.

Using the grocery_inventory table as an example, you have five fields: id, item_name, item_desc, item_price, and curr_qty. To insert a complete record, you could use either of these statements:

▶ A statement with all columns named:

```
INSERT INTO grocery_inventory
(id, item_name, item_desc, item_price, curr_qty)
VALUES ('1', 'Apples', 'Beautiful, ripe apples.', '0.25', 1000);
```

▶ A statement that uses all columns but does not explicitly name them:

```
INSERT INTO grocery_inventory VALUES ('2', 'Bunches of Grapes',
'Seedless grapes.', '2.99', 500);
```

Give both of them a try and see what happens. You should get a successful response to both commands.

Now for some more interesting methods of using INSERT. Because id was defined at creation time as an auto-incrementing integer in the grocery_inventory table, you do not have to put it in your value list. However, if there's a value you specifically do *not* want to list (such as id), you then must list the remaining columns in use. For example, the following statement does not list the columns and does not give a value for id:

```
INSERT INTO grocery_inventory VALUES
 ('Bottled Water (6-pack)', '500ml spring water.', 2.29, 250);
```

The preceding statement produces an error, such as this:

```
ERROR 1136: Column count doesn't match value count at row 1
```

Because you did not list any columns in this query, MySQL expects all of them to be in the value list; since you did not, the query results in an error. If your goal was to let MySQL do the work for you by auto-incrementing the id field, you could use either of these statements:

- A statement with all columns named except id:

  ```
  INSERT INTO grocery_inventory (item_name, item_desc, item_price, curr_qty)
  VALUES ('Bottled Water (6-pack)', '500ml spring water.', '2.29', 250);
  ```

- A statement that uses all columns, but does not explicitly name them *and* indicates a NULL entry for id (so one is filled in for you):

  ```
  INSERT INTO grocery_inventory VALUES ('NULL', 'Bottled Water (12-pack)',
  '500ml spring water.', 4.49, 500);
  ```

Go ahead and try both so that your grocery_inventory table has four records in total. It makes no different to MySQL which one you use, but as with everything based on your own preferences, be consistent in your application development. Consistent structures are easier for you to debug later because you know what to expect.

Using the SELECT Command

SELECT is the SQL command used to retrieve records from your tables. This command syntax can be totally simple or very complicated, depending on which fields you want to select, whether you want to select from multiple tables, and what conditions you plan to impose. As you become more comfortable with database programming, you will learn to enhance your SELECT statements, ultimately making your database do as much work as possible and not overworking your programming language.

The most basic SELECT syntax looks like this:

```
SELECT expressions_and_columns FROM table_name
[WHERE some_condition_is_true]
[ORDER BY some_column [ASC ¦ DESC]]
[LIMIT offset, rows]
```

Look at the first line:

```
SELECT expressions_and_columns FROM table_name
```

One handy expression is the * symbol, which stands for *everything*. So, to select everything (all rows, all columns) from the grocery_inventory table, your SQL statement would be

```
SELECT * FROM grocery_inventory;
```

Depending on how much data is in the grocery_inventory table, your results will vary, but the results might look something like this:

```
+----+-----------------------+-----------------------+------------+----------+
| id | item_name             | item_desc             | item_price | curr_qty |
+----+-----------------------+-----------------------+------------+----------+
| 1  | Apples                | Beautiful, ripe apples. | 0.25     | 1000     |
| 2  | Bunches of Grapes     | Seedless grapes.      | 2.99       | 500      |
| 3  | Bottled Water (6-pack)| 500ml spring water.   | 2.29       | 250      |
| 4  | Bottled Water (12-pack)| 500ml spring water.  | 4.49       | 500      |
+----+-----------------------+-----------------------+------------+----------+
4 rows in set (0.00 sec)
```

> **NOTE**
>
> This output comes from the MySQL command line interface; it creates a lovely, formatted table with the names of the columns along the first row as part of the resultset. If you are using a different interface to MySQL, your results will look different. (Focus on observing the expected data and not the interface differences.)

If you want to select specific columns only, replace the * with the names of the columns, separated by commas. The following statement selects just the id, item_name, and curr_qty fields from the grocery_inventory table:

```
SELECT id, item_name, curr_qty FROM grocery_inventory;
```

The results are displayed as:

```
+----+------------------------+----------+
| id | item_name              | curr_qty |
+----+------------------------+----------+
| 1  | Apples                 | 1000     |
| 2  | Bunches of Grapes      | 500      |
| 3  | Bottled Water (6-pack) | 250      |
| 4  | Bottled Water (12-pack)| 500      |
+----+------------------------+----------+
4 rows in set (0.00 sec)
```

Ordering SELECT Results

Results of SELECT queries are ordered as they were inserted into the table and should not be relied on as a meaningful ordering system. If you want to order results a specific way, such as by date, ID, name, and so on, specify your requirements using the ORDER

BY clause. In the following statement, the intention is a resultset ordered alphanumerically by item_name:

```
SELECT id, item_name, curr_qty FROM grocery_inventory
ORDER BY item_name;
```

Success! The results are as follows:

```
+----+------------------------+----------+
| id | item_name              | curr_qty |
+----+------------------------+----------+
| 1  | Apples                 | 1000     |
| 4  | Bottled Water (12-pack)| 500      |
| 3  | Bottled Water (6-pack) | 250      |
| 2  | Bunches of Grapes       | 500      |
+----+------------------------+----------+
4 rows in set (0.03 sec)
```

TIP

When selecting results from a table without specifying a sort order, the results may or may not be ordered by their key value. This occurs because MySQL reuses the space taken up by previously deleted rows. In other words, if you add records with ID values of 1 through 5, delete the record with ID number 4, and then add another record (ID number 6), the records might appear in the table in this order: 1, 2, 3, 6, 5.

The default sorting of ORDER BY results is ascending (ASC); strings sort from A to Z, integers start at 0, and dates sort from oldest to newest. You can also specify a descending sort, using DESC:

```
SELECT id, item_name, curr_qty FROM grocery_inventory
ORDER BY item_name DESC;
```

Here are the results:

```
+----+------------------------+----------+
| id | item_name              | curr_qty |
+----+------------------------+----------+
| 2  | Bunches of Grapes       | 500      |
| 3  | Bottled Water (6-pack) | 250      |
| 4  | Bottled Water (12-pack)| 500      |
| 1  | Apples                 | 1000     |
+----+------------------------+----------+
4 rows in set (0.00 sec)
```

You're not limited to sorting by just one field—you can specify as many fields as you want as long as they are separated by commas. The sorting priority is the order in which you list the fields.

Limiting Your Results

You can use the LIMIT clause to return only a certain number of records from your SELECT query result. Two requirements apply when using the LIMIT clause: the offset and the number of rows. The *offset* is the starting position, and the *number of rows* should be self-explanatory.

Suppose that you have more than two or three records in the grocery_inventory table, and you want to select the ID, name, and quantity of the first two, ordered by curr_qty. In other words, you want to select the two items with the least inventory. The following single-parameter limit starts at the 0 position and goes to the second record:

```
SELECT id, item_name, curr_qty FROM grocery_inventory
ORDER BY curr_qty LIMIT 2;
```

Here are the results:

```
+----+-------------------------+----------+
| id | item_name               | curr_qty |
+----+-------------------------+----------+
| 3  | Bottled Water (6-pack)  | 250      |
| 2  | Bunches of Grapes       | 500      |
+----+-------------------------+----------+
2 rows in set (0.00 sec)
```

The LIMIT clause can prove useful in an actual application. For example, you can use the LIMIT clause within a series of SELECT statements to travel through results in steps (first two items, next two items, next two items after that):

1. `SELECT * FROM grocery_inventory ORDER BY curr_qty LIMIT 0, 2;`

2. `SELECT * FROM grocery_inventory ORDER BY curr_qty LIMIT 2, 2;`

3. `SELECT * FROM grocery_inventory ORDER BY curr_qty LIMIT 4, 2;`

If you specify an offset and number of rows in your query, and no results are found, you won't see an error—just an empty resultset. For example, if the grocery_inventory table contains only six records, a query with a LIMIT offset of 6 produces no results.

In web-based applications, when you see lists of data display with links such as "previous 10" and "next 10," it's a safe bet that a LIMIT clause is at work.

Using WHERE in Your Queries

You have learned numerous ways to retrieve particular columns from your tables but not specific rows. This is when the WHERE clause comes in to play. From the example SELECT syntax, you see that WHERE is used to specify a particular condition:

```
SELECT expressions_and_columns FROM table_name
[WHERE some_condition_is_true]
```

An example is to retrieve all the records for items with a quantity of 500:

```
SELECT * FROM grocery_inventory WHERE curr_qty = 500;
```

Here are the results:

```
+----+----------------------+----------------------+------------+----------+
| id | item_name            | item_desc            | item_price | curr_qty |
+----+----------------------+----------------------+------------+----------+
| 2  | Bunches of Grapes    | Seedless grapes.     | 2.99       | 500      |
| 4  | Bottled Water (12-pack) | 500ml spring water. | 4.49       | 500      |
+----+----------------------+----------------------+------------+----------+
2 rows in set (0.00 sec)
```

As shown previously, if you use an integer as part of your WHERE clause, quotation marks are not required. Quotation marks are required around strings, however, and the same rules apply with regard to escaping characters as you learned in the section on INSERT.

Using Operators in WHERE Clauses

You've used the equal sign (=) in your WHERE clauses to determine the truth of a condition—that is, whether one thing is equal to another. You can use many types of operators, with comparison operators and logical operators being the most popular types. Table 16.1 lists the comparison operators and their meanings.

TABLE 16.1   Basic Comparison Operators and Their Meanings

Operator	Meaning
=	Equal to
!=	Not equal to
<=	Less than or equal to
<	Less than
>=	Greater than or equal to
>	Greater than

There's also a handy operator called BETWEEN, which is useful with integer or date comparisons because it searches for results between a minimum and maximum value. For example:

```
SELECT * FROM grocery_inventory WHERE item_price BETWEEN 1.50 AND 3.00;
```

Here are the results:

```
+----+-----------------------+----------------------+------------+----------+
| id | item_name             | item_desc            | item_price | curr_qty |
+----+-----------------------+----------------------+------------+----------+
| 2  | Bunches of Grapes     | Seedless grapes.     | 2.99       | 500      |
| 3  | Bottled Water (6-pack)| 500ml spring water.  | 2.29       | 250      |
+----+-----------------------+----------------------+------------+----------+
2 rows in set (0.00 sec)
```

Other operators include logical operators, which enable you to use multiple comparisons within your WHERE clause. The basic logical operators are AND and OR. When using AND, all comparisons in the clause must be true to retrieve results, whereas using OR allows a minimum of one comparison to be true. Also, you can use the IN operator to specify a list of items that you want to match.

String Comparison Using LIKE

You were introduced to matching strings within a WHERE clause by using = or !=, but there's another useful operator for the WHERE clause when comparing strings: the LIKE operator. This operator uses two characters as wildcards in pattern matching:

▶ %—Matches multiple characters

▶ _—Matches exactly one character

For example, if you want to find records in the grocery_inventory table where the first name of the item starts with the letter A, you would use the following:

```
SELECT * FROM grocery_inventory WHERE item_name LIKE 'A%';
```

Here are the results:

```
+----+-----------+-------------------------+------------+----------+
| id | item_name | item_desc               | item_price | curr_qty |
+----+-----------+-------------------------+------------+----------+
| 1  | Apples    | Beautiful, ripe apples. | 0.25       | 1000     |
+----+-----------+-------------------------+------------+----------+
1 row in set (0.00 sec)
```

<u>NOTE</u>

> Unless performing a LIKE comparison on a binary string, the comparison is not case sensitive. You can force a case-sensitive comparison using the BINARY keyword.

Selecting from Multiple Tables

You are not limited to selecting only one table at a time. That would certainly make application programming a long and tedious task! When you select from more than one table in one SELECT statement, you are really joining the tables together.

Suppose that you have two tables: fruit and color. You can select all rows from each of the two tables by using two separate SELECT statements:

SELECT * FROM fruit;

This query might result in something like this:

```
+----+-----------+
| id | fruitname |
+----+-----------+
|  1 | apple     |
|  2 | orange    |
|  3 | grape     |
|  4 | banana    |
+----+-----------+
4 rows in set (0.00 sec)
```

SELECT * FROM color;

The second query could result in data like this:

```
+----+-----------+
| id | colorname |
+----+-----------+
|  1 | red       |
|  2 | orange    |
|  3 | purple    |
|  4 | yellow    |
+----+-----------+
4 rows in set (0.00 sec)
```

When you want to select from both tables at once, the syntax of the SELECT statement differs somewhat. First, you must ensure that all the tables you're using in your query appear in the FROM clause of the SELECT statement. Using the fruit and color example, if you simply want to select all columns and rows from both tables, you might think you would use the following SELECT statement:

```
SELECT * FROM fruit, color;
```

With this query, you get results like this:

```
+----+-----------+----+-----------+
| id | fruitname | id | colorname |
+----+-----------+----+-----------+
|  1 | apple     |  1 | red       |
|  2 | orange    |  1 | red       |
|  3 | grape     |  1 | red       |
|  4 | banana    |  1 | red       |
|  1 | apple     |  2 | orange    |
|  2 | orange    |  2 | orange    |
|  3 | grape     |  2 | orange    |
|  4 | banana    |  2 | orange    |
|  1 | apple     |  3 | purple    |
|  2 | orange    |  3 | purple    |
|  3 | grape     |  3 | purple    |
|  4 | banana    |  3 | purple    |
|  1 | apple     |  4 | yellow    |
|  2 | orange    |  4 | yellow    |
|  3 | grape     |  4 | yellow    |
|  4 | banana    |  4 | yellow    |
+----+-----------+----+-----------+
16 rows in set (0.00 sec)
```

Sixteen rows of repeated information are probably not what you were looking for. What this query did is *literally* join a row in the color table to each row in the fruit table. Because there are 4 records in the fruit table and 4 entries in the color table, that's 16 records returned to you.

When you select from multiple tables, you must build proper WHERE clauses to ensure that you really get what you want. In the case of the fruit and color tables, what you really want is to see the fruitname and colorname records from these two tables where the IDs of each match up. This brings us to the next nuance of the query: how to indicate exactly which field you want when the fields are named the same in both tables.

Simply, you append the table name to the field name, like this:

```
tablename.fieldname
```

So, the query for selecting fruitname and colorname from both tables where the IDs match would be as follows:

```
SELECT fruitname, colorname FROM fruit, color WHERE fruit.id = color.id;
```

This query produces a better result for you:

```
+-----------+-----------+
| fruitname | colorname |
+-----------+-----------+
| apple     | red       |
| orange    | orange    |
| grape     | purple    |
| banana    | yellow    |
+-----------+-----------+
4 rows in set (0.00 sec)
```

However, if you attempt to select a column that appears in both tables with the same name, you get an ambiguity error:

SELECT id, fruitname, colorname FROM fruit, color
WHERE fruit.id = color.id;

This query produces the following error:

```
ERROR 1052: Column: 'id' in field list is ambiguous
```

If you want to select the ID from the fruit table, you use this:

SELECT fruit.id, fruitname, colorname FROM fruit,
color WHERE fruit.id = color.id;

This query produces these results:

```
+------+-----------+-----------+
| id   | fruitname | colorname |
+------+-----------+-----------+
|    1 | apple     | red       |
|    2 | orange    | orange    |
|    3 | grape     | purple    |
|    4 | banana    | yellow    |
+------+-----------+-----------+
4 rows in set (0.00 sec)
```

This was a basic example of joining two tables together for use in a single SELECT query. The JOIN keyword is an actual part of SQL, which enables you to build more complex queries.

Using JOIN

You can use several types of JOINs in MySQL, all of which refer to the order in which the tables are put together and the results are displayed. The type of JOIN used with the fruit and color tables is an INNER JOIN, although it wasn't written explicitly as such. To rewrite the SQL statement using the proper INNER JOIN syntax, you use the following:

```
SELECT fruitname, colorname FROM fruit
INNER JOIN color ON fruit.id = color.id;
```

Your resultset looks like this:

```
+-----------+-----------+
| fruitname | colorname |
+-----------+-----------+
| apple     | red       |
| orange    | orange    |
| grape     | purple    |
| banana    | yellow    |
+-----------+-----------+
4 rows in set (0.00 sec)
```

The ON clause replaces the WHERE clause you've seen before; in this instance, it tells MySQL to join together the rows in the tables where the IDs match each other. When joining tables using ON clauses, you can use any conditions that you would use in a WHERE clause, including all the various logical and arithmetic operators.

Another common type of JOIN is the LEFT JOIN. When joining two tables with LEFT JOIN, all rows from the first table are returned, no matter whether there are matches in the second table. Suppose that you have two tables in an address book, one called master_name, containing basic records, and one called email, containing email records. Any records in the email table would be tied to a particular ID of a record in the master_name table. For example, look at these two tables (the master_name and email tables, respectively):

```
+---------+-----------+----------+
| name_id | firstname | lastname |
+---------+-----------+----------+
| 1       | John      | Smith    |
| 2       | Jane      | Smith    |
| 3       | Jimbo     | Jones    |
| 4       | Andy      | Smith    |
| 5       | Chris     | Jones    |
| 6       | Anna      | Bell     |
| 7       | Jimmy     | Carr     |
| 8       | Albert    | Smith    |
| 9       | John      | Doe      |
+---------+-----------+----------+
```

```
+---------+-------------------+
| name_id | email             |
+---------+-------------------+
| 2       | jsmith@jsmith.com |
| 6       | annabell@aol.com  |
| 9       | jdoe@yahoo.com    |
+---------+-------------------+
```

Using LEFT JOIN on these two tables, you can see that if a value from the email table does not exist, an empty value appears in place of an email address:

```
SELECT firstname, lastname, email FROM master_name
LEFT JOIN email ON master_name.name_id = email.name_id;
```

The LEFT JOIN query here produces these results:

```
+-----------+----------+--------------------+
| firstname | lastname | email              |
+-----------+----------+--------------------+
| John      | Smith    |                    |
| Jane      | Smith    | jsmith@jsmith.com  |
| Jimbo     | Jones    |                    |
| Andy      | Smith    |                    |
| Chris     | Jones    |                    |
| Anna      | Bell     | annabell@aol.com   |
| Jimmy     | Carr     |                    |
| Albert    | Smith    |                    |
| John      | Doe      | jdoe@yahoo.com     |
+-----------+----------+--------------------+
9 rows in set (0.00 sec)
```

A RIGHT JOIN works like LEFT JOIN but with the table order reversed. In other words, when using a RIGHT JOIN, all rows from the second table are returned, no matter whether matches exist in the first table. However, in the case of the master_name and email tables, there are only three rows in the email table, whereas there are nine rows in the master_name table. This means that only three of the nine rows are returned by this query:

```
SELECT firstname, lastname, email FROM master_name
RIGHT JOIN email ON master_name.name_id = email.name_id;
```

The results are as expected:

```
+-----------+----------+--------------------+
| firstname | lastname | email              |
+-----------+----------+--------------------+
| Jane      | Smith    | jsmith@jsmith.com  |
| Anna      | Bell     | annabell@aol.com   |
| John      | Doe      | jdoe@yahoo.com     |
+-----------+----------+--------------------+
3 rows in set (0.00 sec)
```

Several different types of JOINs are available in MySQL, and you have learned about the most common types. To learn more about JOINs such as CROSS JOIN, STRAIGHT JOIN, and NATURAL JOIN, visit the MySQL Manual at http://dev.mysql.com/doc/refman/5.5/en/join.html. As you continue your learning elsewhere, I highly recommend learning more about and practicing JOINs; they can be one of the most powerful tools in your SQL toolkit.

Using Subqueries

Simply stated, a *subquery* is a SELECT statement that appears within another SQL statement. Such queries can prove extremely useful because they often eliminate the need for bulky JOIN queries, and in the case of application programming, sub-queries can eliminate the need for multiple queries within loops.

An example of the basic subquery syntax is shown here:

```
SELECT expressions_and_columns FROM table_name WHERE somecolumn = (SUBQUERY);
```

You can also use subqueries with UPDATE and DELETE statements, as shown here:

```
DELETE FROM table_name WHERE somecolumn = (SUBQUERY);
```

or

```
UPDATE table_name SET somecolumn = 'something' WHERE somecolumn = (SUBQUERY);
```

> The outer statement of a subquery can be SELECT, INSERT, UPDATE, DELETE, SET, or DO.

NOTE

The subquery must always appear in parentheses—no exceptions!

When using subqueries, the WHERE portion of the outer statement does not have to use the = comparison operator. In addition to =, you can use any of the basic comparison operators as well as keywords such as IN.

The following example uses a subquery to obtain records from users in the mas-ter_name table who have an email address in the email table:

```
SELECT firstname, lastname FROM master_name
WHERE name_id IN (SELECT name_id FROM email);
```

The results of this query may look something like this:

```
+ - - - - - -+- - - - - +
| firstname | lastname |
+-----------+----------+
| Jane      | Smith    |
| Anna      | Bell     |
| John      | Doe      |
+-----------+----------+
3 rows in set (0.00 sec)
```

For a more detailed discussion of subqueries, including limitations, see the Subqueries section of the MySQL Manual at http://dev.mysql.com/doc/refman/5.5/en/subqueries.html.

Using the UPDATE **Command to Modify Records**

UPDATE is the SQL command used to modify the contents of one or more columns in an existing record or set of records. The most basic UPDATE syntax looks like this:

```
UPDATE table_name
SET column1='new value',
column2='new value2'
[WHERE some_condition_is_true]
```

The guidelines for updating a record are similar to those used when inserting a record: The data you're entering must be appropriate to the data type of the field, and you must enclose your strings in single or double quotes, escaping where necessary.

For example, assume that you have a table called fruit containing an ID, a fruit name, and the status of the fruit (ripe or rotten):

```
+----+------------+--------+
| id | fruit_name | status |
+----+------------+--------+
|  1 | apple      | ripe   |
|  2 | orange     | rotten |
|  3 | grape      | ripe   |
|  4 | banana     | rotten |
+----+------------+--------+
4 rows in set (0.00 sec)
```

To update the status of the fruit to ripe, use

UPDATE fruit SET status = 'ripe';

You receive a response from the database like so:

```
Query OK, 2 rows affected (0.00 sec)
Rows matched: 4  Changed: 2  Warnings: 0
```

Take a close look at the result of the query. It was successful, as you can tell from the Query OK message. Also note that only two rows were affected—if you try to set the value of a column to the value it already is, the update won't occur for that column.

The second line of the response shows that four rows were matched, and only two were changed. If you're wondering what matched, the answer is simple: Because you did not specify a particular condition for matching, the match is all rows.

You must be careful and use a condition when updating a table, unless you really intend to change all the columns for all records to the same value. For the sake of argument, assume that the word *grape* is spelled incorrectly in its row in the table, and you want to use UPDATE to correct this mistake:

```
UPDATE fruit SET fruit_name = 'grape';
```

This query would have horrible results:

```
Query OK, 4 rows affected (0.00 sec)
Rows matched: 4  Changed: 4  Warnings: 0
```

When you read the result, you *should* be filled with dread: Four of four records were changed, instead of only the one you intended, meaning your fruit table now looks like this:

```
+----+------------+--------+
| id | fruit_name | status |
+----+------------+--------+
|  1 | grape      | ripe   |
|  2 | grape      | ripe   |
|  3 | grape      | ripe   |
|  4 | grape      | ripe   |
+----+------------+--------+
4 rows in set (0.00 sec)
```

All your fruit records are now grapes. While you were attempting to correct the spelling of one field, all fields were changed because you failed to specify a condition.

When doling out UPDATE privileges to your users, think about the responsibility you're giving to someone—one wrong move and your entire table could be grapes. In the preceding example, you could have used the id or fruit_name field in your WHERE clause, as you will see in the following section.

Conditional UPDATEs

Making a conditional UPDATE means that you are using WHERE clauses to match specific records. Using a WHERE clause in an UPDATE statement is just like using a WHERE clause in a SELECT statement. All the same comparison and logical operators can be used, such as equal to, greater than, OR, and AND.

Assume that your fruit table has not been completely filled with grapes but instead contains four records, one with a spelling mistake (grappe instead of grape). The UPDATE statement to fix the spelling mistake is as follows:

```
UPDATE fruit SET fruit_name = 'grape' WHERE fruit_name = 'grappe';
```

In this case, only one row was matched and one row was changed, as shown with this result:

```
Query OK, 1 row affected (0.00 sec)
Rows matched: 1  Changed: 1  Warnings: 0
```

Your `fruit` table should be intact, and all fruit names should be spelled properly:

```
SELECT * FROM fruit;
```

This SELECT query shows the following:

```
+----+------------+--------+
| id | fruit_name | status |
+----+------------+--------+
|  1 | apple      | ripe   |
|  2 | pear       | ripe   |
|  3 | banana     | ripe   |
|  4 | grape      | ripe   |
+----+------------+--------+
4 rows in set (0.00 sec)
```

Using Existing Column Values with UPDATE

Another feature of UPDATE is the capability to use the current value in the record as the base value. For example, go back to the `grocery_inventory` table example, with a table that looks like this:

```
+----+-----------------------+-----------------------+------------+----------+
| id | item_name             | item_desc             | item_price | curr_qty |
+----+-----------------------+-----------------------+------------+----------+
|  1 | Apples                | Beautiful, ripe apples. | 0.25     | 1000     |
|  2 | Bunches of Grapes     | Seedless grapes.      | 2.99       | 500      |
|  3 | Bottled Water (6-pack)| 500ml spring water.   | 2.29       | 250      |
|  4 | Bottled Water (12-pack)| 500ml spring water.  | 4.49       | 500      |
|  5 | Bananas               | Bunches, green.       | 1.99       | 150      |
|  6 | Pears                 | Anjou, nice and sweet.| 0.5        | 500      |
|  7 | Avocado               | Large Haas variety.   | 0.99       | 750      |
+----+-----------------------+-----------------------+------------+----------+
7 rows in set (0.00 sec)
```

When someone purchases a product, such as an apple (id = 1), the inventory table should be updated accordingly. However, you won't know exactly what number to enter in the `curr_qty` column, just that you sold one. In this case, use the current value of the column and subtract 1:

```
UPDATE grocery_inventory SET curr_qty = curr_qty - 1 WHERE id = 1;
```

This query should give you a new value of 999 in the `curr_qty` column, and indeed it does:

```
SELECT * FROM grocery_inventory;
```

The SELECT query shows the new inventory quantity:

```
+----+---------------------+-------------------------+------------+----------+
| id | item_name           | item_desc               | item_price | curr_qty |
+----+---------------------+-------------------------+------------+----------+
| 1  | Apples              | Beautiful, ripe apples. | 0.25       | 999      |
| 2  | Bunches of Grapes   | Seedless grapes.        | 2.99       | 500      |
| 3  | Bottled Water (6-pack) | 500ml spring water.  | 2.29       | 250      |
| 4  | Bottled Water (12-pack)| 500ml spring water.  | 4.49       | 500      |
| 5  | Bananas             | Bunches, green.         | 1.99       | 150      |
| 6  | Pears               | Anjou, nice and sweet.  | 0.5        | 500      |
| 7  | Avocado             | Large Haas variety.     | 0.99       | 750      |
+----+---------------------+-------------------------+------------+----------+
7 rows in set (0.00 sec)
```

Using the REPLACE Command

Another method for modifying records is to use the REPLACE command, which is remarkably similar to the INSERT command.

```
REPLACE INTO table_name (column list) VALUES (column values);
```

The REPLACE statement works like this: If the record you are inserting into the table contains a primary key value that matches a record already in the table, the record in the table is deleted and the new record inserted in its place.

> **NOTE**
>
> The REPLACE command is a MySQL-specific extension to ANSI SQL. This command mimics the action of a DELETE and re-INSERT of a particular record. In other words, you get two commands for the price of one.

Using the grocery_inventory table, the following command replaces the entry for Apples:

```
REPLACE INTO grocery_inventory VALUES
  (1, 'Granny Smith Apples', 'Sweet!', '0.50', 1000);
```

You should see the following result:

```
Query OK, 2 rows affected (0.00 sec)
```

In the query result, notice that the result states 2 rows affected. In this case, because id is a primary key that had a matching value in the grocery_inventory table, the original row was deleted and the new row was inserted: 2 rows affected.

Use a SELECT query to verify that the entry is correct, which it is:

```
+----+------------------------+------------------------+------------+----------+
| id | item_name              | item_desc              | item_price | curr_qty |
+----+------------------------+------------------------+------------+----------+
|  1 | Granny Smith Apples    | Sweet!                 | 0.50       | 1000     |
|  2 | Bunches of Grapes      | Seedless grapes.       | 2.99       | 500      |
|  3 | Bottled Water (6-pack) | 500ml spring water.    | 2.29       | 250      |
|  4 | Bottled Water (12-pack)| 500ml spring water.    | 4.49       | 500      |
|  5 | Bananas                | Bunches, green.        | 1.99       | 150      |
|  6 | Pears                  | Anjou, nice and sweet. | 0.5        | 500      |
|  7 | Avocado                | Large Haas variety.    | 0.99       | 750      |
+----+------------------------+------------------------+------------+----------+
7 rows in set (0.00 sec)
```

If you use a REPLACE statement, and the value of the primary key in the new record does not match a value for a primary key already in the table, the record is simply inserted, and only one row is affected.

Using the DELETE Command

The basic DELETE syntax is as follows:

```
DELETE FROM table_name
[WHERE some_condition_is_true]
[LIMIT rows]
```

Notice that no column specification is used in the DELETE command—when you use DELETE, the entire record is removed. You might recall the fiasco earlier in this chapter regarding grapes in the fruit table, when updating a table without specifying a condition caused an update of all records. You must be similarly careful when using DELETE.

Assuming the following structure and data in a table called fruit

```
+----+------------+--------+
| id | fruit_name | status |
+----+------------+--------+
|  1 | apple      | ripe   |
|  2 | pear       | rotten |
|  3 | banana     | ripe   |
|  4 | grape      | rotten |
+----+------------+--------+
4 rows in set (0.00 sec)
```

the following statement removes all records in the table:

DELETE FROM fruit;

You can always verify the deletion by attempting to SELECT data from the table. If you were to issue this command after removing all the records:

```
SELECT * FROM fruit;
```

You would see that all your fruit is gone:

```
Empty set (0.00 sec)
```

Conditional DELETE

A conditional DELETE statement, just like a conditional SELECT or UPDATE statement, means you are using WHERE clauses to match specific records. You have the full range of comparison and logical operators available to you, so you can pick and choose which records you want to delete.

A prime example is to remove all records for rotten fruit from the fruit table:

```
DELETE FROM fruit WHERE status = 'rotten';
```

Two records were deleted:

```
Query OK, 2 rows affected (0.00 sec)
```

Only ripe fruit remains:

```
+----+------------+--------+
| id | fruit_name | status |
+----+------------+--------+
|  1 | apple      | ripe   |
|  3 | banana     | ripe   |
+----+------------+--------+
2 rows in set (0.00 sec)
```

You can also use ORDER BY clauses in your DELETE statements; look at the basic DELETE syntax with the ORDER BY clause added to its structure:

```
DELETE FROM table_name
[WHERE some_condition_is_true]
[ORDER BY some_column [ASC | DESC]]
[LIMIT rows]
```

At first glance, you might wonder, "Why does it matter in what order I delete records?" The ORDER BY clause isn't for the deletion order; it's for the sorting order of records.

In this example, a table called `access_log` shows access time and username:

```
+----+---------------------+----------+
| id | date_accessed       | username |
+----+---------------------+----------+
|  1 | 2012-01-06 06:09:13 | johndoe  |
|  2 | 2012-01-06 06:09:22 | janedoe  |
|  3 | 2012-01-06 06:09:39 | jsmith   |
|  4 | 2012-01-06 06:09:44 | mikew    |
+----+---------------------+----------+
4 rows in set (0.00 sec)
```

To remove the oldest record, first use `ORDER BY` to sort the results appropriately, and then use `LIMIT` to remove just one record:

```
DELETE FROM access_log ORDER BY date_accessed DESC LIMIT 1;
```

Select all from `access_log` and verify that only three records exist:

```
SELECT * FROM access_log;
```

The results are as follows:

```
+----+---------------------+----------+
| id | date_accessed       | username |
+----+---------------------+----------+
|  2 | 2012-01-06 06:09:22 | janedoe  |
|  3 | 2012-01-06 06:09:39 | jsmith   |
|  4 | 2012-01-06 06:09:44 | mikew    |
+----+---------------------+----------+
3 rows in set (0.00 sec)
```

Frequently Used String Functions in MySQL

MySQL's built-in string-related functions can be used several ways. You can use functions in `SELECT` statements without specifying a table to retrieve a result of the function. Or you can use functions to enhance your `SELECT` results by concatenating two fields to form a new string. The following examples are by no means a complete library of MySQL string-related functions. For more, see the MySQL Manual at http://dev.mysql.com/doc/refman/5.5/en/string-functions.html.

Length and Concatenation Functions

The group of length and concatenation functions focuses on the length of strings and concatenating strings together. Length-related functions include `LENGTH()`,

`OCTET_LENGTH()`, `CHAR_LENGTH()`, and `CHARACTER_LENGTH()`, which do almost the same thing: count characters in a string.

```
SELECT LENGTH('This is cool!');
```

The result is this:

```
+------------------------+
| LENGTH('This is cool!') |
+------------------------+
|                     13 |
+------------------------+
1 row in set (0.00 sec)
```

The fun begins with the `CONCAT()` function, which concatenates two or more strings:

```
SELECT CONCAT('My', 'S', 'QL');
```

This query results in the following:

```
+------------------------+
| CONCAT('My', 'S', 'QL') |
+------------------------+
| MySQL                  |
+------------------------+
1 row in set (0.00 sec)
```

Imagine using this function with a table containing names, split into `firstname` and `lastname` fields. Instead of using two strings, use two field names to concatenate the `firstname` and the `lastname` fields. By concatenating the fields, you reduce the lines of code necessary to achieve the same result in your application:

```
SELECT CONCAT(firstname, lastname) FROM master_name;
```

This query results in the following:

```
+----------------------------+
| CONCAT(firstname, lastname) |
+----------------------------+
| JohnSmith                  |
| JaneSmith                  |
| JimboJones                 |
| AndySmith                  |
| ChrisJones                 |
| AnnaBell                   |
| JimmyCarr                  |
| AlbertSmith                |
| JohnDoe                    |
+----------------------------+
9 rows in set (0.00 sec)
```

TIP

If you're using a field name and not a string in a function, do not enclose the field name within quotation marks. If you do, MySQL interprets the string literally. In a CONCAT() example, like this

```
SELECT CONCAT('firstname', 'lastname') FROM master_name;
```

you get the following result:

```
+------------------------------+
| CONCAT('firstname', 'lastname') |
+------------------------------+
| firstnamelastname            |
| firstnamelastname            |
| firstnamelastname            |
| firstnamelastname            |
| firstnamelastname            |
| firstnamelastname            |
| firstnamelastname            |
| firstnamelastname            |
| firstnamelastname            |
+------------------------------+
9 rows in set (0.00 sec)
```

The CONCAT() function would be useful if there were some sort of separator between the names, and that's where the next function comes in: CONCAT_WS().

As you might have figured out, CONTACT_WS() stands for *concatenate with separator*. The separator can be anything you choose, but the following example uses whitespace:

```
SELECT CONCAT_WS(' ', firstname, lastname) FROM master_name;
```

This query results in the following:

```
+------------------------------------+
| CONCAT_WS(' ', firstname, lastname) |
+------------------------------------+
| John Smith                         |
| Jane Smith                         |
| Jimbo Jones                        |
| Andy Smith                         |
| Chris Jones                        |
| Anna Bell                          |
| Jimmy Carr                         |
| Albert Smith                       |
| John Doe                           |
+------------------------------------+
9 rows in set (0.00 sec)
```

If you want to shorten the width of your result table, you can use AS to name the custom result field:

```
SELECT CONCAT_WS(' ', firstname, lastname) AS fullname FROM master_name;
```

With this, you get the following results:

```
+--------------+
| fullname     |
+--------------+
| John Smith   |
| Jane Smith   |
| Jimbo Jones  |
| Andy Smith   |
| Chris Jones  |
| Anna Bell    |
| Jimmy Carr   |
| Albert Smith |
| John Doe     |
+--------------+
9 rows in set (0.00 sec)
```

Trimming and Padding Functions

MySQL provides several functions for adding and removing extra characters (including whitespace) from strings. The RTRIM() and LTRIM() functions remove whitespace from either the right or left side of a string:

```
SELECT RTRIM('stringstring    ');
```

This query results in the following, although it is difficult to see the change:

```
+-----------------------+
| RTRIM('stringstring    ') |
+-----------------------+
| stringstring          |
+-----------------------+
1 row in set (0.00 sec)
```

The LTRIM() function results are easier to see:

```
SELECT LTRIM('    stringstring');
```

This query results in the following, with the whitespace clearly stripped:

```
+----------------------+
| LTRIM('   stringstring') |
+----------------------+
| stringstring         |
+----------------------+
1 row in set (0.00 sec)
```

You may have padded strings to trim if the string is coming out of a fixed-width field and either doesn't need to carry along the additional padding or is being inserted into a varchar or other non-fixed-width field. If your strings are padded with a character besides whitespace, use the TRIM() function to name the characters you want to remove. For example, to remove the leading X characters from the string XXXneedleXXX, use

```
SELECT TRIM(LEADING 'X' FROM 'XXXneedleXXX');
```

Here is the result of this query:

```
+--------------------------------------+
| TRIM(LEADING 'X' FROM 'XXXneedleXXX') |
+--------------------------------------+
| needleXXX                            |
+--------------------------------------+
1 row in set (0.00 sec)
```

You can use TRAILING to remove the characters from the end of the string:

```
SELECT TRIM(TRAILING 'X' FROM 'XXXneedleXXX');
```

The results of this query are as follows:

```
+---------------------------------------+
| TRIM(TRAILING 'X' FROM 'XXXneedleXXX') |
+---------------------------------------+
| XXXneedle                             |
+---------------------------------------+
1 row in set (0.00 sec)
```

If neither LEADING nor TRAILING is indicated, both are assumed:

```
SELECT TRIM('X' FROM 'XXXneedleXXX');
```

This query results in this:

```
+------------------------------+
| TRIM('X' FROM 'XXXneedleXXX') |
+------------------------------+
| needle                       |
+------------------------------+
1 row in set (0.00 sec)
```

Just as RTRIM() and LTRIM()remove padding characters, RPAD() and LPAD() add characters to a string. For example, you might want to add specific identification characters to a string that is part of an order number, in a database used for sales.

When you use the padding functions, the required elements are the string, the target length, and the padding character. For example, pad the string `needle` with the X character until the string is 10 characters long using this query:

```
SELECT RPAD('needle', 10, 'X');
```

You will see this result:

```
+------------------------+
| RPAD('needle', 10, 'X') |
+------------------------+
| needleXXXX             |
+------------------------+
1 row in set (0.00 sec)
```

Location and Position Functions

The group of location and position functions is useful for finding parts of strings within other strings. The `LOCATE()` function returns the position of the first occurrence of a given substring within the target string. For example, you can look for a needle in a haystack:

```
SELECT LOCATE('needle', 'haystackneedlehaystack');
```

You should see this result:

```
+------------------------------------------+
| LOCATE('needle', 'haystackneedlehaystack') |
+------------------------------------------+
|                                        9 |
+------------------------------------------+
1 row in set (0.00 sec)
```

The substring `needle` begins at position 9 in the target string. If the substring cannot be found in the target string, MySQL returns 0 as a result.

> **NOTE**
>
> Unlike position counting within most programming languages, which start at 0, position counting using MySQL starts at 1.

An extension of the `LOCATE()` function is to use a third argument for starting position. If you start looking for `needle` in `haystack` before position 9, you'll receive a result. Otherwise, because `needle` starts at position 9, you'll receive a 0 result if you specify a greater starting position.

Substring Functions

If your goal is to extract a substring from a target string, several functions fit the bill. Given a string, starting position, and length, you can use the SUBSTRING() function. This example gets three characters from the string MySQL, starting at position 2:

```
SELECT SUBSTRING("MySQL", 2, 3);
```

The result is as follows:

```
+------------------------+
| SUBSTRING("MySQL", 2, 3) |
+------------------------+
| ySQ                    |
+------------------------+
1 row in set (0.00 sec)
```

If you just want a few characters from the left or right ends of a string, use the LEFT() and RIGHT() functions:

```
SELECT LEFT("MySQL", 2);
```

The result of this query is as follows:

```
+----------------+
| LEFT("MySQL", 2) |
+----------------+
| My             |
+----------------+
1 row in set (0.00 sec)
```

Similarly, using RIGHT()

```
SELECT RIGHT("MySQL", 3);
```

produces the following results:

```
+-----------------+
| RIGHT("MySQL", 3) |
+-----------------+
| SQL             |
+-----------------+
1 row in set (0.00 sec)
```

One of the many common uses of substring functions is to extract parts of order numbers to find out who placed the order. In some applications, the system is designed to automatically generate an order number containing a date, customer identification, and other information. If this order number always follows a particular pattern, such as XXXX-YYYYY-ZZ, you can use substring functions to extract the individual parts of the whole. For example, if ZZ always represents the state to which the order was shipped, you can use the RIGHT() function to extract these characters and report the number of orders shipped to a particular state.

String Modification Functions

PHP has numerous functions to modify the appearance of strings, but if you can perform the task as part of the SQL statement, all the better—let the database system do as much work as possible.

The MySQL LCASE() and UCASE() functions transform a string into lowercase or uppercase:

```
SELECT LCASE('MYSQL');
```

This query produces the following results:

```
+----------------+
| LCASE('MYSQL') |
+----------------+
| mysql          |
+----------------+
1 row in set (0.00 sec)
```

For uppercasing, use the following

```
SELECT UCASE('mysql');
```

This query produces the following results:

```
+----------------+
| UCASE('mysql') |
+----------------+
| MYSQL          |
+----------------+
1 row in set (0.00 sec)
```

> **TIP**
>
> A practical use of the LCASE() and UCASE() functions is when you are validating user input against data stored in MySQL—such as in the case of a user login form. If you want the login process to appear not case sensitive, you could attempt to match the uppercase (or lowercase) version of the user input against the uppercase (or lowercase) version of the data stored in the table.

Remember, if you use the functions with field names, don't use quotation marks:

```
SELECT UCASE(lastname) FROM master_name;
```

Use the preceding query to produce results like this:

```
+-----------------+
| UCASE(lastname) |
+-----------------+
| BELL            |
| CARR            |
| DOE             |
| JONES           |
| JONES           |
| SMITH           |
| SMITH           |
| SMITH           |
| SMITH           |
+-----------------+
9 rows in set (0.00 sec)
```

Another fun string-manipulation function is REPEAT(), which does just what it sounds like—repeats a string for a given number of times:

```
SELECT REPEAT("bowwow", 4);
```

You should see this result:

```
+--------------------------+
| REPEAT("bowwow", 4)      |
+--------------------------+
| bowwowbowwowbowwowbowwow |
+--------------------------+
1 row in set (0.00 sec)
```

The REPLACE() function replaces all occurrences of a given string with another string:

```
SELECT REPLACE('bowwowbowwowbowwowbowwow', 'wow', 'WOW');
```

This query produces the following:

```
+------------------------------------------------------+
| REPLACE('bowwowbowwowbowwowbowwow', 'wow', 'WOW')    |
+------------------------------------------------------+
| bowWOWbowWOWbowWOWbowWOW                             |
+------------------------------------------------------+
1 row in set (0.00 sec)
```

Using Date and Time Functions in MySQL

You can use MySQL's built-in date-related functions in SELECT statements, with or without specifying a table, to retrieve a result of the function. Or you can use the functions with any type of date field: date, datetime, timestamp, and year. Depending on the type of field in use, the results of the date-related functions are more or less useful. The following examples are by no means a complete library of MySQL date and time-related functions. For more, see the MySQL Manual at http://dev.mysql.com/doc/refman/5.5/en/date-and-time-functions.html.

Working with Days

The DAYOFWEEK() and WEEKDAY() functions do similar things with slightly different results. Both functions find the weekday index of a date, but the difference lies in the starting day and position.

If you use DAYOFWEEK(), the first day of the week is Sunday, at position 1, and the last day of the week is Saturday, at position 7. For example:

```
SELECT DAYOFWEEK('2012-01-09');
```

This query produces the following result:

```
+-----------------------+
| DAYOFWEEK('2012-01-09') |
+-----------------------+
|                     2 |
+-----------------------+
1 row in set (0.00 sec)
```

The result shows that January 9, 2012, was weekday index 2, or Monday. Using the same date with WEEKDAY() gives you a different result with the same meaning:

```
+----------------------+
| WEEKDAY('2012-01-09') |
+----------------------+
|                    0 |
+----------------------+
1 row in set (0.00 sec)
```

The result shows that January 9, 2012, was weekday index 0. Because WEEKDAY() uses Monday as the first day of the week at position 0 and Sunday as the last day at position 6, 0 is accurate: Monday.

The DAYOFMONTH() and DAYOFYEAR() functions are more straightforward, with only one result and a range that starts at 1 and ends at 31 for DAYOFMONTH() and 366 for DAYOFYEAR(). Some examples follow:

```
SELECT DAYOFMONTH('2012-01-09');
```

This query produces the following results:

```
+-------------------------+
| DAYOFMONTH('2012-01-09') |
+-------------------------+
|                       9 |
+-------------------------+
1 row in set (0.00 sec)
```

Now try:

```
SELECT DAYOFYEAR('2012-01-09');
```

This query produces the following results:

```
+------------------------+
| DAYOFYEAR('2012-01-09') |
+------------------------+
|                     09 |
+------------------------+
1 row in set (0.00 sec)
```

It might seem odd to have a function that returns the day of the month on a particular date because the day is right there in the string. But think about using these types of functions in WHERE clauses to perform comparisons on records. If you have a table that holds online orders with a field containing the date the order was placed, you can quickly get a count of the orders placed on any given day of the week, or see how many orders were placed during the first half of the month versus the second half.

The following two queries show how many orders were placed during the first three days of the week (throughout all months) and then the remaining days of the week:

```
SELECT COUNT(id) FROM orders WHERE DAYOFWEEK(date_ordered) < 4;
```

```
SELECT COUNT(id) FROM orders WHERE DAYOFWEEK(date_ordered) > 3;
```

Using DAYOFMONTH(), the following examples show the number of orders placed during the first half of any month versus the second half:

```
SELECT COUNT(id) FROM orders WHERE DAYOFMONTH(date_ordered) < 16;
```

```
SELECT COUNT(id) FROM orders WHERE DAYOFMONTH(date_ordered) > 15;
```

You can use the DAYNAME() function to add more life to your results because it returns the name of the weekday for any given date:

```
SELECT DAYNAME(date_ordered) FROM orders;
```

This query produces results such as these:

```
+----------------------+
| DAYNAME(date_ordered) |
+----------------------+
| Thursday             |
| Monday               |
| Thursday             |
| Thursday             |
| Wednesday            |
| Thursday             |
| Sunday               |
| Sunday               |
+----------------------+
8 rows in set (0.00 sec)
```

Functions aren't limited to WHERE clauses—you can use them in ORDER BY clauses as well, such as the following:

```
SELECT DAYNAME(date_ordered) FROM orders ORDER BY DAYOFWEEK(date_ordered);
```

Working with Months and Years

Days of the week are not the only parts of the calendar, and MySQL has functions specifically for months and years as well. Just like the DAYOFWEEK() and DAYNAME() functions, MONTH() and MONTHNAME() return the number of the month in a year and the name of the month for a given date. For example:

```
SELECT MONTH('2012-01-09'), MONTHNAME('2012-01-09');
```

This query produces the following:

```
+---------------------+-------------------------+
| MONTH('2012-01-09') | MONTHNAME('2012-01-09') |
+---------------------+-------------------------+
| 1                   | January                 |
+---------------------+-------------------------+
1 row in set (0.00 sec)
```

334

Using MONTHNAME() on the orders table shows the proper results but can show a lot of repeated data:

```
+------------------------+
| MONTHNAME(date_ordered) |
+------------------------+
| November               |
| November               |
| November               |
| November               |
| November               |
| November               |
| November               |
| October                |
+------------------------+
8 rows in set (0.00 sec)
```

You can use DISTINCT to get nonrepetitive results:

```
SELECT DISTINCT MONTHNAME(date_ordered) FROM orders;
```

This query produces results like these:

```
+------------------------+
| MONTHNAME(date_ordered) |
+------------------------+
| November               |
| October                |
+------------------------+
2 rows in set (0.00 sec)
```

For work with years, the YEAR() function returns the year of a given date:

```
SELECT DISTINCT YEAR(date_ordered) FROM orders;
```

This query produces results like the following:

```
+-------------------+
| YEAR(date_ordered) |
+-------------------+
|              2011 |
|              2012 |
+-------------------+
1 row in set (0.00 sec)
```

Working with Weeks

Weeks can be tricky things—there can be 53 weeks in a year if Sunday is the first day of the week and December hasn't ended. For example, December 30 of 2001 was a Sunday:

```
SELECT DAYNAME('2001-12-30');
```

Here's proof:

```
+----------------------+
| DAYNAME('2001-12-30') |
+----------------------+
| Sunday               |
+----------------------+
1 row in set (0.00 sec)
```

That fact made December 30 of 2001 part of the 53rd week of the year, which you can see using this query:

```
SELECT WEEK('2001-12-30');
```

The week of the year is shown appropriately in the results:

```
+--------------------+
| WEEK('2001-12-30') |
+--------------------+
|                 53 |
+--------------------+
1 row in set (0.00 sec)
```

The 53rd week contained December 30 and 31 and was only 2 days long; the first week of 2002 began with January 1.

If you want your weeks to start on Mondays but still want to find the week of the year, the optional second argument enables you to change the start day. A 1 indicates a week that starts on Monday. In the following examples, a Monday start day makes December 30 part of the 52nd week of 2001, but December 31 is still part of the 53rd week of 2001:

```
SELECT WEEK('2001-12-30',1);
```

This query produces the following results:

```
+----------------------+
| WEEK('2001-12-30',1) |
+----------------------+
|                   52 |
+----------------------+
1 row in set (0.00 sec)
```

While this query:

```
SELECT WEEK('2001-12-31',1);
```

produces this result:

```
+----------------------+
| WEEK('2001-12-31',1) |
+----------------------+
|                   53 |
+----------------------+
1 row in set (0.00 sec)
```

Working with Hours, Minutes, and Seconds

If you're using a date that includes the exact time, such as `datetime` or `timestamp`, or even just a `time` field, there are functions to find the hours, minutes, and seconds from that string. Not surprisingly, these functions are called `HOUR()`, `MINUTE()`, and `SECOND()`. `HOUR()` returns the hour in a given time, which is between 0 and 23. The range for `MINUTE()` and `SECOND()` is 0 to 59.

Here is an example:

```
SELECT HOUR('2012-01-09 07:27:49') AS hour,
MINUTE('2012-01-09 07:27:49') AS minute,
SECOND('2012-01-09 07:27:49') AS second;
```

This query produces the following:

```
+------+--------+--------+
| hour | minute | second |
+------+--------+--------+
|    7 |     27 |     49 |
+------+--------+--------+
1 row in set (0.00 sec)
```

That's a lot of queries to get at one time from a `datetime` field—you can put the hour and minute together and even use `CONCAT_WS()` to put the : between the results and get a representation of the time:

```
SELECT CONCAT_WS(':',HOUR('2012-01-09 07:27:49'),
MINUTE('2012-01-09 07:27:49')) AS sample_time;
```

This query produces the following:

```
+-------------+
| sample_time |
+-------------+
| 7:27        |
+-------------+
1 row in set (0.00 sec)
```

In the next section, you learn how to use the `DATE_FORMAT()` function to properly format dates and times.

Formatting Dates and Times with MySQL

The DATE_FORMAT() function formats a date, datetime, or timestamp field into a string by using options that tell it exactly how to display the results. The syntax of DATE_FORMAT() is as follows:

```
DATE_FORMAT(date,format)
```

Table 16.2 lists many formatting options for DATE_FORMAT().

TABLE 16.2   DATE_FORMAT() Format String Options

Option	Result
%M	Month name (January through December)
%b	Abbreviated month name (Jan through Dec)
%m	Month, padded digits (01 through 12)
%c	Month (1 through 12)
%W	Weekday name (Sunday through Saturday)
%a	Abbreviated weekday name (Sun through Sat)
%D	Day of the month using the English suffix, such as first, second, third, and so on
%d	Day of the month, padded digits (00 through 31)
%e	Day of the month (0 through 31)
%j	Day of the year, padded digits (001 through 366)
%Y	Year, four digits
%y	Year, two digits
%X	Four-digit year for the week where Sunday is the first day; used with %V
%x	Four-digit year for the week where Monday is the first day; used with %v
%w	Day of the week (0=Sunday...6=Saturday)
%U	Week (0 through 53) where Sunday is the first day of the week
%u	Week (0 through 53) where Monday is the first day of the week
%V	Week (1 through 53) where Sunday is the first day of the week; used with %X
%v	Week (1 through 53) where Monday is the first day of the week; used with %x
%H	Hour, padded digits (00 through 23)

TABLE 16.2   Continued

%k	Hour (0 through 23)
%h	Hour, padded digits (01 through 12)
%l	Hour (1 through 12)
%i	Minutes, padded digits (00 through 59)
%S	Seconds, padded digits (00 through 59)
%s	Seconds, padded digits (00 through 59)
%r	Time, 12-hour clock (hh:mm:ss [AP]M)
%T	Time, 24-hour clock (hh:mm:ss)
%p	AM or PM

NOTE

> Any other characters used in the DATE_FORMAT() option string appear literally.

To display the 02:02 result that we rigged in the previous section, you use the %h and %i options to return the hour and minute from the date with a : between the two options. For example:

```
SELECT DATE_FORMAT('2012-01-09 02:02:00', '%h:%i') AS sample_time;
```

This query produces the following:

```
+-------------+
| sample_time |
+-------------+
| 02:02       |
+-------------+
1 row in set (0.00 sec)
```

The following are just a few more examples of the DATE_FORMAT() function in use, but this function is best understood by practicing it yourself.

```
SELECT DATE_FORMAT('2012-01-09', '%W, %M %D, %Y') AS sample_time;
```

This query produces the following output:

```
+----------------------------+
| sample_time                |
+----------------------------+
| Monday, January 9th, 2012  |
+----------------------------+
1 row in set (0.00 sec)
```

Here's a query to format the time right now (well, when I wrote this):

```
SELECT DATE_FORMAT(NOW(),'%W the %D of %M, %Y
around %l o\'clock %p') AS sample_time;
```

The output as I ran the query just this moment was this:

```
+----------------------------------------------------+
| sample_time                                        |
+----------------------------------------------------+
| Tuesday the 10th of January, 2012 around 8 o'clock PM |
+----------------------------------------------------+
1 row in set (0.04 sec)
```

Take some time to play around with date formatting options on your own; there are plenty, and you'll find them easy to follow.

Performing Date Arithmetic with MySQL

MySQL has several functions to help perform date arithmetic, and this is one of the areas where it is typically more efficient to allow MySQL to do the math than your PHP script. The DATE_ADD() and DATE_SUB() functions return a result given a starting date and an interval. The syntax for both functions is as follows:

```
DATE_ADD(date,INTERVAL value type)
```

```
DATE_SUB(date,INTERVAL value type)
```

Table 16.3 shows the possible types and their expected value format.

TABLE 16.3   Values and Types in Date Arithmetic

Value	Type
Number of seconds	SECOND
Number of minutes	MINUTE
Number of hours	HOUR
Number of days	DAY
Number of months	MONTH
Number of years	YEAR
"minutes:seconds"	MINUTE_SECOND
"hours:minutes"	HOUR_MINUTE
"days hours"	DAY_HOUR
"years-months"	YEAR_MONTH
"hours:minutes:seconds"	HOUR_SECOND
"days hours:minutes"	DAY_MINUTE
"days hours:minutes:seconds"	DAY_SECOND

For example, to find the date of the current day plus 21 days, use the following:

```
SELECT DATE_ADD(NOW(), INTERVAL 21 DAY);
```

The query as I ran it just now produced the following result:

```
+---------------------------------+
| DATE_ADD(NOW(), INTERVAL 21 DAY) |
+---------------------------------+
| 2012-01-31 21:02:16             |
+---------------------------------+
1 row in set (0.02 sec)
```

Using DATE_SUB() produced this result:

```
+---------------------------------+
| DATE_SUB(NOW(), INTERVAL 21 DAY) |
+---------------------------------+
| 2011-12-20 21:02:23             |
+---------------------------------+
1 row in set (0.00 sec)
```

Use the expression DAY as shown in Table 16.3, despite what might be a natural tendency to use DAYS instead of DAY. Using DAYS results in an error:

```
ERROR 1064: You have an error in your SQL syntax near 'DAYS)' at line 1
```

If you use DATE_ADD() or DATE_SUB() with a date value rather than a datetime value, the result is shown as a date value unless you use expressions related to hours, minutes, and seconds. In that case, your result is a datetime result.

For example, the result of the first query here remains a date field, whereas the second becomes a datetime:

```
SELECT DATE_ADD("2011-12-31", INTERVAL 1 DAY);
```

This query produces the following results:

```
+----------------------------------------+
| DATE_ADD("2011-12-31", INTERVAL 1 DAY) |
+----------------------------------------+
| 2012-01-01                             |
+----------------------------------------+
1 row in set (0.00 sec)
```

While this query:

```
SELECT DATE_ADD("2011-12-31", INTERVAL 12 HOUR);
```

produces this result:

```
+------------------------------------------+
| DATE_ADD("2011-12-31", INTERVAL 12 HOUR) |
+------------------------------------------+
| 2011-12-31 12:00:00                      |
+------------------------------------------+
1 row in set (0.00 sec)
```

You can also perform date arithmetic using the + and - operators instead of
DATE_ADD() and DATE_SUB() functions, such as here:

```
SELECT "2011-12-31" + INTERVAL 1 DAY;
```

This query produces the following result:

```
+------------------------------+
| "2011-12-31" + INTERVAL 1 DAY |
+------------------------------+
| 2012-01-01                   |
+------------------------------+
1 row in set (0.00 sec)
```

Special Functions and Conversion Features

The MySQL NOW() function returns a current datetime result and is useful for time-
stamping login or access times, as well as for numerous other tasks. MySQL has a
few other functions that perform similarly.

The CURDATE() and CURRENT_DATE() functions are synonymous, and each returns
the current date in YYYY-MM-DD format:

```
SELECT CURDATE(), CURRENT_DATE();
```

This query produces results like the following:

```
+------------+---------------+
| CURDATE()  | CURRENT_DATE() |
+------------+---------------+
| 2012-01-10 | 2012-01-10    |
+------------+---------------+
1 row in set (0.01 sec)
```

Similarly, the CURTIME() and CURRENT_TIME() functions return the current time in
HH:MM:SS format:

```
SELECT CURTIME(), CURRENT_TIME();
```

This query produces results like the following:

```
+----------+----------------+
| CURTIME() | CURRENT_TIME() |
+----------+----------------+
| 09:14:26  | 09:14:26       |
+----------+----------------+
1 row in set (0.00 sec)
```

The NOW(), SYSDATE(), and CURRENT_TIMESTAMP() functions return values in full datetime format (YYYY-MM-DD HH:MM:SS):

```
SELECT NOW(), SYSDATE(), CURRENT_TIMESTAMP();
```

This query produces results like the following:

```
+---------------------+---------------------+---------------------+
| NOW()               | SYSDATE()           | CURRENT_TIMESTAMP() |
+---------------------+---------------------+---------------------+
| 2012-01-10 15:23:52 | 2012-01-10 15:23:52 | 2012-01-10 15:23:52 |
+---------------------+---------------------+---------------------+
1 row in set (0.00 sec)
```

The UNIX_TIMESTAMP() function returns the current date in—or converts a given date to—UNIX timestamp format. UNIX timestamp format is in seconds since the epoch, or seconds since midnight, January 1, 1970. For example:

```
SELECT UNIX_TIMESTAMP();
```

This query produces results like the following for the time the query is run:

```
+------------------+
| UNIX_TIMESTAMP() |
+------------------+
|       1326247953 |
+------------------+
1 row in set (0.00 sec)
```

This query gets the UNIX timestamp for a specific date:

```
SELECT UNIX_TIMESTAMP('1973-12-30');
```

```
The result of this query  is:
+----------------------------+
| UNIX_TIMESTAMP('1973-12-30') |
+----------------------------+
|                  126086400 |
+----------------------------+
1 row in set (0.00 sec)
```

The FROM_UNIXTIME() function performs a conversion of a UNIX timestamp to a full datetime format when used without any options:

```
SELECT FROM_UNIXTIME('1326247953');
```

The result of this query is as follows:

```
+-----------------------------+
| FROM_UNIXTIME('1326247953') |
+-----------------------------+
| 2012-01-10 21:12:33         |
+-----------------------------+
1 row in set (0.00 sec)
```

You can use the format options from the DATE_FORMAT() functions to display a timestamp in a more appealing manner:

```
SELECT FROM_UNIXTIME(UNIX_TIMESTAMP(), '%D %M %Y at %h:%i:%s');
```

The result of this query at the moment I wrote this is this:

```
+------------------------------------------------------------+
| FROM_UNIXTIME(UNIX_TIMESTAMP(), '%D %M %Y at %h:%i:%s')    |
+------------------------------------------------------------+
| 10th January 2012 at 09:15:38                              |
+------------------------------------------------------------+
1 row in set (0.00 sec)
```

Summary

In this chapter, you learned the basics of SQL, from table creation to manipulating records. The table-creation command requires three important pieces of information: the table name, the field name, and the field definitions. Field definitions are important because a well-designed table helps speed along your database. MySQL has three different categories of data types: numeric, date and time, and string.

The INSERT command, used to add records to a table, names the table and columns you want to populate and then defines the values. When placing values in the INSERT statement, you must enclose strings within single or double quotes. The SELECT SQL command is used to retrieve records from specific tables. The * character enables you to easily select all fields for all records in a table, but you can also specify particular column names. If the resultset is too long, the LIMIT clause provides a simple method for extracting slices of results if you indicate a starting position and the number of records to return. To order the results, use the ORDER BY clause to select the columns to sort. Sorts can be performed on integers, dates, and strings, in either ascending or descending order. The default order is ascending. Without specifying an order, results display in the order they appear in the table.

You can pick and choose which records you want to return using WHERE clauses to test for the validity of conditions. Comparison or logical operators are used in WHERE clauses, and sometimes both types are used for compound statements. Selecting records from multiple tables within one statement is as advanced as it gets because this type of statement—called JOIN—requires forethought and planning to produce correct results. Common types of JOIN are INNER JOIN, LEFT JOIN, and RIGHT JOIN, although MySQL supports many different kinds of JOIN. You also learned that you can use subqueries instead of JOINs when working with multiple tables.

The UPDATE and REPLACE commands modify existing data in your MySQL tables. UPDATE is good for changing values in specific columns and for changing values in multiple records based on specific conditions. REPLACE is a variation of INSERT that deletes and then reinserts a record with a matching primary key. Be careful when using UPDATE to change values in a column because failure to add a condition results in the given column being updated throughout all records in the table.

The DELETE command is simple: It removes whole records from tables. This also makes it dangerous, so be sure you give DELETE privileges only to users who can handle the responsibility. You can specify conditions when using DELETE so that records are removed only if a particular expression in a WHERE clause is true. Also, you can delete smaller sets of records in your table using a LIMIT clause. If you have an exceptionally large table, deleting portions is less resource-intensive than deleting each record in a huge table.

You were introduced to MySQL functions that perform actions on strings, dates, and times. If you have strings in MySQL that you want to concatenate or for which you want to count characters, you can use functions such as CONCAT(), CONCAT_WS(), and LENGTH(). To pad or remove padding from strings, use RPAD(), LPAD(), TRIM(), LTRIM(), and RTRIM() to get just the strings you want. You can also find the location of a string within another string, or return a part of a given string using the LOCATE(), SUBSTRING(), LEFT(), and RIGHT() functions. Functions such as LCASE(), UCASE(), REPEAT(), and REPLACE() also return variations of the original strings. MySQL's built-in date and time functions can definitely take some of the load off your application by internally formatting dates and times and performing the date and time arithmetic. The formatting options used for the DATE_FORMAT() function provide a simple method to produce a custom display string from any sort of date field. The DATE_ADD() and DATE_SUB() functions and their numerous available interval types help you determine dates and times in the past or future. In addition, functions such as DAY(), WEEK(), MONTH(), and YEAR() prove useful for extracting parts of dates for use in WHERE or ORDER BY clauses.

Q&A

Q. *What characters can I use to name my tables and fields, and what is the character limit?*

A. The maximum length of database, table, or field names is 64 characters. Any character you can use in a directory name or filename, you can use in database and table names, except / and .. These limitations are in place because MySQL creates directories and files in your filesystem, which correspond to database and table names. No character limitations (besides length) apply in field names.

Q. *Can I use multiple functions in one statement, such as making a concatenated string all uppercase?*

A. Sure. Just be mindful of your opening and closing parentheses. This example shows how to uppercase the concatenated first and last names from the master_name table:

```
SELECT UCASE(CONCAT_WS(' ', firstname, lastname)) FROM master_name;
```

The results would be something like this:

```
+-------------------------------------------+
| UCASE(CONCAT_WS(' ', firstname, lastname)) |
+-------------------------------------------+
| JOHN SMITH                                |
| JANE SMITH                                |
| JIMBO JONES                               |
| ANDY SMITH                                |
| CHRIS JONES                               |
| ANNA BELL                                 |
| JIMMY CARR                                |
| ALBERT SMITH                              |
| JOHN DOE                                  |
+-------------------------------------------+
9 rows in set (0.00 sec)
```

If you want to uppercase just the last name, use this:

```
SELECT CONCAT_WS(' ', firstname, UCASE(lastname)) FROM master_name;
```

The results would be something like this:

```
+-------------------------------------------+
| CONCAT_WS(' ', firstname, UCASE(lastname)) |
+-------------------------------------------+
| John SMITH                                |
| Jane SMITH                                |
```

```
| Jimbo JONES                              |
| Andy SMITH                               |
| Chris JONES                              |
| Anna BELL                                |
| Jimmy CARR                               |
| Albert SMITH                             |
| John DOE                                 |
+-----------------------------------------+
9 rows in set (0.00 sec)
```

Workshop

The workshop is designed to help you review what you've learned and begin putting your knowledge into practice.

Quiz

1. The integer 56678685 could be which data type(s)?

2. How would you define a field that could contain only the following strings: apple, pear, banana, cherry?

3. What would be the LIMIT clauses for selecting the first 25 records of a table? Then the next 25?

4. How do you formulate a string comparison using LIKE to match first names of John or Joseph?

5. How do you explicitly refer to a field called id in a table called table1?

6. Write a SQL statement that joins two tables, orders and items_ordered, each of which has a primary key of order_id. From the orders table, select the following fields: order_name and order_date. From the items_ordered table, select the item_description field.

7. Write a SQL query to find the starting position of a substring "grape" in a string "applepearbananagrape".

8. Write a query that selects the last five characters from the string "applepear-bananagrape".

Answers

1. MEDIUMINT, INT, or BIGINT.

2. ENUM ('apple', 'pear', 'banana', 'cherry')

   or

   SET ('apple', 'pear', 'banana', 'cherry')

3. LIMIT 0, 25 and LIMIT 25, 25

4. LIKE 'Jo%'

5. Use table1.id instead of id in your query.

6. SELECT orders.order_name, orders.order_date, items_ordered.item_description FROM orders LEFT JOIN items_ordered ON orders.order_id = items_ordered.id;

7. SELECT LOCATE('grape', 'applepearbananagrape');

8. SELECT RIGHT("applepearbananagrape", 5);

Activity

Take the time to create some sample tables and practice using basic INSERT and SELECT commands.

## CHAPTER 17

Using Transactions and Stored Procedures in MySQL

In this chapter, you learn the following:

▶ The basics of transactions and how to use them in MySQL

▶ The basics of stored procedures and how to create and access them in MySQL

In the preceding chapter, you learned the basics of SQL and how to use the MySQL command-line interface to issue queries and retrieve the results. Armed with only that knowledge, you can successfully complete the projects found in the remaining chapters of this book. However, when you move forward with your knowledge and think about building applications suitable for use in an enterprise environment, you might require more advanced tactics to maintain the integrity of your data and enhance your application's communication with MySQL.

Although the remaining chapters in this book do not contain elements from this chapter—keeping the examples as simple as possible so that your foundational knowledge is strong—you can easily update the code on your own to include the information you learn in this chapter.

What Are Transactions?

Database transactions are sets of queries that must execute in such a way so that if one query fails to execute completely they all fail. For instance, suppose that you have a set of three queries, the second dependent on the results of the first, and the third dependent on the results of the second. If the second query fails, you need to have a way to negate the results of the first query; similarly, if the third query fails, you need to negate the results of the first and second queries, as well.

By instituting transactional processing in your database-driven applications, you ensure the integrity of the data stored in your database. The following sections describe the process of using transactions both through the command-line interface and PHP functions.

> **NOTE**
>
> Fully transactional tables in MySQL are available when using the InnoDB storage engine. Beginning with MySQL 5.5.5, InnoDB is the default storage engine for new tables (see http://dev.mysql.com/doc/refman/5.5/en/innodb-default-se.html for more information). If your tables are of the MyISAM type, they will not be fully transactional.

Basic Syntax Used in Transactions

You need to understand the following key terms when thinking about using transactions with MySQL:

▶ COMMIT—This command occurs at the end of the series of queries in your transaction and is issued only if all the required queries have executed successfully.

▶ ROLLBACK—This command is used when one or more of the series of queries in your transaction fails and resets the affected tables to their pretransaction state.

Going back to the scenario mentioned at the start of this discussion, of three queries dependent on each other, a sequence of events in the MySQL command-line interface might look something like this:

1. Issue the BEGIN command to begin a new transaction.

2. Select a value from table1 to insert into table2.

3. If a value cannot be selected from table1, issue a ROLLBACK command to ensure that the transaction ends and that the tables return to their previous state.

4. If a value can be selected from table1, insert a value into table2.

5. If the insertion of a record into table2 fails, issue a ROLLBACK command to ensure that the transaction ends and that the tables return to their previous state.

6. If a value can be inserted into table1, insert a value into table2.

7. If the insertion of a record into `table3` fails, issue a `ROLLBACK` command to ensure that the transaction ends and that the tables return to their previous state.

8. However, if the insertion of a record into `table3` is successful, issue a `COMMIT` command to ensure that the transaction ends and that the tables update appropriately.

For more information on the inner workings of transactions in MySQL, see the MySQL Manual at http://dev.mysql.com/doc/refman/5.5/en/sql-syntax-transactions.html.

The next section provides an example of transactions as used with inventory and sales records tables.

Working Example Using Transactions

For the purposes of this example, suppose that you've created an online storefront with database tables that hold inventory, sales records, and the line items for the sales records. The `CREATE` statements might look something like this:

```
CREATE TABLE store_inventory (
    id int not null primary key auto_increment,
    item_name varchar(50),
    item_price float(6,2),
    item_qty int
) ENGINE=InnoDB;

CREATE TABLE store_orders (
    id int not null primary key auto_increment,
    purchaser_name varchar(50),
    purchase_date datetime
) ENGINE=InnoDB;

CREATE TABLE store_orders_items (
    id int not null primary key auto_increment,
    order_id int,
    inventory_id int,
    item_qty int
) ENGINE=InnoDB;
```

In the `store_inventory` table for this example, you can find two records:

```
+----+------------+------------+----------+
| id | item_name  | item_price | item_qty |
+----+------------+------------+----------+
| 1  | Great Book | 19.99      | 10       |
| 2  | Awesome CD | 9.99       | 20       |
+----+------------+------------+----------+
```

If a shopper wants to purchase two Great Books and one Awesome CD through your online store, the process would go something like this:

1. The user completes an online form and attempts to pay for the purchases, so issue a BEGIN command for the transaction that would be part of the checkout script:

```
BEGIN;
```

2. Decrement the quantity of items in the store_inventory table:

```
UPDATE store_inventory SET item_qty = item_qty - 2 WHERE id = 1;
UPDATE store_inventory SET item_qty = item_qty - 1 WHERE id = 2;
```

3. Add a record to the store_orders table:

```
INSERT INTO store_orders (purchaser_name, purchase_date)
        VALUES ('John Smith', now());
```

4. If adding the record fails, issue a ROLLBACK command to reset the available quantity of the items:

```
ROLLBACK;
```

5. If adding the record succeeds, get the ID of the record just added and use it in your query to add line items to the sales record by inserting records in the store_orders_items table:

```
INSERT INTO store_orders_items (order_id, inventory_id, item_qty)
        VALUES ('1', '1', '2');
INSERT INTO store_orders_items (order_id, inventory_id, item_qty)
        VALUES ('1', '2', '1');
```

6. If adding the records fails, issue a ROLLBACK command to reset the available quantity of the items and remove the record in store_orders:

```
ROLLBACK;
```

7. If adding the records succeeds but the subsequent charging of a credit card or other payment method fails, issue a ROLLBACK command to reset the available quantity of the items, remove the record in store_orders, and remove the records in store_orders_items:

```
ROLLBACK;
```

8. If adding the records succeeds and the subsequent charging of a credit card or other payment method succeeds, issue a COMMIT command to ensure that all the changes are stored and the transaction ends:

```
COMMIT;
```

Of course, an online storefront does not directly interface with MySQL via the command-line interface but rather through a scripting language such as PHP. However, if you understand the processes behind the transaction, plugging it into PHP is simple—issuing the queries and commands listed previously is no different from any other PHP-to-MySQL communication, which you learn about in Chapter 18, "Interacting with MySQL Using PHP."

In addition to the information you learn in Chapter 18, be sure to review these function definitions in the PHP Manual if you intend to use transactions in your scripts:

- `mysqli_autocommit()`—http://www.php.net/mysqli_autocommit

- `mysqli_commit()`—http://www.php.net/mysqli_commit

- `mysqli_rollback()`—http://www.php.net/mysqli_rollback

I also can't stress enough that you review the MySQL Manual for more information on transactions, at http://dev.mysql.com/doc/refman/5.5/en/sql-syntax-transactions.html, especially the areas that discuss the types of transactions that cannot be rolled back—administrative actions, for the most part, but still useful to know.

What Are Stored Procedures?

Simply put, a stored procedure is a procedure in SQL that is stored in the database server rather than the web server. You might be thinking that you don't store any procedures on the web server, but in fact you do: Any script that contains SQL queries counts as a procedure stored on the web server. For example, every query in your application that selects, deletes, updates, or inserts data into tables—which you will have painstakingly coded in your scripts—can be stored in the database as a stored procedure and referenced as such in your scripts.

Proponents of using stored procedures in code point to performance and maintenance as key reasons for doing so:

- **Better performance**—Stored procedures exist as precompiled SQL in the database, so a typical two-step process (compile and execute) becomes a single-step process (execute).

- **Ease of maintenance**—Maintaining one statement in one place (the database) is significantly less time-consuming than maintaining one statement in numerous places, such as all through scripts on your web server. In addition, storing all your statements in the database as opposed to actual text files in your web server document root is one more line of defense should someone gain access to the files on your web server; all that person has are queries that call stored procedures instead of the logic of the procedure itself.

An example of a useful stored procedure is the SQL query used to generate a report of some sort—be it financial data, sales inventory, or otherwise; just imagine a complex query that involves a lot of processing. Creating a stored procedure out of this type of query goes along with the performance benefits of stored procedures. If you have a simple query used often throughout your application, creating a stored procedure for it would go along with the maintenance benefits of stored procedures. Regardless of the simplicity or complexity of the stored procedure, creating and using it follows the same basic process.

This stored procedure example uses the following table:

```
CREATE TABLE testSP (
    id int not null primary key auto_increment,
    field_name varchar(25),
    date_added datetime
) ENGINE=InnoDB;
```

The values of this table for testing purposes are as follows:

```
+----+------------+---------------------+
| id | field_name | date_added          |
+----+------------+---------------------+
|  1 | Value 1    | 2012-01-23 09:40:24 |
|  2 | Value 2    | 2012-01-24 09:40:24 |
|  3 | Value 3    | 2012-01-25 09:40:24 |
|  4 | Value 4    | 2012-01-26 09:40:24 |
|  5 | Value 5    | 2012-01-27 09:40:24 |
|  6 | Value 6    | 2012-01-30 09:40:24 |
|  7 | Value 7    | 2012-01-31 09:40:24 |
|  8 | Value 8    | 2012-02-01 09:40:24 |
|  9 | Value 9    | 2012-02-02 09:40:24 |
| 10 | Value 10   | 2012-02-14 09:40:24 |
+----+------------+---------------------+
```

Moving past this sample table and into the stored procedure syntax, you next must ensure that MySQL knows the delimiter character you'll be using in your stored procedures. This example uses // as the delimiter, so you issue the following query:

```
DELIMITER //
```

The syntax for creating a basic stored procedure is as follows:

```
CREATE PROCEDURE procedure_name () query //
```

For this example, the stored procedure simply selects all data from the `testSP` table that has been added in the past 7 days. The name of the stored procedure is sp1:

```
CREATE PROCEDURE sp1 () SELECT * FROM testSP WHERE  date_added BETWEEN
    DATE_SUB(NOW(), INTERVAL 7 DAY) AND NOW() //
```

To call the stored procedure, use the `CALL` command:

```
CALL sp1 () //
```

The results of the stored procedure (the `SELECT` query) are returned to you:

```
+----+------------+---------------------+
| id | field_name | date_added          |
+----+------------+---------------------+
|  2 | Value 2    | 2012-01-24 09:40:24 |
|  3 | Value 3    | 2012-01-25 09:40:24 |
|  4 | Value 4    | 2012-01-26 09:40:24 |
|  5 | Value 5    | 2012-01-27 09:40:24 |
|  6 | Value 6    | 2012-01-30 09:40:24 |
+----+------------+---------------------+
```

In Chapter 18, you learn the process for issuing these and all SQL queries using PHP.

Clearly, these few pages do not even begin to scratch the surface of working with stored procedures. This section intends only to introduce you to the concept. Additional recommended reading includes the MySQL Manual entries on stored procedures, at http://dev.mysql.com/doc/refman/5.5/en/stored-routines.html.

Summary

This short chapter provided an introduction to the concepts of transactional processing and the use of stored procedures in MySQL when using the InnoDB storage engine. In addition to a brief overview of both topics, real-life examples described each of these advanced topics. The overall purpose of this chapter was to introduce you to some concepts and keywords you should understand by the time you are developing enterprise applications on your own. Keep these ideas in the back of your mind as you work through the examples in this book and try to find ways to improve on the basic queries used.

Q&A

Q. *Do I have to use transactions all the time now that MySQL supports them?*

A. No, especially not if the dynamic aspect of your application or site is for dynamic *display* of data and not for dynamic *insertion* of data. In addition, if the insertion of data is not necessarily related to any financial- or inventory-related actions, you could get away with not using transactions. In other words, if you do not use transactions and an insert or update query fails, be sure that you can live with the failure—either because no money or crucial customer data would be lost.

Workshop

The workshop is designed to help you review what you've learned and begin putting your knowledge into practice.

Quiz

1. True or False: MyISAM is the default and fully transactional storage engine in MySQL.

2. If step two of a three-step transaction fails, what command would you issue?

3. What are two advantages of using stored procedures?

Answers

1. False. InnoDB is the default storage engine and supports full transactions.

2. ROLLBACK

3. Better performance and ease of maintenance

Activities

1. Think of some additional types of database interactions that might require transactions, and create your own set of tables like those shown in this chapter. Practice issuing and rolling back commands in all the logical places where your interactions could call for them.

2. Create a stored procedure (and its required tables) that reports on all sales transactions that include a specific item, that took place between two given dates.

## CHAPTER 18

Interacting with MySQL Using PHP

In this chapter, you learn the following:

▶ How to connect to MySQL using PHP

▶ How to insert and select data through PHP scripts

Now that you have learned the basics of PHP and the basics of working with MySQL, you are ready to make the two interact. Think of PHP as a conduit to MySQL: The commands you learned in the previous chapter are the same commands that you send to MySQL in this chapter, only this time you send them with PHP.

MySQL or MySQLi Functions?

If you are returning to PHP from working with it years earlier, or have worked with current versions of PHP but with very old versions of MySQL, you *might* have used the mysql_* family of functions. You might also find code examples all over the Internet that use the mysql_* family of functions.

However, since MySQL 4.1.3 (well over 7 years ago at this point), the database system includes functionality necessitating new communications methods in PHP, all encompassed in the mysqli_* family of functions.

All code in this chapter, and throughout the rest of this book, uses the mysqli_* family of functions. For more information, see the PHP Manual chapter "MySQL Improved Extension," at http://www.php.net/mysqli.

Connecting to MySQL with PHP

To successfully use the PHP functions to talk to MySQL, you must have MySQL running at a location to which your web server can connect (not necessarily the same machine as your web server). You also must have created a user (with a password), and you must know the name of the database to which you want to connect. If you followed the instructions in Chapter 2, "Installing and Configuring MySQL," and Chapter 4, "Installing and Configuring PHP," you should already have taken care of this. If you are using PHP and MySQL as part of a hosting package at an Internet service provider, make sure that you have either been given or have created a username, password, and database name before proceeding.

In all script examples in this chapter, the database name is testDB, the user is joeuser, and the password is somepass. Substitute your own information when you use these scripts.

<u>NOTE</u>

> All code in this chapter (as well as other chapters moving forward) reflect the procedural use of the mysqli_* family of functions. You can also use these functions in an object-oriented way. For more information on that, visit the PHP Manual at http://www.php.net/mysqli.
>
> If you are coming to PHP from an object-oriented programming language or have an object-oriented mindset, I recommend reviewing the object-oriented functionality in the PHP Manual and substituting it where appropriate—conceptually, these processes are all quite similar.
>
> However, if you are new to programming, or have not yet embraced an object-oriented mindset, there is nothing wrong with learning the procedural style or using it in your daily work. I continue to use procedural programming throughout this book because it has proven the best way for new programmers to understand the processes.

Making a Connection

The basic syntax for a connection to MySQL is as follows:

```
$mysqli = mysqli_connect("hostname", "username", "password", "database");
```

The value of $mysqli is the result of the function and is used in later functions for communicating with MySQL.

With sample values inserted, the connection code looks like this:

```
$mysqli = mysqli_connect("localhost", "joeuser", "somepass", "testDB");
```

Listing 18.1 is a working example of a connection script. It creates a new connection in line 2 and then tests to see whether an error occurred. If an error occurred, line 5 prints an error message and uses the `mysqli_connect_error()` function to print the message. If no error occurs, line 8 prints a message that includes host information resulting from calling the `mysqli_get_host_info()` function.

LISTING 18.1 A Simple Connection Script

```
1:  <?php
2:  $mysqli = new mysqli("localhost", "joeuser", "somepass", "testDB");
3:
4:  if (mysqli_connect_errno()) {
5:      printf("Connect failed: %s\n", mysqli_connect_error());
6:      exit();
7:  } else {
8:      printf("Host information: %s\n", mysqli_get_host_info($mysqli));
9:  }
10: ?>
```

Save this script as `mysqlconnect.php` and place it in the document area of your web server. Access the script with your web browser and you will see something like the following, if the connection was successful:

```
Host information: localhost via TCP/IP
```

You might also see this:

```
Host information: Localhost via UNIX socket
```

If the connection fails, an error message is printed. Line 5 generates an error via the `mysqli_connect_error()` function. An example is shown here:

```
Connect failed: Access denied for user 'joeuser'@'localhost' (using password:
  YES)
```

```
However, if the connection is successful, line 8 prints the output of
  mysqli_get_host_info(), such as examples above.
```

Although the connection closes when the script finishes its execution, it is a good practice to close the connection explicitly. You can see how to do this in line 9 of Listing 18.2, using the `mysqli_close()` function.

LISTING 18.2 The Modified Simple Connection Script

```
1:  <?php
2:  $mysqli = new mysqli("localhost", "joeuser", "somepass", "testDB");
3:
4:  if (mysqli_connect_errno()) {
5:      printf("Connect failed: %s\n", mysqli_connect_error());
6:      exit();
```

LISTING 18.2   Continued

```
7:  } else {
8:    printf("Host information: %s\n", mysqli_get_host_info($mysqli));
9:    mysqli_close($mysqli);
10:  }
11:  ?>
```

We did not use the `mysql_close()` function after line 5 because if line 5 is executed, it is because no connection was made in the first place.

That's all there is to basic connectivity to MySQL using PHP. The next section covers the query execution functions, which are much more interesting than simply opening a connection and letting it sit there.

Executing Queries

Half the battle in executing MySQL queries using PHP is knowing how to write the SQL—and you've already learned the basics of this in previous chapters. The `mysqli_query()` function in PHP is used to send your SQL query to MySQL.

In your script, first make the connection and then execute a query. The script in Listing 18.3 creates a simple table called `testTable`.

LISTING 18.3   A Script to Create a Table

```
1:  <?php
2:  $mysqli = mysqli_connect("localhost", "joeuser", "somepass", "testDB");
3:
4:  if (mysqli_connect_errno()) {
5:      printf("Connect failed: %s\n", mysqli_connect_error());
6:      exit();
7:  } else {
8:      $sql = "CREATE TABLE testTable
9:              (id INT NOT NULL PRIMARY KEY AUTO_INCREMENT,
10:             testField VARCHAR(75))";
11:     $res = mysqli_query($mysqli, $sql);
12:
13:     if ($res === TRUE) {
14:         echo "Table testTable successfully created.";
15:     } else {
16:         printf("Could not create table: %s\n", mysqli_error($mysqli));
17:     }
18:
19:     mysqli_close($mysqli);
20:  }
21:  ?>
```

NOTE

When you issue queries via a script, the semicolon at the end of the SQL statement is not required.

In lines 8–10, the text that makes up the SQL statement is assigned to the variable $sql. This is arbitrary, and you do not even need to place the content of your SQL query in a separate variable. (It appears as such in the example so that the different parts of this process are clear.)

The mysqli_query function returns a value of true or false, and this value is checked in the if...else statement beginning in line 13. If the value of $res is true, a success message is printed to the screen. If you access MySQL through the command-line interface to verify the creation of the testTable table, you will see the following output of DESCRIBE testTable:

```
+-----------+-------------+------+-----+---------+----------------+
| Field     | Type        | Null | Key | Default | Extra          |
+-----------+-------------+------+-----+---------+----------------+
| id        | int(11)     |      | PRI | NULL    | auto_increment |
| testField | varchar(75) | YES  |     | NULL    |                |
+-----------+-------------+------+-----+---------+----------------+
```

If this is the case, congratulations; you have successfully created a table in your MySQL database using PHP.

However, if the value of $res is not true and the table was not created, an error message appears, generated by the mysqli_error() function.

Retrieving Error Messages

Take some time to familiarize yourself with the mysqli_error() function; it will become your friend. When used in conjunction with the PHP die() function, which simply exits the script at the point at which it appears, the mysqli_error() function returns a helpful error message when you make a mistake.

For example, now that you have created a table called testTable, you cannot execute that script again without an error. Try to execute the script again; when you execute the script, you should see something like the following in your web browser:

```
Could not create table: Table 'testtable' already exists
```

How exciting! Move on to the next section to start inserting data into your table, and soon you'll be retrieving and formatting it via PHP.

Working with MySQL Data

Inserting, updating, deleting, and retrieving data all revolve around the use of the mysqli_query() function to execute the basic SQL queries you learned about in Chapter 16, "Learning Basic SQL Commands." For INSERT, UPDATE, and DELETE queries, no additional scripting is required after the query has been executed because you're not displaying any results (unless you want to). When using SELECT queries, you have a few options for displaying the data retrieved by your query. After an important message about SQL Injection, we start with the basics and insert some data so that you'll have something to retrieve later.

Avoiding SQL Injection

In the table-creation script in Listing 18.3, the data used in the SQL query was hard-coded into the script. However, in the types of dynamic websites or web-based applications that you are likely to build, you will most often be INSERTing data into a table or SELECTing from a table based on user input from a form or other process. If you do not pay attention to this user input and sanitize it before using it in your queries, you are vulnerable to SQL injection.

SQL injection happens when nefarious individuals take the opportunity to type full or partial SQL queries in your form fields, with the assumption that when the script processes these queries, security will be breached and data potentially exposed.

NOTE

> A famous XKCD comic strip, informally known as the "Little Bobby Tables" strip, perfectly illustrates the issue of SQL injections. This strip is often referenced in discussion forums and other programming-related help sites, with respondents saying "Don't forget Little Bobby Tables!" when providing answers to form input and query-related questions. You can see the strip at http://xkcd.com/327/.

Take the following example, which attempts to gather user information from a table called users where the name field matches a value completed in a form; this is much like a web-based login process:

```
SELECT * FROM users
WHERE name = '".$_POST['username_from_form']."';
```

Imagine the value entered in the username_from_form field is something like this:

```
' or '1'='1
```

This results in a full query as follows:

```
SELECT * FROM users
WHERE name = ' ' or '1'='1';
```

This query always results in a valid response, because 1 = 1 always returns true.

You probably get the idea, but if not, the PHP Manual has several more examples on the SQL Injection page at http://www.php.net/manual/en/security.database.sql-injection.php. Throughout this book, the code examples limit vulnerability to SQL injection, with one exception: displaying error messages. While you are learning, and operating in a development rather than production environment, I support the printing of error messages to the screen so that you understand what is happening (or not). In a production environment, you should suppress error messages, especially when they show the names of database users or tables.

After you have mastered the concepts involved with working with MySQL and PHP in the procedural ways as indicated throughout this book, take a look at the PDO (PHP Data Objects) abstraction layer for further hardening of your production applications: http://www.php.net/manual/en/book.pdo.php. A good place to start would be the section on prepared statements and stored procedures: http://www.php.net/manual/en/pdo.prepared-statements.php.

TIP

Inserting Data with PHP

The easiest (and safest) method for inserting data at this stage in the game is to simply hard-code the INSERT statement, as shown in Listing 18.4.

LISTING 18.4 A Script to Insert a Record

```
1:   <?php
2:   $mysqli = mysqli_connect("localhost", "joeuser", "somepass", "testDB");
3:
4:   if (mysqli_connect_errno()) {
5:       printf("Connect failed: %s\n", mysqli_connect_error());
6:       exit();
7:   } else {
8:       $sql = "INSERT INTO testTable (testField) VALUES ('some value')";
9:       $res = mysqli_query($mysqli, $sql);
10:
11:      if ($res === TRUE) {
12:            echo "A record has been inserted.";
13:      } else {
14:          printf("Could not insert record: %s\n", mysqli_error($mysqli));
15:      }
16:
17:      mysqli_close($mysqli);
18:  }
19:  ?>
```

The only change between this script—for record insertion—and the script in Listing 18.3 for table creation is the SQL query stored in the $sql variable on line 8 and text modifications on lines 12 and 14. The connection code and the structure for issuing a query remain the same. In fact, most procedural code for accessing MySQL falls into this same type of code template.

Call this script mysqlinsert.php and place it on your web server. Running this script results in the addition of a row to the testTable table. To enter more records than the one shown in the script, you can either make a long list of hard-coded SQL statements and use mysqli_query() multiple times to execute these statements or you can create a form-based interface to the record addition script, which we do next.

To create the form for this script, you need only one field, because the id field can automatically increment. The action of the form is the name of the record-addition script; let's call it insert.php. Your HTML form might look something like Listing 18.5.

LISTING 18.5   An Insert Form

```
1:   <!DOCTYPE html>
2:   <html>
3:   <head>
4:   <title>Record Insertion Form</title>
5:   </head>
6:   <body>
7:   <form action="insert.php" method="POST">
8:   <p><label for="testfield">Text to Add:</label><br/>
9:   <input type="text" id="testfield" name="testfield" size="30" /></p>
10:  <button type="submit" name="submit" value="insert">Insert Record</button>
11:  </form>
12:  </body>
13:  </html>
```

Save this file as insert_form.html and put it in the document root of your web server. Next, create the insert.php script shown in Listing 18.6. The value entered in the form replaces the hard-coded values in the SQL query with a variable called $_POST['testfield'] (guarded against SQL injection, of course).

LISTING 18.6   An Insert Script Used with the Form

```
1:   <?php
2:   $mysqli = mysqli_connect("localhost", "joeuser", "somepass", "testDB");
3:
4:   if (mysqli_connect_errno()) {
5:       printf("Connect failed: %s\n", mysqli_connect_error());
6:       exit();
7:   } else {
8:       $clean_text = mysqli_real_escape_string($mysqli, $_POST['testfield']);
9:       $sql = "INSERT INTO testTable (testField)
```

```
10:               VALUES ('".$clean_text."')";
11:     $res = mysqli_query($mysqli, $sql);
12:
13:     if ($res === TRUE) {
14:             echo "A record has been inserted.";
15:     } else {
16:         printf("Could not insert record: %s\n", mysqli_error($mysqli));
17:     }
18:
19:     mysqli_close($mysqli);
20: }
21: ?>
```

The only changes between this script and the script in Listing 18.4 is line 8, where the form input is sanitized to avoid SQL injection, and in line 10, where we use the sanitized string $clean_text in place of the hard-coded text string from the previous example. To sanitize the input, we use the mysqli_real_escape_string() function; this function requires that a connection has already been made, and so it is placed in this position within the else portion of the if...else statement.

Save the script as insert.php and put it in the document root of your web server. In your web browser, access the HTML form that you created. It should look something like Figure 18.1.

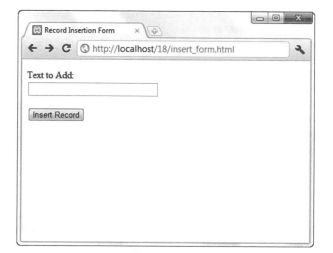

FIGURE 18.1
The HTML form for adding a record.

Enter a string in the Text to Add field, as shown in Figure 18.2.

FIGURE 18.2
Text typed in
the form field.

Finally, click the Insert Record button to execute the insert.php script and insert the record. If successful, you will see results similar to Figure 18.3.

FIGURE 18.3
The record has
been success-
fully added.

To verify the work that has been done with PHP, you can use the MySQL command-line interface to view the records in the table using a SELECT query:

```
SELECT * FROM testTable;
```

The output should be as follows:

```
+----+--------------------+
| id | testField          |
+----+--------------------+
|  1 | some value         |
|  2 | Little Bobby Tables |
+----+--------------------+
2 rows in set (0.00 sec)
```

Next you learn how to retrieve and format results with PHP, and not just the command-line interface.

Retrieving Data with PHP

Because you have a few rows in your testTable table, you can write a PHP script to retrieve that data. Starting with the basics, we write a script that issues a SELECT query but doesn't overwhelm you with result data. Let's just get the number of rows. To do this, use the mysqli_num_rows() function; see line 12 of Listing 18.7.

LISTING 18.7 A Script to Retrieve Data

```
1:  <?php
2:  $mysqli = mysqli_connect("localhost", "joeuser", "somepass", "testDB");
3:
4:  if (mysqli_connect_errno()) {
5:      printf("Connect failed: %s\n", mysqli_connect_error());
6:      exit();
7:  } else {
8:      $sql = "SELECT * FROM testTable";
9:      $res = mysqli_query($mysqli, $sql);
10:
11:     if ($res) {
12:         $number_of_rows = mysqli_num_rows($res);
13:         printf("Result set has %d rows.\n", $number_of_rows);
14:     } else {
15:         printf("Could not retrieve records: %s\n", mysqli_error($mysqli));
16:     }
17:
18:     mysqli_free_result($res);
19:     mysqli_close($mysqli);
20: }
21: ?>
```

Save this script as count.php, place it in your web server document directory, and access it through your web browser. You should see a message like this (the actual number will vary depending on how many records you inserted into the table):

```
Result set has 4 rows.
```

Line 12 uses the `mysqli_num_rows()` function to retrieve the number of rows in the resultset ($res), and it places the value in a variable called $number_of_rows. Line 13 prints this number to your browser. The number should be equal to the number of records you inserted during testing.

There's a new function in this listing that was not in previous listings. Line 18 shows the use of the `mysqli_free_result()` function. Using `mysqli_free_result()` before closing the connection with `mysqli_close()` ensures that all memory associated with the query and result is freed for use by other scripts.

Now that you know there are some records in the table (four, according to the output), you can get fancy and fetch the actual contents of those records. You can do this in a few ways, but the easiest method is to retrieve each row from the table as an array.

You use a `while` statement to go through each record in the resultset, placing the values of each field into a specific variable and then displaying the results onscreen. The syntax of `mysqli_fetch_array()` is as follows:

```
$newArray = mysqli_fetch_array($result_set);
```

Follow along using the sample script in Listing 18.8.

LISTING 18.8   A Script to Retrieve Data and Display Results

```
 1:  <?php
 2:  $mysqli = mysqli_connect("localhost", "joeuser", "somepass", "testDB");
 3:
 4:  if (mysqli_connect_errno()) {
 5:      printf("Connect failed: %s\n", mysqli_connect_error());
 6:      exit();
 7:  } else {
 8:      $sql = "SELECT * FROM testTable";
 9:      $res = mysqli_query($mysqli, $sql);
10:
11:      if ($res) {
12:          while ($newArray = mysqli_fetch_array($res, MYSQLI_ASSOC)) {
13:              $id  = $newArray['id'];
14:              $testField = $newArray['testField'];
15:              echo "The ID is ".$id." and the text is: ".$testField."<br/>";
16:              }
17:      } else {
18:          printf("Could not retrieve records: %s\n", mysqli_error($mysqli));
19:      }
20:
21:      mysqli_free_result($res);
22:      mysqli_close($mysqli);
23:  }
24:  ?>
```

Save this script as `select.php`, place it in your web server document directory, and access it through your web browser. You should see a message for each record entered into `testTable`, as shown in Figure 18.4. This message is created in the `while` loop in lines 12 through 15.

FIGURE 18.4
Selecting records from MySQL.

As you can see, you can create an entire database-driven application using just four or five MySQLi functions. This chapter barely scratched the surface of using PHP with MySQL; there are many more MySQLi functions in PHP.

Additional MySQL Functions in PHP

More than 100 MySQL-specific functions are available through the MySQLi interface in PHP. Most of these functions are simply alternative methods of retrieving data or are used to gather information about the table structure in question. Throughout this book, especially in the project-related chapters a little later, you'll gradually be introduced to more of the MySQL-specific functions in PHP. However, for a complete list of functions, with practical examples, visit the MySQLi section of the PHP Manual at http://www.php.net/mysqli.

Summary

Using PHP and MySQL to create dynamic, database-driven websites is a breeze. Just remember that the PHP functions are essentially a gateway to the database server; anything you can enter using the MySQL command-line interface, you can use with the `mysqli_query()` function. You also learned how to avoid SQL injections when receiving user input from a form.

To connect to MySQL with PHP, you need to know your MySQL username, password, and database name. When connected, you can issue standard SQL commands with the mysqli_query() function. If you have issued a SELECT command, you can use mysqli_num_rows() to count the records returned in the resultset. If you want to display the data found, you can use mysqli_fetch_array() to get all the results during a loop and display them onscreen.

Q&A

Q. *Is it possible to use both mysql_* and mysqli_* functions in one application?*

A. If PHP was built with both libraries enabled, you can use either set of functions to talk to MySQL. However, be aware that if you use the mysql_* set of functions with a version of MySQL later than 4.1.3, you cannot access certain new functionality. In addition, if you are inconsistent with your usage throughout your application, maintenance and upkeep of your application will be time-consuming and produce less-than-optimal results.

Workshop

The workshop is designed to help you review what you've learned and begin putting your knowledge into practice.

Quiz

1. What is the primary function used to make the connection between PHP and MySQL, and what information is necessary?

2. Which PHP function retrieves the text of a MySQL error message?

3. Which PHP function counts the number of records in a resultset?

Answers

1. The mysqli_connect() function creates a connection to MySQL and requires the hostname, username, and password.

2. The mysqli_error() function returns a MySQL error message.

3. The mysqli_num_rows() function counts the number of records in a resultset.

Activities

1. Using an HTML form and PHP script, create a table that contains fields for a person's first and last names. Create another script that adds records to the table.

2. Once you have records in your table, create a PHP script that retrieves and displays these records in alphabetical order by last name.

CHAPTER 19

Managing a Simple Mailing List

In this chapter, you learn the following:

▶ How to create a subscribe/unsubscribe form and script

▶ How to create a front end for sending your message

▶ How to create the script that sends your message

This chapter provides the first of several hands-on, small projects designed to pull together your PHP and MySQL knowledge. In this chapter, you learn how to create a managed distribution list that you can use to send out newsletters or anything else to a list of email addresses in a database.

NOTE

As with all the small sample projects in this book, these projects might not be exactly what you plan to build with your new PHP and MySQL knowledge. However, I cannot stress enough that the concepts and examples shown in this and other projects are similar to those you will encounter when developing any application that uses CRUD functionality (create, read, update, delete).

The mailing mechanism you use in this chapter is not meant to be a replacement for mailing list software, which is specifically designed for bulk messages. You should use the type of system you build in this chapter only for small lists, fewer than a few hundred email addresses.

Developing the Subscription Mechanism

You learned in earlier chapters that planning is the most important aspect of creating any product. In this case, think of the elements you need for your subscription mechanism:

▶ A table to hold email addresses

▶ A way for users to add or remove their email addresses

▶ A form and script for sending the message

The following sections describe each item individually.

Creating the subscribers Table

You really need only one field in the subscribers table: to hold the email address of the user. However, you should have an ID field just for consistency among your tables, and because referencing an ID is much simpler than referencing a long email address in where clauses. So, in this case, your MySQL query would look something like this:

```
CREATE TABLE subscribers (
    id INT NOT NULL PRIMARY KEY AUTO_INCREMENT,
    email VARCHAR (150) UNIQUE NOT NULL
);
```

Note the use of UNIQUE in the field definition for email. This means that although id is the primary key, duplicates should not be allowed in the email field either. The email field is a unique key, and id is the primary key.

Log in to MySQL via the command line and issue this query. After creating the table, issue a DESC or DESCRIBE query to verify that the table has been created to your specifications, such as the following:

```
mysql> DESC subscribers;
+-------+--------------+------+-----+---------+----------------+
| Field | Type         | Null | Key | Default | Extra          |
+-------+--------------+------+-----+---------+----------------+
| id    | int(11)      | NO   | PRI | NULL    | auto_increment |
| email | varchar(150) | NO   | UNI | NULL    |                |
+-------+--------------+------+-----+---------+----------------+
2 rows in set (0.00 sec)
```

Now that you have a table in your database, you can create the form and script that place values in there.

Creating an Include File for Common Functions

Although there are only two scripts in this process, some common functions exist between them—namely, the database connection information. To make your scripts more concise in situations like this, take the common functions or code snippets and put them in a file to be included in your other scripts via the include() function that you learned about in Chapter 13, "Working with Files and Directories." Listing 19.1 contains the code shared by the scripts in this chapter.

LISTING 19.1   Common Functions in an Included File

```
1:   <?php
2:   // function to connect to database
3:   function doDB() {
4:       global $mysqli;
5:
6:       //connect to server and select database
7:       $mysqli = mysqli_connect("localhost", "joeuser",
8:           "somepass", "testDB");
9:
10:      //if connection fails, stop script execution
11:      if (mysqli_connect_errno()) {
12:          printf("Connect failed: %s\n", mysqli_connect_error());
13:          exit();
14:      }
15:  }
16:  // function to check email address
17:  function emailChecker($email) {
18:      global $mysqli, $safe_email, $check_res;
19:
20:      //check that email is not already in list
21:      $safe_email = mysqli_real_escape_string($mysqli, $email);
22:      $check_sql = "SELECT id FROM SUBSCRIBERS
23:          WHERE email = '".$safe_email."'";
24:      $check_res = mysqli_query($mysqli, $check_sql)
25:          or die(mysqli_error($mysqli));
26:  }
27:  ?>
```

Lines 3–15 set up the first function, doDB(), which is simply the database connection function. If the connection cannot be made, the script exits when this function is called; otherwise, it makes the value of $mysqli available to other parts of your script.

Lines 17–26 define a function called emailChecker(), which takes an input and returns an output—like most functions do. We look at this one in the context of the script, as we get to it in Listing 19.2

Save this file as ch19_include.php and place it on your web server. In Listing 19.2, you will see how to include this file when necessary in your scripts.

Creating the Subscription Form

The subscription form is actually an all-in-one form and script called `manage.php`, which handles both subscribe and unsubscribe requests. Listing 19.2 shows the code for `manage.php`, which uses a few user-defined functions to eliminate repetitious code and to start you thinking about creating functions on your own. The code looks long, but a line-by-line description follows (and a lot of the code just displays an HTML form, so no worries).

LISTING 19.2   Subscribe and Unsubscribe with `manage.php`

```
 1:  <?php
 2:  include 'ch19_include.php';
 3:  //determine if they need to see the form or not
 4:  if (!$_POST) {
 5:      //they need to see the form, so create form block
 6:      $display_block = <<<END_OF_BLOCK
 7:      <form method="POST" action="$_SERVER[PHP_SELF]">
 8:
 9:      <p><label for="email">Your E-Mail Address:</label><br/>
10:      <input type="email" id="email" name="email"
11:            size="40" maxlength="150" /></p>
12:
13:      <fieldset>
14:      <legend>Action:</legend><br/>
15:      <input type="radio" id="action_sub" name="action"
16:            value="sub" checked />
17:      <label for="action_sub">subscribe</label><br/>
18:      <input type="radio" id="action_unsub" name="action"
19:            value="unsub" />
20:      <label for="action_unsub">unsubscribe</label>
21:      </fieldset>
22:
23:      <button type="submit" name="submit" value="submit">Submit</button>
24:      </form>
25:  END_OF_BLOCK;
26:  } else if (($_POST) && ($_POST['action'] == "sub")) {
27:      //trying to subscribe; validate email address
28:      if ($_POST['email'] == "") {
29:          header("Location: manage.php");
30:          exit;
31:      } else {
32:          //connect to database
33:          doDB();
34:
35:          //check that email is in list
36:          emailChecker($_POST['email']);
37:
38:          //get number of results and do action
39:          if (mysqli_num_rows($check_res) < 1) {
40:              //free result
41:              mysqli_free_result($check_res);
42:
43:              //add record
44:              $add_sql = "INSERT INTO subscribers (email)
45:                      VALUES('".$safe_email."')";
```

```
46:                $add_res = mysqli_query($mysqli, $add_sql)
47:                         or die(mysqli_error($mysqli));
48:                $display_block = "<p>Thanks for signing up!</p>";
49:
50:                //close connection to MySQL
51:                mysqli_close($mysqli);
52:            } else {
53:                //print failure message
54:                $display_block = "<p>You're already subscribed!</p>";
55:            }
56:        }
57: } else if (($_POST) && ($_POST['action'] == "unsub")) {
58:        //trying to unsubscribe; validate email address
59:        if ($_POST['email'] == "") {
60:            header("Location: manage.php");
61:            exit;
62:        } else {
63:            //connect to database
64:            doDB();
65:
66:            //check that email is in list
67:            emailChecker($_POST['email']);
68:
69:            //get number of results and do action
70:            if (mysqli_num_rows($check_res) < 1) {
71:                //free result
72:                mysqli_free_result($check_res);
73:
74:                //print failure message
75:                $display_block = "<p>Couldn't find your address!</p>
76:                <p>No action was taken.</p>";
77:            } else {
78:                //get value of ID from result
79:                while ($row = mysqli_fetch_array($check_res)) {
80:                    $id = $row['id'];
81:                }
82:
83:                //unsubscribe the address
84:                $del_sql = "DELETE FROM subscribers
85:                        WHERE id = ".$id;
86:                $del_res = mysqli_query($mysqli, $del_sql)
87:                        or die(mysqli_error($mysqli));
88:                $display_block = "<p>You're unsubscribed!</p>";
89:            }
90:            mysqli_close($mysqli);
91:        }
92: }
93: ?>
94: <!DOCTYPE html>
95: <html>
96: <head>
97: <title>Subscribe/Unsubscribe to a Mailing List</title>
98: </head>
99: <body>
100: <h1>Subscribe/Unsubscribe to a Mailing List</h1>
101: <?php echo "$display_block"; ?>
102: </body>
103: </html>
```

Listing 19.2 might be long, but it's not complicated. In fact, it could be longer were it not for the user-defined functions placed in `ch19_include.php` and included on line 2 of this script.

Line 4 starts the main logic of the script. Because this script performs several actions, you need to determine which action it is currently attempting. If the presence of `$_POST` is `false`, you know that the user has not submitted the form; therefore, you must show the form to the user.

Lines 6–25 create the subscribe/unsubscribe form by storing a string in the `$display_block` variable using the heredoc format. In the heredoc format, the string delimiter can be any string identifier following <<<, as long as the ending identifier is on its own line, as you can see in this example on line 25.

NOTE

> You can learn more about the heredoc and other string formats in the PHP Manual at http://www.php.net/manual/en/language.types.string.php.

In the form, we use `$_SERVER[PHP_SELF]` as the action (line 7), and then create a text field called `email` for the user's email address (lines 9–11) and set up a set of radio buttons (lines 13–21) to find the desired task. At the end of the string creation, the script breaks out of the `if...else` construct, skips down to line 101, and proceeds to print the HTML stored in the `$display_block` variable. The form displays as shown in Figure 19.1.

FIGURE 19.1
The subscribe/
unsubscribe
form.

Back inside the `if...else` construct, if the presence of `$_POST` is `true`, you need to do something. There are two possibilities: the subscribing and unsubscribing actions for the email address provided in the form. You determine which action to take by looking at the value of `$_POST['action']` from the radio button group.

In line 26, if the presence of $_POST is true and the value of $_POST['action'] is "sub", you know the user is trying to subscribe. To subscribe, the user needs an email address, so check for one in lines 28–30. If no address is present, redirect the user back to the form.

However, if an address is present, call the doDB() function (stored in ch19_include.php) in line 34 to connect to the database so that you can issue queries. In line 36, you call the second of our user-defined functions: emailChecker(). This function takes an input ($_POST['email'], in this case) and processes it. If you look back to lines 21–25 of Listing 19.1, you'll see code within the emailChecker() function that issues a query in an attempt to find an id value in the subscribers table for the record containing the email address passed to the function. The function then returns the resultset, called $check_res, for use within the larger script.

NOTE

> Note the definition of global variables at the beginning of both user-defined functions in Listing 19.1. These variables need to be shared with the entire script, and so are declared global.

Jump down to line 39 of Listing 19.2 to see how the $check_res variable is used: The number of records referred to by the $check_res variable is counted to determine whether the email address already exists in the table. If the number of rows is less than 1, the address is not in the list, and it can be added. The record is added, the response is stored in lines 44–48, and the failure message (if the address is already in the table) is stored in line 54. At that point, the script breaks out of the if...else construct, skips down to line 101, and proceeds to print the HTML currently stored in $display_block. You'll test this functionality later.

The last combination of inputs occurs if the presence of $_POST is true and the value of the $_POST['action'] variable is "unsub". In this case, the user is trying to unsubscribe. To unsubscribe, an existing email address is required, so check for one in lines 59–61. If no address is present, send the user back to the form.

If an address is present, call the doDB() function in line 64 to connect to the database. Then, in line 67, you call emailChecker(), which again returns the resultset, $check_res. Line 70 counts the number of records in the result set to determine whether the email address already exists in the table. If the number of rows is less than 1, the address is not in the list and it cannot be unsubscribed.

In this case, the response message is stored in lines 75–76. However, if the number of rows is not less than 1, the user is unsubscribed (the record deleted) and the response is stored in lines 84–88. At that point, the script breaks out of the `if...else` construct, skips down to line 101, and proceeds to print the HTML.

Figures 19.2 through 19.5 show the various results of the script, depending on the actions selected and the status of email addresses in the database.

FIGURE 19.2
Successful
subscription.

FIGURE 19.3
Subscription
failure.

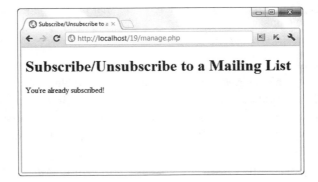

FIGURE 19.4
Successful
unsubscribe
action.

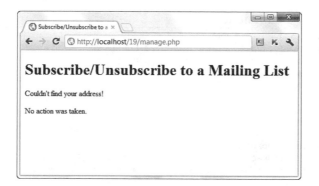

FIGURE 19.5
Unsuccessful
unsubscribe
action.

Next, you create the form and script that sends along mail to each of your subscribers.

Developing the Mailing Mechanism

With the subscription mechanism in place, you can create a basic form interface for a script that takes the content of your form and sends it to every address in your subscribers table. This is another one of those all-in-one scripts, called sendmymail.php, and it is shown in Listing 19.3.

Before attempting to use the script in this section, make sure that you have read the section in Chapter 11, "Working with Forms," regarding the configuration in your php.ini file. The php.ini file is required to send mail.

NOTE

LISTING 19.3   Send Mail to Your List of Subscribers

```
1: <?php
2: include 'ch19_include.php';
3: if (!$_POST) {
4:     //haven't seen the form, so display it
5:     $display_block = <<<END_OF_BLOCK
6:     <form method="POST" action="$_SERVER[PHP_SELF]">
7:
8:     <p><label for="subject">Subject:</label><br/>
9:     <input type="text" id="subject" name="subject" size="40" /></p>
10:
11:     <p><label for="message">Mail Body:</label><br/>
12:     <textarea id="message" name="message" cols="50"
          rows="10"></textarea></p>
13:     <button type="submit" name="submit" value="submit">Submit</button>
14:     </form>
15: END_OF_BLOCK;
16: } else if ($_POST) {
```

LISTING 19.3   Continued

```
17:        //want to send form, so check for required fields
18:        if (($_POST['subject'] == "") || ($_POST['message'] == "")) {
19:            header("Location: sendmymail.php");
20:            exit;
21:        }
22:
23:        //connect to database
24:        doDB();
25:
26:        if (mysqli_connect_errno()) {
27:            //if connection fails, stop script execution
28:            printf("Connect failed: %s\n", mysqli_connect_error());
29:            exit();
30:        } else {
31:            //otherwise, get emails from subscribers list
32:            $sql = "SELECT email FROM subscribers";
33:            $result = mysqli_query($mysqli, $sql)
34:                    or die(mysqli_error($mysqli));
35:
36:            //create a From: mailheader
37:            $mailheaders = "From: Your Mailing List
38:                <you@yourdomain.com>";
39:            //loop through results and send mail
40:            while ($row = mysqli_fetch_array($result)) {
41:                set_time_limit(0);
42:                $email = $row['email'];
43:                mail("$email", stripslashes($_POST['subject']),
44:                        stripslashes($_POST['message']), $mailheaders);
45:                $display_block .= "newsletter sent to: ".$email."<br/>";
46:            }
47:            mysqli_free_result($result);
48:            mysqli_close($mysqli);
49:        }
50: }
51: ?>
52: <!DOCTYPE html>
53: <html>
54: <head>
55: <title>Sending a Newsletter</title>
56: </head>
57: <body>
58: <h1>Send a Newsletter</h1>
59: <?php echo $display_block; ?>
60: </body>
61: </html>
```

As in Listing 19.2, the file of user-defined functions is included on line 2. Although only the database connection function is used in this file, there's no harm in having the other function in the file, as well.

The main logic of the script starts at line 3, where you determine whether the user has seen the form yet. If the presence of the $_POST variable is false, you know the user has not submitted the form; therefore, you must show the form.

Lines 5–15 create the form for sending the newsletter to your subscriber list, which uses $_SERVER[PHP_SELF] as the action (line 6), creates a text field called subject for the subject of the mail, and creates a textarea called message for the body of the mail to be sent.

At this point, the script breaks out of the if...else construct, and the HTML is printed. The form displays as shown in Figure 19.6.

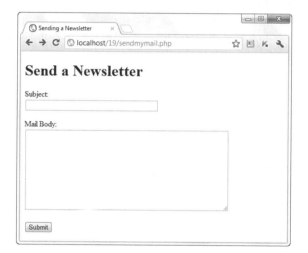

FIGURE 19.6
Form for sending the bulk mail.

If the presence of $_POST is not false, the script should send the form to the email addresses in the subscribers table. Before sending the message, you must check for the two required items from the form in lines 18–20: $_POST['subject'] and $_POST['message']. If either of these items is not present, redirect the user to the form again.

If the required items are present, the script moves on to line 24, which calls the database connection function. A query is issued in line 33, which grabs all the email addresses from the subscribers table. There is no order to these results, although you could throw an order by clause in there if you want to send them out in alphabetic order for whatever reason.

Lines 37–38 create a From: mail header, which is used inside the upcoming while loop, when the mail is sent. This header ensures that the mail looks like it is from a person and not a machine because you've specifically provided a value in this string. The while loop, which begins on line 40, extracts the email addresses from the resultset one at a time. On line 41, you use the set_time_limit() function to set the time limit to 0, or "no limit." Doing so allows the script to run for as long as it needs to.

CAUTION Because the script in Listing 19.3 simply executes the `mail()` function numerous times, it does not take into account the queuing factors in actual mailing list software, which are designed to ease the burden on your outgoing mail server. Using `set_time_limit()` does not ease its burden; it just allows the script to continue to run when it might have timed out before.

In lines 43–44, the mail is sent using the `mail()` function, inserting the values from the form where appropriate. Line 45 adds to a string that is later printed to the screen, which shows to whom the mail was sent. Figures 19.7 and 19.8 show the outcome of the script.

FIGURE 19.7
Mail has been sent!

FIGURE 19.8
The mail arrived safely.

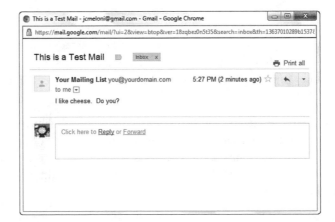

Summary

In this chapter, you applied your basic PHP and MySQL knowledge to the creation of a personal mailing list. Included were the database table creation, the subscribe and unsubscribe mechanisms, and the form and script for sending the mail.

Q&A

Q. *How can I ease the burden on my mail server?*

A. Besides looking into packaged mailing list software, you can bypass the `mail()` function and talk directly to your SMTP server via a socket connection. Such an example is shown in the PHP manual for the `fsockopen()` function (http://www.php.net/fsockopen), as well as in other developer resource sites.

Q. *Where do bounced messages go?*

A. As with any email (not just those sent in the manner described in this chapter), bounces go to whatever address you specify in your `From:` or `Reply-to:` mail headers.

Workshop

The workshop is designed to help you review what you've learned and begin putting your knowledge into practice.

Quiz

1. Which PHP function sends mail?

2. Why is `$mysqli` named as a global variable in Listing 19.1?

3. What PHP function call causes the script to execute for as long as it needs to run?

Answers

1. This is not a trick question. It's the `mail()` function!

2. Because the variable `$mysqli` is created and assigned a value in a function that is included in one script for use by another, the variable must be declared as global to ensure it is usable outside of the confines of the function in which it was created.

3. `set_time_limit(0)`

Activities

1. Modify the `manage.php` script to display the user's email as part of the response message for any action that is taken.

2. Modify the `sendmymail.php` script to add additional form fields that will correspond to section headings in the message string itself. Remember that when the form is submitted, those strings will have to be concatenated into one message string that is sent to the `mail()` function.

CHAPTER 20

Creating an Online Address Book

In this chapter, you learn the following:

- ▶ How to create relational tables for an online address book
- ▶ How to create the forms and scripts for adding and deleting records in the address book
- ▶ How to create the forms and scripts for viewing records

In this chapter, you create a manageable online address book. You learn how to create the relevant database tables, as well as the forms and scripts for adding, deleting, and viewing database records.

> **NOTE**
>
> These basic concepts are the foundations of developing any application that uses CRUD functionality (create, read, update, delete), which is precisely what a *lot* of web-based applications are.

Planning and Creating the Database Tables

When you think of an address book, the obvious fields come to mind: name, address, telephone number, email address. However, if you look at (or remember) a paper-based address book, you might note there are several entries for one person. Maybe that person has three telephone numbers, or two email addresses, and so forth—whatever *didn't* fit in the original template. In an online address book, a set of related tables helps alleviate the redundancy and repetition of information and allows you to display all information in a unified view.

Table 20.1 shows sample table and field names to use for your online address book. In a minute, you use actual SQL statements to create the tables, but first you should look at this information and try to see the relationships appear. Ask yourself which of the fields should be primary or unique keys.

TABLE 20.1   Address Book Table and Field Names

Table Name	Field Names
master_name	id, date_added, date_modified, f_name, l_name
address	id, master_id, date_added, date_modified, address, city, state, zipcode, type
telephone	id, master_id, date_added, date_modified, tel_number, type
fax	id, master_id, date_added, date_modified, fax_number, type
email	id, master_id, date_added, date_modified, email, type
personal_notes	id, master_id, date_added, date_modified, note

Notice the use of date-related fields; each table has a date_added and date_modified field in it. The fields help maintain your data; you might at some point want to issue a query that removes all records older than a certain number of months or years, or removes all records that haven't been updated within a certain period.

As you can see in the following SQL statements, the master_name table has two fields besides the ID and date-related fields: f_name and l_name, for first name and last name. The id field is the primary key. No other keys need to be primary or unique unless you really want to limit your address book to one John Smith, one Mary Jones, and so forth.

NOTE

> The field lengths for the text fields in the following statements are arbitrary; you can make them as long or as short as you want, within the allowable definition of the field type.

The following SQL statement creates the master_name table:

```
CREATE TABLE master_name (
    id INT NOT NULL PRIMARY KEY AUTO_INCREMENT,
    date_added DATETIME,
    date_modified DATETIME,
    f_name VARCHAR (75),
    l_name VARCHAR (75)
);
```

Next, you create the supplementary tables, which all relate back to the `master_name` table. For instance, the `address` table has the basic primary key `id` field, the `date_added` field, and the `date_modified` field, plus the field through which the relationship will be made—the `master_id` field.

The `master_id` is equal to the `id` field in the `master_name` table, matching the person whose address this is. The `master_id` field is not a unique key because it is a perfectly valid assumption that one person may have several address entries. You see this in the `type` field, defined as an enumerated list containing three options: `home`, `work`, or `other`. A person may have one or more of all three types, so no other keys are present in this table besides the primary key `id`. Assuming that this particular address book contains only U.S. addresses, round out the table with `address`, `city`, `state`, and `zipcode` fields:

```
CREATE TABLE address (
    id INT NOT NULL PRIMARY KEY AUTO_INCREMENT,
    master_id INT NOT NULL,
    date_added DATETIME,
    date_modified DATETIME,
    address VARCHAR (255),
    city VARCHAR (30),
    state CHAR (2),
    zipcode VARCHAR (10),
    type ENUM ('home', 'work', 'other')
);
```

The `telephone`, `fax`, and `email` tables are all variations on the same theme:

```
CREATE TABLE telephone (
    id INT NOT NULL PRIMARY KEY AUTO_INCREMENT,
    master_id INT NOT NULL,
    date_added DATETIME,
    date_modified DATETIME,
    tel_number VARCHAR (25),
    type ENUM ('home', 'work', 'other')
);
CREATE TABLE fax (
    id INT NOT NULL PRIMARY KEY AUTO_INCREMENT,
    master_id INT NOT NULL,
    date_added DATETIME,
    date_modified DATETIME,
    fax_number VARCHAR (25),
    type ENUM ('home', 'work', 'other')
);
CREATE TABLE email (
    id INT NOT NULL PRIMARY KEY AUTO_INCREMENT,
    master_id INT NOT NULL,
    date_added DATETIME,
    date_modified DATETIME,
    email VARCHAR (150),
    type ENUM ('home', 'work', 'other')
);
```

The personal_notes table also follows the same sort of pattern, except that master_id is a unique key and allows only one notes record per person:

```
CREATE TABLE personal_notes (
    id int NOT NULL PRIMARY KEY AUTO_INCREMENT,
    master_id INT NOT NULL UNIQUE,
    date_added DATETIME,
    date_modified DATETIME,
    note TEXT
);
```

Now that your tables are created, you can work through the forms and scripts for managing and viewing your records.

Creating an Include File for Common Functions

In Chapter 19, "Managing a Simple Mailing List," an included file of common functions was used to make your scripts more concise. The same thing is true in this chapter. Although the only content in the common functions file is the database connection function, this process serves two purposes: to make your scripts more concise and to eliminate the need to modify the database connection information throughout multiple files should that information change. Listing 20.1 contains the code shared by the scripts in this chapter.

LISTING 20.1   Common Functions in an Included File

```
1:  <?php
2:  function doDB() {
3:      global $mysqli;
4:
5:      //connect to server and select database; you may need it
6:      $mysqli = mysqli_connect("localhost", "joeuser",
7:          "somepass", "testDB");
8:
9:      //if connection fails, stop script execution
10:     if (mysqli_connect_errno()) {
11:         printf("Connect failed: %s\n", mysqli_connect_error());
12:         exit();
13:     }
14: }
15: ?>
```

Lines 2–14 set up the database connection function, doDB. If the connection cannot be made, the script exits when this function is called; otherwise, it makes the value of $mysqli available to other parts of your script.

Save this file as `ch20_include.php` and place it on your web server. The other code listings in this chapter include this file within the first few lines of the script.

Creating a Menu

Your online address book contains several actions, so it makes sense to create a menu for your links. Listing 20.2 creates a simple menu for all the scripts you create in this chapter, called `mymenu.html`

LISTING 20.2 Address Book Menu

```
1: <!DOCTYPE html>
2: <html>
3: <head>
4: <title>My Address Book</title>
5: </head>
6: <body>
7: <h1>My Address Book</h1>
8:
9: <p><strong>Management</strong></p>
10: <ul>
11: <li><a href="addentry.php">Add an Entry</a></li>
12: <li><a href="delentry.php">Delete an Entry</a></li>
13: </ul>
14:
15: <p><strong>Viewing</strong></p>
16: <ul>
17: <li><a href="selentry.php">Select a Record</a></li>
18: </ul>
19: </body>
20: </html>
```

Figure 20.1 shows the output of Listing 20.2. You tackle each of these items in order, starting with "Add an Entry" in the next section.

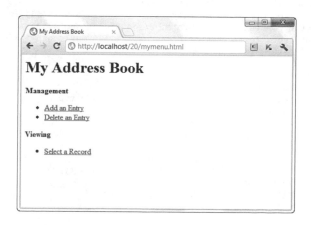

FIGURE 20.1
Address book menu.

Creating the Record-Addition Mechanism

Just because you'll potentially be adding information to six different tables doesn't mean your form or script will be monstrous. In fact, your scripts won't look much different from any of the ones you created in previous lessons. With practice, you can make these verbose scripts much more streamlined and efficient.

Listing 20.3 shows a basic record-addition script, called addentry.php, which has two parts: what to do if the form should be displayed (lines 4–89) and what actions to take if the form is being submitted (lines 91–187). Lines 3–89 simply place the contents of the HTML form into a string called $display_block.

LISTING 20.3   **Basic Record-Addition Script Called** addentry.php

```
1:    <?php
2:    include 'ch20_include.php';
3:
4:    if (!$_POST) {
5:        //haven't seen the form, so show it
6:        $display_block = <<<END_OF_TEXT
7:        <form method="post" action="$_SERVER[PHP_SELF]">
8:        <fieldset>
9:        <legend>First/Last Names:</legend><br/>
10:       <input type="text" name="f_name" size="30"
11:            maxlength="75" required="required" />
12:       <input type="text" name="l_name" size="30"
13:            maxlength="75" required="required" />
14:       </fieldset>
15:
16:       <p><label for="address">Street Address:</label><br/>
17:       <input type="text" id="address" name="address"
18:            size="30" /></p>
19:
20:       <fieldset>
21:       <legend>City/State/Zip:</legend><br/>
22:       <input type="text" name="city" size="30" maxlength="50" />
23:       <input type="text" name="state" size="5" maxlength="2" />
24:       <input type="text" name="zipcode" size="10" maxlength="10" />
25:       </fieldset>
26:
27:       <fieldset>
28:       <legend>Address Type:</legend><br/>
29:       <input type="radio" id="add_type_h" name="add_type"
30:            value="home" checked />
31:            <label for="add_type_h">home</label>
32:       <input type="radio" id="add_type_w" name="add_type"
33:            value="work" />
34:            <label for="add_type_w">work</label>
35:       <input type="radio" id="add_type_o" name="add_type"
36:            value="other" />
37:            <label for="add_type_o">other</label>
38:       </fieldset>
```

```
39:
40:       <fieldset>
41:       <legend>Telephone Number:</legend><br/>
42:       <input type="text" name="tel_number" size="30" maxlength="25" />
43:       <input type="radio" id="tel_type_h" name="tel_type"
44:              value="home" checked />
45:              <label for="tel_type_h">home</label>
46:       <input type="radio" id="tel_type_w" name="tel_type"
47:              value="work" />
48:              <label for="tel_type_w">work</label>
49:       <input type="radio" id="tel_type_o" name="tel_type"
50:              value="other" />
51:              <label for="tel_type_o">other</label>
52:       </fieldset>
53:
54:       <fieldset>
55:       <legend>Fax Number:</legend><br/>
56:       <input type="text" name="fax_number" size="30" maxlength="25" />
57:       <input type="radio" id="fax_type_h" name="fax_type"
58:              value="home" checked />
59:              <label for="fax_type_h">home</label>
60:       <input type="radio" id="fax_type_w" name="fax_type"
61:              value="work" />
62:              <label for="fax_type_w">work</label>
63:       <input type="radio" id="fax_type_o" name="fax_type"
64:              value="other" />
65:              <label for="fax_type_o">other</label>
66:       </fieldset>
67:
68:       <fieldset>
69:       <legend>Email Address:</legend><br/>
70:       <input type="email" name="email" size="30" maxlength="150" />
71:       <input type="radio" id="email_type_h" name="email_type"
72:              value="home" checked />
73:              <label for="email_type_h">home</label>
74:       <input type="radio" id="email_type_w" name="email_type"
75:              value="work" />
76:              <label for="email_type_w">work</label>
77:       <input type="radio" id="email_type_o" name="email_type"
78:              value="other" />
79:              <label for="email_type_o">other</label>
80:       </fieldset>
81:
82:       <p><label for="note">Personal Note:</label><br/>
83:       <textarea id="note" name="note" cols="35"
84:                 rows="3"></textarea></p>
85:
86:       <button type="submit" name="submit"
87:              value="send">Add Entry</button>
88:       </form>
89:  END_OF_TEXT;
```

Stop here for a minute and make sure you know what is going on in the listing so
far. Before any other code, note that the file with a user-defined function is included
on line 2. After that, as already noted, this script performs one of two tasks at any

given time: It either shows the record-addition form or it performs the SQL queries related to adding a new record.

The logic that determines the task begins at line 4, with a test for the value of $_POST. If there is no value in the $_POST superglobal, the user has not submitted the form and therefore needs to see the form. The HTML for the form is placed in a string called $display_block, from lines 6–89. The script then breaks out of the if...else construct and jumps down to line 189, which outputs the HTML and prints the value of $display_block, in this case the form. Figure 20.2 displays the outcome.

FIGURE 20.2
The record-addition form.

Pick up the code in the listing with the else if statement, or what happens if the form *has* been submitted.

LISTING 20.3   (continued)

```
90:  } else if ($_POST) {
91:      //time to add to tables, so check for required fields
92:      if (($_POST['f_name'] == "") || ($_POST['l_name'] == "")) {
93:          header("Location: addentry.php");
94:          exit;
95:      }
96:
```

```
97:      //connect to database
98:      doDB();
99:
100:     //create clean versions of input strings
101:     $safe_f_name = mysqli_real_escape_string($mysqli,
102:         $_POST['f_name']);
103:     $safe_l_name = mysqli_real_escape_string($mysqli,
104:         $_POST['l_name']);
105:     $safe_address = mysqli_real_escape_string($mysqli,
106:         $_POST['address']);
107:     $safe_city = mysqli_real_escape_string($mysqli,
108:         $_POST['city']);
109:     $safe_state = mysqli_real_escape_string($mysqli,
110:         $_POST['state']);
111:     $safe_zipcode = mysqli_real_escape_string($mysqli,
112:         $_POST['zipcode']);
113:     $safe_tel_number = mysqli_real_escape_string($mysqli,
114:         $_POST['tel_number']);
115:     $safe_fax_number = mysqli_real_escape_string($mysqli,
116:         $_POST['fax_number']);
117:     $safe_email = mysqli_real_escape_string($mysqli,
118:         $_POST['email']);
119:     $safe_note = mysqli_real_escape_string($mysqli,
120:         $_POST['note']);
121:
122:  //add to master_name table
123:  $add_master_sql = "INSERT INTO master_name (date_added,
124:      date_modified, f_name, l_name) VALUES
125:      (now(), now(), '".$safe_f_name."', '".$safe_l_name."')";
126:  $add_master_res = mysqli_query($mysqli, $add_master_sql)
127:      or die(mysqli_error($mysqli));
128:
129:  //get master_id for use with other tables
130:  $master_id = mysqli_insert_id($mysqli);
131:
132:  if (($_POST['address']) || ($_POST['city']) ||
133:      ($_POST['state']) || ($_POST['zipcode'])) {
134:      //something relevant, so add to address table
135:      $add_address_sql = "INSERT INTO address (master_id,
136:          date_added, date_modified, address, city, state,
137:          zipcode, type)  VALUES
138:          ('".$master_id."', now(), now(),
139:          '".$safe_address."', '".$safe_city."',
140:          '".$safe_state."' , '".$safe_zipcode."' ,
141:          '".$_POST['add_type']."')";
142:      $add_address_res = mysqli_query($mysqli, $add_address_sql)
143:          or die(mysqli_error($mysqli));
144:  }
145:
146:  if ($_POST['tel_number']) {
147:      //something relevant, so add to telephone table
148:      $add_tel_sql = "INSERT INTO telephone (master_id, date_added,
149:          date_modified, tel_number, type)  VALUES
150:          ('".$master_id."', now(), now(),
151:          '".$safe_tel_number."', '".$_POST['tel_type']."')";
152:      $add_tel_res = mysqli_query($mysqli, $add_tel_sql)
153:          or die(mysqli_error($mysqli));
154:  }
```

LISTING 20.3   (continued)

```
155:
156:    if ($_POST['fax_number']) {
157:        //something relevant, so add to fax table
158:        $add_fax_sql = "INSERT INTO fax (master_id, date_added,
159:            date_modified, fax_number, type)  VALUES
160:            ('".$master_id."', now(), now(), '".$safe_fax_number."',
161:            '".$_POST['fax_type']."')";
162:        $add_fax_res = mysqli_query($mysqli, $add_fax_sql)
163:            or die(mysqli_error($mysqli));
164:    }
165:    if ($_POST['email']) {
166:        //something relevant, so add to email table
167:        $add_email_sql = "INSERT INTO email (master_id, date_added,
168:            date_modified, email, type)  VALUES
169:            ('".$master_id."', now(), now(), '".$safe_email."',
170:            '".$_POST['email_type']."')";
171:        $add_email_res = mysqli_query($mysqli, $add_email_sql)
172:            or die(mysqli_error($mysqli));
173:    }
174:
175:    if ($_POST['note']) {
176:        //something relevant, so add to notes table
177:        $add_notes_sql = "INSERT INTO personal_notes (master_id,
178:            date_added, date_modified, note)  VALUES
179:            ('".$master_id."', now(), now(),
180:            '".$safe_note."')";
181:        $add_notes_res = mysqli_query($mysqli, $add_notes_sql)
182:            or die(mysqli_error($mysqli));
183:    }
184:    mysqli_close($mysqli);
185:    $display_block = "<p>Your entry has been added.  Would you
186:        like to <a href=\"addentry.php\">add another</a>?</p>";
187: }
188: ?>
189: <!DOCTYPE html>
190: <head>
191: <title>Add an Entry</title>
192: </head>
193: <body>
194: <h1>Add an Entry</h1>
195: <?php echo $display_block; ?>
196: </body>
197: </html>
```

The `else` condition on Line 90 is invoked if there is a value in $_POST, meaning that the user has submitted the form. In this simple example, two fields were designated as required fields: the first name and last name of the person. So, lines 92–95 check for values in $_POST['f_name'] and $_POST['l_name'] and redirect the user back to the form if either value is missing.

NOTE

> Because the two required fields in the form are marked as such using the HTML5 `required` attribute, the form will not be submitted without text in the fields. However, for older browsers or those devices not supporting the HTML5 `required` attribute in `INPUT` fields, this server-side check does the trick.

After making it through the check for required fields, the code connects to the database in line 98. Once the database connection is made, you can safely use `mysqli_real_escape_string()` to sanitize the user input and create "safe" versions of those strings for use in `INSERT` statements.

Next comes the multitude of insertion statements, only one of which is required: the insertion of a record into the `master_name` table. This occurs on lines 123–127. After the insertion is made, the id of this record is extracted using `mysqli_insert_id()` on line 130. You use this value, now referred to as `$master_id`, in your remaining SQL queries.

The SQL queries for inserting records into the remaining tables are all conditional, meaning they occur only if some condition is true. In lines 132–133, you see that the condition that must be met is that a value exists for any of the following variables: `$_POST['address']`, `$_POST['city']`, `$_POST['state']`, and `$_POST['zipcode']`. Lines 135–143 create and issue the query if this condition is met.

The same principle holds true for adding to the `telephone` table (lines 146–154), the `fax` table (lines 156–164), the `email` table (lines 165–173), and the `personal_notes` table (lines 175–183). If the conditions are met, records are inserted into those tables.

Once through this set of conditions, the message for the user is placed in the `$display_block` variable, and the script exits this `if...else` construct and prints HTML from lines 189–197. Figure 20.3 shows an output of the record-addition script.

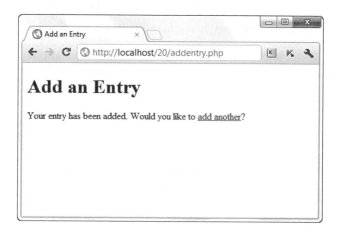

FIGURE 20.3
A record has been added.

Add a few records using this form so that you have some values to play with in the following sections. On your own, try to modify this script in such a way that the values entered in the form print to the screen after successful record insertion.

Viewing Records

If you verified your work in the preceding section by issuing queries through the MySQL monitor or other interface, you probably became tired of typing SELECT * FROM... for every table. In this section, you create the two-part script that shows you how to select and view records in your database.

Listing 20.4 shows the select-and-view script called selentry.php, which has three parts: the record-selection form (lines 5–42), the code to display the record contents (lines 43–172), and the HTML template that displays the dynamically generated strings (lines 176–184). Because this code is long, the listing is broken into smaller chunks for discussion.

LISTING 20.4   Script Called selentry.php for Selecting and Viewing a Record

```
1:  <?php
2:  include 'ch20_include.php';
3:  doDB();
4:
5:  if (!$_POST) {
6:      //haven't seen the selection form, so show it
7:      $display_block = "<h1>Select an Entry</h1>";
8:
9:      //get parts of records
10:     $get_list_sql = "SELECT id,
11:                     CONCAT_WS(', ', l_name, f_name) AS display_name
12:                     FROM master_name ORDER BY l_name, f_name";
13:     $get_list_res = mysqli_query($mysqli, $get_list_sql)
14:                     or die(mysqli_error($mysqli));
15:
16:     if (mysqli_num_rows($get_list_res) < 1) {
17:         //no records
18:         $display_block .= "<p><em>Sorry, no records to select!</em></p>";
19:
20:     } else {
21:         //has records, so get results and print in a form
22:         $display_block .= "
23:         <form method=\"post\" action=\"".$_SERVER['PHP_SELF']."\">
24:         <p><label for=\"sel_id\">Select a Record:</label><br/>
25:         <select id=\"sel_id\" name=\"sel_id\" required=\"required\">
26:         <option value=\"\">-- Select One --</option>";
27:
28:         while ($recs = mysqli_fetch_array($get_list_res)) {
29:             $id = $recs['id'];
```

```
30:                    $display_name = stripslashes($recs['display_name']);
31:                    $display_block .=
32:                    "<option value=\"".$id."\">".$display_name."</option>";
33:                }
34:
35:                $display_block .= "
36:                </select>
37:                <button type=\"submit\" name=\"submit\"
38:                        value=\"view\">View Selected Entry\"></button>
39:                </form>";
40:            }
41:            //free result
42:            mysqli_free_result($get_list_res);
```

As with the addentry.php script, the selentry.php script performs one of two tasks at any given time: It either shows the selection form or it performs all the SQL queries related to viewing the record. No matter which of the two tasks the script performs, the database still comes into play. Given that, include the file with the connection function on line 2, and call that function on line 3.

The logic that determines the task begins at line 5, with a test for the value of the $_POST superglobal. If $_POST has no value, the user is not coming from the selection form and therefore needs to see it. A string called $display_block is started in line 7, and this string will ultimately hold the HTML that makes up the record-selection form.

Lines 10–12 select specific fields from the records in the master_name table to build the selection drop-down options in the form. For this step, you need only the name and ID of the person whose record you want to select. Line 16 tests for results of the query; if the query has no results, you cannot build a form. If this were the case, the value of $display_block would be filled with an error message and the script would end, printing the resulting HTML to the screen.

However, assume that you have a few records in the master_name table. In this case, you have to extract the information from the query results to be able to build the form. This is done in lines 28–33, with form elements written to the $display_block string both above and below it.

This listing stops at line 42, but you'll soon see lines 43 through the end of the script. If you were to close up the if statement and the PHP block and print the value of $display_block to the screen at this point, you would see a form something like that shown in Figure 20.4 (with different entries, depending on what is in your database, of course).

FIGURE 20.4
The record-
selection form.

However, you must finish the `selentry.php` script in order for it to be useful, so continue Listing 20.4 at line 43, which begins the `else` portion of the `if...else` statement.

LISTING 20.4   (continued)

```
43:    } else if ($_POST) {
44:        //check for required fields
45:        if ($_POST['sel_id'] == "")  {
46:             header("Location: selentry.php");
47:            exit;
48:        }
49:
50:        //create safe version of ID
51:        $safe_id = mysqli_real_escape_string($mysqli, $_POST['sel_id']);52:
52:
53:        //get master_info
54:        $get_master_sql = "SELECT concat_ws(' ',f_name,l_name) as display_name
55:                           FROM master_name WHERE id = '".$safe_id."'";
56:        $get_master_res = mysqli_query($mysqli, $get_master_sql)
57:                          or die(mysqli_error($mysqli));
58:
59:        while ($name_info = mysqli_fetch_array($get_master_res)) {
60:            $display_name = stripslashes($name_info['display_name']);
61:        }
62:
63:        $display_block = "<h1>Showing Record for ".$display_name."</h1>";
64:
65:        //free result
66:        mysqli_free_result($get_master_res);
67:
68:        //get all addresses
69:        $get_addresses_sql = "SELECT address, city, state, zipcode, type FROM
70:                              address WHERE master_id = '".$safe_id."'";
71:        $get_addresses_res = mysqli_query($mysqli, $get_addresses_sql)
72:                             or die(mysqli_error($mysqli));
73:
74:        if (mysqli_num_rows($get_addresses_res) > 0) {
75:            $display_block .= "<p><strong>Addresses:</strong><br/>
```

```
76:             <ul>";
77:
78:             while ($add_info = mysqli_fetch_array($get_addresses_res)) {
79:                 address = stripslashes($add_info['address']);
80:                 $city = stripslashes($add_info['city']);
81:                 $state = stripslashes($add_info['state']);
82:                 $zipcode = stripslashes($add_info['zipcode']);
83:                 $address_type = $add_info['type'];
84:
85:                 $display_block .= "<li>$address $city $state $zipcode
86:                                 ($address_type)</li>";
87:             }
88:             $display_block .= "</ul>";
89:         }
90:     //free result
91:     mysqli_free_result($get_addresses_res);
```

Line 43 contains the else portion of the if...else statement and is invoked if the user submits the form and wants to see a specific record. It first checks for a required field, in line 45; in this case, it is checking for the value of $_POST['sel_id']. This value matches the ID from the master_name table to that of the selection made in the record-selection form. If that value does not exist, the user is redirected back to the selection form—you can't very well gather information from a set of tables when the primary key isn't present!

Assuming that a value was present for $_POST['sel_id'], a safe version of it is created in line 51. Next, you create and issue a query in lines 54–57 that obtains the name of the user whose record you want to view. This information is placed in the now-familiar $display_block string, which will continue to be built as the script continues.

Lines 69–89 represent the query against the address table, and the resulting display string that is built. If the selected individual has no records in the address table, nothing is added to the $display_block string. However, if there are one or more entries, the addresses for this person are added to the $display_block string as one or more unordered list elements, as shown in lines 78–87.

Lines 92–168 of Listing 20.4 perform the same type of looping and writing to the $display_block variable, but the tables are different. For instance, lines 92–109 look for information in the telephone table and create an appropriate string to be added to $display_block, if any information is present. The same structure is repeated in lines 114–130 for information from the fax table, lines 135–150 for information from the email table, and lines 155–172 for any content present in the personal_notes table.

LISTING 20.4   (continued)

```
92:        //get all tel
93:        $get_tel_sql = "SELECT tel_number, type FROM telephone WHERE
94:                       master_id = '".$safe_id."'";
95:        $get_tel_res = mysqli_query($mysqli, $get_tel_sql)
96:                      or die(mysqli_error($mysqli));
97:
98:        if (mysqli_num_rows($get_tel_res) > 0) {
99:            $display_block .= "<p><strong>Telephone:</strong><br/>
100:           <ul>";
101:
102:           while ($tel_info = mysqli_fetch_array($get_tel_res)) {
103:               $tel_number = stripslashes($tel_info['tel_number']);
104:               $tel_type = $tel_info['type'];
105:
106:               $display_block .= "<li>$tel_number ($tel_type)</li>";
107:           }
108:           $display_block .= "</ul>";
109:       }
110:       //free result
111:       mysqli_free_result($get_tel_res);
112:
113:       //get all fax
114:       $get_fax_sql = "SELECT fax_number, type FROM fax WHERE
115:                      master_id = '".$safe_id."'";
116:       $get_fax_res = mysqli_query($mysqli, $get_fax_sql)
117:                     or die(mysqli_error($mysqli));
118:
119:       if (mysqli_num_rows($get_fax_res) > 0) {
120:           $display_block .= "<p><strong>Fax:</strong><br/>
121:           <ul>";
122:
123:           while ($fax_info = mysqli_fetch_array($get_fax_res)) {
124:               $fax_number =  stripslashes($fax_info['fax_number']);
125:               $fax_type = $fax_info['type'];
126:
127:               $display_block .= "<li>$fax_number ($fax_type)</li>";
128:           }
129:            $display_block .= "</ul>";
130:       }
131:       //free result
132:       mysqli_free_result($get_fax_res);
133:
134:       //get all email
135:       $get_email_sql = "SELECT email, type FROM email WHERE
136:                        master_id = '".$safe_id."'";
137:       $get_email_res = mysqli_query($mysqli, $get_email_sql)
138:                       or die(mysqli_error($mysqli));
139:       if (mysqli_num_rows($get_email_res) > 0) {
140:           $display_block .= "<p><strong>Email:</strong><br/>
141:           <ul>";
142:
143:           while ($email_info = mysqli_fetch_array($get_email_res)) {
144:               $email = stripslashes($email_info['email']);
145:               $email_type = $email_info['type'];
146:
147:               $display_block .= "<li>$email ($email_type)</li>";
```

```
148:        }
149:        $display_block .= "</ul>";
150:     }
151:     //free result
152:     mysqli_free_result($get_email_res);
153:
154:     //get personal note
155:     $get_notes_sql = "SELECT note FROM personal_notes WHERE
156:                       master_id = '".$safe_id."'";
157:     $get_notes_res = mysqli_query($mysqli, $get_notes_sql)
158:                       or die(mysqli_error($mysqli));
159:
160:     if (mysqli_num_rows($get_notes_res) == 1) {
161:         while ($note_info = mysqli_fetch_array($get_notes_res)) {
162:             $note = nl2br(stripslashes($note_info['note']));
163:         }
164:         $display_block .= "<p><strong>Personal Notes:</strong><br/>
165:         $note</p>";
166:     }
167:     //free result
168:     mysqli_free_result($get_notes_res);
```

You still have to do a little housekeeping and finish up the script, as shown in the last portion of Listing 20.4.

LISTING 20.4   (continued)

```
169:     $display_block .= "<br/>
170:     <p style=\"text-align:center\">
171:     <a href=\"".$_SERVER['PHP_SELF']."\">select another</a></p>";
172: }
173: //close connection to MySQL
174: mysqli_close($mysqli);
175: ?>
176: <!DOCTYPE html>
177: <html>
178: <head>
179: <title>My Records</title>
180: </head>
181: <body>
182: <?php echo $display_block; ?>
183: </body>
184: </html>
```

Lines 169–171 simply print a link back to the selection form before closing up the if...else statement in line 172 and the PHP block in the line following. Lines 176 through the end of the script are the generic HTML template that surround the contents of the $display_block string.

After selecting a record from the form shown in Figure 20.4, you will see a result like that shown in Figure 20.5—your data will vary, of course.

FIGURE 20.5
An individual's
record.

When you try this script for yourself, against your own records, you should see information only for those individuals who have additional data associated with them. For example, if you have an entry for a friend, and all you have is an email address entered in the email table, you shouldn't see any text relating to address, telephone, fax, or personal notes—no associated records were entered in those tables.

Creating the Record-Deletion Mechanism

The record-deletion mechanism is nearly identical to the script used to view a record. In fact, you can just take the first 42 lines of Listing 20.4, paste them into a new file called delentry.php, and change "View" to "Delete" in lines 24 and 38. Starting with a new line 43, the remainder of the code for delentry.php is shown in Listing 20.5.

LISTING 20.5 Script Called delentry.php for Selecting and Deleting a Record

```
43: } else if ($_POST) {
44:     //check for required fields
45:     if ($_POST['sel_id'] == "") {
46:         header("Location: delentry.php");
47:         exit;
48:     }
49:
50:     //create safe version of ID
51:     $safe_id = mysqli_real_escape_string($mysqli, $_POST['sel_id']);
52:
```

```
53:     //issue queries
54:     $del_master_sql = "DELETE FROM master_name WHERE
55:                         id = '".$safe_id."'";
56:     $del_master_res = mysqli_query($mysqli, $del_master_sql)
57:                         or die(mysqli_error($mysqli));
58:
59:     $del_address_sql = "DELETE FROM address WHERE
60:                         id = '".$safe_id."'";
61:     $del_address_res = mysqli_query($mysqli, $del_address_sql)
62:                         or die(mysqli_error($mysqli));
63:
64:     $del_tel_sql = "DELETE FROM telephone WHERE id = '".$safe_id."'";
65:     $del_tel_res = mysqli_query($mysqli, $del_tel_sql)
66:                         or die(mysqli_error($mysqli));
67:
68:     $del_fax_sql = "DELETE FROM fax WHERE id = '".$safe_id."'";
69:     $del_fax_res = mysqli_query($mysqli, $del_fax_sql)
70:                         or die(mysqli_error($mysqli));
71:
72:     $del_email_sql = "DELETE FROM email WHERE id = '".$safe_id."'";
73:     $del_email_res = mysqli_query($mysqli, $del_email_sql)
74:                         or die(mysqli_error($mysqli));
75:
76:     $del_note_sql = "DELETE FROM personal_notes WHERE
77:                         id = '".$safe_id."'";
78:     $del_note_res = mysqli_query($mysqli, $del_note_sql)
79:                         or die(mysqli_error($mysqli));
80:
81:     mysqli_close($mysqli);
82:
83:     $display_block = "<h1>Record(s) Deleted</h1>
84:     <p>Would you like to
85:     <a href=\"".$_SERVER['PHP_SELF']."\">delete another</a>?</p>";
86: }
87: ?>
88: <!DOCTYPE html>
89: <html>
90: <head>
91: <title>My Records</title>
92: </head>
93: <body>
94: <?php echo $display_block; ?>
95: </body>
96: </html>
```

Picking up in line 45, the script looks for the required field, $_POST['sel_id'], just
as it did in the selentry.php script. If that required value does not exist, the script
redirects the user to the selection form, but if it does exist, a safe version is created in
line 51. In lines 54–79, queries delete all information related to the selected individual from all tables. Lines 83–85 place a nice message in $display_block, and the
script exits and prints the HTML to the screen. Figure 20.6 shows an output of the
record-deletion script.

FIGURE 20.6
Deleting a
record.

When you go back to the record-selection form after deleting a record, you'll note that the individual you deleted is no longer in the selection menu—as it should be!

Adding Subentries to a Record

At this point in the chapter, you've learned how to add, remove, and view records. What's missing is adding additional entries to the related tables after you've already entered a master record—entries for home versus work telephone number, for example. All you need to do is make a few changes to existing scripts.

In the `selentry.php` script in Listing 20.4, change lines 185–186 to read as follows:

```
$display_block .= "<p style=\"text-align:center\">
<a href=\"addentry.php?master_id=".$_POST['sel_id']."\">add info</a> ...
<a href=\"".$_SERVER['PHP_SELF']."\">select another</a></p>";
```

This change simply adds a link to the `addentry.php` script and also passes it a variable that will become accessible to the next script via `$_GET['master_id']`.

Now you need to modify the `addentry.php` script from Listing 20.3 to account for its dual purposes. Here is a summary of the changes to the original script.

Replace the first 16 lines of the original `addentry.php` script with the following snippet:

```
<?php
include 'ch20_include.php';
doDB();

if ((!$_POST) || ($_GET['master_id'] != "")) {
    //haven't seen the form, so show it
    $display_block = "
    <form method=\"post\" action=\"".$_SERVER['PHP_SELF']."\">";
    if (isset($_GET['master_id'])) {
```

```
            //create safe version of ID
            $safe_id = mysqli_real_escape_string($mysqli, $_GET['master_id']);

            //get first, last names for display/tests validity
            $get_names_sql = "SELECT concat_ws(' ', f_name, l_name) AS display_name
                              FROM master_name WHERE id = '".$safe_id."'";
            $get_names_res = mysqli_query($mysqli, $get_names_sql)
                             or die(mysqli_error($mysqli));

            if (mysqli_num_rows($get_names_res) == 1) {
                while ($name_info = mysqli_fetch_array($get_names_res)) {
                    $display_name = stripslashes($name_info['display_name']);
                }
            }
        }

    if (isset($display_name)) {
        $display_block .= "<p>Adding information for
        <strong>$display_name</strong>:</p>";
    } else {
        $display_block .= <<<END_OF_TEXT
        <fieldset>
        <legend>First/Last Names:</legend><br/>
        <input type="text" name="f_name" size="30"
            maxlength="75" required="required" />
        <input type="text" name="l_name" size="30"
            maxlength="75" required="required" />
        </fieldset>
END_OF_TEXT;
    }
    $display_block .= <<<END_OF_TEXT

    <p><label for="address">Street Address:</label><br/>
```

This snippet simply moves around the form elements, printing the first and last name fields only if they contain a new record. If they contain an addition to a record, the individual's name is extracted from the database for aesthetic purposes as well as for a validity check of the ID.

Next, find this line in the original addentry.php script:

```
<button type="submit" name="submit" value="send">Add Entry</button>
```

Directly above it, add the following:

```
END_OF_TEXT;
if ($_GET) {
    $display_block .= "<input type=\"hidden\" name=\"master_id\"
        value=\""".$_GET['master_id']."\">";
}

    $display_block .= <<<END_OF_TEXT
```

This modification ensures that the known value of master_id is passed along to the next task, if it is present.

Identify what were lines 91–130 of the original script, beginning with the comment time to add to tables and ending with obtaining the value of $master_id. Replace those lines with the following:

```
//time to add to tables, so check for required fields
if ((($_POST['f_name'] == "") || ($_POST['l_name'] == "")) &&
(!isset($_POST['master_id']))) {
    header("Location: addentry.php");
    exit;
}

//connect to database
doDB();

//create clean versions of input strings
$safe_f_name = mysqli_real_escape_string($mysqli,
        $_POST['f_name']);
$safe_l_name = mysqli_real_escape_string($mysqli,
        $_POST['l_name']);
$safe_address = mysqli_real_escape_string($mysqli,
        $_POST['address']);
$safe_city = mysqli_real_escape_string($mysqli,
        $_POST['city']);
$safe_state = mysqli_real_escape_string($mysqli,
        $_POST['state']);
$safe_zipcode = mysqli_real_escape_string($mysqli,
        $_POST['zipcode']);
$safe_tel_number = mysqli_real_escape_string($mysqli,
        $_POST['tel_number']);
$safe_fax_number = mysqli_real_escape_string($mysqli,
        $_POST['fax_number']);
$safe_email = mysqli_real_escape_string($mysqli,
        $_POST['email']);
$safe_note = mysqli_real_escape_string($mysqli,
        $_POST['note']);

if (!$_POST['master_id']) {
    //add to master_name table
    $add_master_sql = "INSERT INTO master_name (date_added, date_modified,
                    f_name, l_name) VALUES (now(), now(),
                    '".$safe_f_name."', '".$safe_l_name."')";
    $add_master_res = mysqli_query($mysqli, $add_master_sql)
                    or die(mysqli_error($mysqli));

    //get master_id for use with other tables
    $master_id = mysqli_insert_id($mysqli);
} else {
    $master_id = mysqli_real_escape_string($mysqli, $_POST['master_id']);
}
```

These lines modify the check for required fields, allowing the script to continue without values for first and last names, but only if it has a $_POST['master_id'] value. Then the script connects to the database to perform all the additions you want it to, but it skips the addition to the master_name table if a value for $_POST['master_id'] exists.

Finally, in the section of the script that handles the insertion into the personal_
notes table, change INSERT into to UPDATE to handle an update of the notes field:

```
$add_notes_sql = "UPDATE personal_notes set note = '".$safe_note."',
                    date_modified = now() WHERE master_id = '".$master_id."'";
```

The new script should look like Listing 20.6.

LISTING 20.6　New addentry.php Script

```
1:   <?php
2:   include 'ch20_include.php';
3:   doDB();
4:
5:   if ((!$_POST) || ($_GET['master_id'] != "")) {
6:       //haven't seen the form, so show it
7:       $display_block = "
8:       <form method=\"post\" action=\"".$_SERVER['PHP_SELF']."\">";
9:       if (isset($_GET['master_id'])) {
10:          //create safe version of ID
11:          $safe_id = mysqli_real_escape_string($mysqli, $_GET['master_id']);
12:
13:          //get first, last names for display/tests validity
14:          $get_names_sql = "SELECT concat_ws(' ', f_name, l_name) AS
               display_name
15:                              FROM master_name WHERE id = '".$safe_id."'";
16:          $get_names_res = mysqli_query($mysqli, $get_names_sql)
17:                              or die(mysqli_error($mysqli));
18:
19:          if (mysqli_num_rows($get_names_res) == 1) {
20:              while ($name_info = mysqli_fetch_array($get_names_res)) {
21:                  $display_name = stripslashes($name_info['display_name']);
22:              }
23:          }
24:       }
25:
26:       if (isset($display_name)) {
27:          $display_block .= "<p>Adding information for
28:          <strong>$display_name</strong>:</p>";
29:       } else {
30:          $display_block .= <<<END_OF_TEXT          <fieldset>
31:          <legend>First/Last Names:</legend><br/>
32:          <input type="text" name="f_name" size="30"
33:              maxlength="75" required="required" />
34:          <input type="text" name="l_name" size="30"
35:              maxlength="75" required="required" />
36:          </fieldset>
37:   END_OF_TEXT;
38:       }
39:       $display_block .= <<<END_OF_TEXT
40:       <p><label for="address">Street Address:</label><br/>
41:       <input type="text" id="address" name="address"
42:           size="30" /></p>
43:
44:       <fieldset>
```

LISTING 20.6 Continued

```
45:        <legend>City/State/Zip:</legend><br/>
46:        <input type="text" name="city" size="30" maxlength="50" />
47:        <input type="text" name="state" size="5" maxlength="2" />
48:        <input type="text" name="zipcode" size="10" maxlength="10" />
49:        </fieldset>
50:
51:        <fieldset>
52:        <legend>Address Type:</legend><br/>
53:        <input type="radio" id="add_type_h" name="add_type"
54:              value="home" checked />
55:              <label for="add_type_h">home</label>
56:        <input type="radio" id="add_type_w" name="add_type"
57:              value="work" />
58:              <label for="add_type_w">work</label>
59:        <input type="radio" id="add_type_o" name="add_type"
60:              value="other" />
61:              <label for="add_type_o">other</label>
62:        </fieldset>
63:
64:        <fieldset>
65:
66:        <legend>Telephone Number:</legend><br/>
67:        <input type="text" name="tel_number" size="30" maxlength="25" />
68:        <input type="radio" id="tel_type_h" name="tel_type"
69:              value="home" checked />
70:              <label for="tel_type_h">home</label>
71:        <input type="radio" id="tel_type_w" name="tel_type"
72:              value="work" />
73:              <label for="tel_type_w">work</label>
74:        <input type="radio" id="tel_type_o" name="tel_type"
75:              value="other" />
76:              <label for="tel_type_o">other</label>
77:        </fieldset>
78:
79:        <fieldset>
80:        <legend>Fax Number:</legend><br/>
81:        <input type="text" name="fax_number" size="30" maxlength="25" />
82:        <input type="radio" id="fax_type_h" name="fax_type"
83:              value="home" checked />
84:              <label for="fax_type_h">home</label>
85:        <input type="radio" id="fax_type_w" name="fax_type"
86:              value="work" />
87:              <label for="fax_type_w">work</label>
88:        <input type="radio" id="fax_type_o" name="fax_type"
89:              value="other" />
90:              <label for="fax_type_o">other</label>
91:        </fieldset>
92:
93:        <fieldset>
94:        <legend>Email Address:</legend><br/>
95:        <input type="email" name="email" size="30" maxlength="150" />
96:        <input type="radio" id="email_type_h" name="email_type"
97:              value="home" checked />
98:              <label for="email_type_h">home</label>
99:        <input type="radio" id="email_type_w" name="email_type"
100:             value="work" />
101:             <label for="email_type_w">work</label>
```

```
102:        <input type="radio" id="email_type_o" name="email_type"
103:               value="other" />
104:               <label for="email_type_o">other</label>
105:        </fieldset>
106:
107:        <p><label for="note">Personal Note:</label><br/>
108:        <textarea id="note" name="note" cols="35"
109:                  rows="3"></textarea></p>
110: END_OF_TEXT;
111:        if ($_GET) {
112:            $display_block .= "<input type=\"hidden\" name=\"master_id\"
113:                value=\"".$_GET['master_id']."\">";
114:        }
115:        $display_block .= <<<END_OF_TEXT
116:        <button type="submit" name="submit"
117:                value="send">Add Entry</button>
118:        </form>
119: END_OF_TEXT;
120: } else if ($_POST) {
121:        //time to add to tables, so check for required fields
122:        if ((($_POST['f_name'] == "") || ($_POST['l_name'] == "")) &&
123:            (!isset($_POST['master_id']))) {
124:                header("Location: addentry.php");
125:                exit;
126:        }
127:
128:        //connect to database
129:        doDB();
130:        //create clean versions of input strings
131:        $safe_f_name = mysqli_real_escape_string($mysqli,
132:            $_POST['f_name']);
133:        $safe_l_name = mysqli_real_escape_string($mysqli,
134:            $_POST['l_name']);
135:        $safe_address = mysqli_real_escape_string($mysqli,
136:            $_POST['address']);
137:        $safe_city = mysqli_real_escape_string($mysqli,
138:            $_POST['city']);
139:        $safe_state = mysqli_real_escape_string($mysqli,
140:            $_POST['state']);
141:        $safe_zipcode = mysqli_real_escape_string($mysqli,
142:            $_POST['zipcode']);
143:        $safe_tel_number = mysqli_real_escape_string($mysqli,
144:            $_POST['tel_number']);
145:        $safe_fax_number = mysqli_real_escape_string($mysqli,
146:            $_POST['fax_number']);
147:        $safe_email = mysqli_real_escape_string($mysqli,
148:            $_POST['email']);
149:        $safe_note = mysqli_real_escape_string($mysqli,
150:            $_POST['note']);
151:
152:        if (!$_POST['master_id']) {
153:            //add to master_name table
154:            $add_master_sql = "INSERT INTO master_name (date_added,
                date_modified,
155:                            f_name, l_name) VALUES (now(), now(),
156:                            '".$safe_f_name."', '".$safe_l_name."')";
157:            $add_master_res = mysqli_query($mysqli, $add_master_sql)
```

LISTING 20.6   Continued

```
158:                              or die(mysqli_error($mysqli));
159:
160:          //get master_id for use with other tables
161:          $master_id = mysqli_insert_id($mysqli);
162:      } else {
163:          $master_id = mysqli_real_escape_string($mysqli,
                 $_POST['master_id']);
164:      }
165:
166:      if (($_POST['address']) || ($_POST['city']) ||
167:          ($_POST['state']) || ($_POST['zipcode'])) {
168:          //something relevant, so add to address table
169:          $add_address_sql = "INSERT INTO address (master_id,
170:              date_added, date_modified, address, city, state,
171:              zipcode, type)  VALUES
172:              ('".$master_id."', now(), now(),
173:              '".$safe_address."', '".$safe_city."',
174:              '".$safe_state."' , '".$safe_zipcode."' ,
175:              '".$_POST['add_type']."')";
176:          $add_address_res = mysqli_query($mysqli, $add_address_sql)
177:              or die(mysqli_error($mysqli));
178:      }
179:
180:      if ($_POST['tel_number']) {
181:          //something relevant, so add to telephone table
182:          $add_tel_sql = "INSERT INTO telephone (master_id, date_added,
183:              date_modified, tel_number, type)  VALUES
184:              ('".$master_id."', now(), now(),
185:              '".$safe_tel_number."', '".$_POST['tel_type']."')";
186:          $add_tel_res = mysqli_query($mysqli, $add_tel_sql)
187:              or die(mysqli_error($mysqli));
188:      }
189:
190:      if ($_POST['fax_number']) {
191:          //something relevant, so add to fax table
192:          $add_fax_sql = "INSERT INTO fax (master_id, date_added,
193:              date_modified, fax_number, type)  VALUES
194:              ('".$master_id."', now(), now(), '".$safe_fax_number."',
195:              '".$_POST['fax_type']."')";
196:          $add_fax_res = mysqli_query($mysqli, $add_fax_sql)
197:              or die(mysqli_error($mysqli));
198:      }
199:      if ($_POST['email']) {
200:          //something relevant, so add to email table
201:          $add_email_sql = "INSERT INTO email (master_id, date_added,
202:              date_modified, email, type)  VALUES
203:              ('".$master_id."', now(), now(), '".$safe_email."',
204:              '".$_POST['email_type']."')";
205:          $add_email_res = mysqli_query($mysqli, $add_email_sql)
206:              or die(mysqli_error($mysqli));
207:      }
208:
209:      if ($_POST['note']) {
210:          //something relevant, so add to notes table
211:          $add_notes_sql = "UPDATE personal_notes set note =
212:                          '".$safe_note."', date_modified = now()
```

```
213:                          WHERE master_id = '".$master_id."'";
214:     }
215:     mysqli_close($mysqli);
216:     $display_block = "<p>Your entry has been added.  Would you
217:          like to <a href=\"addentry.php\">add another</a>?</p>";
218: }
219: ?>
220: <!DOCTYPE html>
221: <head>
222: <title>Add an Entry</title>
223: </head>
224: <body>
225: <h1>Add an Entry</h1>
226: <?php echo $display_block; ?>
227: </body>
228: </html>
```

You can try out this revised script by selecting a record to view and then following the add info link. You should see a form like that shown in Figure 20.7.

FIGURE 20.7
Adding to a record.

After submitting this form, you can go back through the selection sequence and view the record to verify that your changes have been made.

Summary

In this chapter, you applied your basic PHP and MySQL knowledge to create a personal address book. You learned how to create the database table and scripts for record addition, removal, and simple viewing. You also learned how to add multiple records attached to a single master entry.

Q&A

Q. *What do I do if I want to add additional sections to my address book, such as entries for a person's birthday or other information?*

A. Different tables are used for address, telephone, fax, email, and personal notes because it is possible for a person to have more than one record containing those types of information. In the case of a person's birthday, a person has just one of those, so a relational database is overkill because only one record would ever exist per user. So, to add a person's birthday you should add a field to the `master_name` table. In the case of adding tables for other information, ask yourself whether a person will only ever have one instance of that information (such as birthday) or multiple instances (such as email addresses). If the latter case, create a table much like the `address`, `telephone`, `fax`, `email`, or `personal_notes` tables, which use `master_id` as a foreign key.

Workshop

The workshop is designed to help you review what you've learned and begin putting your knowledge into practice.

Quiz

1. When you are passing a variable through the query string, which superglobal does it belong in?

2. How many records in the `address`, `email`, `telephone`, and `fax` tables can you have for each individual in your `master_name` table?

3. Through which database field are additional records attached to a master record?

Answers

1. The $_GET superglobal.

2. As many as you want—it's relational!

3. The `master_id` field.

Activities

1. Go through each of the administration scripts and modify the code so that a link to the menu prints at the bottom of each screen.

2. Use the second version of the `addentry.php` script to add secondary contact information to records in your database. Figure 20.8 shows what a record will look like after the script adds secondary contact information to it.

FIGURE 20.8
An individual's record with multiple entries in tables.

## CHAPTER 21

Creating a Simple Discussion Forum

In this chapter, you learn the following:

- ▶ How to create tables for a simple discussion forum
- ▶ How to create input forms for a simple discussion forum
- ▶ How to display a simple discussion forum

In this chapter, you learn the design process behind a simple discussion forum. This includes developing the database tables and user input forms and displaying the results. When broken into pieces like this, such a task seems simple—and it is! The ultimate goal is to understand the concepts and relationships that go into making something like a discussion forum, not to create the world's most full-functioned system. In fact, you'll see it's quite sparse, but it sure is relational.

Designing the Database Tables

Think of the basic components of a forum: topics and posts. A forum—if properly used by its patrons—should have several topics, and each of those topics will have one or more posts submitted by users. Knowing that, you should realize that the posts are tied to the topics through a key field. This key forms the relationship between the two tables.

Think about the requirements for the topics themselves. You definitely need a field for the title, and subsequently you might want fields to hold the creation time and the identification of the user who created the topic. Similarly, think of the requirements for the posts: You want to store the text of the post, the time of its creation, and the identity of person who created it. Most important, you need that key to tie the post to the topic.

The following two table creation statements create these tables, called `forum_topics` and `forum_posts`:

```
CREATE TABLE forum_topics (
    topic_id INT NOT NULL PRIMARY KEY AUTO_INCREMENT,
    topic_title VARCHAR (150),
    topic_create_time DATETIME,
    topic_owner VARCHAR (150)
);
CREATE TABLE forum_posts (
    post_id INT NOT NULL PRIMARY KEY AUTO_INCREMENT,
    topic_id INT NOT NULL,
    post_text TEXT,
    post_create_time DATETIME,
    post_owner VARCHAR (150)
);
```

NOTE

> This simple forum example identifies users by their email addresses and does not require any sort of login sequence.

You should now have two empty tables waiting for some input. In the next section, you create the input forms for adding a topic and a post.

Creating an Include File for Common Functions

Previous chapters used an included file of common functions to make your scripts more concise and to help manage information that might change over time, such as a database username and password. The same thing is true in this chapter. Listing 21.1 contains the code shared by the scripts in this chapter.

LISTING 21.1   Common Functions in an Included File

```
1:  <?php
2:  function doDB() {
3:      global $mysqli;
4:
5:      //connect to server and select database; you may need it
6:      $mysqli = mysqli_connect("localhost", "joeuser",
7:          "somepass", "testDB");
8:
9:      //if connection fails, stop script execution
10:     if (mysqli_connect_errno()) {
11:         printf("Connect failed: %s\n", mysqli_connect_error());
12:         exit();
13:     }
14: }
15: ?>
```

Lines 2–14 set up the database connection function, doDB. If the connection cannot be made, the script exits when this function is called; otherwise, it makes the value of $mysqli available to other parts of your script.

Save this file as **ch21_include.php** and place it on your web server. The other code listings in this chapter include this file within the first few lines of the script.

Creating the Input Forms and Scripts

Before you can add any posts, you must add a topic to the forum. It is common practice in forum creation to add the topic and the first post in that topic at the same time, because from a user's point of view, it doesn't make much sense to add a topic and then go back, select the topic, and add a reply. You want the process to be as smooth as possible. Listing 21.2 shows the form for a new topic creation, which includes a space for the first post in the topic.

LISTING 21.2 Form for Adding a Topic

```
1:  <!DOCTYPE html>
2:  <html>
3:  <head>
4:  <title>Add a Topic</title>
5:  </head>
6:  <body>
7:  <h1>Add a Topic</h1>
8:  <form method="post" action="do_addtopic.php">
9:
10: <p><label for="topic_owner">Your Email Address:</label><br/>
11: <input type="email" id="topic_owner" name="topic_owner" size="40"
12:        maxlength="150" required="required" /></p>
13:
14: <p><label for="topic_title">Topic Title:</label><br/>
15: <input type="text" id="topic_title" name="topic_title" size="40"
16:        maxlength="150" required="required" /></p>
17: <p><label for="post_text">Post Text:</label><br/>
18: <textarea id="post_text" name="post_text" rows="8"
19:           cols="40" ></textarea></p>
20:
21: <button type="submit" name="submit" value="submit">Add Topic</button>
22:
23: </form>
24: </body>
25: </html>
```

Seems simple enough: The three fields shown in the form, which you can see in Figure 21.1, are all you need to complete both tables; your script and database can fill in the rest. Save Listing 21.2 as something like **addtopic.html** and put it in your web server document root so that you can follow along.

FIGURE 21.1
The topic-
creation form.

To create the entry in the `forum_topics` table, you use the values from the `$_POST['topic_title']` and `$_POST['topic_owner']` variables from the input form. The `topic_id` and `topic_create_time` fields will be automatically incremented and added via the `now()` MySQL function, respectively.

Similarly, in the `forum_posts` table, you use the values of `$_POST['post_text']` and `$_POST['topic_owner']` from the input form, and the `post_id`, `post_create_time`, and the `topic_id` fields will be automatically incremented or otherwise supplied. Because you need a value for the `topic_id` field to be able to complete the entry in the `forum_posts` table, you know that query must happen after the query to insert the record in the `forum_topics` table. Listing 21.3 creates the script to add these records to the table.

LISTING 21.3   Script for Adding a Topic

```
1:  <?php
2:  include 'ch21_include.php';
3:  doDB();
4:
5:  //check for required fields from the form
6:  if ((!$_POST['topic_owner']) || (!$_POST['topic_title']) ||
7:      (!$_POST['post_text'])) {
8:      header("Location: addtopic.html");
9:      exit;
10: }
11:
12: //create safe values for input into the database
13: $clean_topic_owner = mysqli_real_escape_string($mysqli,
14:                      $_POST['topic_owner']);
15: $clean_topic_title = mysqli_real_escape_string($mysqli,
```

```
16:                          $_POST['topic_title']);
17: $clean_post_text = mysqli_real_escape_string($mysqli,
18:                          $_POST['post_text']);
19:
20: //create and issue the first query
21: $add_topic_sql = "INSERT INTO forum_topics
22:                     (topic_title, topic_create_time, topic_owner)
23:                     VALUES ('".$clean_topic_title ."', now(),
24:                     '".$$clean_topic_owner."')";
25:
26: $add_topic_res = mysqli_query($mysqli, $add_topic_sql)
27:                     or die(mysqli_error($mysqli));
28:
29: //get the id of the last query
30: $topic_id = mysqli_insert_id($mysqli);
31:
32: //create and issue the second query
33: $add_post_sql = "INSERT INTO forum_posts
34:                     (topic_id, post_text, post_create_time, post_owner)
35:                     VALUES ('".$topic_id."', '".$clean_post_text."',
36:                     now(), '".$clean_topic_owner."')";
37:
38: $add_post_res = mysqli_query($mysqli, $add_post_sql)
39:                     or die(mysqli_error($mysqli));
40: //close connection to MySQL
41: mysqli_close($mysqli);
42:
43: //create nice message for user
44: $display_block = "<p>The <strong>".$_POST["topic_title"]."</strong>
45:     topic has been created.</p>";
46: ?>
47: <!DOCTYPE html>
48: <html>
49: <head>
50: <title>New Topic Added</title>
51: </head>
52: <body>
53: <h1>New Topic Added</h1>
54: <?php echo $display_block; ?>
55: </body>
56: </html>
```

Lines 2–3 include the file of user-created functions and call the database connection function. Next, lines 6–10 check for the three required fields needed to complete both tables (the topic owner, a topic title, and some text for the post). If any one of these fields is not present, the user is redirected to the original form. Lines 13–18 create database-safe versions of the contents of those variables.

Lines 21–27 create and insert the first query, which adds the topic to the forum_topics table. Note that no value is entered for the id field in the table; the automatically incrementing value is added by the system per the original table definition. The MySQL now() function is used to timestamp the record with the current time at insertion. The other fields in the record are completed using values from the form.

Line 30 shows the use of a handy function: `mysqli_insert_id()`. This function retrieves the primary key ID of the last record inserted into the database by this script. In this case, `mysqli_insert_id()` gets the id value from the `forum_topics` table, which will become the entry for the `topic_id` field in the `forum_posts` table.

Lines 33–39 create and insert the second query, again using a mixture of information known and supplied by the system. The second query adds the text of the user's post to the `forum_posts` table. Lines 44–45 simply create a display string for the user, and the rest of the script rounds out the HTML that is rendered by the browser.

Save this listing as **do_addtopic.php**—the name of the action in the previous script—and place it in the document root of your web server. Complete the form you created from Listing 21.1 and then submit it, and you should see the New Topic Added message. Figures 21.2 and 21.3 show the sequence of events.

FIGURE 21.2
Adding a topic and first post.

FIGURE 21.3
Successful addition of a topic and first post.

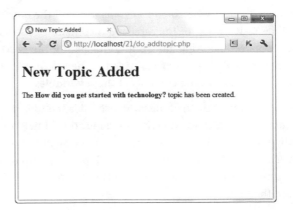

In the next section, you put together two more pieces of the puzzle: displaying the topics and posts and replying to a topic.

Displaying the Topic List

Now that you have a topic and at least one post in your database, you can display this information and let people add new topics or reply to existing ones. In Listing 21.4, you take a step back and create a page that lists all the topics in the forum. This page shows the basic information of each topic and provides the user with a link to add a new topic; you have already created the form and script for that. The code in Listing 21.4 represents an entry page for your forum.

Although Listing 21.4 looks like a lot of code, it's actually many small, simple concepts you've already encountered, starting with the include() function and database connection function in lines 2–3.

LISTING 21.4   Topic Listing Script

```
1:  <?php
2:  include 'ch21_include.php';
3:  doDB();
4:
5:  //gather the topics
6:  $get_topics_sql = "SELECT topic_id, topic_title,
7:                      DATE_FORMAT(topic_create_time,  '%b %e %Y at %r') AS
8:                      fmt_topic_create_time, topic_owner FROM forum_topics
9:                      ORDER BY topic_create_time DESC";
10: $get_topics_res = mysqli_query($mysqli, $get_topics_sql)
11:                    or die(mysqli_error($mysqli));
12:
13: if (mysqli_num_rows($get_topics_res) < 1) {
14:     //there are no topics, so say so
15:     $display_block = "<p><em>No topics exist.</em></p>";
16: } else {
17:     //create the display string
18:     $display_block <<<END_OF_TEXT
19:     <table>
20:     <tr>
21:     <th>TOPIC TITLE</th>
22:     <th># of POSTS</th>
23:     </tr>
24: END_OF_TEXT;
25:
26:     while ($topic_info = mysqli_fetch_array($get_topics_res)) {
27:         $topic_id = $topic_info['topic_id'];
28:         $topic_title = stripslashes($topic_info['topic_title']);
29:         $topic_create_time = $topic_info['fmt_topic_create_time'];
30:         $topic_owner = stripslashes($topic_info['topic_owner']);
31:
32:         //get number of posts
33:         $get_num_posts_sql = "SELECT COUNT(post_id) AS post_count FROM
34:                         forum_posts WHERE topic_id = '".$topic_id."'";
```

LISTING 21.4   Continued

```
35:        $get_num_posts_res = mysqli_query($mysqli, $get_num_posts_sql)
36:                       or die(mysqli_error($mysqli));
37:
38:        while ($posts_info = mysqli_fetch_array($get_num_posts_res)) {
39:            $num_posts = $posts_info['post_count'];
40:        }
41:
42:        //add to display
43:        $display_block .= <<<END_OF_TEXT
44:        <tr>
45:        <td><a href="showtopic.php?topic_id=$topic_id">
46:        <strong>$topic_title</strong></a><br/>
47:        Created on $topic_create_time by $topic_owner</td>
48:        <td class="num_posts_col">$num_posts</td>
49:        </tr>
50: END_OF_TEXT;
51:    }
52:    //free results
53:    mysqli_free_result($get_topics_res);
54:    mysqli_free_result($get_num_posts_res);
55:
56:    //close connection to MySQL
57:    mysqli_close($mysqli);
58:
59:    //close up the table
60:    $display_block .= "</table>";
61: }
62: ?>
63: <!DOCTYPE html>
64: <html>
65: <head>
66: <title>Topics in My Forum</title>
67: <style type="text/css">
68:    table {
69:       border: 1px solid black;
70:       border-collapse: collapse;
71:    }
72:    th {
73:       border: 1px solid black;
74:       padding: 6px;
75:       font-weight: bold;
76:       background: #ccc;
77:    }
78:    td {
79:       border: 1px solid black;
80:       padding: 6px;
81:    }
82:    .num_posts_col { text-align: center; }
83: </style>
84: </head>
85: <body>
86: <h1>Topics in My Forum</h1>
87: <?php echo $display_block; ?>
88: <p>Would you like to <a href="addtopic.html">add a topic</a>?</p>
89: </body>
90: </html>
```

Lines 6–11 show the first of the database queries, and this particular one selects all the topic information in order by descending date. In other words, these lines gather the data in such a way that the topic that was created most recently will appear at the top of the list. In the query, notice the use of the date_format() function to create a much nicer date display than the raw value stored in the database.

Line 13 checks for the presence of any records returned by the query. If no records are returned, and therefore no topics are in the table, you want to tell the user. Line 15 creates this message. At this point, if no topics existed, the script would break out of the if...else construct and be over with; the next action would occur at line 63, which is the start of the static HTML. If the script ended here, the message created in line 15 would be printed in line 87.

If you have topics in your forum_topics table, however, the script continues at line 16. At line 18, a block of text is assigned to the $display_block variable, containing the beginnings of an HTML table. Lines 19–23 set up a table with two columns: one for the title and one for the number of posts. At line 26, you begin to loop through the results of the original query.

The while loop in line 26 says that while there are elements to be extracted from the resultset, extract each row as an array called $topic_info, and use the field names as the array element to assign the value to a new variable. So, the first element the script tries to extract is the topic_id field, on line 27. It assigns the value of $topic_info['topic_id'] to the $topic_id variable, meaning that it gets a local value for $topic_id from an array called $topic_info, containing a field called topic_id. Continue doing this for the $topic_title, $topic_create_time, and $topic_owner variables in lines 28–30. The stripslashes() function removes any escape characters that may have been input into the table at the time of record insertion.

Lines 33–36 create and issue another query, in the context of the while loop, to get the number of posts for that particular topic. In line 43, the script continues the creation of the $display_block string, using the concatenation operator (.=) to make sure that this string is tacked on to the end of the display string we have built so far. In lines 45–47, you create the HTML table column to display the link to the file that will show the topic (showtopic.php) and print the topic owner and creation time.

The second HTML table column, on line 48, shows the number of posts. The script breaks out of the while loop on line 51, and in line 60 adds the last bit to the $display_block string to close the table. The remaining lines print the HTML for the page, including the value of the $display_block string.

If you save this file as topiclist.php and place it in your web server document root, and if you have topics in your database tables, you might see something like Figure 21.4.

FIGURE 21.4
Topics are available.

Displaying the Posts in a Topic

As you might have guessed, the next item on the task list is to build that show-topic.php file to show the topic's postings. Listing 21.5 does just that. In this listing, lines 6–9 check for the existence of a value for topic_id in the GET query string. Because you intend to show all the posts within a selected topic, you need to know which topic to use in your query, and this is the manner in which the information is given to you. If a value in $_GET['topic_id'] does not exist, the user is redirected back to the topic listing page, presumably to try again.

LISTING 21.5 Script to Show Topic Posts

```
1:   <?php
2:   include 'ch21_include.php';
3:   doDB();
4:
5:   //check for required info from the query string
6:   if (!isset($_GET['topic_id'])) {
7:       header("Location: topiclist.php");
8:       exit;
9:   }
10:
11:  //create safe values for use
12:  $safe_topic_id = mysqli_real_escape_string($mysqli, $_GET['topic_id']);
13:
14:  //verify the topic exists
15:  $verify_topic_sql = "SELECT topic_title FROM forum_topics
16:                      WHERE topic_id = '".$safe_topic_id."'";
17:  $verify_topic_res =  mysqli_query($mysqli, $verify_topic_sql)
18:                      or die(mysqli_error($mysqli));
19:
```

```
20:    if (mysqli_num_rows($verify_topic_res) < 1) {
21:        //this topic does not exist
22:        $display_block = "<p><em>You have selected an invalid topic.<br/>
23:        Please <a href=\"topiclist.php\">try again</a>.</em></p>";
24:    } else {
25:        //get the topic title
26:        while ($topic_info = mysqli_fetch_array($verify_topic_res)) {
27:            $topic_title = stripslashes($topic_info['topic_title']);
28:        }
29:
30:        //gather the posts
31:        $get_posts_sql = "SELECT post_id, post_text,
             DATE_FORMAT(post_create_time,
32:                              '%b %e %Y<br/>%r') AS fmt_post_create_time, post_owner
33:                           FROM forum_posts
34:                           WHERE topic_id = '".$safe_topic_id."'
35:                           ORDER BY post_create_time ASC";
36:        $get_posts_res = mysqli_query($mysqli, $get_posts_sql)
37:                           or die(mysqli_error($mysqli));
38:
39:        //create the display string
40:        $display_block = <<<END_OF_TEXT
41:        <p>Showing posts for the <strong>$topic_title</strong> topic:</p>
42:        <table>
43:        <tr>
44:        <th>AUTHOR</th>
45:        <th>POST</th>
46:        </tr>
47:    END_OF_TEXT;
48:
49:        while ($posts_info = mysqli_fetch_array($get_posts_res)) {
50:            $post_id = $posts_info['post_id'];
51:            $post_text = nl2br(stripslashes($posts_info['post_text']));
52:            $post_create_time = $posts_info['fmt_post_create_time'];
53:            $post_owner = stripslashes($posts_info['post_owner']);
54:
55:            //add to display
56:            $display_block .= <<<END_OF_TEXT
57:            <tr>
58:            <td>$post_owner<br/><br/>
59:            created on:<br/>$post_create_time</td>
60:            <td>$post_text<br/><br/>
61:            <a href="replytopost.php?post_id=$post_id">
62:            <strong>REPLY TO POST</strong></a></td>
63:            </tr>
64:    END_OF_TEXT;
65:        }
66:
67:        //free results
68:        mysqli_free_result($get_posts_res);
69:        mysqli_free_result($verify_topic_res);
70:
71:        //close connection to MySQL
72:        mysqli_close($mysqli);
73:
74:        //close up the table
75:        $display_block .= "</table>";
76:    }
```

LISTING 21.5　Continued

```
77:  ?>
78:  <!DOCTYPE html>
79:  <html>
80:  <head>
81:  <title>Posts in Topic</title>
82:  <style type="text/css">
83:     table {
84:        border: 1px solid black;
85:        border-collapse: collapse;
86:     }
87:     th {
88:        border: 1px solid black;
89:        padding: 6px;
90:        font-weight: bold;
91:        background: #ccc;
92:     }
93:     td {
94:        border: 1px solid black;
95:        padding: 6px;
96:        vertical-align: top;
97:     }
98:     .num_posts_col { text-align: center; }
99:     </style>
100: </head>
101: <body>
102: <h1>Posts in Topic</h1>
103: <?php echo $display_block; ?>
104: </body>
105: </html>
```

Lines 15–18 show the first of these queries, and this one is used to validate that the `topic_id` sent in the query string is actually a valid entry by selecting the associated `topic_title` for the topic in question. If the validation fails the test in line 20, a message is created in lines 22–23, and the script breaks out of the `if...else` statement and finishes up by printing HTML. This output looks like Figure 21.5.

FIGURE 21.5
Invalid topic
selected.

If, however, the topic is valid, extract the value of topic_title in line 27, again using stripslashes() to remove any escape characters that may have been automatically added upon insertion. Next, the script creates and issues a query in lines 31–37 to gather all the posts associated with that topic in ascending order by time. In this case, newest posts are at the bottom of the list. Line 40 starts a block of text, containing the beginnings of an HTML table. Lines 42–46 set up a table with two columns: one for the author of the post and one for the post text itself. The script stops writing the text block momentarily, and at line 49 begins to loop through the results of the original query.

The while loop in line 49 says that although there are elements to be extracted from the resultset, extract each row as an array called $posts_info, and use the field names as the array element to assign the value to a new variable. So, the first element the script tries to extract is the post_id field on line 50. It assigns the value of $posts_info['post_id'] to the variable $post_id, meaning that it gets a local value for $post_id from an array called $posts_info, containing a field called post_id. Continue doing this for the $post_text, $post_create_time, and $post_owner variables in lines 51–53. The stripslashes() function is again used to remove any escape characters, and the nl2br() function is used on the value of $posts_info[post_text] to replace all newline characters with line-break characters.

In line 56, the script continues to write to the $display_block string, using the concatenation operator (.=) to make sure that this string is tacked on to the end of the string we have created so far. Lines 58–59 create the HTML table column to display the author and creation time of the post. The second HTML table row, on lines 60–63, shows the text of the post as well as a link to reply to the post. The script breaks out of the while loop on line 65, and on line 75 adds the last bit to the $display_block string to close the table. The remaining lines print the HTML for the page, including the value of the $display_block string.

If you save this file as showtopic.php and place it in your web server document root, and if you have posts in your database tables, you might see something like Figure 21.6.

FIGURE 21.6
Posts in a topic.

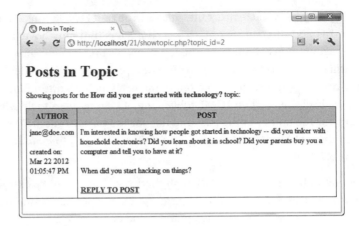

A one-post topic is boring, so let's finish up this chapter by creating the script to add a post to a topic.

Adding Posts to a Topic

In this final step, you create the `replytopost.php` script, which contains code that looks similar to the script used to add a new topic. Listing 21.6 shows the code for this all-in-one form and script, which begins with the inclusion of the functions file and the initiation of the database connection on lines 2–3. Although the script performs different tasks depending on the status of the form (whether it's being shown or submitted), both conditions require database interaction at some point.

LISTING 21.6 Script to Add Replies to a Topic

```
1:  <?php
2:  include 'ch21_include.php';
3:  doDB();
4:
5:  //check to see if we're showing the form or adding the post
6:  if (!$_POST) {
7:      // showing the form; check for required item in query string
8:      if (!isset($_GET['post_id'])) {
9:          header("Location: topiclist.php");
10:         exit;
11: }
12:
13:     //create safe values for use
14:     $safe_post_id = mysqli_real_escape_string($mysqli, $_GET['post_id']);
15:
16:     //still have to verify topic and post
17:     $verify_sql = "SELECT ft.topic_id, ft.topic_title FROM forum_posts
18:                     AS fp LEFT JOIN forum_topics AS ft ON fp.topic_id =
19:                     ft.topic_id WHERE fp.post_id = '".$safe_post_id."'";
20:
```

```
21:       $verify_res = mysqli_query($mysqli, $verify_sql)
22:                     or die(mysqli_error($mysqli));
23:
24:       if (mysqli_num_rows($verify_res) < 1) {
25:           //this post or topic does not exist
26:           header("Location: topiclist.php");
27:           exit;
28:       } else {
29:           //get the topic id and title
30:           while($topic_info = mysqli_fetch_array($verify_res)) {
31:               $topic_id = $topic_info['topic_id'];
32:               $topic_title = stripslashes($topic_info['topic_title']);
33:           }
34: ?>
35: <!DOCTYPE html>
36: <html>
37: <head>
38: <title>Post Your Reply in <?php echo $topic_title; ?></title>
39: </head>
40: <body>
41: <h1>Post Your Reply in <?php echo $topic_title; ?></h1>
42: <form method="post" action="<?php echo $_SERVER['PHP_SELF']; ?>">
43: <p><label for="post_owner">Your Email Address:</label><br/>
44: <input type="email" id="post_owner" name="post_owner" size="40"
45: maxlength="150" required="required"></p>
46: <p><label for="post_text">Post Text:</label><br/>
47: <textarea id="post_text" name="post_text" rows="8" cols="40"
48: required="required"></textarea></p>
49: <input type="hidden" name="topic_id" value="<?php echo $topic_id; ?>">
50: <button type="submit" name="submit" value="submit">Add Post</button>
51: </form>
52: </body>
53: </html>
54: <?php
55:       }
56:       //free result
57:       mysqli_free_result($verify_res);
58:
59:       //close connection to MySQL
60:       mysqli_close($mysqli);
61:
62: } else if ($_POST) {
63:       //check for required items from form
64:       if ((!$_POST['topic_id']) || (!$_POST['post_text']) ||
65:       (!$_POST['post_owner'])) {
66:           header("Location: topiclist.php");
67:           exit;
68:       }
69:
70:       //create safe values for use
71:       $safe_topic_id = mysqli_real_escape_string($mysqli, $_POST['topic_id']);
72:       $safe_post_text = mysqli_real_escape_string($mysqli, $_POST['post_text']);
73:       $safe_post_owner = mysqli_real_escape_string($mysqli, $_POST['post_owner']);
74:
75:       //add the post
76:       $add_post_sql = "INSERT INTO forum_posts (topic_id,post_text,
77:                       post_create_time,post_owner) VALUES
78:                       ('".$safe_topic_id."', '".$safe_post_text."',
```

LISTING 21.6   Continued

```
79:                           now(),'".$safe_post_owner."')";
80:       $add_post_res = mysqli_query($mysqli, $add_post_sql)
81:                           or die(mysqli_error($mysqli));
82:
83:       //close connection to MySQL
84:       mysqli_close($mysqli);
85:
86:       //redirect user to topic
87:       header("Location: showtopic.php?topic_id=".$_POST['topic_id']);
88:       exit;
89: }
90: ?>
```

Line 6 checks to see whether the form is being submitted. If $_POST does not have a value, the form has not yet been submitted, and it must be shown. Before showing the form, however, you must check for that one required item; lines 8–11 check for the existence of a value for post_id in the GET query string. If a value in $_GET['post_id'] does not exist, the user is redirected back to the topic listing page.

If you made it past the check for a value in $_GET['post_id'], lines 17–22 create and issue a complicated-looking query that gets the values of the topic_id and topic_title fields from the forum_topics table, based on the only value that you know: a now-database-safe (thanks to line 14) value of $_GET['post_id']. This query both validates the existence of the post and gets information you will need later in the script. Lines 24–27 act on the results of this validity test, again redirecting the user back to the topiclist.php page if the test fails.

If the value of $_GET['post_id'] represents a valid post, you extract the value of topic_id and topic_title in lines 30–33, again using stripslashes() to remove any escape characters. Next, the script prints to the screen the entirety of the form for adding a post, and that's it for this script until the user clicks the form submission button. In the form, you see that the action is $_SERVER['PHP_SELF'] on line 42, indicating that this script will be recalled into action. A hidden field in line 49 holds the information that needs to be passed along to the next iteration of the script.

Moving on to line 62, this block of code is executed when the script is reloaded and $_POST contains a value. This block checks for the presence of all required fields from the form (lines 64–68) and then, if they are all present, issues the query to add the post to the database (lines 76–81) using safe values created in lines 71–73. After the post is added to the database, the user is redirected to the showtopic.php page (lines 87–88), using the appropriate query string to display the active topic.

If you save this file as `replytopost.php` and place it in your web server document root, try it out and you may see something like Figures 21.7 and 21.8.

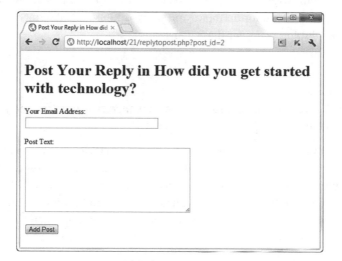

FIGURE 21.7
Preparing to add
a post.

FIGURE 21.8
A post was
added to the
list.

Summary

To take an idea from inception through to fruition, you should follow a design process. This process essentially says, "Think before you act." Discuss rules, requirements, and objectives; then create the final version of your normalized tables.

In this chapter, you saw how forums are hierarchical in nature: Forums contain topics; topics contain posts. You cannot have a topic without a post, and posts do not exist in forums without belonging to a topic. You applied this knowledge to the creation of tables to hold forum topics and posts, and used PHP scripts to create the input and display pages for these items.

Q&A

Q. *What if I want multiple forums? This sequence assumes that only one forum is available.*

A. If you want to have multiple forums in your discussion board, create a table called `forums` (or something to that effect) containing fields for an ID, name, and perhaps a forum description. Then, in the `forum_topics` and `forum_posts` tables, add a field called `forum_id` so that these elements lower in the hierarchy are tied to the master forum. Be sure to amend the SQL queries for record insertion to account for the value of the `forum_id`.

Next, instead of starting your display at the topic level, begin it at the forum level. Just as you created a script to display topics, create a script to show the forums. The link to the forum display would contain the `forum_id`, and the page itself would show all the topics within that forum.

Workshop

The workshop is designed to help you review what you've learned and begin putting your knowledge into practice.

Quiz

1. How is the topic ID value passed to the `showtopic.php` script?

2. What else, besides telling the user that the topic was successfully added, could we do at the end of the `do_addtopic.php` script?

3. Why does the script use the `mysqli_real_escape_string()` function on values from forms?

Answers

1. Through the $_GET superglobal, named as the the value of
   $_GET['topic_id'].

2. Just as with the replytopost.php script, we could eliminate the message display and simply redirect the user to the topic she just created, showing the
   new topic and post in all its glory.

3. The mysqli_real_escape_string() function guards against SQL injection
   attacks by preparing "safe" strings for insertion into the database tables.

Activities

1. You'll notice that none of these pages are really tied together with any sort of
   navigation. Take these basic framework scripts and apply some navigational
   flow to them. Make sure that users can always add a topic or return to the
   topic list from any given page, for example.

2. Use the information provided in the Q&A section to integrate and display
   multiple forums into your tidy little discussion board. While you're at it, apply
   some text styles and colors to jazz up these bare-bones examples.

CHAPTER 22

Creating an Online Storefront

In this chapter, you learn the following:

▶ Create relational tables for an online store
▶ Create scripts to display store categories
▶ Create scripts to display individual items

In this short chapter, you create a generic online storefront. As with the previous project chapters, you learn how to create the relevant database tables as well as the scripts for displaying the information to the user. The examples used in this chapter represent one of an infinite number of possibilities to complete these tasks and are meant to provide a foundation of knowledge rather than a definitive method for completing this task.

Planning and Creating the Database Tables

Before you tackle the process of creating database tables for an online store, think about the real-life shopping process. When you walk into a store, items are ordered in some fashion: The hardware and the baby clothes aren't mixed together, the electronics and the laundry detergent aren't side by side, and so on. Applying that knowledge to database normalization, already you can see that you need a table to hold categories and a table to hold items. In this simple store, each item belongs to one category.

Next, think about the items themselves. Depending on the type of store you have, your items might or might not have colors, and might or might not have sizes. But all your items will have a name, a description, and a price. Again, thinking in terms of normalization, you can imagine that you might have one general items table and two additional tables that relate to the general items table.

Table 22.1 shows sample table and field names to use for your online storefront. In a minute, you create the actual SQL statements, but first you should look at this information and try to see the relationships. Ask yourself which of the fields should be primary or unique keys.

TABLE 22.1   Storefront Table and Field Names

Table Name	Field Names
store_categories	id, cat_title, cat_desc
store_items	id, cat_id, item_title, item_price, item_desc, item_image
store_item_size	item_id, item_size
store_item_color	item_id, item_color

As you can see in the following SQL statements, the store_categories table has two fields besides the id field: cat_title and cat_desc, for title and description, respectively. The id field is the primary key, and cat_title is a unique field because there's no reason you would have two identical categories:

```
CREATE TABLE store_categories (
    id INT NOT NULL PRIMARY KEY AUTO_INCREMENT,
    cat_title VARCHAR (50) UNIQUE,
    cat_desc TEXT
);
```

Next we tackle the store_items table, which has five fields besides the id field—none of which are unique keys. The lengths specified in the field definitions are arbitrary; you should use whatever best fits your store.

The cat_id field relates the item to a particular category in the store_categories table. This field is not unique because you will want more than one item in each category. The item_title, item_price, and item_desc (for description) fields are self-explanatory. The item_image field holds a filename (in this case, the file is assumed to be local to your server) that you use to build an HTML <img> tag when it is time to display your item information:

```
CREATE TABLE store_items (
    id INT NOT NULL PRIMARY KEY AUTO_INCREMENT,
    cat_id INT NOT NULL,
    item_title VARCHAR (75),
    item_price FLOAT (8,2),
    item_desc TEXT,
    item_image VARCHAR (50)
);
```

Both the store_item_size and store_item_color tables contain optional information: If you sell books, they won't have sizes or colors, but if you sell shirts, they will. For each of these tables, the item_id and item_size fields are not unique keys because you can associate as many colors and sizes with a particular item as you want:

```
CREATE TABLE store_item_size (
    id INT NOT NULL PRIMARY KEY AUTO_INCREMENT,
    item_id INT NOT NULL,
    item_size VARCHAR (25)
);
CREATE TABLE store_item_color (
    id INT NOT NULL PRIMARY KEY AUTO_INCREMENT,
    item_id INT NOT NULL,
    item_color VARCHAR (25)
);
```

These are all the tables necessary for a basic storefront—that is, for displaying the items you have for sale. Chapter 23, "Creating a Shopping Cart Mechanism," integrates the user experience into the mix. For now, just concentrate on your inventory.

In Chapter 20, "Creating an Online Address Book," you learned how to use PHP forms and scripts to add or delete records in your tables. If you apply the same principles to this set of tables, you can easily create an administrative front end to your storefront. We do not go through that process in this book, but feel free to do it on your own. (If you understood what was going on in Chapter 20, you know enough about PHP and MySQL to complete the tasks.)

For now, you can simply issue MySQL queries, via the MySQL monitor or other interface, to add information to your tables. Following are some examples, if you want to follow along with sample data.

Inserting Records into the store_categories Table

The following queries create three categories in your store_categories table: hats, shirts, and books.

```
INSERT INTO store_categories VALUES
  ('1', 'Hats', 'Funky hats in all shapes and sizes!');

INSERT INTO store_categories VALUES ('2', 'Shirts', 'From t-shirts to
sweatshirts to polo shirts and beyond.');

INSERT INTO store_categories VALUES ('3', 'Books', 'Paperback, hardback,
books for school or play.');
```

In the next section, we add some items to the categories.

Inserting Records into the `store_items` Table

The following queries add three item records to each category. Feel free to add many more.

```
INSERT INTO store_items VALUES ('1', '1', 'Baseball Hat', '12.00',
'Fancy, low-profile baseball hat.', 'baseballhat.gif');

INSERT INTO store_items VALUES ('2', '1', 'Cowboy Hat', '52.00',
'10 gallon variety', 'cowboyhat.gif');

INSERT INTO store_items VALUES ('3', '1', 'Top Hat', '102.00',
'Good for costumes.', 'tophat.gif');

INSERT INTO store_items VALUES ('4', '2', 'Short-Sleeved T-Shirt',
'12.00', '100% cotton, pre-shrunk.', 'sstshirt.gif');

INSERT INTO store_items VALUES ('5', '2', 'Long-Sleeved T-Shirt',
'15.00', 'Just like the short-sleeved shirt, with longer sleeves.',
'lstshirt.gif');

INSERT INTO store_items VALUES ('6', '2', 'Sweatshirt', '22.00',
'Heavy and warm.', 'sweatshirt.gif');

INSERT INTO store_items VALUES ('7', '3', 'Jane\'s Self-Help Book',
'12.00', 'Jane gives advice.', 'selfhelpbook.gif');

INSERT INTO store_items VALUES ('8', '3', 'Generic Academic Book',
'35.00', 'Some required reading for school, will put you to sleep.',
'boringbook.gif');

INSERT INTO store_items VALUES ('9', '3', 'Chicago Manual of Style',
'9.99', 'Good for copywriters.', 'chicagostyle.gif');
```

NOTE

> The preceding queries refer to various graphics, such as `baseballhat.gif`, which are not included in the code. You can find sample images or make some placeholder graphics of your own.

Inserting Records into the `store_item_size` Table

The following queries associate sizes with one of the three items in the shirts category and a generic "one size fits all" size to each of the hats (assume that they're strange hats). On your own, insert the same set of size associations for the remaining items in the shirts category:

```
INSERT INTO store_item_size (item_id, item_size) VALUES (1,'One Size Fits All');
INSERT INTO store_item_size (item_id, item_size) VALUES (2,'One Size Fits All');
INSERT INTO store_item_size (item_id, item_size) VALUES (3,'One Size Fits All');
INSERT INTO store_item_size (item_id, item_size) VALUES (4,'S');
INSERT INTO store_item_size (item_id, item_size) VALUES (4,'M');
INSERT INTO store_item_size (item_id, item_size) VALUES (4,'L');
INSERT INTO store_item_size (item_id, item_size) VALUES (4,'XL');
```

Inserting Records into the `store_item_color` Table

The following queries associate colors with one of the three items in the `shirts` category. On your own, insert color records for the remaining shirts and hats.

```
INSERT INTO store_item_color (item_id, item_color) VALUES (1,'red');
INSERT INTO store_item_color (item_id, item_color) VALUES (1,'black');
INSERT INTO store_item_color (item_id, item_color) VALUES (1,'blue');
```

Displaying Categories of Items

Believe it or not, the most difficult task in this project is now complete. Compared to thinking up categories and items, creating the scripts used to display the information is easy!

The first script you make is one that lists categories and items. Obviously, you do not want to list all categories and all items all at once as soon as the user walks in the door, but you do want to give the user the option of immediately picking a category, seeing its items, and then picking another category. In other words, this script serves two purposes: It shows the categories, and then if a user clicks a category link, it shows the items in that category.

Listing 22.1 shows the full code for `seestore.php`. If you have worked through this book sequentially, you will notice a lot of the same basic construction you saw in previous chapters; as I mentioned earlier in this book, these projects are all examples of foundational CRUD (create, read, update, delete) applications. Even so, the code is still explained in detail after the listing.

LISTING 22.1 Script to View Categories

```
1:  <?php
2:  //connect to database
3:  $mysqli = mysqli_connect("localhost", "joeuser", "somepass", "testDB");
4:
5:  $display_block = "<h1>My Categories</h1>
6:  <p>Select a category to see its items.</p>";
7:
8:  //show categories first
9:  $get_cats_sql = "SELECT id, cat_title, cat_desc FROM
10:                  store_categories ORDER BY cat_title";
11: $get_cats_res =  mysqli_query($mysqli, $get_cats_sql)
12:                  or die(mysqli_error($mysqli));
13:
14: if (mysqli_num_rows($get_cats_res) < 1) {
15:     $display_block = "<p><em>Sorry, no categories to browse.</em></p>";
16: } else {
17:     while ($cats = mysqli_fetch_array($get_cats_res)) {
18:         $cat_id  = $cats['id'];
19:         $cat_title = strtoupper(stripslashes($cats['cat_title']));
```

LISTING 22.1 Continued

```
20:        $cat_desc = stripslashes($cats['cat_desc']);
21:
22:        $display_block .= "<p><strong><a href=\"".$_SERVER['PHP_SELF'].
23:        "?cat_id=".$cat_id."\">".$cat_title."</a></strong><br/>"
24:        .$cat_desc."</p>";
25:
26:        if (isset($_GET['cat_id']) && ($_GET['cat_id'] == $cat_id)) {
27:            //create safe value for use
28:            $safe_cat_id = mysqli_real_escape_string($mysqli,
29:                $_GET['cat_id']);
30:
31:            //get items
32:            $get_items_sql = "SELECT id, item_title, item_price
33:                              FROM store_items WHERE
34:                              cat_id = '".$cat_id."' ORDER BY item_title";
35:            $get_items_res = mysqli_query($mysqli, $get_items_sql)
36:                              or die(mysqli_error($mysqli));
37:
38:            if (mysqli_num_rows($get_items_res) < 1) {
39:                $display_block = "<p><em>Sorry, no items in this
40:                category.</em></p>";
41:            } else {
42:                $display_block .= "<ul>";
43:                while ($items = mysqli_fetch_array($get_items_res)) {
44:                    $item_id = $items['id'];
45:                    $item_title = stripslashes($items['item_title']);
46:                    $item_price = $items['item_price'];
47:
48:                    $display_block .= "<li><a
                        href=\"showitem.php?item_id=".
49:                    $item_id."\">".$item_title."</a>
50:                    (\$".$item_price.")</li>";
51:                }
52:
53:                $display_block .= "</ul>";
54:            }
55:            //free results
56:            mysqli_free_result($get_items_res);
57:        }
58:    }
59: }
60: }
61: //free results
62: mysqli_free_result($get_cats_res);
63: //close connection to MySQL
64: mysqli_close($mysqli);
65: ?>
66: <!DOCTYPE html>
67: <html>
68: <head>
```

```
69: <title>My Categories</title>
70: </head>
71: <body>
72: <?php echo $display_block; ?>
73: </body>
74: </html>
```

Given the length of scripts you saw in Chapter 20, these 74 fully functional lines should be a welcome change. Line 3 opens the database connection because regardless of which action the script is taking—showing categories or showing items in categories—the database is necessary.

Line 5 starts the $display_block string, with some basic page title information added to it. Lines 9–12 create and issue the query to retrieve the category information. Line 14 checks for categories; if none are in the table, a message is stored in the $display block variable for display to the user, and that's all this script does. (It jumps to the HTML in line 66 and prints to the screen after freeing up some database results.) However, if categories are found, the script moves on to line 17, which begins a while loop to extract the information.

In the while loop, lines 18–20 retrieve the ID, title, and description of the category. String operations are performed to ensure that no slashes are in the text and that the category title is in uppercase for display purposes. Lines 22–24 place the category information, including a self-referential page link, in the $display_block string. If a user clicks the link displayed by that string, she returns to this same script, except with a category ID passed in the query string. The script checks for this value in line 26.

If a $_GET['cat_id'] value has been passed to the script (and has been verified as a valid ID) because the user clicked on a category link in hopes of seeing listed items, the script builds and issues another query using a safe version of that value (lines 32–36) to retrieve the items in the category. Lines 38–51 check for items and then build an item string as part of $display_block. Part of the information in the string is a link to a script called showitem.php, which you create in the next section.

After reaching that point, the script has nothing left to do besides free up some resources, and it prints the HTML and value of $display_block. Figure 22.1 shows the outcome of the script when accessed directly; only the category information shows.

FIGURE 22.1
Categories in
the store.

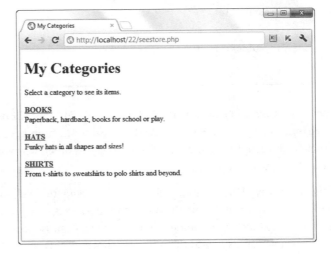

In Figure 22.2, you see what happens when the user clicks on the HATS link: The script gathers all the items associated with the category and prints them on the screen. The user can still jump to another category on this same page, and the script will gather the items for that category.

FIGURE 22.2
Items within a
category in the
store.

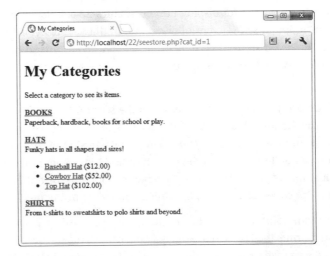

The last piece of the puzzle for this chapter is the creation of the item display page.

Displaying Items

The item display page in this chapter simply shows all the item information. In Chapter 23, you add a few lines to it to make it function with an Add to Cart button, but for now we focus on the display. Listing 22.2 shows the code for showitem.php.

LISTING 22.2   Script to View Item Information

```
1:  <?php
2:  //connect to database
3:  $mysqli = mysqli_connect("localhost", "joeuser", "somepass", "testDB");
4:
5:  $display_block = "<h1>My Store - Item Detail</h1>";
6:
7:  //create safe values for use
8:  $safe_item_id = mysqli_real_escape_string($mysqli, $_GET['item_id']);
9:
10: //validate item
11: $get_item_sql = "SELECT c.id as cat_id, c.cat_title, si.item_title,
12:                   si.item_price, si.item_desc, si.item_image FROM store_items
13:                   AS si LEFT JOIN store_categories AS c on c.id = si.cat_id
14:                   WHERE si.id = '".$safe_item_id."'";
15: $get_item_res = mysqli_query($mysqli, $get_item_sql)
16:                   or die(mysqli_error($mysqli));
17:
18: if (mysqli_num_rows($get_item_res) < 1) {
19:     //invalid item
20:     $display_block .= "<p><em>Invalid item selection.</em></p>";
21: } else {
22:     //valid item, get info
23:     while ($item_info = mysqli_fetch_array($get_item_res)) {
24:         $cat_id = $item_info['cat_id'];
25:         $cat_title = strtoupper(stripslashes($item_info['cat_title']));
26:         $item_title = stripslashes($item_info['item_title']);
27:         $item_price = $item_info['item_price'];
28:         $item_desc = stripslashes($item_info['item_desc']);
29:         $item_image = $item_info['item_image'];
30:     }
31:
32:     //make breadcrumb trail & display of item
33:     $display_block .= <<<END_OF_TEXT
34:     <p><em>You are viewing:</em><br/>
35:     <strong><a href="seestore.php?cat_id=$cat_id">$cat_title</a> &gt;
36:       $item_title</strong></p>
36:     <div style="float: left;"><img src="$item_image" alt="$item_title"
37:       /></div>
37:     <div style="float: left; padding-left: 12px">
38:     <p><strong>Description:</strong><br/>$item_desc</p>
39:     <p><strong>Price:</strong> \$$item_price</p>
40: END_OF_TEXT;
41:
42:     //free result
43:     mysqli_free_result($get_item_res);
44:
```

LISTING 22.2   Continued

```
45:     //get colors
46:     $get_colors_sql = "SELECT item_color FROM store_item_color WHERE
47:                        item_id = '".$safe_item_id."' ORDER BY item_color";
48:     $get_colors_res = mysqli_query($mysqli, $get_colors_sql)
49:                       or die(mysqli_error($mysqli));
50:
51:     if (mysqli_num_rows($get_colors_res) > 0) {
52:         $display_block .= "<p><strong>Available Colors:</strong><br/>";
53:         while ($colors = mysqli_fetch_array($get_colors_res)) {
54:             item_color = $colors['item_color'];
55:             $display_block .= $item_color."<br/>";
56:         }
57:     }
58:     //free result
59:     mysqli_free_result($get_colors_res);
60:
61:     //get sizes
62:     $get_sizes_sql = "SELECT item_size FROM store_item_size WHERE
63:                       item_id = ".$safe_item_id." ORDER BY item_size";
64:     $get_sizes_res = mysqli_query($mysqli, $get_sizes_sql)
65:                      or die(mysqli_error($mysqli));
66:
67:     if (mysqli_num_rows($get_sizes_res) > 0) {
68:         $display_block .= "<p><strong>Available Sizes:</strong><br/>";
69:         while ($sizes = mysqli_fetch_array($get_sizes_res)) {
70:             $item_size = $sizes['item_size'];
71:             $display_block .= $item_size."<br/>";
72:         }
73:     }
74:     //free result
75:     mysqli_free_result($get_sizes_res);
76:
77:     $display_block .= "</div>";
78: }
79: //close connection to MySQL
80: mysqli_close($mysqli);
81: ?>
82: <!DOCTYPE html>
83: <html>
84: <head>
85: <title>My Store</title>
86: </head>
87: <body>
88: <?php echo $display_block; ?>
89: </body>
90: </html>
```

Line 3 makes the database connection because information in the database forms all the content of this page. Line 5 starts the $display_block string, with some basic page title information.

Lines 11–13 create and issue the query to retrieve the category and item information, using the safe value created in line 8. This particular query is a table join. Instead of selecting the item information from one table and then issuing a second query to find the name of the category, this query simply joins the table on the category ID to find the category name.

Line 15 checks for a result; if there is no matching item in the table, a message is printed to the user and that's all this script does. However, if item information is found, the script moves on and gathers the information in lines 23–30.

In lines 34–35, you first create what's known as a *breadcrumb trail*. This is simply a navigational device used to get back to the top-level item in the architecture. In other words, you're going to print a link so the user can get back to the category. The category ID, retrieved from the master query in this script, is appended to the link in the breadcrumb trail.

In lines 36–39, you continue to add to the $display_block, setting up a display of information about the item. You use the values gathered in lines 23–30 to create an image link, print the description, and print the price. What's missing are the colors and sizes, so lines 46–57 select and print any colors associated with this item, and lines 62–73 gather the sizes associated with the item.

Lines 77–78 wrap up the $display_block string and the master if...else statement. Because the script has nothing left to do after closing the connection to MySQL, it prints the HTML (lines 82–90) including the value of $display_block. Figure 22.3 shows the outcome of the script when selecting the baseball hat from the hats category. Of course, your display will differ from mine because you won't have the same images I used, but you get the idea.

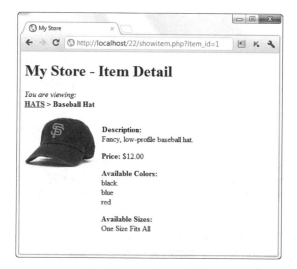

FIGURE 22.3
The baseball hat item page.

That's all there is to creating a simple item display. In Chapter 23, you modify this script so that it can add the item to a shopping cart.

Summary

In this chapter, you applied your basic PHP and MySQL knowledge to the creation of a storefront display. You learned how to create the database table and scripts for viewing categories, item lists, and single items.

Q&A

Q. *In the item detail record, you use single filenames in the `item_image` field. What if I want to link to items on a different server?*

A. You can enter a URL in the `item_image` field as long as you define the field to hold a long string such as a URL.

Workshop

The workshop is designed to help you review what you've learned and begin putting your knowledge into practice.

Quiz

1. Which PHP function was used to uppercase the category title strings?

2. Why don't the `store_item_size` and `store_item_color` tables contain any unique keys?

3. Why do you continue to use `mysqli_real_escape_string()` on values that will be used in database queries?

Answers

1. `strtoupper()`

2. Presumably, you will have items with more than one color and more than one size. Therefore, `item_id` is not a unique key. Also, items may have the same colors or sizes, so the `item_color` and `item_size` fields must not be primary or unique either.

3. You should use `mysqli_real_escape_string()` to ensure values from the user, which will be used in database queries, are safe to use, no matter if you've created one script, ten scripts, or one hundred.

Activities

1. Create three more categories, with an item or two in each, by issuing queries of your own in MySQL.

2. Make some images (or use Creative Commons licensed images) for each of the items in your store, and put them in an `images` directory on your server. Doing so necessitates one change to the `showitem.php` script: adding the image directory to the file path of the generated `<img/>` tag.

## CHAPTER 23

Creating a Shopping Cart Mechanism

In this chapter, you learn the following:

▶ How to create relational tables for the shopping cart and checkout portion of an online store

▶ How to create the scripts to add and remove cart items

▶ Some methods for processing transactions, and how to create your checkout sequence

In this chapter, you integrate a shopping cart mechanism and checkout procedure into the basic storefront display that you created in Chapter 22, "Creating an Online Storefront." You learn the methods for creating relevant database tables as well as what goes into scripts for adding and deleting cart items. The examples used in this chapter again represent only a few of an infinite number of possibilities to complete these tasks and are meant as working examples rather than the definitive guide for building an online store.

Planning and Creating the Database Tables

Because the goal of this chapter is to provide the user with a way to select and order items, you can imagine what the tables will be—first and foremost, you need a table to hold the shopping cart information. In addition to the cart table, you need a table to store orders, along with one to store the items purchased as part of each order.

The following SQL statements were used to create the three new tables, starting with the store_shoppertrack table. This is the table used to hold items as users add them to their shopping cart.

NOTE

The field lengths used to define these tables were chosen arbitrarily to accommodate several possible inputs. Feel free to modify the lengths to meet your specific needs.

```
CREATE TABLE store_shoppertrack (
    id INT NOT NULL PRIMARY KEY AUTO_INCREMENT,
    session_id VARCHAR (32),
    sel_item_id INT,
    sel_item_qty SMALLINT,
    sel_item_size VARCHAR(25),
    sel_item_color VARCHAR(25),
    date_added DATETIME
);
```

In this table, the only key is the id field for the record. The session_id cannot be unique; otherwise, users could order only one item from your store, which is not a good business practice.

The value stored in the session_id field identifies the user; it matches the value of the PHP session ID assigned to that particular user. The sel_* fields hold the selections by the user: the selected item, the selected quantity of the item, and the selected color and size of the item. Finally, there's a date_added field. Many times, users place items in their cart and never go through the checkout process. This practice leaves straggling items in your tracking table, which you might want to clear out periodically. For example, you might want to delete all cart items more than a week old—this is where the date_added field is helpful.

The next table holds the order information:

```
CREATE TABLE store_orders (
    id INT NOT NULL PRIMARY KEY AUTO_INCREMENT,
    order_date DATETIME,
    order_name VARCHAR (100),
    order_address VARCHAR (255),
    order_city VARCHAR (50),
    order_state CHAR(2),
    order_zip VARCHAR(10),
    order_tel VARCHAR(25),
    order_email VARCHAR(100),
    item_total FLOAT(6,2),
    shipping_total FLOAT(6,2),
    authorization VARCHAR (50),
    status ENUM('processed', 'pending')
);
```

The only key field in the store_orders table is the id. For the sake of brevity in this chapter, we make an assumption that the billing and shipping addresses of the user are the same and that this store sells only to U.S. addresses. It's simple enough for you to add another block of fields for shipping address information, if you want to do so. If this were a live example, you certainly would want to; otherwise, you would lose business from shoppers who purchase items for gifts, for instance.

Also, this table assumes that you are not storing credit card information, which you absolutely should not do unless you have super-encrypted the information and are sure that your firewalled server is secure. Instead, this table is based on the idea of real-time, credit card processing. You learn about a few real-time transaction options at the end of this chapter.

The final table holds the line items in each order, store_orders_items:

```
CREATE TABLE store_orders_items (
    id INT NOT NULL PRIMARY KEY AUTO_INCREMENT,
    order_id INT,
    sel_item_id INT,
    sel_item_qty SMALLINT,
    sel_item_size VARCHAR(25),
    sel_item_color VARCHAR(25),
    sel_item_price FLOAT(6,2)
);
```

The sel_* fields should look familiar. With the exception of sel_item_price, they are the same fields that appear in the store_shoppertrack table because what you are tracking in that table are the line items that people want to purchase. The primary key in this table is the id field, and the order_id field ties each line item to the appropriate record in store_orders.

The sel_item_price field is included here, as opposed to simply relating to the item record, because you might have occasion to change the pricing in your item record. If you change the price in the item record, and you relate the sold line items to the current catalog price, your line item prices won't reflect what the user actually paid.

With your tables all squared away, we can move on to adding an item to the user's shopping cart.

Integrating the Cart with Your Storefront

In this section, you make modifications to the showitem.php script from Chapter 22. The goal is to transform the item information page into an item information page with a form for selecting colors, sizes, and quantities.

In the original script, insert the following before line 2:

```
session_start();
```

Because the shopping cart elements are attached to the user through a session ID, the session must be started. The next changes do not occur until what was line 39 of the showitem.php script from Chapter 22, so that's where we start in Listing 23.1.

LISTING 23.1   New Lines in showitem.php

```
39:    <p><strong>Price:</strong> \$$item_price</p>
40:    <form method="post" action="addtocart.php">
41: END_OF_TEXT;
42:
43:    //free result
44:    mysqli_free_result($get_item_res);
45:
46:    //get colors
47:    $get_colors_sql = "SELECT item_color FROM store_item_color WHERE
48:                       item_id = '".$safe_item_id."' ORDER BY item_color";
49:    $get_colors_res = mysqli_query($mysqli, $get_colors_sql)
50:                      or die(mysqli_error($mysqli));
51:
52:    if (mysqli_num_rows($get_colors_res) > 0) {
53:        $display_block .= "<p><label for=\"sel_item_color\">
54:        Available Colors:</label><br/>
55:        <select id=\"sel_item_color\" name=\"sel_item_color\">";
56:
57:        while ($colors = mysqli_fetch_array($get_colors_res)) {
58:            $item_color = $colors['item_color'];
59:            $display_block .= "<option value=\"".$item_color."\">".
60:            $item_color."</option>";
61:        }
62:        $display_block .= "</select></p>";
63:    }
64:
65:    //free result
66:    mysqli_free_result($get_colors_res);
67:
68:    //get sizes
69:    $get_sizes_sql = "SELECT item_size FROM store_item_size WHERE
70:                      item_id = ".$safe_item_id." ORDER BY item_size";
71:    $get_sizes_res = mysqli_query($mysqli, $get_sizes_sql)
72:                     or die(mysqli_error($mysqli));
73:
74:    if (mysqli_num_rows($get_sizes_res) > 0) {
75:        $display_block .= "<p><label for=\"sel_item_size\">
76:        Available Sizes:</label><br/>
77:        <select id=\"sel_item_size\" name=\"sel_item_size\">";
78:
79:        while ($sizes = mysqli_fetch_array($get_sizes_res)) {
80:            $item_size = $sizes['item_size'];
81:            $display_block .= "<option value=\"".$item_size."\">".
82:            $item_size."</option>";
83:        }
```

```
84:     }
85:
86:     $display_block .= "</select></p>";
87:
88:     //free result
89:     mysqli_free_result($get_sizes_res);
90:
91:     $display_block .= "
92:     <p><label for=\"sel_item_qty\">Select Quantity:</label>
93:     <select id=\"sel_item_qty\" name=\"sel_item_qty\">";
94:
95:     for($i=1; $i<11; $i++) {
96:         $display_block .= "<option value=\"".$i."\">".$i."</option>";
97:     }
98:
99:     $display_block .= <<<END_OF_TEXT
100:    </select></p>
101:    <input type="hidden" name="sel_item_id"
102:    value="$_GET[item_id]" />
103:    <button type="submit" name="submit" value="submit">
104:    Add to Cart</button>
105:    </form>
106:    </div>
107: END_OF_TEXT;
108: }
109:
110: //close connection to MySQL
111: mysqli_close($mysqli);
112: ?>
113: <!DOCTYPE html>
114: <html>
115: <head>
116: <title>My Store</title>
117: <style type="text/css">
118:     label {font-weight: bold;}
119: </style>
120: </head>
121: <body>
122: <?php echo $display_block; ?>
123: </body>
124: </html>
```

The first change is at the new line 40, where the $display_block string is continued to include the beginning <form> element. The action of the form is a script called addtocart.php, which you create in the next section.

The next change occurs at line 55, where the $display_block string is continued to include the opening tag of a <select> element named sel_item_color (and the "Available Colors" text is now surrounded by a <label> tag in lines 53–54, because it is labeling a form element). In lines 58–60, the colors are put into <option> elements for the user to choose from instead of simply printing on the screen. Line 62 closes the <select> element.

The same types of changes are made for item sizes. Lines 75–77 reflect the continuation of the `$display_block` string to include the `<select>` element, named `sel_item_size`. Lines 80–82 write the colors in `<option>` elements, and line 86 closes the `<select>` element.

Lines 91–97 are additions to the script. These lines create a `<select>` element, called `sel_item_qty`, for the user to pick how many items to purchase (a `for` loop iterates through numbers from 1 to 10 to create the `<option>` elements). Line 100 closes this `<select>` element, and lines 101–102 adds a hidden field for the `item_id`. Lines 103–104 adds the submit button, and line 105 closes the form. We close the connection to MySQL in line 111, and the remaining lines include the bits of HTML used to render the page, with the addition of a stylesheet entry for the `<label>` tag to make it bold like the nonlabels used in the display.

When viewing the baseball hat item using the new version of `showitem.php`, you would see Figure 23.1, reflecting the addition of the form elements.

FIGURE 23.1
The new baseball hat item page.

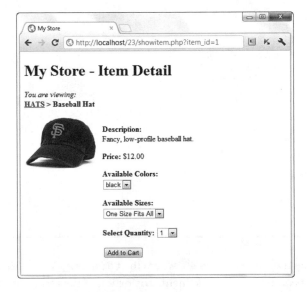

The next step is to create the `addtocart.php` script so that the form you just created actually does something.

Adding Items to Your Cart

The `addtocart.php` script simply writes information to the `store_shoppertrack` table and redirects the user to the view of the shopping cart. We create the `addtocart.php` script first in Listing 23.2, and then tackle the `showcart.php` script next.

LISTING 23.2 The `addtocart.php` **Script**

```php
1:  <?php
2:  session_start();
3:
4:  if (isset($_POST['sel_item_id'])) {
5:      //connect to database
6:      $mysqli = mysqli_connect("localhost", "joeuser", "somepass", "testDB");
7:
8:      //create safe values for use
9:      $safe_sel_item_id = mysqli_real_escape_string($mysqli,
10:             $_POST['sel_item_id']);
11:     $safe_sel_item_qty = mysqli_real_escape_string($mysqli,
12:             $_POST['sel_item_qty']);
13:     $safe_sel_item_size = mysqli_real_escape_string($mysqli,
14:             $_POST['sel_item_size']);
15:     $safe_sel_item_color = mysqli_real_escape_string($mysqli,
16:             $_POST['sel_item_color']);
17:
18:     //validate item and get title and price
19:     $get_iteminfo_sql = "SELECT item_title FROM store_items WHERE
20:                          id = '".$safe_sel_item_id."'";
21:     $get_iteminfo_res = mysqli_query($mysqli, $get_iteminfo_sql)
22:                         or die(mysqli_error($mysqli));
23:
24:     if (mysqli_num_rows($get_iteminfo_res) < 1) {
25:
26:         //free result
27:         mysqli_free_result($get_iteminfo_res);
28:
29:         //close connection to MySQL
30:         mysqli_close($mysqli);
31:
32:         //invalid id, send away
33:         header("Location: seestore.php");
34:         exit;
35:     } else {
36:         //get info
37:         while ($item_info = mysqli_fetch_array($get_iteminfo_res)) {
38:             $item_title =  stripslashes($item_info['item_title']);
39:         }
40:
41:         //free result
42:         mysqli_free_result($get_iteminfo_res);
43:
44:         //add info to cart table
45:         $addtocart_sql = "INSERT INTO store_shoppertrack
46:                           (session_id, sel_item_id, sel_item_qty,
47:                           sel_item_size, sel_item_color, date_added)
48:                           VALUES ('".$_COOKIE['PHPSESSID']."',
49:                           '".$safe_sel_item_id."',
50:                           '".$safe_sel_item_qty."',
51:                           '".$safe_sel_item_size."',
52:                           '".$safe_sel_item_color."', now())";
53:         $addtocart_res = mysqli_query($mysqli, $addtocart_sql)
54:                          or die(mysqli_error($mysqli));
55:
56:
```

LISTING 23.2   Continued

```
57:            //close connection to MySQL
58:            mysqli_close($mysqli);
59:
60:            //redirect to showcart page
61:            header("Location: showcart.php");
62:            exit;
63:     }
64:
65: } else {
66:     //send them somewhere else
67:     header("Location: seestore.php");
68:     exit;
69: }
70: ?>
```

Line 2 continues the user session, which is important because you need to capture the user's session ID to write to the `store_shoppertrack` table.

In line 4, the script verifies that a value is present in `$_POST['sel_item_id']`, meaning that the user came to this script after submitting the proper form. If there is no value, the script jumps down to line 51 and sends the user away in line 53, and that's it for the script.

However, if there is a value in `$_POST['sel_item_id']`, line 6 makes the database connection, lines 9–16 create safe versions of the form information, and line 17 issues a query to verify that the selected item ID is for a valid item. Lines 19–22 create and issue a SQL query to gather the title of the selected item. Line 24 checks for a result; if there is no result, the user is again redirected away in line 33 because the item selection was not valid.

If the item selection is valid, the script continues to line 38 and extracts this value from the resultset. The script now has enough information to add the item selection to the `store_shoppertrack` table, which it does in lines 45–54.

After the query has been issued, the user is redirected to `showcart.php`, which contains all cart items. You create this script in the next section.

Viewing the Cart

Now that you can add items to a cart, you want to see them! Listing 23.3 shows the code for `showcart.php`.

LISTING 23.3   The `showcart.php` Script

```
1:    <?php
2:    session_start();
3:
4:    //connect to database
```

```
 5:   $mysqli = mysqli_connect("localhost", "joeuser", "somepass", "testDB");
 6:
 7:   $display_block = "<h1>Your Shopping Cart</h1>";
 8:
 9:   //check for cart items based on user session id
10:   $get_cart_sql = "SELECT st.id, si.item_title, si.item_price,
11:                       st.sel_item_qty, st.sel_item_size, st.sel_item_color FROM
12:                       store_shoppertrack AS st LEFT JOIN store_items AS si ON
13:                       si.id = st.sel_item_id WHERE session_id =
14:                       '".$_COOKIE['PHPSESSID']."'";
15:   $get_cart_res = mysqli_query($mysqli, $get_cart_sql)
16:                       or die(mysqli_error($mysqli));
17:
18:   if (mysqli_num_rows($get_cart_res) < 1) {
19:       //print message
20:        $display_block .= "<p>You have no items in your cart.
21:        Please <a href=\"seestore.php\">continue to shop</a>!</p>";
22:   } else {
23:       //get info and build cart display
24:       $display_block .= <<<END_OF_TEXT
25:       <table>
26:       <tr>
27:       <th>Title</th>
28:       <th>Size</th>
29:       <th>Color</th>
30:       <th>Price</th>
31:       <th>Qty</th>
32:       <th>Total Price</th>
33:       <th>Action</th>
34:       </tr>
35: END_OF_TEXT;
36:
37:       while ($cart_info = mysqli_fetch_array($get_cart_res)) {
38:           $id = $cart_info['id'];
39:           $item_title = stripslashes($cart_info['item_title']);
40:           $item_price = $cart_info['item_price'];
41:           $item_qty = $cart_info['sel_item_qty'];
42:           $item_color = $cart_info['sel_item_color'];
43:           $item_size = $cart_info['sel_item_size'];
44:           $total_price = sprintf("%.02f", $item_price * $item_qty);
45:
46:           $display_block .= <<<END_OF_TEXT;
47:           <tr>
48:           <td>$item_title <br></td>
49:           <td>$item_size <br></td>
50:           <td>$item_color <br></td>
51:           <td>\$ $item_price <br></td>
52:           <td>$item_qty <br></td>
53:           <td>\$ $total_price</td>
54:           <td><a href="removefromcart.php?id=$id">remove</a></td>
55:           </tr>
56: END_OF_TEXT;
57:     }
58:     $display_block .= "</table>";
59: }
60: //free result
61: mysqli_free_result($get_cart_res);
62:
```

LISTING 23.3   Continued

```
63: //close connection to MySQL
64: mysqli_close($mysqli);
65: ?>
66: <!DOCTYPE html>
67: <html>
68: <head>
69: <title>My Store</title>
70: <style type="text/css">
71:     table {
72:         border: 1px solid black;
73:         border-collapse: collapse;
74:     }
75:     th {
76:         border: 1px solid black;
77:         padding: 6px;
78:         font-weight: bold;
79:         background: #ccc;
80:         text-align: center;
81:     }
82:     td {
83:         border: 1px solid black;
84:         padding: 6px;
85:         vertical-align: top;
86:         text-align: center;
87:     }
88: </style>
89: </head>
90: <body>
91: <?php echo $display_block; ?>
92: </body>
93: </html>
```

Line 2 continues the user session, which is important because you need to match the user's session ID with the records in the store_shoppertrack table. Line 5 makes the database connection, and line 7 begins the $display_block string, with a heading for the page.

Lines 10–14 represent a joined query, in which the user's saved items are retrieved. The id, sel_item_qty, sel_item_size, and sel_item_color fields are extracted from store_shoppertrack, and the item_title and item_price fields are retrieved from the store_items table based on the matching information from store_shoppertrack. In other words, instead of printing 2 for the selected item, Baseball Hat is shown as the title. Lines 15–16 issue the query, and line 18 checks for results.

If there are no results, the user has no items in the store_shoppertrack table. A message is written to the $display_block string, and the script exits and shows the message.

If there are indeed results, the beginning of an HTML table is created in lines 24–34, with columns defined for all the information in the cart (plus one column for an action link). Line 37 begins the while loop to extract each item from the store_shoppertrack, and this loop continues until line 56, printing the information in the proper table cell.

In line 54, you see a link created for an item removal script, which you create in the next section. Line 58 closes the table, and the script finishes and prints HTML to the screen in lines 66–93, including some stylesheet entries for your table headings and other cells.

Now, go back to an item page and add the item to your cart. After the items are written to the store_shoppertrack table, you should be redirected to the show-cart.php page, and your newly selected items should be displayed. Figure 23.2 shows my cart after adding some items.

FIGURE 23.2
Items added to cart.

The next step is to create the removefromcart.php script.

Removing Items from Your Cart

The removefromcart.php script is short because all it does is issue a query and redirect the user to another script. Inevitably, a user will want to weed items out of his cart, and this script enables him to do just that. Listing 23.4 shows the complete script.

LISTING 23.4 The `removefromcart.php` Script

```
1:  <?php
2:  session_start();
3:
4:  if (isset($_GET['id'])) {
5:      //connect to database
6:      $mysqli = mysqli_connect("localhost", "joeuser", "somepass", "testDB");
7:
8:      //create safe values for use
9:      $safe id = mysqli_real_escape_string($mysqli, $_GET['id']);
10:
11:     $delete_item_sql = "DELETE FROM store_shoppertrack WHERE
12:                         id = '".$safe_id."' and session_id =
13:                         '".$_COOKIE['PHPSESSID']'";
14:     $delete_item_res = mysqli_query($mysqli, $delete_item_sql)
15:                        or die(mysqli_error($mysqli));
16:
17:     //close connection to MySQL
18:     mysqli_close($mysqli);
19:
20:     //redirect to showcart page
21:     header("Location: showcart.php");
22:     exit;
23: } else {
24:     //send them somewhere else
25:     header("Location: seestore.php");
26:     exit;
27: }
28: ?>
```

Line 2 continues the user session because you need to match the user's session ID with the records in the `store_shoppertrack` table. Line 4 checks for a value in `$_GET['id']`. If a value does not exist in `$_GET['id']`, the user is not clicking the link from her cart and, therefore, is sent away in line 22.

If a value exists in `$_GET['id']`, line 6 makes the database connection, line 9 creates a database-safe version of the variable, and a SQL query (lines 11–13) is issued (lines 14–15), and the user is redirected to the `showcart.php` script (line 21), where the item should no longer be displayed in the user's shopping cart. Try it and see!

Payment Methods and the Checkout Sequence

Several commerce methods exist when it comes time to pay for the purchases in the shopping cart. The "right" method for you depends on your business—merchant accounts through banking institutions often require you to have a business license, a reseller's permit, and other pieces of paper proving that you're a legitimate business. If you're simply a person who has a few items to sell, you might not want to go through all that paperwork. However, you still have options.

Regardless of the payment method you choose, one thing is certain: If you are passing credit card information over the Web, you must do so over an SSL (Secure Sockets Layer) connection. Obtaining an SSL certificate and installing it on your system is covered in Chapter 30, "Setting Up a Secure Web Server." You do not have to use this secure connection during the user's entire shopping experience, just from the point at which sensitive information will be captured, such as when you send the user to the checkout form.

Creating the Checkout Form

At this point in the book, you should be well versed in creating a simple form. At the beginning of this chapter, you created the store_orders table with fields to use as a guideline for your form:

- ▶ order_name
- ▶ order_address
- ▶ order_city
- ▶ order_state
- ▶ order_zip
- ▶ order_tel
- ▶ order_email

In addition, your form needs fields for the credit card number, expiration date, and the name on the credit card. Another nice feature is to repeat the user's shopping cart contents with an item subtotal so that the customer remembers what he's paying for and approximately how much the order will cost. Also at this point of the checkout sequence, you offer any shipping options you might have. Shipping and sales tax would be calculated in the next step of the process.

From the point of clicking the submit button on the form, the checkout sequence depends on the payment method you are using. The next section goes through the basic steps and offers suggestions on various methods of payment processing.

Performing the Checkout Actions

If you have obtained a merchant account through your bank, you can utilize real-time payment services such as Authorize.Net's payment gateway services or PayPal's PayFlo product. For more information about these services, see http://www.authorize.net and https://www.paypal.com/webapps/mpp/merchant, respectively.

PHP does not contain built-in functions that enable direct access to these payment gateways, but when you have an account with merchant services of these types, you can download scripts that you can use in your own applications, or you are given information on an API for application developers.

Authorize.Net and PayPal are two of several transaction-processing gateways that exist for use by merchants—I include them here because I have personally (and successfully) used both gateway services since their inception. However, be aware that your bank will usually provide a list of merchants it prefers you to use. So if you stray from your bank's list of preferred vendors, be sure to research your selected vendor thoroughly to avoid any delays with deposits and to ensure that you're getting the best deal.

After you have selected a transaction processor, your checkout script should follow a path such as the following:

1. Total the items, add tax, and add shipping. This gives you the total amount to authorize from the credit card.

2. Perform credit card authorization for the total amount.

3. You receive either a success or failure response from your card-processing routine. If the response is a failure, print a message to the user and the transaction is over. If the response is a success, continue to step 4.

4. Write the basic order information to a table such as `store_orders`, including the authorization code you receive on successful authorization. Get the `id` value of this record using `mysql_insert_id()`.

5. For each item in the shopping cart tied to this user, insert a record into `store_orders_itemmap`. Each record references the `id` (as `order_id`) gathered in the previous step.

6. Delete the shopping cart items for this user.

7. Display the order with the authorization code in place of the credit card information on the screen so that the user can print it and hold it as a receipt. You can also send this information via email to the user.

The steps listed here—with the exception of the actual payment authorization code—are the same simple steps you have been using throughout this book, and there's no reason to make them more difficult than they need to be.

Summary

In this chapter, you applied your basic PHP and MySQL knowledge to the integration of a shopping cart into the storefront from Chapter 22. Included were the database table creation, modifications to the item detail page, and new scripts for adding and removing cart items.

Q&A

Q. *How can users be sure that an item is in stock when they add it to their cart?*

A. If the store_items table were modified to contain a field for the current quantity, and when a user completed the checkout sequence that quantity was decreased by the number of items that the user ordered, then in the showitem.php script you could generate a drop-down list that had a maximum selection of the number of items remaining in inventory. Of course, if you are working with thousands of items in inventory it shouldn't matter if your drop-down selector only allows the purchase of 10 at a time. However, for a better user experience you would want the user to be able to add as many to their cart as possible, and in that case you might also add an inventory check before finishing the add-to-cart sequence, and disallow the addition of a quantity greater than the quantity in stock.

Workshop

The workshop is designed to help you review what you've learned and begin putting your knowledge into practice.

Quiz

1. When removing an item from the cart, why do you suppose that the query validates the session ID of the user against the record?

2. What would be a reason not to store the price in a hidden field when adding to the cart?

3. What would you do to the database and form to handle the need for different shipping and billing addresses?

Answers

1. Users should be able to remove only their own items.

2. If you stored the price in a hidden field, a rogue user could change that value before posting the form (writing whatever price he wanted into the store_shoppertrack table as opposed to the actual price).

3. Modify the existing address-related fields in the store_orders table so that it is clear they are either for shipping or billing addresses, then duplicate the set of fields in the table (and give them a name indicating they're for either shipping or billing—whichever you didn't use already) and also the form and the eventual INSERT statement.

Activities

1. Even if you do not have a merchant account, set up the checkout form as described in the "Creating the Checkout Form" section. Don't forget to add a link to the shopping cart (or any other page in the store) to this "checkout" functionality.

2. After creating the checkout form, save the order information and line items to the database tables created at the beginning of this chapter. Don't worry about the merchant account or payment processing at this point. Just get the process going that allows users to save items in their shopping cart, check out by giving you some dummy credit card and address information, and then store that basic order information in the store_orders table and the items in the order in the store_orders_items table.

CHAPTER 24

Creating a Simple Calendar

In this chapter, you learn the following:

▶ How to build a simple calendar script

▶ How to view and add events in your calendar

▶ How to build a class library to generate date pull-downs in HTML forms

This chapter pulls together the skills you've learned so far regarding the PHP language and building small CRUD applications—those that create, retrieve, update, and delete data. In this chapter, you continue your learning in the context of creating a small calendar application.

Building a Simple Display Calendar

You'll use the date and time functions you learned in Chapter 10, "Working with Strings, Dates, and Time," to build a calendar that displays the dates for any month between 1990 and 2020. Those are randomly selected years and have no significance—you can make your calendar go from 1980 to 2025 if you want, or any other range of dates that make sense to you. The user can select both month and year with pull-down menus, and the dates for the selected month will be organized according to the days of the week.

In this script, we work with two variables—one for month and one for year—which are supplied by user input. These pieces of information are used to build a timestamp based on the first day of the selected month. If user input is invalid or absent, the default value is the first day of the current month.

Checking User Input

When the user accesses the calendar application for the first time, no information will have been submitted. Therefore, we must ensure that the script can handle the fact that the variables for month and year might not be defined. We could use the `isset()` function for this because it returns `false` if the variable passed to it has not been defined. However, let's use the `checkdate()` function instead, which not only will see whether the variable exists but will also do something meaningful with it, namely, validate that it is a date. Listing 24.1 shows the fragment of code that checks for `month` and `year` variables coming from a form, and builds a timestamp based on them.

LISTING 24.1   Checking User Input for the Calendar Script

```
 1: <?php
 2: if ((!isset($_POST['month'])) || (!isset($_POST['year']))) {
 3:     $nowArray = getdate();
 4:     $month = $nowArray['mon'];
 5:     $year = $nowArray['year'];
 6: } else {
 7:     $month = $_POST['month'];
 8:     $year = $_POST['year'];
 9: }
10: $start = mktime (12, 0, 0, $month, 1, $year);
11: $firstDayArray = getdate($start);
12: ?>
```

Listing 24.1 is a fragment of a larger script, so it does not produce any output itself. But it's an important fragment to understand, which is why it sits all alone here, ready for an explanation.

In the `if` statement on line 2, we test whether the month and year have been provided by a form. If the month and year have not been defined, the `mktime()` function used later in the fragment will not be able to make a valid date from undefined `month` and `year` arguments.

If the values are present, we use `getdate()` on line 3 to create an associative array based on the current time. We then set values for `$month` and `$year` ourselves, using the array's `mon` and `year` elements (lines 4 and 5). If the variables have been set from the form, we put the data into `$month` and `$year` variables so as not to touch the values in the original `$_POST` superglobal.

Now that we are sure that we have valid data in `$month` and `$year`, we can use `mktime()` to create a timestamp for the first day of the month (line 10). We will need information about this timestamp later on, so on line 11, we create a variable called `$firstDayArray` that will store an associative array returned by `getdate()` and based on this timestamp.

Building the HTML Form

We now need to create an interface by which users can ask to see data for a month and year. For this, we use SELECT elements. Although we could hard-code these in HTML, we must also ensure that the pull-downs default to the currently chosen month, so we will dynamically create these pull-downs, adding a SELECT attribute to the OPTION element where appropriate. The form is generated in Listing 24.2.

LISTING 24.2   Building the HTML Form for the Calendar Script

```
1: <?php
2: if ((!isset($_POST['month'])) || (!isset($_POST['year']))) {
3:     $nowArray = getdate();
4:     $month = $nowArray['mon'];
5:     $year = $nowArray['year'];
6: } else {
7:     $month = $_POST['month'];
8:     $year = $_POST['year'];
9: }
10: $start = mktime (12, 0, 0, $month, 1, $year);
11: $firstDayArray = getdate($start);
12: ?>
13: <!DOCTYPE html>
14: <html>
15: <head>
16: <title><?php echo "Calendar:".$firstDayArray['month']."
17:   ".$firstDayArray['year']; ?></title>
18: <body>
19: <h1>Select a Month/Year Combination</h1>
20: <form method="post" action="<?php echo $_SERVER['PHP_SELF']; ?>">
21: <select name="month">
22: <?php
23: $months = Array("January", "February", "March", "April", "May",
24: "June", "July", "August", "September", "October", "November", "December");
25: for ($x=1; $x <= count($months); $x++) {
26:     echo"<option value=\"$x\"";
27:     if ($x == $month) {
28:         echo " selected";
29:     }
30:     echo ">".$months[$x-1]."</option>";
31: }
32: ?>
33: </select>
34: <select name="year">
35: <?php
36: for ($x=1990; $x<=2020; $x++) {
37:     echo "<option";
38:     if ($x == $year) {
39:         echo " selected";
40:     }
41:     echo ">$x</option>";
42: }
43: ?>
44: </select>
```

LISTING 24.2   Continued

```
45: <button type="submit" name="submit" value="submit">Go!</button>
46: </form>
47: </body>
48: </html>
```

Having created the $start timestamp and the $firstDayArray date array in lines 2–11, let's begin to write the HTML for the page. Notice that we use $firstDayArray to add the month and year to the TITLE element on lines 16 and 17.

Line 20 is the beginning of our form. To create the SELECT element for the month pull-down, we drop back into PHP mode on line 22 to write the individual OPTION tags. First, for display purposes, we create in lines 23 and 24 an array called $months that contains the names of the 12 months. We then loop through this array, creating an OPTION tag for each name (lines 25–31).

This is an overcomplicated way of writing a simple SELECT element were it not for the fact that we are testing $x (the counter variable in the for statement) against the $month variable on line 27. If $x and $month are equivalent, we add the string SELECTED to the OPTION tag, ensuring that the correct month will be selected automatically when the page loads. We use a similar technique to write the year pull-down on lines 36–42. Finally, back in HTML mode, we create a submit button on line 45.

We now have a form that can send the month and year parameters to itself and will default either to the current month and year or the month and year previously chosen. If you save this listing as dateselector.php, place it in your web server document root, and access it with your web browser, you should see something like Figure 24.1. (Your month and year might differ.)

FIGURE 24.1
The calendar form.

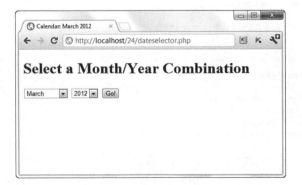

Creating the Calendar Table

We now need to create a table and populate it with dates for the chosen month. We do this in Listing 24.3, which represents the complete calendar display script.

Although line 2 is new, lines 3–64 should be familiar from your work with Listing 24.2, with some stylesheet entries added in lines 19–35. That addition in line 2 simply defines a constant variable, in this case ADAY (for example, "a day") with a value of 86400. This value represents the number of seconds in a day, which the script uses later.

LISTING 24.3   The Complete Calendar Display Script

```
1: <?php
2: define("ADAY", (60*60*24));
3: if ((!isset($_POST['month'])) || (!isset($_POST['year']))) {
4:     $nowArray = getdate();
5:     $month = $nowArray['mon'];
6:     $year = $nowArray['year'];
7: } else {
8:     $month = $_POST['month'];
9:     $year = $_POST['year'];
10:  }
11: $start = mktime (12, 0, 0, $month, 1, $year);
12: $firstDayArray = getdate($start);
13: ?>
14: <!DOCTYPE html>
15: <html>
16: <head>
17: <title><?php echo "Calendar: ".$firstDayArray['month']."
18:    ".$firstDayArray['year'']; ?></title>
19: <style type="text/css">
20:     table {
21:         border: 1px solid black;
22:         border-collapse: collapse;
23:     }
24:     th {
25:         border: 1px solid black;
26:         padding: 6px;
27:         font-weight: bold;
28:         background: #ccc;
29:     }
30:     td {
31:         border: 1px solid black;
32:         padding: 6px;
33:         vertical-align: top;
34:         width: 100px;
35:     }
36: </style>
37: <body>
38: <h1>Select a Month/Year Combination</h1>
39: <form method="post" action="<?php echo $_SERVER['PHP_SELF']; ?>">
40: <select name="month">
```

LISTING 24.3   Continued

```
41: <?php
42: $months = Array("January", "February", "March", "April", "May",
43: "June", "July", "August", "September", "October", "November", "December");
44: for ($x=1; $x <= count($months); $x++) {
45:     echo"<option value=\"$x\"";
46:     if ($x == $month) {
47:         echo " selected";
48:     }
49:     echo ">".$months[$x-1]."</option>";
50: }
51: ?>
52: </select>
53: <select name="year">
54: <?php
55: for ($x=1980; $x<=2010; $x++) {
56:     echo "<option";
57:     if ($x == $year) {
58:         echo " selected";
59:     }
60:     echo ">$x</option>";
61: }
62: ?>
63: </select>
64: <button type="submit" name="submit" value="submit">Go!</button>
65: </form>
66: <br/>
67: <?php
68: $days = Array("Sun", "Mon", "Tue", "Wed", "Thu", "Fri", "Sat");
69: echo "<table><tr>\n";
70: foreach ($days as $day) {
71:     echo "<td>".$day.</td>\n";
72: }
73: for ($count=0; $count < (6*7); $count++) {
74:     $dayArray = getdate($start);
75:     if (($count % 7) == 0) {
76:         if ($dayArray['mon'] != $month) {
77:             break;
78:         } else {
79:             echo "</tr><tr>\n";
80:         }
81:     }
82:     if ($count < $firstDayArray['wday'] || $dayArray['mon'] != $month) {
83:         echo "<td> </td>\n";
84:     } else {
85:         echo "<td>".$dayArray['mday']."</td>\n";
86:         $start += ADAY;
87:     }
88: }
89: echo "</tr></table>";
90: ?>
91: </body>
92: </html>
```

We pick up the entirely new code at line 66 of Listing 24.3. Because the table will be indexed by days of the week, we loop through an array of day names in lines 70–72, printing each in its own table cell, on line 71. All the real magic of the script happens in the final for statement beginning on line 73.

In line 73, we initialize a variable called $count and ensure that the loop will end after 42 iterations. This is to make sure that we will have enough cells to populate with date information, taking into consideration that a four-week month might actually have partial weeks at the beginning and the end, thus the need for six 7-day weeks (rows).

Within this for loop, we transform the $start variable into a date array with getdate(), assigning the result to $dayArray (line 73). Although $start is the first day of the month during the loop's initial execution, we will increment this timestamp by the value of ADAY (24 hours) for every iteration (see line 85).

On line 75, we test the $count variable against the number 7, using the modulus operator. The block of code belonging to this if statement will therefore be run only when $count is either zero or a multiple of 7. This is our way of knowing whether we should end the loop altogether or start a new row, where rows represent weeks.

After we have established that we are in the first iteration or at the end of a row, we can go on to perform another test on line 76. If the mon (month number) element of the $dayArray is no longer equivalent to the $month variable, we are finished. Remember that $dayArray contains information about the $start timestamp, which is the current place in the month that we are displaying. When $start goes beyond the current month, $dayArray["mon"] will hold a different figure than the $month number provided by user input. Our modulus test demonstrated that we are at the end of a row, and the fact that we are in a new month means that we can leave the loop altogether. Assuming, however, that we are still in the month that we are displaying, we end the row and start a new one on line 79.

In the next if statement, on line 82, we determine whether to write date information to a cell. Not every month begins on a Sunday, so it's likely that our rows will contain an empty cell or two. Similarly, few months will finish at the end of one of our rows, so it's also likely that we will have a few empty cells before we close the table.

We have stored information about the first day of the $firstDayArray; in particular, we can access the number of the day of the week in $firstDayArray['wday']. If the value of $count is smaller than this number, we know that we haven't yet reached the correct cell for writing. By the same token, if the value of the $month variable is no longer equal to $dayArray['mon'], we know that we have reached the end of the month (but not the end of the row, as we determined in our earlier modulus test). In either case, we write an empty cell to the browser on line 83.

In the final else clause on line 84, we can do the fun stuff. We have already determined that we are within the month that we want to list, and that the current day column matches the day number stored in $firstDayArray['wday']. Now we must use the $dayArray associative array that we established early in the loop to write the day of the month and some blank space into a cell.

Finally, on line 86, we need to increment the $start variable, which contains our date stamp. We just add the number of seconds in a day to it (we defined this value in line 2), and we're ready to begin the loop again with a new value in $start to be tested. If you save this listing as showcalendar.php, place it in your web server document root, and access it with your web browser, you should see something like Figure 24.2 (your month and year might differ).

FIGURE 24.2
The calendar form and script.

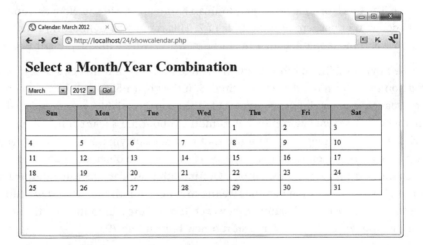

Adding Events to the Calendar

Displaying the calendar is great, but with just a few extra lines of code, you can make it interactive—that is, you can add and view events on a given day. To begin, let's create a simple database table that holds event information. For purposes of simplicity, these events will occur on only a single day and only their start date and time will be shown. Although you can make the event entries as complex as you want, this example is here just to show the basic process involved.

The calendar_events table will include fields for the start date and time, the event title, and an event short description:

```
CREATE TABLE calendar_events (
    id INT NOT NULL PRIMARY KEY AUTO_INCREMENT,
    event_title VARCHAR (25),
    event_shortdesc VARCHAR (255),
    event_start DATETIME
);
```

We can use the code in Listing 24.3 as our base (the script called showcalendar.php). In this new script, we add a link to a pop-up window as part of the calendar display. Each date is a link; the pop-up window calls another script that displays the full text of an event as well as provide the capability to add an event. To begin, add the following JavaScript code in the <head> area, before the opening <body> tag—after line 36 of the original script in Listing 24.3:

```
<script type="text/javascript">
function eventWindow(url) {
    event_popupWin = window.open(url, 'event', 'resizable=yes, scrollbars=yes,
            toolbar=no,width=400,height=400');
    event_popupWin.opener = self;
}
</script>
```

This JavaScript function defines a 400×400 window that will call a URL we provide. We use this JavaScript function to replace what was line 85 of the original script in Listing 24.3; we now wrap the date display in this link to the JavaScript-based pop-up window, which calls a script named event.php. The new code is as follows:

```
echo "<td><a href=\"javascript:eventWindow('event.php?m=".$month.
"&amp;d=".$dayArray['mday']."&amp;y=$year');\">".$dayArray['mday']."</a>
<br/><br/>".$event_title."</td>\n";
```

Not only do we call the event.php file, but we also have to send along with it the date information for the particular link that is clicked. This is done via the query string, and you can see we're sending along three variables—what will become $_GET['m'] for the month, $_GET['d'] for the day, and $_GET['y'] for the year.

Only one change remains for this particular script before we tackle the event.php script—adding an indicator to this particular view, if events do indeed exist. The query that checks for existing events on a given day appears at the onset of the else statement that was originally found at line 84. An entirely new else statement is shown; you can see that the database connection is made, a query is issued, and, if results are found, text is printed within the table cell for that day:

```
} else {
    $mysqli = mysqli_connect("localhost", "joeuser", "somepass", "testDB");
    $chkEvent_sql = "SELECT event_title FROM calendar_events WHERE
                    month(event_start) = '".$month."' AND
                    dayofmonth(event_start) = '".$dayArray['mday']."'
                    AND year(event_start) = '".$year."' ORDER BY event_start";
```

```
$chkEvent_res = mysqli_query($mysqli, $chkEvent_sql)
              or die(mysqli_error($mysqli));

if (mysqli_num_rows($chkEvent_res) > 0) {
    while ($ev = mysqli_fetch_array($chkEvent_res)) {
        $event_title = stripslashes($ev['event_title']);
    }
} else {
    $event_title = "";
}

echo "<td><a href=\"javascript:eventWindow('event.php?m=".$month.
"&amp;d=".$dayArray['mday']."&amp;y=$year');\">".
$dayArray['mday']."</a><br/><br/>".$event_title."</td>\n";

unset($event_title);

$start += ADAY;
}
```

In Listing 24.4, you can see the entirely new script, which we'll call
showcalendar_withevent.php.

LISTING 24.4   Calendar Display Script with Entry-Related Modifications

```
1:  <?php
2:  define("ADAY", (60*60*24));
3:  if ((!isset($_POST['month'])) || (!isset($_POST['year']))) {
4:      $nowArray = getdate();
5:      $month = $nowArray['mon'];
6:      $year = $nowArray['year'];
7:  } else {
8:      $month = $_POST['month'];
9:      $year = $_POST['year'];
10: }
11: $start = mktime (12, 0, 0, $month, 1, $year);
12: $firstDayArray = getdate($start);
13: ?>
14: <!DOCTYPE html>
15: <html>
16: <head>
17: <title><?php echo "Calendar: ".$firstDayArray['month']." ".
18: $firstDayArray['year'] ?></title>
19: <head>
20: <style type="text/css">
21:     table {
22:         border: 1px solid black;
23:         border-collapse: collapse;
24:     }
25:     th {
26:         border: 1px solid black;
27:         padding: 6px;
28:         font-weight: bold;
29:         background: #ccc;
30:     }
31:     td {
```

```
32:            border: 1px solid black;
33:            padding: 6px;
34:            vertical-align: top;
35:            width: 100px;
36:        }
37: </style>
38: <script type="text/javascript">
39: function eventWindow(url) {
40:     event_popupWin = window.open(url, 'event',
41:     'resizable=yes,scrollbars=yes,toolbar=no,width=400,height=400');
42:     event_popupWin.opener = self;
43: }
44: </script>
45: <body>
46: <h1>Select a Month/Year Combination</h1>
47: <form method="post" action="<?php echo $_SERVER['PHP_SELF']; ?>">
48: <select name="month">
49: <?php
50: $months = Array("January", "February", "March", "April", "May", "June",
51: "July", "August", "September", "October", "November", "December");
52: for ($x=1; $x <= count($months); $x++) {
53:     echo"<option value=\"$x\"";
54:     if ($x == $month) {
55:         echo " selected";
56:     }
57:     echo ">".$months[$x-1]."</option>";
58: }
59: ?>
60: </select>
61: <select name="year">
62: <?php
63: for ($x=1990; $x<=2020; $x++) {
64:     echo "<option";
65:     if ($x == $year) {
66:         echo " selected";
67:     }
68:     echo ">$x</option>";
69: }
70: ?>
71: </select>
72: <button type="submit" name="submit" value="submit">Go!</button>
73: </form>
74: <br/>
75: <?php
76: $days = Array("Sun", "Mon", "Tue", "Wed", "Thu", "Fri", "Sat");
77: echo "<table><tr>\n";
78: foreach ($days as $day) {
79:     echo "<th>$day</th>\n";
80: }
81:
82: for ($count=0; $count < (6*7); $count++) {
83:     $dayArray = getdate($start);
84:     if (($count % 7) == 0) {
85:         if ($dayArray['mon'] != $month) {
86:             break;
87:         } else {
88:             echo "</tr><tr>\n";
89:         }
```

LISTING 24.4   Continued

```
90:        }
91:        if ($count < $firstDayArray['wday'] || $dayArray['mon'] != $month) {
92:            echo "<td> </td>\n";
93:        } else {
94:            $mysqli = mysqli_connect("localhost", "joeuser", "somepass",
                   "testDB");
95:            $chkEvent_sql = "SELECT event_title FROM calendar_events WHERE
96:                            month(event_start) = '".$month."' AND
97:                            dayofmonth(event_start) = '".$dayArray['mday']."'
98:                            AND year(event_start) = '".$year."' ORDER BY
                               event_start";
99:            $chkEvent_res = mysqli_query($mysqli, $chkEvent_sql)
100:                           or die(mysqli_error($mysqli));
101:
102:           if (mysqli_num_rows($chkEvent_res) > 0) {
103:               while ($ev = mysqli_fetch_array($chkEvent_res)) {
104:                   $event_title .= stripslashes($ev['event_title']."<br/>";
105:               }
106:           } else {
107:               $event_title = "";
108:           }
109:
110:           echo "<td><a href=\"javascript:eventWindow('event.php?m=".$month.
111:           "&amp;d=".$dayArray['mday']."&amp;y=$year');\">".
112:           $dayArray['mday']."</a><br/><br/>".$event_title."</td>\n";
113:
114:           unset($event_title);
115:           $start += ADAY;
116:        }
117: }
118: echo "</tr></table>";
119:
120: //close connection to MySQL
121: mysqli_close($mysqli);
122: ?>
123: </body>
124: </html>
```

In Figure 24.3, you can see the new calendar, including the representation of the event title on a date that, for illustrative purposes here, I've prepopulated with an event in the calendar_events table.

All that remains is adding the all-in-one event.php script used in the pop-up window to display and also add an event to the calendar (on a particular day). Listing 24.5 contains all the necessary code; the fun part starts at line 8, which connects to the MySQL database. Line 11 checks whether the event entry form has been submitted; if it has, database-safe values are created in lines 14–24, and an INSERT statement is created and issued to add the event to the calendar_events table before continuing (lines 29–34).

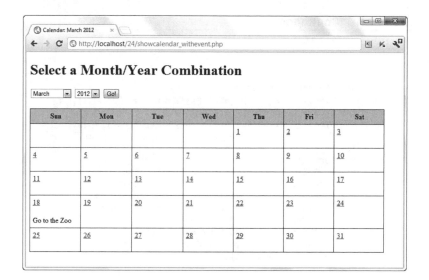

FIGURE 24.3
Showing the calendar with an event.

LISTING 24.5 Showing Events/Adding Events via Pop-Up

```
1:   <!DOCTYPE html>
2:   <html>
3:   <head>
4:   <title>Show/Add Events</title>
5:   <body>
6:   <h1>Show/Add Events</h1>
7:   <?php
8:   $mysqli = mysqli_connect("localhost", "joeuser", "somepass", "testDB");
9:
10:  //add any new event
11:  if ($_POST) {
12:
13:      //create database-safe strings
14:      $safe_m = mysqli_real_escape_string($mysqli, $_POST['m']);
15:      $safe_d = mysqli_real_escape_string($mysqli, $_POST['d']);
16:      $safe_y = mysqli_real_escape_string($mysqli, $_POST['y']);
17:      $safe_event_title = mysqli_real_escape_string($mysqli,
18:         $_POST['event_title']);
19:      $safe_event_shortdesc = mysqli_real_escape_string($mysqli,
20:         $_POST['event_shortdesc']);
21:      $safe_event_time_hh = mysqli_real_escape_string($mysqli,
22:         $_POST['event_time_hh']);
23:      $safe_event_time_mm = mysqli_real_escape_string($mysqli,
24:         $_POST['event_time_mm']);
25:
26:      $event_date = $safe_y."-".$safe_m."-".$safe_d."
27:         ".$safe_event_time_hh.":".$safe_event_time_mm.":00";
28:
29:      $insEvent_sql = "INSERT INTO calendar_events (event_title,
30:                  event_shortdesc, event_start) VALUES
31:                  ('".$safe_event_title."', '".$safe_event_shortdesc."',
32:                  '".$event_date."')";
33:       $insEvent_res = mysqli_query($mysqli, $insEvent_sql)
```

LISTING 24.5   Continued

```
34:            or die(mysqli_error($mysqli));
35:
36: } else {
37:
38:     //create database-safe strings
39:     $safe_m = mysqli_real_escape_string($mysqli, $_GET['m']);
40:     $safe_d = mysqli_real_escape_string($mysqli, $_GET['d']);
41:     $safe_y = mysqli_real_escape_string($mysqli, $_GET['y']);
42: }
43:
44: //show events for this day
45: $getEvent_sql = "SELECT event_title, event_shortdesc,
46:                  date_format(event_start, '%l:%i %p') as fmt_date
47:                  FROM calendar_events WHERE month(event_start) =
48:                  '".$safe_m."' AND dayofmonth(event_start) =
49:                  '".$safe_d."' AND year(event_start) =
50:                  '".$safe_y."' ORDER BY event_start";
51: $getEvent_res = mysqli_query($mysqli, $getEvent_sql)
52:      or die(mysqli_error($mysqli));
53:
54: if (mysqli_num_rows($getEvent_res) > 0) {
55:     $event_txt = "<ul>";
56:     while ($ev = @mysqli_fetch_array($getEvent_res)) {
57:        $event_title = stripslashes($ev['event_title']);
58:        $event_shortdesc = stripslashes($ev['event_shortdesc']);
59:        $fmt_date = $ev['fmt_date'];
60:        $event_txt .= "<li><strong>".$fmt_date."</strong>:
61:              ".$event_title."<br/>".$event_shortdesc."</li>";
62:        }
63:     $event_txt .= "</ul>";
64:     mysqli_free_result($getEvent_res);
65: } else {
66:     $event_txt = "";
67: }
68: // close connection to MySQL
69: mysqli_close($mysqli);
70:
71: if ($event_txt != "") {
72:     echo "<p><strong>Today's Events:</strong></p>
73:     $event_txt
74:     <hr/>";
75: }
76:
77: // show form for adding an event
78: echo <<<END_OF_TEXT
79: <form method="post" action="$_SERVER[PHP_SELF]">
80: <p><strong>Would you like to add an event?</strong><br/>
81: Complete the form below and press the submit button to
82: add the event and refresh this window.</p>
83:
```

```
84:    <p><label for="event_title">Event Title:</label><br/>
85:    <input type="text" id="event_title" name="event_title"
86:          size="25" maxlength="25" /></p>
87:
88:    <p><label for="event_shortdesc">Event Description:</label><br/>
89:    <input type="text" id="event_shortdesc" name="event_shortdesc"
90:          size="25" maxlength="255" /></p>
91:    <fieldset>
92:    <legend>Event Time (hh:mm):</legend>
93:    <select name="event_time_hh">
94:    END_OF_TEXT;
95:
96:    for ($x=1; $x <= 24; $x++) {
97:        echo "<option value=\"$x\">$x</option>";
98:    }
99:
100: echo <<<END_OF_TEXT
101: </select> :
102: <select name="event_time_mm">
103: <option value="00">00</option>
104: <option value="15">15</option>
105: <option value="30">30</option>
106: <option value="45">45</option>
107: </select>
108: </fieldset>
109: <input type="hidden" name="m" value="$safe_m">
110: <input type="hidden" name="d" value="$safe_d">
111: <input type="hidden" name="y" value="$safe_y">
112:
113: <button type="submit" name="submit" value="submit">Add Event</button>
114: </form>
115: END_OF_TEXT;
116: ?>
117: </body>
118: </html>
```

Lines 45–52 create and issue the query and retrieve all records that correspond to events on this given day. The text block used to display entries is created in lines 54–67. However, users also need to see the form for adding an event, and this is built in lines 79–114, effectively the end of the script.

Figure 24.4 shows how a pop-up looks when a link is followed from the calendar and an entry is already present. In this example, we wanted to add another event on this day, so the form has been completed in preparation for adding the additional event.

FIGURE 24.4
Showing the day detail, ready to add another event.

In Figure 24.5, a second event has been added to this particular day.

FIGURE 24.5
A second event has been added.

Obviously, this is a simple example, but it shows that it is indeed easy to build a calendar-based application in just a few short scripts.

Creating a Calendar Library

Because dates are ubiquitous in web-based application interfaces, and because working with dates can be complicated, let's look at creating a class library to automate some of the work you might do with dates. Along the way, we revisit some of the techniques we have already covered in this book—especially in Chapter 9, "Working with Objects."

The simple date_pulldown library created in this instance will consist of three separate select elements: one for day of the month, one for month, and one for year. When a user submits a page, the script will verify the form input. If there is a problem with the input, we will refresh the page with the user's input still in place. This is easy to accomplish with text boxes but is more of a chore with pull-down menus.

Pages that display information pulled from a database present a similar problem. Data can be entered straight into the value attributes of text-type input elements. Dates will need to be split into month, day, and year values, and then the correct option elements selected.

The date_pulldown class aims to make date pull-downs sticky (so that they will remember settings from page to page) and easy to set. To create our class, we first need to declare it and create a constructor.

NOTE

A *constructor* is a function that exists within a class and is automatically called when a new instance of the class is created.

We can also declare some class properties. We will step through Listing 24.6; this first snippet shows the beginning of the class.

LISTING 24.6 The Calendar Library Class

```
 1: class date_pulldown {
 2:     public $name;
 3:     public $timestamp = -1;
 4:     public $months = array("Jan", "Feb", "Mar", "Apr", "May", "Jun",
 5:             "Jul", "Aug", "Sep", "Oct", "Nov", "Dec");
 6:     public $yearstart = -1;
 7:     public $yearend = -1;
 8:
 9:     function date_pulldown($name) {
10:         $this->name = $name;
11:     }
```

We first declare the $name property on line 2. We use it to name the HTML select elements. The $timestamp property, defined on line 3, will hold a UNIX timestamp.

The $months array property, defined on lines 4–5, contains the strings we display in our month pull-down. The $yearstart and $yearend properties (lines 6 and 7) are both set to –1, pending initialization. They will eventually hold the first and last years of the range that will be presented in the year pull-down.

The constructor is simple. It accepts a string, which we assign to the $name property. Now that we have the basis of our class, we need a set of methods by which the client code can set the date. Listing 24.6 continues as follows.

LISTING 24.6   (continued)

```
12:    function setDate_global( ) {
13:        if (!$this->setDate_array($GLOBALS[$this->name])) {
14:            return $this->setDate_timestamp(time());
15:        }
16:        return true;
17:    }
18:
19:    function setDate_timestamp($time) {
20:        $this->timestamp = $time;
21:        return true;
22:    }
23:
24:    function setDate_array($inputdate) {
25:        if (is_array($inputdate) &&
26:            isset($inputdate['mon']) &&
27:            isset($inputdate['mday']) &&
28:            isset($inputdate['year'])) {
29:
30:            $this->timestamp = mktime(11, 59, 59,
31:                $inputdate['mon'], $inputdate['mday'], $inputdate['year']);
32:            return true;
33:        }
34:        return false;
35:    }
```

Of the methods shown here, setDate_timestamp() is the simplest (lines 19–22). It requires a UNIX timestamp, which it assigns to the $timestamp property. But let's not forget the others.

The setDate_array() method (lines 24–35) expects an associative array with at least three keys: mon, mday, and year. These keys will have data values in the same format as in the array returned by getdate(). This means that setDate_array() will accept a hand-built array such as

```
array("mday"=> 25, "mon"=>3, "year"=> 2012);
```

or the result of a call to getdate():

```
getdate(1208052013);
```

It is no accident that the pull-downs we build later will be constructed to produce an array containing mon, mday, and year keys. The method uses the mktime() function to construct a timestamp, which is then assigned to the $timestamp variable.

The setDate_global() method (lines 12–17) is called by default. It attempts to find a global variable with the same name as the object's $name property. This is passed to setDate_array(). If this method discovers a global variable of the right structure, it uses that variable to create the $timestamp variable. Otherwise, the current date is used.

The ranges for days and months are fixed, but years are a different matter. As Listing 24.6 continues, we create a few methods to allow the client code to set a range of years, although we also provide default behavior.

LISTING 24.6 (continued)

```
36:     function setYearStart($year) {
37:         $this->yearstart = $year;
38:     }
38:
40:     function setYearEnd($year) {
41:         $this->yearend = $year;
42:     }
43:
44:     function getYearStart() {
45:         if ($this->yearstart < 0) {
46:             $nowarray = getdate(time());
47:             $this->yearstart = $nowarray['year']-5;
48:         }
49:
50:         return $this->yearstart;
51:     }
52:
53:     function getYearEnd() {
54:         if ($this->yearend < 0) {
55:             $nowarray = getdate(time());
56:             $this->yearend = $nowarray['year']+5;
57:         }
58:         return $this->yearend;
59:     }
```

The setYearStart() and setYearEnd() methods (lines 36–43) are straightforward in that a year is directly assigned to the appropriate property. The getYearStart() method tests whether the $yearstart property has been set, and if it has not, the method assigns a $yearstart value 5 years before the current year. The getYearEnd() method performs a similar operation.

We're now ready to create the business end of the class as Listing 24.6 continues.

LISTING 24.6 (continued)

```
60:     function output() {
61:         if ($this->timestamp < 0) {
62:             $this->setDate_global();
63:         }
64:         $datearray = getdate($this->timestamp);
65:         $out  = $this->day_select($this->name, $datearray);
66:         $out .= $this->month_select($this->name, $datearray);
67:         $out .= $this->year_select($this->name, $datearray);
68:         return $out;
69:     }
70:
71:     function day_select($fieldname, $datearray)  {
72:         $out = "<select name=\"$fieldname"."['mday']\">\n";
73:         for ($x=1; $x<=31; $x++) {
74:             $out .= "<option value=\"$x\""($datearray['mday']==($x)
75:             ?" selected":"").">".sprintf("%02d", $x) ."</option>\n";
76:         }
77:         $out .= "</select>\n";
78:         return $out;
79:     }
80:
81:     function month_select($fieldname, $datearray) {
82:         $out = "<select name=\"$fieldname"."['mon']\">\n";
83:         for ($x = 1; $x <= 12; $x++) {
84:             $out .= "<option value=\"".($x)."\"".($datearray['mon']==($x)
85:             ?" selected":"")."> ".$this->months[$x-1]."</option>\n";
86:         }
87:         $out .= "</select>\n";
88:         return $out;
89:     }
90:
91:     function year_select($fieldname, $datearray) {
92:         $out = "<select name=\"$fieldname"."['year']\">";
93:         $start = $this->getYearStart();
94:         $end = $this->getYearEnd();
95:         for ($x= $start; $x < $end; $x++) {
96:             $out .= "<option value=\"$x\""($datearray['year']==($x)
97:             ?" selected":"").">".$x."</option>\n";
98:         }
99:         $out .= "</select>\n";
100:        return $out;
101:    }
102: }
```

The output() method orchestrates most of this code (lines 60–69). It first checks the $timestamp property, and, unless one of the setDate methods has been called, the value of $timestamp will be set to –1 and setDate_global() will be called by default. The timestamp is passed to the getdate() function to construct a date array, and a method is called to produce each pull-down.

The day_select() method (lines 71–79) simply constructs an HTML select element with an option element for each of the 31 possible days in a month. The object's current date is stored in the $datearray argument variable, which is used during the construction of the element to set the selected attribute of the relevant option element. The sprintf() function formats the day number, adding a leading zero to days 1–9. The month_select() and year_select() methods (lines 81–101) use similar logic to construct the month and year pull-downs.

Why did we break down the output code into four methods, rather than simply creating one block of code? When we build a class, we have two kinds of programmer in mind: one who will want to instantiate a date_pulldown object, and one who will want to subclass the date_pulldown class to refine its functionality.

For the former, we want to provide a simple and clear interface to the class's functionality. The programmer can then instantiate an object, set its date, and call the output() method. For the latter, we want to make it easy to change discrete elements of the class's functionality. By putting all the output code into one method, we would force a child class that needed to tweak output to reproduce a lot of code that is perfectly usable. By breaking this code into discrete methods, we allow for subclasses that can change limited aspects of functionality without disturbing the whole. If a child class needs to represent the year pull-down as two radio buttons, for example, you can simply override the year_select() method.

Listing 24.7 contains some code that calls the library class. Before you try to execute this code, take the code from Listing 24.6, surround it with PHP opening and closing tags, and save it into a file called date_pulldown.class.php. Place this file in the document root of your web server because Listing 24.7 uses it and it had better be there!

LISTING 24.7   Using the date_pulldown Class

```
1:   <!DOCTYPE html>
2:   <html>
3:   <head>
4:   <title>Using the date_pulldown Class</title>
5:   </head>
6:   <?php
7:   include("date_pulldown.class.php");
8:   $date1 = new date_pulldown("fromdate");
9:   $date2 = new date_pulldown("todate");
10:  $date3 = new date_pulldown("foundingdate");
11:  $date3->setYearStart("1972");
12:  if (empty($foundingdate)) {
13:      $date3->setDate_array(array('mday'=>26, 'mon'=>4, 'year'=>1984));
14:  }
15:  ?>
16:  <body>
17:  <form>
18:  <p><strong>From:</strong><br/>
19:  <?php echo $date1->output(); ?></p>
20:
```

LISTING 24.7   Continued

```
21: <p><strong>To:</strong><br/>
22: <?php echo $date2->output(); ?></p>
23:
24: <p><strong>Company Founded:</strong><br/>
25: <?php echo $date3->output(); ?></p>
26:
27: <button type="submit" name="submit" value="submit">Submit</button>
28: </form>
29: </body>
30: </html>
```

On line 7, we include the date_pulldown.class.php; after we have included the class file, we can use all of its methods. We use the class's default behavior for all the pull-downs, apart from "foundingdate". For this particular object, we override the default year start, setting it to 1972 on line 11. On line 13, we assign this pull-down an arbitrary date that will be displayed until the form is submitted (see Figure 24.6).

FIGURE 24.6
The pull-downs generated by the date_pulldown class.

NOTE

This is only the front end of a form, with no action or method; you need to supply your own action or method for this to actually do something.

Summary

In this chapter, you pulled together the PHP date-related functions you learned about earlier in the book to work within a basic calendar application display. You learned how to test the validity of an input date using checkdate(), and you worked through a sample script that applied some of the tools you have learned. You also saw one method for adding and viewing events within your calendar application. You also learned how to build a date-related class library that can be used to automate some of the more tedious aspects of working with dates within HTML forms.

Q&A

Q. *Are there any functions for converting between different calendars?*

A. Yes. PHP provides an entire suite of functions that cover alternative calendars. You can read about these in the official PHP Manual at http://www.php.net/manual/en/ref.calendar.php.

Workshop

The workshop is designed to help you review what you've learned and begin putting your knowledge into practice.

Quiz

1. What PHP function did we use to create a timestamp?

2. What PHP function did we use to create an associative array of date-related information?

3. Why are the variables in the date_pulldown class declared as public?

Answers

1. `mktime()`

2. `getdate()`

3. Public variables are available outside of the class, as these variables need to be.

Activities

1. Modify the calendar display script to show an entire year of the calendar—from January through December. After that, display the calendar as a 3×4 grid, or four rows of three months on each row.

2. Modify the event-creation script to use the `date` pull-down class.

## CHAPTER 25

Restricting Access to Your Applications

In this chapter, you learn the following:

▶ How to restrict access based on the user, client IP address, domain name, and browser version

▶ How to use the user management tools provided with Apache

▶ How to store and retrieve cookie information

▶ How to use cookies for authentication

This chapter explains how to use Apache to restrict access to parts of a website based on the identity of the user or on information about the request. On the application side of things, you can create your own mechanism for user validation and check the validity of your users through cookies.

Authentication Overview

Authorization and authentication are common requirements for many websites. Before continuing, a few definitions are in order.

Authentication establishes the identity of parties in a communication. You can authenticate yourself through something you know such as a password or a cookie, through something tangible such as an ID card or a key, through something intrinsically part of you such as your fingerprint or your retina, or through any combination of these elements. In the context of a website, authentication is usually restricted to the use of passwords and certificates.

Authorization deals with protecting access to resources. You can authorize access based on several factors, such as the IP address the user is coming from, the user's browser type, the content the user is trying to access, or who the user is (previously determined via authentication).

Apache includes several modules that provide authentication and access control and that you can use to protect both dynamic and static content. You can either use one of these modules or implement your own access control at the application level and provide customized login screens, single sign-on, and other advanced functionality.

Client Authentication

Users are authenticated for tracking or authorization purposes. The HTTP specification provides two authentication mechanisms: basic and digest. In both cases, the process is the following:

1. A client tries to access restricted content in the web server.

2. Apache checks whether the client is providing a username and password. If not, Apache returns an HTTP 401 status code, indicating that user authentication is required.

3. The client reads the response and prompts the user for the required username and password (usually with a pop-up dialog box).

4. The client retries accessing the web page, this time transmitting the username and password as part of the HTTP request. The client remembers the username and password and transmits them in later requests to the same site, so the user does not need to retype them for every request.

5. Apache checks the validity of the credentials and grants or denies access based on the user identity and other access rules.

In the basic authentication scheme, the username and password are transmitted in cleartext as part of the HTTP request headers. This poses a security risk because an attacker could easily peek at the conversation between server and browser, learn the username and password, and reuse them freely afterward.

The digest authentication provides increased security because it transmits a digest instead of the clear text password. The digest is based on a combination of several parameters, including the username, password, and request method. The server can calculate the digest on its own and check that the client knows the password, even when the password itself is not transmitted over the network.

NOTE

A *digest algorithm* is a mathematical operation that takes a text and returns another text, a digest, which uniquely identifies the original one. A good digest algorithm should make sure that, at least for practical purposes, different input texts produce different digests and that the original input text cannot be derived from the digest. MD5 is the name of a commonly used digest algorithm.

Because of potential differences in browser support for digest authentication, you might want to restrict its use to scenarios in which you have control over the browser software of your clients, such as in a corporate intranet.

In any case, for both digest and basic authentication, the requested information itself is transmitted unprotected over the network. A better choice to secure access to your website involves using the HTTP over SSL protocol, as described in Chapter 30, "Setting Up a Secure Web Server."

User Management Methods

When the authentication module receives the username and password from the client, it needs to verify that they are valid against an existing repository of users. The usernames and passwords can be stored in a variety of ways, including the file- and database-based mechanisms provided for by Apache. Third-party modules provide support for additional mechanisms such as *Lightweight Directory Access Protocol* (LDAP) and *Network Information Services* (NIS).

Apache Authentication Module Functionality

Apache provides the basic framework and directives to perform authentication and access control. The authentication modules provide support for validating passwords against a specific back-end method (file, database, and so on). Users can optionally be organized in groups, easing management of access control rules.

Apache provides three built-in directives related to authentication that can be used with any of the authentication modules: AuthName, AuthType, and Require.

AuthName accepts a string argument, the name for the authentication realm. A *realm* is a logical area of the web server that you are asking the password for. It is displayed in the browser pop-up window.

AuthType specifies the type of browser authentication: basic or digest.

`Require` enables you to specify a list of users or groups that will be allowed access. The syntax is `Require user` followed by one or more usernames, or `Require group` followed by one or more group names. For example

```
Require user joe bob
```

or

```
Require group employee contractor
```

If you want to grant access to anyone who provides a valid username and password, you can do so as follows:

```
Require valid-user
```

With the preceding directives, you can control who has access to specific virtual hosts, directories, files, and so on. Although authentication and authorization are separate concepts, in practice they intertwine in Apache. Access is granted based on specific user identity or group membership. Some third-party modules, such as certain LDAP-based modules, allow for clearer separation between authentication and authorization.

The authentication modules included with Apache provide the following

- **Back-end storage**—Provides text or database files containing the username and group information

- **User management**—Supplies tools for creating and managing users and groups in the back-end storage

- **Authoritative information**—Specifies whether the results of the module are authoritative

---

NOTE

Sometimes users will not be allowed access to a particular realm because their information is not found in the user database provided by the module, or because no authentication rules matched their information. In that case, one of two situations will occur:

- If the module specifies its results as authoritative, a user is denied access and Apache returns an error.
- If the module specifies its results as not authoritative, other modules can attempt to authenticate the user.

This enables you to have a main authorization module that knows about most users and have additional modules that can authenticate the rest of the users.

File-Based Authentication

The mod_auth Apache module provides basic authentication via text files containing usernames and passwords, similar to how traditional UNIX authentication works with the /etc/passwd and /etc/groups files.

Back-End Storage

When using back-end storage methods, you need to specify the file containing the list of usernames and passwords and, optionally, the file containing the list of groups.

The users file is a UNIX-style password file, containing names of users and encrypted passwords. The entries look like the following, on UNIX, using the crypt algorithm:

```
admin:iFrlxqg0Q6RQ6
```

On Windows, using the MD5 algorithm, they look like this:

```
admin:$apr1$Ug3.....$jVTedbQWBKTfXsn5jK6UX/
```

The groups file contains a list of groups and the users who belong to each one of them, separated by spaces, such as in the following entry:

```
web: admin joe Daniel
```

The AuthUserFile and the AuthGroupFile directives take a path argument, pointing to the users file and the groups file. The groups file is optional.

User Management

The Apache distribution includes the htpasswd utility on UNIX and htpasswd.exe on Windows; they are designed to help you manage user password files. Both versions are functionally identical, but the Windows version uses a different method to encrypt the password. The encryption is transparent to the user and administrator. On Linux/UNIX, the first time you add a user, you need to type

```
/usr/local/apache2/bin/htpasswd -c file userid
```

where *file* is the password file that will contain the list of usernames and passwords, and *userid* is the username you want to add. You are then prompted for a password, and the file is created. For example, on Linux/UNIX, the command

```
/usr/local/apache2/bin/htpasswd -c /usr/local/apache2/conf/htusers admin
```

creates the password file /usr/local/apache2/conf/htusers and adds the admin user.

Similar functionality exists on Windows, where the command-line operation might look something like this:

```
htpasswd -c "C:\Program Files\Apache Software Foundation\Apache2.2\conf\htusers"
    admin
```

The -c command-line option tells the htpasswd executable that it should create the file. When you want to add users to an existing password file, do not use the -c option; if you do so, the file will be overwritten.

It is important that you store the password file outside the document root and thus make it inaccessible via a web browser. Otherwise, an attacker could download the file and get a list of your usernames and passwords. Although the passwords are encrypted, when you have the file, it is possible to perform a brute-force attack to try to guess them.

Using mod_auth

Listing 25.1 shows a configuration example that restricts access to the private directory in the document root to authenticated users present in the htusers password file. Note that the optional AuthGroupFile directive is not present.

LISTING 25.1   File-Based Authentication Example

```
1: <Directory /usr/local/apache2/htdocs/private>
2: AuthType Basic
3: AuthName "Private Area"
4: AuthUserFile /usr/local/apache2/conf/htusers
5: Require valid-user
6: </Directory>
```

Database File-Based Access Control

Storing usernames and passwords in plaintext files is convenient, but this method does not scale well. Apache would need to open and read the files sequentially to look for a particular user. When the number of users grows, this operation becomes very time-consuming. The mod_auth_dbm module enables you to replace the text-based files with indexed database files, which can handle a much greater number of users without performance degradation. The mod_auth_dbm module is included with Apache, but is not enabled by default. Enabling this module occurs when configuring Apache to be built using the --enable-module=dbm option.

Back-End Storage

The mod_auth_dbm module provides two directives, AuthDBMUserFile and AuthDBMGroupFile, that point to the database files containing the usernames and groups. Unlike plaintext files, both directives can point to the same file, which combines both users and groups.

User Management

Apache provides a utility for both UNIX and Windows users, called htdbm, that enables you to create and manage users and groups stored in a database file.

You can find the utility in the bin directory of the Apache distribution; once there, to add a user to a new database, type the following:

```
htdbm -c databasename userid
```

You are then prompted for the password, and the user is added to a new database file.

If you ever need to delete the user daniel, you can issue the following command:

```
htdbm -x databasename daniel
```

You can find complete syntax information by invoking htdbm without any arguments.

Using Apache for Access Control

The mod_authz_host module, enabled by default, enables you to restrict access to resources based on parameters of the client request, such as the presence of a specific header or the IP address or hostname of the client.

Implementing Access Rules

You can specify access rules using the Allow and Deny directives. Each of these directives takes a list of arguments such as IP addresses, environment variables, and domain names.

Allow/Deny Access by IP Addresses

You can deny or grant access to a client based on its IP address:

```
Allow from 10.0.0.1 10.0.0.2 10.0.0.3
```

You can also specify IP address ranges with a partial IP address or a network/mask pair. In addition, you can specify the first 1, 2, or 3 bytes of an IP address. Any IP address containing those will match this rule. For example, the rule

```
Deny from 10.0
```

matches any address starting with 10.0, such as 10.0.1.0 and 10.0.0.1.

You can also use the IP address and the netmask; the IP address specifies the network, and the mask specifies which bits belong to the network prefix and which ones belong to the nodes. The rule

```
Allow from 10.0.0.0/255.255.255.0
```

matches IP addresses 10.0.0.1, 10.0.0.2, and so on, to 10.0.0.254.

You can also specify the network mask via high-order bits. For example, you could write the previous rule as follows:

```
Allow from 10.0.0.0/24
```

Allow/Deny Access by Domain Name

You can control access based on specific hostnames or partial domain names. For example, `Allow from example.com` matches `www.example.com`, `foo.example.com`, and so on.

<u>NOTE</u>

> Enabling access rules based on domain names forces Apache to do a reverse DNS lookup on the client address, bypassing the settings of the `HostName-Lookups` directive. This has performance implications.

Allow/Deny Access Based on Environment Variables

You can specify access rules based on the presence of a certain environment variable by prefixing the name of the variable with the string `env=`. You can use this feature to grant or deny access to certain browsers or browser versions to prevent specific sites from linking to your resources and so on. For this example to work as intended, the client needs to transmit the `User-Agent` header.

For example:

```
BrowserMatch MSIE iexplorer
Deny from env=iexplorer
```

Because the client sends the `User-Agent` header, it could possibly be omitted or manipulated, but most users will not do so, and this technique will work in most cases.

Allow/Deny Access to All Clients

The keyword `all` matches all clients. You can specify `Allow from all` or `Deny from all` to grant or deny access to all clients.

Evaluating Access Rules

You can have several `Allow` and `Deny` access rules. You can choose the order in which the rules are evaluated by using the `Order` directive. Rules evaluated later have higher precedence. `Order` accepts one argument, which can be `Deny,Allow`, `Allow,Deny`, or `Mutual-Failure`. `Deny,Allow` is the default value for the `Order` directive. Note that there is no space in the value.

Deny,Allow

`Deny,Allow` specifies that `Deny` directives are evaluated before `Allow` directives. With `Deny,Allow`, the client is granted access by default if there are no `Allow` or `Deny` directives or the client does not match any of the rules. If the client matches a `Deny` rule, it is denied access unless it also matches an `Allow` rule, which takes precedence because `Allow` directives are evaluated last and have greater priority.

Listing 25.2 shows how to configure Apache to allow access to the `/private` location to clients coming from the internal network or the domain `example.com` and deny access to everyone else.

LISTING 25.2 `Deny,Allow` **Access Control Configuration Example**

```
1: <Location /private>
2:  Order Deny,Allow
3:  Deny from all
4:  Allow from 10.0.0.0/255.255.255.0  example.com
5: </Location>
```

Allow,Deny

`Allow,Deny` specifies that `Allow` directives are evaluated before `Deny` directives. With `Allow,Deny`, the client is denied access by default if there are no `Allow` or `Deny` directives or if the client does not match any of the rules. If the client matches an `Allow` rule, it is granted access unless it also matches a `Deny` rule, which takes precedence.

Note that the presence of `Order Allow,Deny` without any `Allow` or `Deny` rules causes all requests to the specified resource to be denied because the default behavior is to deny access.

Listing 25.3 allows access to everyone except a specific host.

LISTING 25.3 `Allow,Deny` **Access Control Configuration Example**

```
1: <Location /some/location/>
2:  Order Allow,Deny
3:  Allow from all
```

LISTING 25.3   Continued

```
4: Deny from host.example.com
5: </Location>
```

Mutual-Failure

In the case of Mutual-Failure, the host is granted access only if it matches an Allow directive *and* does not match any Deny directive.

Combining Apache Access Methods

In previous sections, you learned how to restrict access based on user identity or request information. The Satisfy directive enables you to determine whether both types of access restrictions must be satisfied to grant access. Satisfy accepts one parameter, which can be either all or any.

Satisfy all means that the client will be granted access if it provides a valid username and password *and* passes the access restrictions. Satisfy any means the client will be granted access if it provides a valid username and password *or* passes the access restrictions.

Why is this directive useful? For example, you might want to provide free access to your website to users coming from an internal, trusted address, but require users coming from the Internet to provide a valid username and password. Listing 25.4 demonstrates just that.

LISTING 25.4   Mixing Authentication and Access Control Rules

```
1: <Location /restricted>
2: Allow from 10.0.0.0/255.255.255.0
3: AuthType Basic
4: AuthName "Intranet"
5: AuthUserFile /usr/local/apache2/conf/htusers
6: Require valid-user
7: Satisfy any
8: </Location>
```

NOTE

> Access control based on connection or request information is not completely secure. Although it provides an appropriate level of protection for most cases, the rules rely on the integrity of your DNS servers and your network infrastructure. If an attacker gains control of your DNS servers, or your routers or firewalls are incorrectly configured, he can easily change authorized domain name records to point to his machine or pretend he is coming from an authorized IP address.

Limiting Access Based on HTTP Methods

In general, you want your access control directives to apply to all types of client requests, and this is the default behavior. In some cases, however, you want to apply authentication and access rules to only certain HTTP methods such as GET and HEAD.

The <Limit> container takes a list of methods and contains the directives that apply to requests containing those methods. The complete list of methods that you can use is GET, POST, PUT, DELETE, CONNECT, OPTIONS, PATCH, PROPFIND, PROPPATCH, MKCOL, COPY, MOVE, LOCK, and UNLOCK.

The <LimitExcept> section provides complementary functionality, containing directives that will apply to requests not containing the listed methods.

Listing 25.5 shows an example from the default Apache configuration file. The <Limit> and <LimitExcept> sections allow read-only methods but deny requests to any other methods that can modify the content of the file system, such as PUT. For more information on the myriad options available here, see the Apache documentation at http://httpd.apache.org/docs-2.2/mod/core.html.

LISTING 25.5   Restricting Access Based on Rule

```
 1: <Directory /home/*/public_html>
 2:   AllowOverride FileInfo AuthConfig Limit
 3:   Options MultiViews Indexes SymLinksIfOwnerMatch IncludesNoExec
 4:   <Limit GET POST OPTIONS PROPFIND>
 5:    Order Allow,Deny
 6:    Allow from all
 7:   </Limit>
 8:   <LimitExcept GET POST OPTIONS PROPFIND>
 9:    Order Deny,Allow
10:    Deny from all
11:   </LimitExcept>
12: </Directory>
```

In the next section, you learn about restricting access on the application side based on information found in cookies.

Restricting Access Based on Cookie Values

In Chapter 12, "Working with Cookies and User Sessions," you learned all about the structure of a cookie and how to set and access cookie variables in PHP. The next few sections show some practical uses of cookies for authentication purposes.

Suppose that you want to create a login form that checks for values against a database. If the user is authorized, you send a cookie that says as much. Then, for all pages you want to restrict only to authorized users, you check for the specific cookie. If the cookie is present, the user can see the page. If the cookie is not present, the user is either sent back to the login form or a message regarding access restrictions can be printed to the screen. The next few sections go through each of these steps.

Creating the Authorized Users Table

When you're integrating user accounts into a web-based application, it is common to store the user-specific information in a database table. The information in this table can then be used to authorize the user and grant access to areas of the site specifically for these "special" users.

The following table-creation command creates a table called auth_users in your MySQL database, with fields for the ID, first name, last name, email address, username, and password:

```
CREATE TABLE auth_users (
    id int NOT NULL PRIMARY KEY AUTO_INCREMENT,
    f_name VARCHAR(50),
    l_name VARCHAR(50),
    email VARCHAR(150),
    username VARCHAR(25),
    password VARCHAR(41)
);
```

The following INSERT command puts a record in the auth_users table for a user named John Doe, with an email address of john@doe.com, a username of jdoe, and a password of doepass:

```
INSERT INTO auth_users VALUES ('1', 'John', 'Doe', 'john@doe.com',
'jdoe', PASSWORD('doepass'));
```

This INSERT command should be self-explanatory, with the exception of the use of the PASSWORD() function. When this function is used in the INSERT command, what is stored in the table is in fact not the actual password, but a 41-character hash of the password.

When you view the contents of the auth_users table, you will see the hash in the password field, as follows:

```
+----------+------------------------------------------+
| username | password                                 |
+----------+------------------------------------------+
| jdoe     | *0AAD744979343D58A7F17A50E514E6AD6533D04B |
+----------+------------------------------------------+
```

Although it might look like it is encrypted, a *hash* is in fact not an encrypted bit of information. Instead, it is a "fingerprint" of the original information. Hashes are generally used, like fingerprints, to perform matches. In this case, when you check your user's password, you check that the hash of the input matches the stored hash. Using hashes alleviates the need—and security risk—of storing actual passwords.

Creating the Login Form and Script

After you authorize users in your table, you need to give them a mechanism for proving their authenticity. In this case, a simple two-field form will do, as shown in Listing 25.6.

LISTING 25.6   User Login Form

```
1:  <!DOCTYPE html>
2:  <html>
3:  <head>
4:  <title>User Login Form</title>
5:  </head>
6:  <body>
7:  <h1>Login Form</h1>
8:  <form method="post" action="userlogin.php">
9:  <p><label for="username"><strong>username:</strong><br/>
10: <input type="text" id="username" name="username" /></label></p>
11: <p><label for="password"><strong>password:</strong><br/>
12: <input type="password" id="password" name="password" /></label></p>
13: <button type="submit" name="submit" value="login">Login</button>
14: </form>
15: </body>
16: </html>
```

Put these lines into a text file called userlogin.html, and place it in your web server document root. Next, you create the script itself, which the form expects to be called userlogin.php (see Listing 25.7).

LISTING 25.7   User Login Script

```
1:  <?php
2:  //check for required fields from the form
3:  if ((!isset($_POST['username'])) || (!isset($_POST['password']))) {
4:      header("Location: userlogin.html");
5:      exit;
6:  }
7:
8:  //connect to server and select database
9:  $mysqli = mysqli_connect("localhost", "joeuser", "somepass", "testDB")
10:         or die(mysqli_error());
11:
12: //use mysqli_real_escape_string to clean the input
13: $username = mysqli_real_escape_string($mysqli, $_POST['username']);
14: $password = mysqli_real_escape_string($mysqli, $_POST['password']);
```

LISTING 25.7   Continued

```
15:
16: //create and issue the query
17: $sql = "SELECT f_name, l_name FROM auth_users WHERE
18:         username = '".$username."' AND
19:         password = PASSWORD('".$password."')";
20: $result = mysqli_query($mysqli, $sql) or die(mysqli_error($mysqli));
21:
22: //get the number of rows in the result set; should be 1 if a match
23: if (mysqli_num_rows($result) == 1) {
24:
25:     //if authorized, get the values of f_name l_name
26:     while ($info = mysqli_fetch_array($result)) {
27:         $f_name = stripslashes($info['f_name']);
28:         $l_name = stripslashes($info['l_name']);
29:     }
30:
31:     //set authorization cookie
32:     setcookie("auth", "1", 0, "/", "yourdomain.com", 0);
33:
34:     //create display string
35:     $display_block = "
36:     <p>".$f_name." ".$l_name." is authorized!</p>
37:     <p>Authorized Users' Menu:</p>
38:     <ul>
39:     <li><a href=\"secretpage.php\">secret page</a></li>
40:     </ul>";
41: } else {
42:     //redirect back to login form if not authorized
43:     header("Location: userlogin.html");
44:     exit;
45: }
46: //close connection to MySQL
47: mysqli_close($mysqli);
48: ?>
49: <!DOCTYPE html>
50: <html>
51: <head>
52: <title>User Login</title>
53: </head>
54: <body>
55: <?php echo $display_block; ?>
56: </body>
57: </html>
```

Put these lines into a text file called userlogin.php, modify line 32 so that "your-domain.com" is your actual domain name, and place this file in your web server document root. In a moment, you'll try it out, but first let's examine what the script is doing.

Line 3 checks for the two required fields—the only two fields in the form: $_POST['username'] and $_POST['password']. If either of these fields is not present, the script redirects the user back to the original login form. If the two fields *are* present, the script moves along to line 9, which connects to the database server in preparation for issuing the SQL query to check the authenticity of the user. Before issuing the query, though, lines 13 and 14 sanitize the user input. Once sanitized, the query and its execution are found in lines 17–20. Note that the query checks the hash of the password input from the form against the password stored in the table. These two elements must match each other, and belong to the username in question, to authorize the user.

Line 23 tests the result of the query by counting the number of rows in the resultset. The row count should be exactly 1 if the username and password pair represents a valid login. If this is the case, the `mysqli_fetch_array()` function is used in lines 26–29 to extract the first and last names of the user. These names are used for aesthetic purposes only.

Line 32 sets the authorization cookie. The name of the cookie is `auth`, and the value is 1. If a 0 is put in the time slot, the cookie lasts as long as this user's web browser session is open. When the user closes the browser, the cookie expires. Lines 35–40 create a message for display, including a link to a file you create in a moment.

Finally, lines 41–45 handle a failed login attempt. In this case, the user is simply redirected back to the original login form.

Go ahead and access the login form and input the valid values for the John Doe user. When you submit the form, the result should look like Figure 25.1.

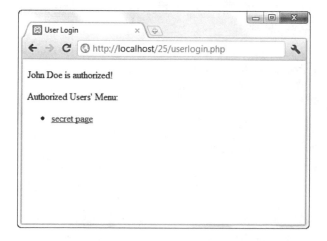

FIGURE 25.1
Successful login result.

Try to log in with an invalid username and password pair, and you should be redirected to the login form. In the next (and final) section, you create the `secretpage.php` script, which reads the authentication cookie you have just set and acts accordingly.

Testing for the `auth` **Cookie**

The last piece of this puzzle is to use the value of the `auth` cookie to allow a user to access a private file. In this case, Listing 25.8 shows the file in question.

LISTING 25.8   Checking for `auth` **Cookie**

```
 1: <?php
 2: if ($_COOKIE['auth'] == "1") {
 3:       $display_block = "<p>You are an authorized user.</p>";
 4: } else {
 5:     //redirect back to login form if not authorized
 6:     header("Location: userlogin.html");
 7:     exit;
 8: }
 9. ?>
10: <!DOCTYPE html>
11: <html>
12: <head>
13: <title>Secret Page</title>
14: </head>
15: <body>
16: <?php echo $display_block; ?>
17: </body>
18: </html>
```

From the menu shown in Figure 25.1, click the Secret Page link. Because you are an authorized user, you should see a result like Figure 25.2.

FIGURE 25.2
Accessing the secret page as an authorized user.

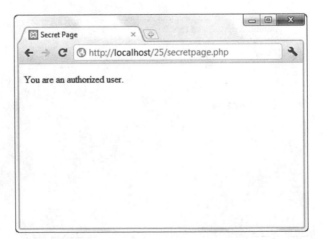

Close your browser and attempt to access `secretpage.php` directly. You will find that you cannot, and you will be redirected to the original login form because the authentication cookie has not been set after a successful login.

Summary

This chapter explained how to use Apache features to restrict access to your website based on the identity of the remote user and information from the HTTP request or network connection. It also covered some authentication modules included with Apache and additional tools that you can use to create and manage your user and group databases.

In addition, you learned one method for using cookie values to allow access to specific parts of your PHP application.

Q&A

Q. *I have a UNIX system. Can I use* `/etc/passwd` *as my user database?*

A. Although using `/etc/passwd` might seem convenient, it is advisable that you do not use the existing `/etc/passwd` file for authenticating users of your website. Otherwise, an attacker who gains access to a user of your website will also gain access to the system. Keep separate databases and encourage users to choose different passwords for their system accounts and web access. Periodically run password checkers that scan for weak passwords and accounts in which the username is also the password.

Q. *Why am I asked for my password twice in some websites?*

A. Your browser keeps track of your password so that you do not have to type it for every request. The stored password is based on the realm (`AuthName` directive) and the hostname of the website. Sometimes you can access a website via different names, such as yourdomain.com and www.yourdomain.com. If you are authorized to access a certain restricted area of yourdomain.com but are redirected or follow a link to www.yourdomain.com, you will be asked again to provide the username and password because your browser thinks it is a completely different website.

Q. *Are there any serious security or privacy issues raised by cookies?*

A. A server can access a cookie set only from its own domain. Although a cookie can be stored on the user's hard drive, there is no other access to the user's file system. It is possible, however, to set a cookie in response to a request for an image. So, if many sites include images served from a third-party ad server or counter script, the third party might be able to track a user across multiple domains.

Workshop

The workshop is designed to help you review what you've learned and begin putting your knowledge into practice.

Quiz

1. What are the advantages of database files over plaintext files for storing user authentication information?

2. Can you name some disadvantages of HTTP basic authentication?

3. What function is designed to allow you to set a cookie on a visitor's browser?

Answers

1. Database files are much more scalable because they can be indexed, and also clustered for robustness. This means that Apache does not need to read the file sequentially until a match is found for a particular user but rather can jump to the exact location.

2. One disadvantage is that the information is transmitted in cleartext over the network. This means that unless you are using SSL, it is possible for an attacker to read the packets your browser sends to the server and steal your password. Another disadvantage is that HTTP authentication does not provide a means for customizing the login (except the realm name). It is common for websites to implement custom login mechanisms using HTML forms and cookies.

3. The `setcookie()` function enables you to set a cookie (although you could also output a `Set-Cookie` header using the `header()` function).

Activity

Practice using the various types of authentication—both server based and with PHP—on your development server. Get a feel for the differences between basic HTTP authentication and something you devise on your own.

CHAPTER 26

Logging and Monitoring Web Server Activity

In this chapter, you learn the following:

▶ How to understand Apache log formats and logging levels

▶ How to rotate and analyze Apache logs

▶ How to interpret common errors that might appear in your logs

▶ How to create scripts that log specific items to database tables

▶ How to create custom reports based on these logging tables

This chapter describes how the logging system in Apache works and how you can customize it (which information to store and where). In addition, you learn a quick way to use PHP and MySQL to log specific items of interest to you outside the realm of the Apache log files.

Standard Apache Access Logging

Using Apache's basic logging features, you can keep track of who visits your websites by logging accesses to the servers hosting them. You can log every aspect of the browser requests and server responses, including the IP address of the client, user, and resource accessed. You need to take three steps to create a request log:

1. Define *what* you want to log—your log format.

2. Define *where* you want to log it—your log files, a database, an external program.

3. Define *whether* to log—conditional logging rules.

The next few sections take a closer look at these steps.

Defining What to Log

As well as logging nearly every aspect associated with the request, you can define how your log entries appear by creating a log format. A *log format* is a string that contains text mixed with log-formatting directives. Log-formatting directives start with a % followed by a directive name or identifier, usually a letter indicating the piece of information to be logged.

When Apache logs a request, it scans the string and substitutes the value for each directive. For example, if the log format is This is the client address %a, the log entry is something like This is the client address 10.0.0.2. That is, the logging directive %a replaces the IP address of the client making the request. Table 26.1 provides a comprehensive list of all formatting directives.

TABLE 26.1   Log Formatting Directives

Formatting Options	Explanation
Data from the Client	
%a	Remote IP address, from the client.
%h	Hostname or IP address of the client making the request. Whether the hostname is logged depends on two factors: The IP address of the client must resolve to a hostname via a reverse DNS lookup, and Apache must be configured to do that lookup using the HostNameLookups directive, explained later in this chapter. If these conditions are not met, the IP address of the client is logged rather than the hostname.
%l	Remote user, obtained via the identd protocol. This option is not very useful because the majority of the client machines do not support this protocol.
%u	Remote user, from the HTTP basic authentication protocol.
Data from the Server	
%A	Local IP address, from the server.
%D	Time it took to serve the request, in microseconds.
%{env_variable}e	Value for an environment variable named *env_variable*. (There are many.)
%{time_format}t	Current time. If {*time_format*} is present, it is interpreted as an argument to the UNIX strftime function. See the logresolve Apache manual page for details.

Formatting Options	Explanation
%T	Time it took to serve the request, in seconds.
%v	Canonical name of the server that answered the request.
%V	Server name according to the UseCanonicalName directive.
%X	Status of the connection to the server. A value of x means the connection was aborted before the server could send the data. A + means the connection will be kept alive for further requests from the same client. A - means the connection will be closed.
Data from the Request	
%{cookie_name}C	Value for a cookie named cookie_name.
%H	Request protocol, such as HTTP or HTTPS.
%m	Request method such as GET, POST, PUT, and so on.
%{header_name}i	Value for a header named header_name in the request from the client. This information can be useful, for example, to log the names and versions of your visitors' browsers.
%r	Text of the original HTTP request.
%q	Query parameters, if any, prefixed by a ?.
%U	Requested URL, without query parameters.
%y	Username for the HTTP authentication (basic or digest).
Data from the Response	
%b, %B	Size, in bytes, of the body of the response sent back to the client (excluding headers). The only difference between the options is that if no data was sent, %b will log a - and %B will log 0.
%f	Path of the file served, if any.
%t	Time when the request was served.
%{header_name}o	Value for a header named header_name in the response to the client.
%>s	Final status code. Apache can process several times the same request (internal redirects). This is the status code of the final response.

The *Common Log Format* (CLF) is a standard log format. Most websites can log requests using this format, and many log processing and reporting tools understand the format. Its format is the following:

```
"%h %l %u %t \"%r\" %>s %b"
```

That is, it includes the hostname or IP address of the client, remote user via `identd`, remote user via HTTP authentication, time when the request was served, text of the request, status code, and size in bytes of the content served.

The following is a CLF entry example:

```
10.0.0.1 - - [19/Jan/2012:17:32:43 -0500] "GET / HTTP/1.0" 200 1101
```

You are now ready to learn how to define log formats using the `LogFormat` directive. This directive takes two arguments: The first argument is a logging string, and the second is a nickname that will be associated with that logging string.

For example, the following directive from the default Apache configuration file defines the CLF and assigns it the nickname `common`:

```
LogFormat "%h %l %u %t \"%r\" %>s %b" common
```

You can also use the `LogFormat` directive with only one argument, either a log format string or a nickname. This has the effect of setting the default value for the logging format used by the `TransferLog` directive, explained in "Defining Where to Log" later in this chapter.

The `HostNameLookups` **Directive**

When a client makes a request, Apache knows only the IP address of the client. Apache must perform what is called a *reverse DNS lookup* to find out the hostname associated with the IP address. This operation can be time-consuming and can introduce a noticeable lag in the request processing. The `HostNameLookups` directive enables you to control whether to perform the reverse DNS lookup.

The `HostNameLookups` directive can take one of the following arguments: `on`, `off`, or `double`. The default is `off`. The `double` lookup argument means that Apache finds out the hostname from the IP and then tries to find the IP from the hostname. This process is necessary if you are really concerned with security, as described in http://httpd.apache.org/docs-2.2/dns-caveats.html. If you are using hostnames as part of your Allow and Deny rules, a double DNS lookup is performed regardless of the HostNameLookups settings.

If HostNameLookups is enabled (on or double), Apache logs the hostname. This causes extra load on your server, which you should be aware of when making the decision to turn HostNameLookups on or off. If you choose to keep HostNameLookups off, which is recommended for medium- to high-traffic sites, Apache logs only the associated IP address. There are plenty of tools to resolve the IP addresses in the logs later. See the "Managing Apache Logs" section later in this chapter. In addition, the result is passed to CGI scripts via the environment variable REMOTE_HOST.

The IdentityCheck **Directive**

At the beginning of the chapter, you learned how to log the remote username via the identd protocol using the %l log formatting directive. The IdentityCheck directive takes a value of on or off to enable or disable checking for that value and making it available for inclusion in the logs. Because the information is not reliable and takes a long time to check, it is switched off by default and should probably never be enabled. %l was mentioned only because it is part of the CLF. For more information on the identd protocol, see RFC 1413 at http://www.rfc-editor.org/rfc/rfc1413.txt.

Status Code

You can specify whether to log specific elements in a log entry. At the beginning of the chapter, you learned that log directives start with a %, followed by a directive identifier. In between, you can insert a list of status codes, separated by commas. If the request status is one of the listed codes, the parameter is logged; otherwise, a - is logged.

For example, the following directive identifier logs the browser name and version for malformed requests (status code 400) and requests with methods not implemented (status code 501). This information can prove useful for tracking which clients are being used to access your website.

```
%400,501{User-agent}i
```

You can precede the method list with an ! to log the parameter if the methods are implemented:

```
%!400,501{User-agent}i
```

Defining Where to Log

Logging to files is the default way of logging requests in Apache. You can define the name of the file using the `TransferLog` and `CustomLog` directives.

The `TransferLog` directive takes a file argument and uses the latest log format defined by a `LogFormat` directive with a single argument (the nickname or the format string). If no log format is present, it defaults to the CLF.

The following example shows how to use the `LogFormat` and `TransferLog` directives to define a log format that is based on the CLF but that also includes the browser name:

```
LogFormat "%h %l %u %t \"%r\" %>s %b \"%{User-agent}i\""
TransferLog logs/access_log
```

The `CustomLog` directive enables you to specify the logging format explicitly. It takes at least two arguments: a logging format and a destination file. The logging format can be specified as a nickname or as a logging string directly.

For example, the directives

```
LogFormat "%h %l %u %t \"%r\" %>s %b \"%{User-agent}i\"" myformat
CustomLog logs/access_log myformat
```

and

```
CustomLog logs/access_log "%h %l %u %t \"%r\" %>s %b \"%{User-agent}i\""
```

are equivalent.

The `CustomLog` directive accepts an environment variable as a third argument. If the environment variable is present, the entry is logged; otherwise, it is not. If the environment variable is negated by prefixing an `!` to it, the entry is logged if the variable is *not* present.

The following example shows how to avoid logging images in GIF and JPEG format in your logs:

```
SetEnvIf Request_URI "(\.gif|\.jpg)$" image
CustomLog logs/access_log common env=!image
```

NOTE

> The regular expression used for pattern matching in this and other areas of the `httpd.conf` file follows the same format for regular expressions in PHP and other programming languages.

Both `TransferLog` and `CustomLog` directives can accept an executable program, prefixed by a pipe sign, `|`, as an argument. Apache writes the log entries to the standard input of this program. The program, in turn, processes the input by logging the entries to a database, transmitting them to another system, and so on.

If the program dies for some reason, the server makes sure that it restarts. If the server stops, the program also stops. The `rotatelogs` utility, bundled with Apache and explained later in this chapter, is an example of a logging program.

As a general rule, unless you have a specific requirement for using a particular program, it is easier and more reliable to log to a file on disk and do the processing, merging, analysis of logs, and so on, at a later time, possibly on a different machine.

NOTE

Make sure that the program you use for logging requests is secure, because it runs as the user Apache was started with. On UNIX, this usually means root because the external program is started before the server changes its user ID to the value of the `User` directive, typically nobody or www.

Standard Apache Error Logging

Apache can be configured to log error messages and debugging information, in addition to client requests. In addition to errors generated by Apache itself, CGI errors can be logged.

Each error log entry is prefixed by the time the error occurred and the client IP address or hostname, if available. As with HTTP request logging, you can log error information to a file or program. On UNIX systems, you can also log to the `syslog` daemon. On Windows, errors can be logged in the Windows event log and are then viewable via the Windows Event Viewer. Use the `ErrorLog` directive to define where you want your logs to go.

Logging Errors to a File

A file argument indicates the path to the error log file. If the path is relative, it is assumed to be relative to the server root. By default, the error log file is located in the logs directory and is named `error_log` on UNIX and `error.log` on Windows. The following is an example:

```
ErrorLog logs/my_error_log
```

Logging Errors to a Program

You can specify the path to a program, prefixed by a pipe |. Apache logs errors to the standard input of the program, and the program further processes them. The following is an example:

```
ErrorLog "|/usr/local/bin/someprogram"
```

The `syslog` Daemon Argument

On a UNIX system, if you specify `syslog` as an argument, you can log error messages to the UNIX system log daemon `syslogd`. By default, log errors are logged to the `syslog` facility `local7`. The facility is the part of the system generating the error. You can specify a facility by providing `syslog:facility` as an argument. Examples of `syslog` facilities are `mail`, `uucp`, `local0`, `local1`, and so on. For a complete list, look at the documentation for `syslog` included with your system. (Try `man syslogd` or `man syslogd.conf` at the command line.) The following is an example of logging to `syslog`:

```
ErrorLog syslog:local6
```

The `LogLevel` Directive

The error information provided by Apache has several degrees of importance. You can choose to log only important messages and disregard informational or trivial warning messages. The `LogLevel` directive takes an error-level argument. Only errors of that level of importance or higher are logged.

Table 26.2 specifies the valid values for the `LogLevel` directive, as specified by the Apache documentation. By default, the `LogLevel` value is `warn`. That should be enough for most Apache installations. If you are trying to troubleshoot a specific configuration, you can alter the level to `debug`.

TABLE 26.2   `LogLevel` Options as Described in the Apache Documentation

Setting	Description	Example
emerg	Emergencies—system is unusable	Child cannot open lock file. Exiting.
alert	Action must be taken immediately	getpwuid: couldn't determine user name from uid.
crit	Critical conditions	socket: Failed to get a socket, exiting child.

Setting	Description	Example
error	Error conditions	Premature end of script headers.
warn	Warning conditions	Child process 1234 did not exit, sending another SIGHUP.
notice	Normal but significant conditions	httpd: caught SIGBUS, attempting to dump core in...
info	Informational	Server seems busy, (You may need to increase StartServers, or Min/MaxSpareServers)...
debug	Debug-level messages	Opening config file...

Managing Apache Logs

Apache provides several tools for managing your logs. Other Apache-specific third-party tools are available and mentioned here. Because Apache can log requests in the CLF, you can use most generic log-processing tools with Apache as well.

Resolving Hostnames

Earlier in the chapter, you learned how to use the HostNameLookups directive to enable or disable hostname resolution at the time the request is made. If HostName-Lookups is set to off (the default), the log file contains only IP addresses. Later, you can use the command-line logresolve utility on UNIX or logresolve.exe on Windows to process the log file and convert the IP addresses to hostnames.

The logresolve utility reads log entries from standard input and outputs the result to its standard output. To read to and from a file, you can use redirection on both UNIX and Windows:

```
logresolve < access.log > resolved.log
```

Log-resolving tools are efficient because they can cache results and do not cause any delay when serving requests to clients.

Log Rotation

In websites with high traffic, access log files can quickly grow in size. You should have a mechanism to rotate logs periodically, archiving and compressing older logs at defined intervals.

Log files should not be removed while Apache is running because the server is writing directly to them. A solution would be to use an intermediate program to log the requests. The program, in turn, takes care of rotating the logs.

Apache provides the `rotatelogs` program on UNIX and `rotatelogs.exe` on Windows for this purpose. It accepts three arguments: a filename, a rotate interval in seconds, and an optional offset in minutes against UTC (coordinated universal time).

For example

```
TransferLog "|bin/rotatelogs /var/logs/apachelog 86400"
```

creates a new log file and moves the current log to the `/var/logs` directory daily. (At the end of the command, `86400` is the number of seconds in 1 day.)

NOTE

> If the path to the program includes spaces, you might need to escape them by prefixing them with a \ (backslash)—for example, `My\ Documents`. This is especially common in the Windows platform.

If the name of the file includes % prefixed options, the name is treated as input to the `strftime` function that converts the % options to time values. The manual page for the `rotatelogs` utility contains a complete listing of options, but here's an example:

```
TransferLog "|bin/rotatelogs /var/logs/apachelog%m_%d_%y 86400"
```

This command adds the current month, day, and year to the log filename.

If the name does not include any %-formatted options, the current time in seconds is added to the name of the archived file.

Log Analysis

Whether you have a single server and log files, or a cluster of servers producing their own log files, after you collect the logs you can analyze them and gain information about traffic and visitor behavior.

Many commercial, shareware, and freeware applications are available for server-side log analysis and reporting. Two popular open source applications are Webalizer (http://www.mrunix.net/webalizer/) and awstats (http://awstats.sourceforge.net/).

Wusage is a nice, inexpensive commercial alternative at http://www.boutell.com/wusage/.

Monitoring Error Logs

If you run Apache on a UNIX system, you can use the `tail` command-line utility to monitor in real-time log entries to both your access and error logs. The syntax is

```
tail -f logname
```

where *logname* is the path to the Apache log file. It prints onscreen the last few lines of the log file and continues to print entries as they are added to the file.

You can find additional programs that enable you to identify problems quickly by scanning your error log files for specific errors, malformed requests, and so on and reporting on them. ScanErrLog is one such program; you can find it at http://www.librelogiciel.com/software/.

Logging Custom Information to a Database

Creating your own logging tables in MySQL, matched up with snippets of PHP code, can help you to capture access-related information for specific pages of your site. Using this information, you can create customized reports. This method can be much less cumbersome than wading through Apache log files, especially when you are just searching for a subset of access information. The following sections outline a simple version of this process.

Creating the Database Table

The first step in your custom logging method is to create the database table. The following table-creation command creates a table called `access_tracker` in your MySQL database, with fields for an ID, page title, user agent, and date of access:

```
CREATE TABLE access_tracker (
    id INT NOT NULL PRIMARY KEY AUTO_INCREMENT,
    page_title VARCHAR(50),
    user_agent TEXT,
    date_accessed DATE
);
```

Next you create the code snippet that writes to this table.

Creating the PHP Code Snippet

As you might have gathered already, *code snippet* simply means *a little bit of code*. In other words, something that doesn't qualify as a long script but just serves a simple purpose. In this case, the code snippet in Listing 26.1 writes some basic information to the `access_tracker` table.

LISTING 26.1   Code Snippet for Access Tracking

```
1:  <?php
2:  //set up static variables
3:  $page_title = "sample page A";
4:  $user_agent = getenv('HTTP_USER_AGENT');
5:
6:  //connect to server and select database
7:  $mysqli = mysqli_connect("localhost", "joeuser", "somepass", "testDB")
8:          or die(mysql_error());
9:
10: //create and issue query
11: $sql = "INSERT INTO access_tracker (page_title,user_agent,date_accessed)
12:         VALUES ('$page_title', '$user_agent', now())";
13: $result = mysqli_query($mysqli, $sql) or die(mysqli_error($mysqli));
14:
15: //close connection to MySQL
16: mysqli_close($mysqli);
17: ?>
```

What you do with this snippet is simple, for purposes of illustration here: Place it at the beginning of every page you want to track. For each page, change the value of `$page_title` in the snippet to represent the actual title of the page.

Now create a script called `sample1.php`, containing the contents of Listing 26.1 and then the contents in Listing 26.2.

LISTING 26.2   HTML Page Example

```
1:  <!DOCTYPE html>
2:  <html>
3:  <head>
4:  <title>Sample Page A</title>
5:  </head>
6:  <body>
7:  <h1>Sample Page A</h1>
8:  <p>blah blah blah.</p>
9:  </body>
10: </html>
```

Create a few copies of this file with different filenames and values for $page_title. Then access these different pages with your web browser to fill up your logging table.

Creating Sample Reports

When you have the data in your access_tracker table, you can create a simple report screen to disseminate this information. The code in Listing 26.3 creates a report that issues queries to count total results as well as the breakdown of browsers in use. Each of these blocks is explained after the code listing.

LISTING 26.3   Creating an Access Report

```
 1:    <?php
 2:    //connect to server and select database
 3:    $mysqli = mysqli_connect("localhost", "joeuser", "somepass", "testDB")
 4:              or die(mysqli_error());
 5:
 6:    //issue query and select results for counts
 7:    $count_sql = "SELECT count(page_title) AS p_count FROM access_tracker";
 8:    $count_res = mysqli_query($mysqli, $count_sql) or
 9:      die(mysqli_error($mysqli));
10:    while ($count_info = mysqli_fetch_array($count_res)) {
11:        $all_count = $count_info['p_count'];
12:    }
13:
14:    //issue query and select results for user agents
15:    $user_agent_sql = "SELECT DISTINCT user_agent, count(user_agent) AS
16:                       ua_count FROM access_tracker GROUP BY user_agent
17:                       ORDER BY ua_count desc";
18:    $user_agent_res = mysqli_query($mysqli, $user_agent_sql)
19:                      or die(mysqli_error($mysqli));
20:
21:    //start user agent display block
22:    $user_agent_block = "<ul>";
23:
24:    //loop through user agent results
25:    while ($row_ua = mysqli_fetch_array($user_agent_res)) {
26:        $user_agent = $row_ua['user_agent'];
27:        $user_agent_count = $row_ua['ua_count'];
28:        $user_agent_block .= "
29:        <li>".$user_agent."
30:           <ul>
31:           <li><em>accesses per browser: ".$user_agent_count."</em>
32:           </ul>
33:        </li>";
34:    }
35:
36:    //finish up the user agent block
37:    $user_agent_block .= "</ul>";
38:
39:    //issue query and select results for pages
40:    $page_title_sql = "SELECT DISTINCT page_title, count(page_title) AS
```

LISTING 26.3   Continued

```
41:                         pt_count FROM access_tracker GROUP BY page_title
42:                         ORDER BY pt_count desc";
43: $page_title_res = mysqli_query($mysqli, $page_title_sql)
44:                   or die(mysqli_error($mysqli));
45:
46: //start page title display block
47: $page_title_block = "<ul>";
48:
49: //loop through results
50: while ($row_pt = mysqli_fetch_array($page_title_res)) {
51:     $page_title = $row_pt['page_title'];
52:     $page_count = $row_pt['pt_count'];
53:     $page_title_block .= "
54:     <li>".$page_title."
55:         <ul>
56:         <li><em>accesses per page: ".$page_count."</em>
57:         </ul>
58:     </li>";
59: }
60:
61: //finish up the page title block
62: $page_title_block .= "</ul>";
63:
64: //close connection to MySQL
65: mysqli_close($mysqli);
66: ?>
67: <!DOCTYPE html>
68: <html>
69: <head>
70: <title>Access Report</title>
71: </head>
72: <body>
73: <h1>Access Report</h1>
74: <p><strong>Total Accesses Tracked:</strong>
75: <?php echo "$all_count"; ?></p>
76: <p><strong>Web Browsers Used:</strong>
77: <?php echo "$user_agent_block"; ?></p>
78: <p><strong>Individual Pages:</strong>
79: <?php echo "$page_title_block"; ?></p>
80: </body>
81: </html>
```

Line 3 connects to the database so that you can issue the queries against the access_tracker table. Lines 7–8 issue the query to select the count of all pages, and lines 15–19 count the user agent accesses. Line 22 starts an unordered list block for the results of the user agent query, and lines 25–34 loop through the results and create the list, which is closed in line 37.

Lines 40–44 create and issue the query to count the individual pages. Line 47 starts an unordered list block for the results of this query, and lines 50–59 loop through the results and create the list of accessed pages, which is closed in line 62.

Put these lines into a text file called `accessreport.php`, and place this file in your web server document root. When you access this report, you will see something like Figure 26.1. Your page names, counts, and browsers will differ, but you get the idea.

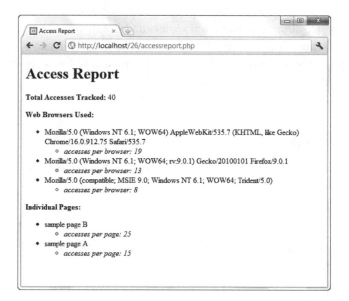

FIGURE 26.1
Custom access report for tracked pages.

This sort of tracking is a lot easier than wading through Apache access logs, but I do not recommend completely replacing your access logs with a database-driven system. That's a bit too much database-connection overhead, even if MySQL is particularly nice on your system. Instead, target your page tracking to something particularly important.

Summary

This chapter explained how to log specific information about the requests and errors generated by Apache. You can store the logs in files or databases or pass them to external programs. You learned about the different utilities available for managing, processing, and analyzing logs, both the ones included with Apache and those available from third parties.

In this chapter, you also learned an easy method for using PHP code snippets and a MySQL database to perform simple access tracking of specific pages. This information was displayed in an easy-to-understand access report built with PHP.

Q&A

Q. *Why wouldn't I want to log images?*

A. In heavily loaded servers, logging can become a bottleneck. If the purpose of logging is to count the number of visitors and analyze their usage of the website, you can achieve this result by logging only the HTML pages, not the images contained in them. This reduces the number of hits stored in the logs and the time spent writing them.

Workshop

The workshop is designed to help you review what you've learned and begin putting your knowledge into practice.

Quiz

1. How can you avoid logging hits from a client accessing your website from a particular network?

2. How can you log images to a different file?

3. Why would you want to turn `HostNameLookups` off in your Apache configuration?

Answers

1. In some situations, you might want to ignore requests coming from a particular network, such as your own, so that they do not skew the results. You can do this either by post-processing the logs and removing them or by using the `SetEnvIf` directive:

```
SetEnvIf Remote_Addr 10\.0\.0\. intranet
CustomLog logs/access_log "%h %l %u %t \"%r\" %>s %b" !intranet
```

2. Earlier in the chapter, you learned how to avoid logging images. Instead of ignoring images altogether, you can easily log them to a separate file, using the same environment variable mechanism:

```
SetEnvIf Request_URI "(\.gif|\.jpeg)$" image
CustomLog logs/access_log common env=!image
CustomLog logs/images_log common env=image
```

3. Having `HostNameLookups` on causes extra load on the server because it looks up the IP of the user accessing the site and writes that to the log file. You can still get the information at a later date by using a hostname resolver when generating usage reports, and the server load is then minimized for the user.

Activities

1. Create a tracking script that logs accesses to a database via PHP. Using the list of possible environment variables, log more than just the page title, user agent, and date accessed.

2. Create a report of the access data you have stored, only this time add a date range selector and only produce results that fall within the selected range.

CHAPTER 27

Application Localization

In this chapter, you learn the following:

▶ How to recognize and prepare for character set differences

▶ How to prepare the structure of your application and produce localized sites

The key phrase in *World Wide Web* is *World Wide*. Creating a website useful to speakers of different languages is a breeze using PHP and MySQL. The process of preparing your applications for use in multiple locales is called *internationalization*; customizing your code for each locale is called *localization*.

About Internationalization and Localization

First and foremost, it's important to understand that neither internationalization nor localization is the same thing as content translation. In fact, you can have a fully translated website—all in German, all in Japanese, or all in whatever language you want—and it will not be considered an internationalized or localized website. It will just be a translated one. The key aspects of an internationalized application are as follows:

▶ Externalizing all strings, icons, and graphics

▶ Modifying the display of formatting functions (dates, currency, numbers, and so on)

After you have constructed your application so that your strings are externalized—when all strings used in functions, classes, and other scripts are managed in one place and included or otherwise referred to as constant variables—and your formatting functions can change per locale, you can begin the process of localization. Translation happens to be a part of localization.

A *locale* is essentially a grouping—in this case, a grouping of the translated strings, graphics, text, and formatting conventions that will be used in the application or website to be localized. These groupings are usually referred to by the name of the pervasive language of the application, such as the German locale. Although it might be obvious that the German locale includes text translated into German, it does not mean that the website is applicable only to people in Germany. Austrians who speak German would probably utilize a localized German website, but it would not be referred to as the Austrian locale.

In the next few sections, you learn about working with different character sets and how to modify your environment to successfully prepare your applications for localization.

About Character Sets

Character sets are usually referred to as *single-byte* or *multibyte*, referring to the number of bytes needed to define a relationship with a character used in a language. English, German, and French (among many others) are single-byte languages; only 1 byte is necessary to represent a character such as the letter *a* or the number *9*. Single-byte code sets have, at most, 256 characters, including the entire set of ASCII characters, accented characters, and other characters necessary for formatting.

Multibyte code sets have more than 256 characters, including all single-byte characters as a subset. Multibyte languages include traditional and simplified Chinese, Japanese, Korean, Thai, Arabic, Hebrew, and so forth. These languages require more than 1 byte to represent a character. A good example is the word *Tokyo*, the capital of Japan. In English, it is spelled with four different characters, using a total of 5 bytes. However, in Japanese, the word is represented by two syllables, *tou* and *kyou*, each of which uses 2 bytes, for a total of 4 bytes used.

This is a complete simplification of character sets and the technology behind them, but the relevance is this: To properly interpret and display the text of web pages in their intended language, it is up to you to tell the web browser which character set to use. This is achieved by sending the appropriate headers before all content.

If you have a set of pages that include Japanese text and you do not send the correct headers regarding language and character set, those pages will render incorrectly in web browsers whose primary language is not Japanese. In other words, because no character set information is included, the browser assumes that it is to render the text using its own default character set. For example, if your Japanese pages use the Shift_JIS or UTF-8 character set and your browser is set for ISO-8859-1, your browser will try to render the Japanese text using the single-byte ISO-8859-1 character set. It will fail miserably in this unless the headers alert it to use Shift_JIS or UTF-8 and you have the appropriate libraries and language packs installed on your operating system.

TIP

> *Mojibake* is the term for this type of unrecognizable characters. For more information, see http://en.wikipedia.org/wiki/Mojibake.

The headers in question are the Content-type and Content-language headers, and these can also be set as HTML5 tag attributes. Because you have all the tools for a dynamic environment, it's best to both send the appropriate headers before your text and print the correct HTML5 attributes tags in your document. The following is an example of the header() function outputting the proper character information for an English site:

```
header("Content-Type: text/html;charset=ISO-8859-1");
header("Content-Language: en");
```

The accompanying HTML5 tags would be these:

```
<html lang="en">
<meta charset="ISO-8859-1">
```

A German site would use the same character set but a different language code:

```
header("Content-Type: text/html;charset=ISO-8859-1");
header("Content-Language: de");
```

The accompanying HTML5 tags would be these:

```
<html lang="de">
<meta charset="ISO-8859-1">
```

A Japanese site uses both a different character set and different language code:

```
header("Content-Type: text/html;charset=Shift_JIS");
header("Content-Language: ja");
```

The accompanying HTML5 tags would be these:

```
<html lang="ja">
<meta charset="Shift_JIS">
```

Environment Modifications

Your environment, as defined in the installation chapters of this book, need not change to handle localized websites. Although you can use several language-related settings in Apache, PHP, and MySQL to accommodate localized websites, you can also perform all the tasks in this chapter without making any language-related changes to your configuration. Just for your own information, the next few sections point you to the appropriate documentation for internationalization using Apache, PHP, and MySQL.

Configuration Changes to Apache

In Chapter 29, "Apache Performance Tuning and Virtual Hosting," you learn about the concept of content negotiation using the mod_mime or mod_negotiation modules and the AddLanguage and AddCharset directives (among others). You use these directives when you manually change the extension of your file and want Apache to interpret the character set to be used, based on that extension. However, that is not what this chapter discusses. You want all your localized websites to have the same file-naming conventions (such as index.html and company_info.html) and not have to manually create multiple pages with different language-based extensions to accommodate translated files. Your goal regarding website localization is to have a single set of pages filled with the appropriately translated text running from one web server.

NOTE _____

There's nothing wrong with Apache-based content negotiation using multiple files with language-based naming conventions. It's just not the focus of this chapter. You can read more about Apache-based content negotiation at http://httpd.apache.org/docs-2.2/content-negotiation.html.

Configuration Changes to PHP

As with Apache, no configuration changes in PHP are required for any tasks in this chapter. However, you can use a host of functions related to the handling of multibyte characters, if you want. These functions are in the PHP manual at http://www.php.net/mbstring and must be enabled during the configuration process using this code. (Windows users enable the php_mbstring.dll extension in php.ini.)

```
--enable-mbstring=LANG
```

Here, LANG is a language code, such as ja for Japanese, cn for Simplified Chinese, and so forth. Or, you can use this line to enable all available languages:

```
--enable-mbstring=all
```

When you enable mbstring functions in PHP, you can set several options in the php.ini configuration file to use these functions properly. After this is configured, you can use any of the more than 40 mbstring-related functions for handling multibtye input in PHP.

The manual entries for these functions are comprehensive and recommended reading for advanced work with multibyte character sets and dynamic content. You will get by just fine in this chapter without them, although it is recommended that at some point you peruse the PHP manual for your own edification.

Configuration Changes to MySQL

No explicit changes are needed in MySQL for the localization examples used in this chapter because the examples are not database-driven. The default character set used in MySQL is ISO-8859-1, but that does not mean that you are limited only to storing single-byte characters in your database tables. For more information on the current language-related elements of MySQL, read the MySQL Manual entry at http://dev.mysql.com/doc/refman/5.5/en/globalization.html.

Creating a Localized Page Structure

In this section, you look at a functioning example of a localized welcome page that uses PHP to enable a user to select a target language and then receive the appropriate text. The goal of this section is to show an example of externalizing the strings used in this script, which is one of the characteristics of internationalization.

In this script, the user happens upon your English-based website but is also presented with an option to browse within the locale of his choice—English, German, or Japanese. Three elements are involved in this process:

- ▶ Creating and using a master file for sending locale-specific header information

- ▶ Creating and using a master file for displaying the information based on the selected locale

- ▶ Using the script itself

Listing 27.1 shows the contents of the master file used for sending locale-specific header information.

LISTING 27.1 Language Definition File

```
1:  <?php
2:  if ((!isset($_SESSION['lang'])) || (!isset($_GET['lang']))) {
3:      $_SESSION['lang'] = "en";
4:      $currLang = "en";
5:  } else {
6:      $currLang = $_GET['lang'];
7:      $_SESSION['lang'] = $currLang;
```

LISTING 27.1   Continued

```
8:    }
9:
10:   switch($currLang) {
11:       case "en":
12:           define("CHARSET","ISO-8859-1");
13:           define("LANGCODE", "en");
14:       break;
15:
16:       case "de":
17:           define("CHARSET","ISO-8859-1");
18:           define("LANGCODE", "de");
19:       break;
20:
21:       case "ja":
22:           define("CHARSET","UTF-8");
23:           define("LANGCODE", "ja");
24:       break;
25:
26:       default:
27:           define("CHARSET","ISO-8859-1");
28:           define("LANGCODE", "en");
29:       break;
30:   }
31:
32:   header("Content-Type: text/html;charset=".CHARSET);
33:   header("Content-Language: ".LANGCODE);
34:   ?>
```

Lines 2–8 of Listing 27.1 set up the session value needed to store the user's selected language choice.

NOTE

The session_start() function is not used in the define_lang.php or the lang_strings.php file listed in the following paragraphs because these files are included via the include() function from within the master file. The master file, which you will create shortly, calls the session_start() function, which will be valid for these included files as well.

If no session value exists, the English locale settings are used. If your site were a German site by default, you would change this file to use the German locale by default. This script prepares for the next script, which contains an input-selection mechanism, by setting the value of $currLang to the result of this input in line 6.

The switch statement beginning on line 10 contains several case statements designed to assign the appropriate values to the constant variables CHARSET and LANGCODE. Lines 32–33 actually utilize these variables for the first time when dynamically creating and sending the headers for Content-type and Content-language.

Save this file as **define_lang.php** and place it in the document root of your web browser. This file defines two constants used in the next script, which is the actual display script. The constants are CHARSET and LANGCODE, corresponding to the character set and language code for each locale. The display script uses these constants to create the proper META tags regarding character set and language code. Although this script sends the headers, it's a good idea to ensure that they are part of the page itself to aid in any necessary input from forms.

Listing 27.2 creates a function that simply stores the externalized strings used in the display script. This example uses two: one to welcome the user to the page (WELCOME_TXT) and one to introduce the language selection process (CHOOSE_TXT) .

LISTING 27.2 String Definition File

```php
1:  <?php
2:  function defineStrings() {
3:    switch($_SESSION['lang']) {
4:        case "en":
5:            define("WELCOME_TXT","Welcome!");
6:            define("CHOOSE_TXT","Choose Language");
7:        break;
8:
9:        case "de":
10:            define("WELCOME_TXT","Willkommen!");
11:            define("CHOOSE_TXT","Sprache auswählen");
12:        break;
13:
14:        case "ja":
15:            define("WELCOME_TXT","[unprintable characters]");
16:            define("CHOOSE_TXT","[unprintable characters]");
17:        break;
18:
19:        default:
20:            define("WELCOME_TXT","Welcome!");
21:            define("CHOOSE_TXT","Choose Language");
22:        break;
23:    }
24: }
25: ?>
```

Use the file lang_strings.php from the CD included with this book to use the actual Japanese characters that cannot be displayed here. Place this file in the document root of your web browser. This file defines two constants, WELCOME_TXT and CHOOSE_TXT, which are used in the display script. These constants are defined within the context of the function called defineStrings(), although you could just as easily make this file a long switch statement outside the context of the function structure. I've simply put it in a function for the sake of organization and for ease of explanation when it comes time to use the display script.

Finally, it's time to create the display script. Remember, one key element of internationalization is to externalize all strings so that only one master file needs to be used. Listing 27.3 is such an example.

LISTING 27.3   Localized Welcome Script

```
1:  <?php
2:  session_start();
3:  include 'define_lang.php';
4:  include 'lang_strings.php';
5:  defineStrings();
6:  ?>
7:  <!DOCTYPE html>
8:  <html lang="<?php echo LANGCODE; ?>">
9:  <head>
10:    <title><?php echo WELCOME_TXT; ?></title>
11:  <meta charset="<?php echo CHARSET; ?>" />
12:  <body>
13:  <h1 style="text-align: center;"><?php echo WELCOME_TXT; ?></h1>
14:  <p style="text-align: center; font-weight: bold;">
15:    <?php echo CHOOSE_TXT; ?><br/><br/>
16:  <a href="<?php echo $_SERVER['PHP_SELF']."?lang=en"; ?>">
17:      <img src="en_flag.gif" alt="English" /></a>
18:  <a href="<?php echo $_SERVER['PHP_SELF']."?lang=de"; ?>">
19:      <img src="de_flag.gif" alt="German"/></a>
20:  <a href="<?php echo $_SERVER['PHP_SELF']."?lang=ja"; ?>">
21:      <img src="ja_flag.gif" alt="Japanese"/></a>
22:  </p>
23:  </body>
24:  </html>
```

Notice that Listing 27.3 is a basic template because all the language-related elements are externalized in the `define_lang.php` or `lang_strings.php` files. All this third file does is display the appropriate results, depending on the selected (or default) locale.

Line 5 calls the `defineStrings()` function, which then makes available the appropriate values for the two constant variables, which are used in lines 8, 10, 11, 13, and 15. Lines 16–18 display flags representing the English, German, and Japanese locales, which are clickable. When the user clicks one of the flags, the locale changes to the new, selected locale, and the strings used are those appropriate to the new locale. These links contain the `lang` variable, which is passed to the script as `$_GET['lang']`. If you look at line 6 of Listing 27.1, you will see how the code uses this to change the setting regarding the user's preferred locale.

NOTE

Despite the use here for illustrative purposes in a development environment, the use of a flag to represent language selection options is not recommended, because there exists no natural graphic representation for a language. Take, for instance, the use of the flag of Great Britain to represent English and the flag of Germany to represent German. English has an official or majority status in over 80 different countries, and German in at least 10—no single flag can represent that information.

Save this file as **lang_selector.php** and place it in the document root of your web browser. When visited for the first time, it should look something like Figure 27.1.

FIGURE 27.1
Viewing the language selector for the first time.

Until another language is selected, the default is English; accordingly, the Welcome and Choose Language text appears in English. When the user clicks the German flag, he sees Figure 27.2; when the user clicks the Japanese flag, he sees Figure 27.3.

FIGURE 27.2
Viewing the German language page.

FIGURE 27.3
Viewing the
Japanese
language
page.

Companies and organizations that offer localized versions of their websites often have long discussions about how to represent the locale selections—flags, names of countries, names of languages, and so forth. There is no clear-cut answer, but please remember that the use of flags is frowned upon. How to display the language selection is definitely a business decision, but if you have gone through the process of externalizing strings, text, and images and created an internationalized website template that is ready to be localized, the format of your locale selection is the least of your concerns.

Localizing Your Application with gettext()

The previous sections walked you through a basic approach to application internationalization and localization. A more advanced approach would be to use the built-in PHP function called gettext(), which is a gateway of sorts (an API, or application programming interface) to the GNU gettext package.

> **NOTE**
>
> For more information about GNU gettext, see http://www.gnu.org/software/gettext/gettext.htm.

The use of gettext and its PHP-related functions requires translation catalog files to be in specific format. A popular cross-platform editor for these files is Poedit (see http://www.poedit.com/). Once a translation catalog template has been created (full of your externalized strings), you can give the template to translators you have hired, or that you use through a crowdsourcing service such as Transifex (https://www.transifex.net/) or Get Localization (http://www.getlocalization.com/). With completed catalog files in hand, you can put them in a directory in your web server document root and begin the process of using gettext functions.

You can learn more about `gettext` and the PHP `gettext`-related functions in the PHP Manual at http://www.php.net/gettext, but in general the process goes something like this:

▶ Use `putenv()` to set the `LC_ALL` environment variable for the locale.

▶ Use `setlocale()` to set a value for `LC_ALL` (see http://www.php.net/setlocale).

▶ Use `bindtextdomain()` to set the location of the translation catalog for the given domain (domain in this case means a name identifying the application, not a domain like www.mydomain.com; see http://www.php.net/bindtextdomain).

▶ Use `textdomain()` to set the default domain to use with `gettext` (see http://www.php.net/textdomain).

▶ From this point forward, use either `gettext("some string")` or `_("some string")` to invoke the `gettext` translation for that string. So, if you have a translation catalog that assigns the German translated string `"Willkommen!"` for `"Welcome"`, and all the environment variables are set as appropriate for German, the following code will output "Willkommen!":

```
echo _("Welcome");
```

Once you have a handle on the basics of application internationalization and localization, if you are going to develop an application used by speakers of many different languages, I recommend looking into a `gettext`-based localization framework and crowdsourced translation services (unless you have a plethora of native language speakers at your disposal or a lot of money to spend on translation services).

Summary

This chapter introduced you to the basics of internationalization and localization. You learned the two keys to creating an internationalized site: All strings, text, and graphics are externalized, as is number, currency, and date formatting. You also learned that neither internationalization nor localization is equivalent to translating text; translation is just one part of localization.

You also learned a little bit about character sets: They can be single-byte or multibyte. You also learned the importance of sending the appropriate language-related headers so that your web browser can interpret and display your text properly.

You also created a practical example of how to store a locale-related session variable, to determine and send the localized strings to a preexisting template. This template can be used by all locales because each element was externalized. As a bit of a bonus, you learned about an advanced step in using application frameworks for localization, using PHP's gettext functions.

Q&A

Q. *How do I go about localizing numbers, dates, and currency using PHP?*

A. Two functions will prove very useful to you in this regard: number_format() and date(). You have already learned about the date() function. To use it in a localized environment, you simply rearrange the month, day, and year elements as appropriate to the locale (MM-DD-YYYY, DD-MM-YYYY, and so forth). The number_format() function is used for numbers and currency; it groups the thousandths with a comma, period, or space, as appropriate to the locale. Read the PHP Manual entry at http://www.php.net/number_format for possible uses.

Workshop

The workshop is designed to help you review what you've learned and begin putting your knowledge into practice.

Quiz

1. Is English a single-byte or multibyte language? What about Japanese?

2. What two headers related to character encoding are crucial in a localized site?

3. In addition to text strings, what other content elements need attention when internationalizing a site?

Answers

1. English is single-byte; Japanese is double-byte.

2. Content-Type with the charset indicator, Content-Language.

3. The formatting of dates, currency, and numbers are other types of content elements that need attention in the internationalization process.

Activities

1. Use Google Translate (or your own knowledge) to add "Welcome!" messages in a few different languages to the language definition and display files you created in this chapter.

2. Because graphical representations of flags are nonoptimal for use in selecting languages, change the flag-based language selection in the sample files from this chapter to something more appropriate.

CHAPTER 28

Working with XML and JSON

This chapter introduces you to working with XML documents and JSON data via PHP, but in no way is it comprehensive—entire books have been written on XML alone. However, for people new to XML, XML manipulation via PHP, and to receiving and working with JSON data, some sets of functions are more manageable than others; this chapter introduces you to a few of them.

What Is XML?

The name *XML* comes from the full name of the language, *Extensible Markup Language*. Although *markup* is in the name of the language, do not think of XML as you do HTML. XML is used for the storage and exchange of data within tag pairs of your own designation, whereas HTML is a presentation language that allows you to delineate the structure and presentation of the document being viewed, regardless of the data it contains.

Basic XML Document Structure

XML documents contain two major elements: the prolog and the body. The *prolog* contains the XML declaration statement and any processing instructions and comments you want to add.

NOTE

> For a complete definition of XML documents, read the XML specification at http://www.w3.org/TR/REC-xml.

The following snippet is a valid prolog:

```
<?xml version="1.0" ?>
<!-- Sample XML document -->
```

After the prolog comes the content structure. XML is hierarchical, like a book—books have titles and chapters, each of which contain paragraphs, and so forth. There is only one root element in an XML document. Continuing the book example, the element might be called `Books`, and the tags `<Books></Books>` surround all other information:

```
<Books>
```

Next, add any subsequent elements—called *children*—to your document. Continuing the book example, you need a master book element and then within it elements for title, author, and publishing information. Call these child elements `Title`, `Author`, and `PublishingInfo`. But the publishing information will likely contain more than one bit of information; you need a publisher's name, location, and year of publication. Not a problem. Just create another set of child elements within your parent element (which also happens to be a child element of the root element). For example, just the `<PublishingInfo>` element could look like this:

```
<PublishingInfo>
    <PublisherName>Sams Publishing</PublisherName>
    <PublisherCity>Indianapolis</PublisherCity>
    <PublishedYear>2012</PublishedYear>
</PublishingInfo>
```

All together, a sample `books.xml` document with one entry could look something like this:

```
<?xml version="1.0" ?>
<!--Sample XML document -->
<Books>
    <Book>
        <Title>A Very Good Book</Title>
        <Author>Jane Doe</Author>
        <PublishingInfo>
            <PublisherName>Sams Publishing</PublisherName>
            <PublisherCity>Indianapolis</PublisherCity>
            <PublishedYear>2012</PublishedYear>
        </PublishingInfo>
    </Book>
</Books>
```

Keep in mind two important rules for creating valid XML documents:

▶ XML is case sensitive, so <Book> and <book> are considered different elements.

▶ All XML tags must be properly closed, XML tags must be properly nested, and no overlapping tags are allowed.

Add some dummy entries to the books.xml file and place it in the document root of your web server for use in later examples. You will use the same XML file throughout the different interface examples shown in this chapter.

When Might You Use XML and PHP?

The short (and snarky) answer to this question is "anytime you want," but the serious answer is, as you can imagine, a little more complex than that. Earlier in this section, I noted that XML defines and carries content. This is still true. But what does that look like in "real life"?

The examples in this chapter use XML to store a small catalog of books. Imagine a large catalog of books stored in a proprietary database format, but one that has the capability to output data in XML format. If you need to get your hands on that catalog of books, but have no intention of purchasing or using the proprietary software in which it lives, XML would be the answer—using XML as a data interchange format. The owner of that data that is stored in a proprietary format, or in a manner that precludes direct access by a third-party (that is, you), exports the catalog into XML format. You can then parse and display the XML however you want, using one of the formats described in this chapter.

You'll next learn about parsing XML documents using two different function families—DOM functions and SimpleXML functions. While they both produce the same results (parsing XML documents to provide you with data you can use later in your script), the approach is slightly different for each of them. For example, while SimpleXML functions are much simpler to use than DOM functions, as you'll see after you work through the code listings, there would be a performance loss when working with large files since the entire XML document is loaded into memory and parsed before you can even begin to work with it. There are tradeoffs to be had with either choice, which is why this chapter simply introduces you to two sets of functions and leaves you to your own devices to figure out what really does (or does not) work for you and your development situation.

Accessing XML in PHP Using DOM Functions

The DOM XML extension has been part of PHP since version 4, but was completely overhauled in PHP 5. The primary change was to include the DOM functionality within a default installation of PHP, which is to say that no additional libraries or extensions need to be installed or configured to use these functions.

NOTE

> *DOM* stands for *Document Object Model*. For more information about DOM, visit http://www.w3.org/TR/DOM-Level-2-Core/core.html.

The purpose of DOM functions is to enable you to work with data stored in an XML document using the DOM API. The most basic DOM function is `DOMDocument->load()`, which creates a new DOM tree from the contents of a file. After you create the DOM tree, you can use other DOM functions to manipulate the data. In Listing 28.1, DOM functions are used to loop through a DOM tree and retrieve stored values for later display.

LISTING 28.1   **Loop Through an XML Document Using DOM Functions**

```
1:   <?php
2:   $dom = new DomDocument;
3:   $dom->load("books.xml");
4:
5:   foreach ($dom->documentElement->childNodes as $books) {
6:       if (($books->nodeType == 1) && ($books->nodeName == "Book")) {
7:
8:           foreach ($books->childNodes  as $theBook) {
9:               if (($theBook->nodeType == 1) &&
10:              ($theBook->nodeName == "Title")) {
11:                  $theBookTitle = $theBook->textContent;
12:              }
13:
14:              if (($theBook->nodeType == 1) &&
15:              ($theBook->nodeName == "Author")) {
16:                  $theBookAuthor = $theBook->textContent;
17:              }
18:
19:              if (($theBook->nodeType == 1) &&
20:              ($theBook->nodeName == "PublishingInfo")) {
21:
22:                  foreach ($theBook->childNodes as $thePublishingInfo) {
23:                      if (($thePublishingInfo->nodeType == 1) &&
24:                      ($thePublishingInfo->nodeName == "PublisherName")) {
25:                          $theBookPublisher = $thePublishingInfo->textContent;
26:                      }
27:
28:                      if (($thePublishingInfo->nodeType == 1) &&
29:                      ($thePublishingInfo->nodeName == "PublishedYear")) {
```

```
30:                              $theBookPublishedYear =
31:                                  $thePublishingInfo->textContent;
32:                          }
33:                      }
34:                  }
35:              }
36:
37:          echo "
38:          <p><em>".$theBookTitle."</em>
39:          by ".$theBookAuthor."<br/>
40:          published by ".$theBookPublisher." in ".$theBookPublishedYear."</p>";
41:
42:          unset($theBookTitle);
43:          unset($theBookAuthor);
44:          unset($theBookPublisher);
45:          unset($theBookPublishedYear);
46:      }
47: }
48: ?>
```

Line 2 creates a new DOM document, and line 3 loads the contents of books.xml into this document. The document tree is now accessible through $dom, as you can see in later lines. Line 5 begins the master loop through the document tree, as it places each node of the document into an array called $books.

Line 6 looks for an element called Book, and processing continues if it finds one. Remember, the <Book></Book> tag pair surrounds each entry for a book in the books.xml file. If processing continues, line 8 gathers all the child nodes into an array called $theBook, and the if statements in lines 9–12 and 14–17 look for specific nodes called Title and Author, respectively, and place the values into the variables $theBookTitle and $theBookAuthor for later use.

Line 19 begins a similar if statement, but because this line looks for a node called Publishing Info and you know that the <PublishingInfo></PublishingInfo> tag pair contains its own set of child nodes, another looping construct is needed to obtain the information in the next level of data. On line 22, child nodes are found and placed in the array called $thePublishingInfo, and then if statements in lines 23–26 and lines 28–32 look for specific nodes called PublisherName and PublishedYear, respectively, and place the values into the variables $theBookPublisher and $theBookPublishedYear for later use.

After the loop created in line 8 is closed in line 35, lines 37–40 echo a marked-up string to the browser, using values stored in $theBookTitle, $theBookAuthor, $theBookPublisher, and $theBookPublishedYear variables. After these values are used, they are unset in lines 42–45, and the loop continues for the next Book entry in the document tree.

Save this listing as `domexample.php` and place it in the document root of your web server. When viewed through your web browser you should see something like Figure 28.1.

FIGURE 28.1
Text extracted and displayed using DOM functions.

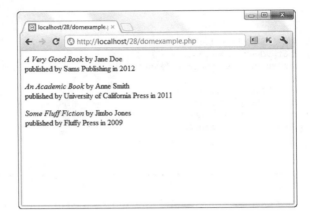

For a complete listing of all DOM-related classes, methods, and related functions in PHP, visit the PHP Manual at http://www.php.net/dom.

In the next section, you use the same `books.xml` file, but retrieve and display its values using the SimpleXML family of functions rather than DOM.

Accessing XML in PHP Using SimpleXML Functions

SimpleXML is enabled by default in PHP5 and requires no additional installation or configuration steps. It lives up to its description in the PHP Manual of being "a very simple and easily usable toolset to convert XML" while still being powerful.

Unlike the DOM family of functions, there are only a few SimpleXML functions and methods. The most basic SimpleXML function parses the XML data into an object that you can directly access and manipulate without SimpleXML-specific functions to do so (in other words, as you would work with any object). The first function you need to know about is `simplexml_load_file()`, which loads a file and creates an object out of the data:

```
$object_with_data = simplexml_load_file("somefile.xml");
```

Listing 28.2 uses a short bit of code to create a SimpleXML object and then displays the hierarchy of the data stored in the object.

LISTING 28.2   Load and Display Data Using SimpleXML

```
1: <?php
2: $theData = simplexml_load_file("books.xml");
3: echo "<pre>";
4: print_r($theData);
5: echo "</pre>";
6: ?>
```

Line 2 uses `simple_load_file()` to load the contents of `books.xml` into an object called $theData. In line 4, the `print_r()` function outputs a human-readable version of the data stored in the object, surrounded by the `<pre></pre>` tag pair.

Save this listing as `simplexml_dump.php` and place it in the document root of your web server. When viewed through your web browser, you should see something like Figure 28.2.

FIGURE 28.2
Data dumped from a SimpleXML object.

Dumping out data is not all that spectacular, but it does show you the structure of the object, which in turn lets you know how to access the data in a hierarchical fashion. For instance, the output of `simplexml_dump.php` shows the entry for a book:

```
[0] => SimpleXMLElement Object
(
    [Title] => A Very Good Book
    [Author] => Jane Doe
```

```
[PublishingInfo] => SimpleXMLElement Object
(
    [PublisherName] => Sams Publishing
    [PublisherCity] => Indianapolis
    [PublishedYear] => 2012
)
)
```

To reference this record directly, you use the following:

`$theData->Book`

You access the elements in the record like this:

- ▶ `$theData->Book->Title` for the Title

- ▶ `$theData->Book->Author` for the Author

- ▶ `$theData->Book->PublishingInfo->PublisherName` for the Publisher Name

- ▶ `$theData->Book->PublishingInfo->PublisherCity` for the Publisher City

- ▶ `$theData->Book->PublishingInfo->PublishedYear` for the Published Year

But because you likely would want to loop through all the records and not just the first one, the references to the data are a little different, as you can see in Listing 28.3.

LISTING 28.3   Through an XML Document Using SimpleXML

```
1:  <?php
2:  $theData = simplexml_load_file("books.xml");
3:
4:  foreach($theData->Book as $theBook) {
5:      $theBookTitle = $theBook->Title;
6:      $theBookAuthor = $theBook->Author;
7:      $theBookPublisher = $theBook->PublishingInfo->PublisherName;
8:      $theBookPublisherCity = $theBook->PublishingInfo->PublisherCity;
9:      $theBookPublishedYear = $theBook->PublishingInfo->PublishedYear;
10:
11:     echo "
12:     <p><em>".$theBookTitle."</em>
13:     by ".$theBookAuthor."<br/>
14:     published by ".$theBookPublisher." (".$theBookPublisherCity.")
15:     in ".$theBookPublishedYear."</p>";
16:
17:     unset($theBookTitle);
18:     unset($theBookAuthor);
19:     unset($theBookPublisher);
```

```
20:     unset($theBookPublishedYear);
21: }
22: ?>
```

In line 2, the contents of books.xml are loaded using simple_load_file() into an object called $theData. In line 4, the contents of $theData->Book, which is to say all the individual records, are put into an array called $theBook. Lines 5–9 gather the value of specific elements, beginning at the level of $theBook, and these values are output in lines 11–15. Lines 17–20 unset the value of the variables for the next pass through the loop.

Save this listing as simplexmlexample.php and place it in the document root of your web server. When viewed through your web browser, you should see something like Figure 28.3.

FIGURE 28.3
Text extracted and displayed using SimpleXML functions.

Note that the output looks quite similar to the output of Listing 28.1, and in fact the SimpleXML example *is* just a simpler (or more concise) version of the DOM-based example you saw earlier.

For more information about the SimpleXML functions in PHP, visit the PHP Manual at http://www.php.net/simplexml.

Working with JSON

JSON, which stands for *JavaScript Object Notation*, is another data interchange format (like XML) that is simple for both humans and machines to read and write. Because of this simplicity, JSON output has become increasingly popular and may one day eclipse (if it hasn't already) the use of XML output for data exposed via application programming interfaces (APIs).

Using JSON, you can have collections of name/value pairs (which take the form of objects) and you can have an ordered list of values (which take the form of an array). If you were to redo an entry in the books.xml file from earlier in the chapter, into JSON format, it might look like the following snippet:

```
{
  "book":[
    {
      "title":"A Very Good Book",
      "author":"Jane Doe",
      "publisher_name":"Sams Publishing",
      "publisher_city":"Indianapolis",
      "publisher_year":"2012"
    }
  ]
}
```

Adding two other entries would give you some JSON-formatted data like that shown in Listing 28.4.

LISTING 28.4   *JSON-Formatted Books Data*

```
 1: {
 2:      "book":[
 3:          {
 4:              "title":"A Very Good Book",
 5:              "author":"Jane Doe",
 6:              "publisher_name":"Sams Publishing",
 7:              "publisher_city":"Indianapolis",
 8:              "publisher_year":"2012"
 9:          },
10:          {
11:              "title":"An Academic Book",
12:              "author":"Anne Smith",
13:              "publisher_name":"University of California Press",
14:              "publisher_city":"Berkeley",
15:              "publisher_year":"2011"
16:          },
17:          {
18:              "title":"Some Fluff Fiction",
19:              "author":"Jimbo Jones",
20:              "publisher_name":"Fluffy Press",
21:              "publisher_city":"New York",
22:              "publisher_year":"2009"
23:          }
24:      ]
25: }
```

NOTE

To learn much more about JSON, see http://www.json.org. A useful tool when creating JSON for the first time is the JSON Parser at http://json.parser.online.fr/, which enables you to paste text and find (and fix) syntax errors.

Once you have some JSON, you can use the PHP json_decode() function to take the well-formatted data and turn it into an object, just as you did with the SimpleXML example earlier. Listing 28.5 uses a short bit of code to load some JSON data and display the hierarchy of the data stored in the object.

LISTING 28.5   Load and Display JSON Data

```
1: <?php
2: $theData = file_get_contents("books.xml");
3: echo "<pre>";
4: print_r(json_decode($theData));
5: echo "</pre>";
6: ?>
```

Line 2 uses file_get_contents() to load the contents of books.txt (a text file containing the JSON data shown in Listing 28.4) into an object called $theData. In line 4, the print_r() function outputs a human-readable version of the decoded JSON data stored in the object, surrounded by the <pre></pre> tag pair.

Save this listing as json_dump.php and place it in the document root of your web server. When viewed through your web browser, you should see something like Figure 28.4.

FIGURE 28.4
Data formerly in JSON format.

To create a formatted version of this data, you access the elements in the record like this:

▶ `$theData->book->title` for the Title

▶ `$theData->book->author` for the Author

▶ `$theData->book->publisher_name` for the Publisher Name

▶ `$theData->book->publisher_city` for the Publisher City

▶ `$theData->book->publisher_year` for the Published Year

As mentioned previously, of the most popular ways of consuming JSON is as output from APIs. The following URL contains an example API endpoint for accessing the Google search API with two variables: v for the API version (1.0 in this case) and u for the search term (PHP in this case):

`http://ajax.googleapis.com/ajax/services/search/web?v=1.0&q=PHP`

Change line 2 of Listing 28.5 to the following and save the file as `json_google_dump.php` and place it in the document root of your web server:

```
$theData = file_get_contents("http://ajax.googleapis.com/ajax/services/
  search/web?v=1.0&q=PHP");
```

When you view this script in your web browser, you should see something like Figure 28.5.

FIGURE 28.5
JSON output
from a Google
search.

Once you know the basics of working with JSON data, which—after you have used the json_decode() function in PHP—is really just the basics of working with objects, you have all the data on the Internet in the palm of your hands. Well, not *all* of it, but a fair portion of it. For a comprehensive list and more information about APIs, visit ProgrammableWeb at http://www.programmableweb.com/.

Summary

This brief chapter introduced you to two sets of PHP functions used to manipulate XML (DOM functions and SimpleXML) and JSON. In addition to a brief overview of both topics, you saw examples of displaying information stored in XML or JSON data using these functions. The purpose of this chapter was just to introduce you to the concept of working with XML and JSON using PHP. If you are interested in using XML and PHP together, you might also want to look into AJAX (Asynchronous JavaScript and XML), which often uses PHP to produce or modify XML or JSON data before it is displayed to the client.

Q&A

Q. Why would I use XML to store data when MySQL is a great (and free) database?

A. XML can be used not only as a storage method, but also as an intermediary for data transfer. For instance, you might use XML in conjunction with a database, by extracting data and sending it to a third-party function that only interprets XML data. In addition, although it is true that MySQL is great (and free), some users might not have access to MySQL or any other database, in which case XML files can play the role of a database system.

Q. How do I create JSON from arrays and objects created in other parts of my scripts?

A. If you want to produce JSON output, you just use the json_encode() function, which takes your existing arrays and objects and puts them into JSON format. See http://www.php.net/json_encode for more information.

Workshop

The workshop is designed to help you review what you've learned and begin putting your knowledge into practice.

Quiz

1. What should be the opening line of a valid XML document?

2. Does the following code put your XML content into a new DOM document?

   ```
   $dom = new DomDocument;
   ```

3. What code would be used to load the contents of a file called my.xml into a SimpleXML object called $myData?

Answers

1. `<?xml version="1.0">`

2. No, it just creates a DOM document referenced as $dom. To load the content you must also use something like this:

   ```
   $dom->load("books.xml");
   ```

3. `$myData = simplexml_load_File("my.xml");`

Activities

1. Create a script that formats the JSON-encoded books data to produce the same result in the browser as shown in Listings 28.1 and 28.3.

2. Make an array of data, either manually or through a script that retrieves information from a database, and then encode it in JSON format. If you then create another script that loads that output and formats it for use, you will have created and used an API for your own application.

## CHAPTER 29

Apache Performance Tuning and Virtual Hosting

In this chapter, you learn the following:

▶ Which operating system and Apache-related settings can limit the server's ability to scale or degrade performance

▶ Several tools for load testing Apache

▶ How to fine-tune Apache for optimum performance

▶ How to configure Apache to detect and prevent abusive behavior from clients

▶ How to configure name-based virtual hosts, IP-based virtual hosts, and the difference between the two

▶ The dependencies virtual hosting has on DNS

▶ How to set up scaled-up cookie-cutter virtual hosts

This administration-related chapter focuses on increasing the performance and scalability of your Apache server. In addition, you learn about name-based and IP-based virtual hosting and *Domain Name System* (DNS)-related issues and issues related to the web browser itself. This chapter also explains different mechanisms that you can use to isolate clients from each other and the associated security trade-offs.

Performance and Scalability Issues

This section covers scalability problems and how to prevent them. This section is more of a "don't do this" list, explaining limiting factors that can degrade performance or prevent the server from scaling. You also learn about the proactive tuning of Apache for optimal performance.

Operating System Limits

Several operating system factors limit Apache's performance. These factors relate to process creation, memory limits, and the maximum simultaneous number of open files or connections.

> **NOTE**
>
> The UNIX `ulimit` command enables you to set several of the limits covered in this section on a per-process basis. Refer to your operating system documentation for details on `ulimit`'s syntax.

Processes

Apache provides settings for preventing the number of server processes and threads from exceeding certain limits. These settings affect scalability because they limit the number of simultaneous connections to the web server, which in turn affects the number of visitors you can service simultaneously from one server.

The *Apache Multi-Processing Module* (MPM) settings are in turn constrained by OS settings limiting the number of processes and threads. How to change those limits varies from operating system to operating system. In Linux kernels, it requires changing the NR_TASKS defined in the /proc/sys/kernel/threads-max file. You can read the contents of the file with this command:

```
# cat /proc/sys/kernel/threads-max
```

You can write to the file using this command:

```
# echo value > /proc/sys/kernel/threads-max
```

In Linux (unlike most other UNIX versions), there is a mapping between threads and processes, and they are similar from the point of view of the OS.

In Solaris, those parameters can be changed in the /etc/system file. Those changes do not require rebuilding the kernel but might require a reboot to take effect. You can change the total number of processes by changing the max_nprocs entry and the number of processes allowed for a given user with maxuproc.

File Descriptors

Whenever a process opens a file (or a socket), a structure called a *file descriptor* is assigned until the file is closed. The OS limits the number of file descriptors that a given process can open, thus limiting the number of simultaneous connections the web server can have. How those settings are changed depends on the operating system. On Linux systems, you can read or modify /proc/sys/fs/file-max. On

Solaris systems, you must edit the value for `rlim_fd_max` in the `/etc/system` file. This change requires a reboot to take effect.

You can find additional information at http://httpd.apache.org/docs/2.4/vhosts/ fd-limits.html.

Controlling External Processes

Apache provides several directives to control the amount of resources external processes use. Such processes include CGI scripts spawned from the server and programs executed via server-side includes, but do not include PHP scripts that are invoked using the module version because the module is part of the server process.

Support for the following Apache directives (used in `httpd.conf`) is available only on UNIX and varies from system to system:

▶ **RLimitCPU**—Accepts two parameters: the soft limit and the hard limit for the amount of CPU time in seconds that a process is allowed. If the `max` keyword is used, it indicates the maximum setting allowed by the operating system. The hard limit is optional. The soft limit can be changed between restarts, and the hard limit specifies the maximum allowed value for that setting.

▶ **RLimitMem**—The syntax is identical to `RLimitCPU`, but this directive specifies the amount (in bytes) of memory used per process.

▶ **RLimitNProc**—The syntax is identical to `RLimitCPU`, but this directive specifies the number of processes.

These three directives help to prevent malicious or poorly written programs from running out of control.

Performance-Related Apache Settings

This section presents different Apache settings that affect performance.

File System Access

From a resource standpoint, accessing files on disk is an expensive process, so you should try to minimize the number of disk accesses required for serving a request. Symbolic links, per-directory configuration files, and content negotiation are some of the factors that affect the number of disk accesses:

▶ **Symbolic links**—In UNIX, a *symbolic link* (or *symlink*) is a special kind of file that points to another file. It is created with the UNIX `ln` command and is useful for making a certain file appear in different places.

Two of the parameters that the `Options` directive allows are `FollowSymLinks` and `SymLinksIfOwnerMatch`. By default, Apache won't follow symbolic links because they can be used to bypass security settings. For example, you can create a symbolic link from a public part of the website to a restricted file or directory not otherwise accessible via the Web. So, also by default, Apache needs to perform a check to verify that the file is not a symbolic link. If `SymLinksIfOwnerMatch` is present, it follows a symbolic link if the same user who created the symbolic link owns the target file.

Because those tests must be performed for every path element and for every path that refers to a filesystem object, they can be taxing on your system. If you control the content creation, you should add an `Options +FollowSymLinks` directive to your configuration and avoid the `SymLinksIfOwnerMatch` argument. In this way, the tests won't take place, and performance isn't affected.

▶ **Per-directory configuration files**—As explained in Chapter 3, "Installing and Configuring Apache," it is possible to have per-directory configuration files. These files, usually named `.htaccess`, provide a convenient way of configuring the server and allow for some degree of delegated administration. However, if this feature is enabled, Apache has to look for these files in each directory in the path leading to the file being requested, resulting in taxing filesystem accesses. If you don't have a need for per-directory configuration files, you can disable this feature by adding `AllowOverride none` to your configuration. Doing so avoids the performance penalty associated with accessing the filesystem looking for `.htaccess` files.

▶ **Content negotiation**—Apache can serve different versions of a file depending on client language or preferences. This can be accomplished using specific language-related file extensions, but in that case, Apache must access the filesystem for every request, looking for files such as extensions. If you need to use content negotiation, make sure that you at least use a type-map file, minimizing accesses to disk. Some application-based alternatives to Apache content negotiation for internationalization purposes can be found in Chapter 27, "Application Localization."

▶ **Scoreboard file**—This is a special file that the main Apache process uses to communicate with its child processes on older operating systems. You can specify its location using the `ScoreBoardFile` directive, but most modern platforms do not require the use of this file. If this file is required, you might find improved performance if you place it on a RAM disk. A *RAM disk* is a mechanism that allows a portion of the system memory to be accessed as a filesystem. The details on creating a RAM disk vary from system to system.

Network and Status Settings

A number options can degrade performance:

▶ **HostnameLookups**—When `HostnameLookups` is set to on or double, Apache performs a DNS lookup to capture the hostname of the client each time the client makes a request. This constant lookup introduces a delay into the response process. The default setting for this directive is `off`. If you want to capture the hostname of the requestor, you can always process the request logs with a log resolver later, offline, and not in real time.

▶ **Accept mechanism**—Apache can use different mechanisms to control how Apache children arbitrate requests. The optimal mechanism depends on the specific platform and number of processors. You can find additional information at http://httpd.apache.org/docs-2.4/misc/perf-tuning.html.

▶ **mod_status**—This module collects statistics about the server, connections, and requests, which slows down Apache. For optimal performance, disable this module, or at least make sure that `ExtendedStatus` is set to `off`, which is the default.

Load Testing with ApacheBench

You can test the performance of your site with benchmarking and traffic-generation tools. Many commercial and open source tools are available, each with varying degrees of sophistication. In general, it is difficult to accurately simulate real-world request traffic because visitors have different navigation patterns, access the Internet using connections with different speeds, stop a download if it is taking too long, click the reload button repeatedly if they get impatient, and so on. As such, some tools record actual network traffic for later replay.

However, for a quick—but accurate—glimpse at basic information regarding your server's capability to handle heavy traffic, the Apache server comes with a simple, but useful, load-testing tool called ApacheBench, or ab. You can find it in the bin directory of the Apache distribution.

This tool enables you to request a certain URL a number of times and display a summary of the result. The following command requests the main page of Google 1,000 times, with 10 simultaneous clients at any given time:

```
# /usr/local/apache2/bin/ab -n 1000 -c 10 http://www.google.com/
```

NOTE

> If you invoke ab without any arguments, you get a complete listing of command-line options and syntax. In addition, the trailing slash on the target URL is required, unless a specific page is named.

The result will look similar to the following:

```
This is ApacheBench, Version 2.3 <$Revision: 655654 $>
Copyright 1996 Adam Twiss, Zeus Technology Ltd, http://www.zeustech.net/
Licensed to The Apache Software Foundation, http://www.apache.org/

Benchmarking www.google.com (be patient)
Completed 100 requests
Completed 200 requests
Completed 300 requests
Completed 400 requests
Completed 500 requests
Completed 600 requests
Completed 700 requests
Completed 800 requests
Completed 900 requests
Finished 1000 requests


Server Software:        gws
Server Hostname:        www.google.com
Server Port:            80

Document Path:          /
Document Length:        11955 bytes

Concurrency Level:      10
Time taken for tests:   50.751 seconds
Complete requests:      1000
Failed requests:        669
   (Connect: 0, Receive: 0, Length: 669, Exceptions: 0)
Write errors:           0
Total transferred:      12710814 bytes
HTML transferred:       11974814 bytes
Requests per second:    19.70 [#/sec] (mean)
Time per request:       507.515 - (mean)
Time per request:       50.751 - (mean, across all concurrent requests)
Transfer rate:          244.58 [Kbytes/sec] received

Connection Times (ms)
```

```
            min   mean[+/-sd] median    max
Connect:     31    50   11.3      46    179
Processing:  88   454   53.8     449    803
Waiting:     84   285  119.0     282    694
Total:      136   504   56.5     499    850

Percentage of the requests served within a certain time (ms)
   50%    499
   66%    512
   75%    521
   80%    527
   90%    540
   95%    564
   98%    711
   99%    754
  100%    850 (longest request)
```

These requests were made over the open Internet; you should get many more requests per second if you conduct the test against a server on the same machine or over a local network, so bear that in mind as you test.

The output of the tool should be self-explanatory; what will be most relevant are the number of requests per second and the average time it takes to fully service a request (the Total time). You can also see how all the requests were served in less than 1 second.

You can play with different settings for the number of requests and with the number of simultaneous clients to find the point at which your server slows down significantly.

Proactive Performance Tuning

The previous sections explained which settings might prevent Apache from scaling. Now it's time for you to learn some techniques to proactively increase the performance of your server.

Mapping Files to Memory

As explained previously, accesses to disk affect performance significantly. Although most modern operating systems keep a cache of the most frequently accessed files, Apache also enables you to explicitly map a file into memory so that access to disk is not necessary. The module that performs this mapping is mod_file_cache. You can specify a list of files to memory map by using the MMapFile directive, which applies to the server as a whole. An additional directive in Apache 2.x, CacheFile, takes a list of files, caches the file descriptors at startup, and keeps them around between requests, saving time and resources for frequently requested files.

Distributing the Load

Another way to increase the overall performance of your web services for your end users is to distribute the load among several servers. You can do so in a variety of ways:

▶ Use a hardware load balancer to direct network and HTTP traffic across several servers, making it look like a single server from the outside.

▶ Use a software load-balancer solution using a reverse proxy with mod_rewrite.

▶ Use separate servers to provide images, large download files, and other static material. For example, you can place your images in a server called images.example.com and link to them from your main server.

Caching

The fastest way to serve content is not to serve it at all! This can be achieved by using appropriate HTTP headers that instruct clients and proxies of the validity in time of the requested resources. In this way, some resources that appear in multiple pages but do not change frequently, such as logos or navigation buttons, are transmitted only once for a certain period of time.

In addition, you can use mod_cache in Apache 2.x to cache dynamic content so that it does not have to be created for every request. This is potentially a big performance boost because dynamic content usually requires accessing databases, processing templates, and so on, which can take significant resources.

NOTE

> Apache 2.4 has many caching features that were considered experimental in earlier versions of Apache. See the Apache Caching Guide for more information on this topic: http://httpd.apache.org/docs/2.4/caching.html.

Reducing Transmitted Data

Another method for reducing server load is to reduce the amount of data being transferred to the client. This in turn makes your clients' websites operate faster, especially those over slow links. You can do a number of things to achieve this:

▶ Reduce the number of images.

▶ Reduce the size of your images.

▶ Compress large, downloadable files.

▶ Precompress static HTML and use content negotiation.

▶ Use `mod_deflate` to compress HTML content. This can be useful if CPU power is available and clients are connecting over slow links. The content will be delivered quicker, and the process will be free sooner to answer additional requests.

Network Settings

HTTP 1.1 allows multiple requests to be served over a single connection. HTTP 1.0 enables the same thing with keepalive extensions. The `KeepAliveTimeout` directive enables you to specify the maximum time in seconds that the server waits before closing an inactive connection. Increasing the timeout means that you increase the chance of the connection being reused. However, it also ties up the connection and Apache process during the waiting time, which can degrade performance, as discussed earlier in the chapter.

Preventing Abuse

Denial of service (DoS) attacks work by swamping your web server with a great number of simultaneous requests, slowing down the server or preventing access altogether. DoS attacks are difficult to prevent in general, and usually the most effective way to address them is at the network or operating system level. One example is to block specific addresses from making requests to the server; although you can block addresses at the web server level, it is more efficient to block them at the network firewall/router or with the operating system network filters.

Other kinds of abuse include posting extremely big requests or opening many simultaneous connections. You can limit the size of requests and timeouts to minimize the effect of attacks. The default request timeout is 300 seconds, but you can change it with the `TimeOut` directive. A number of directives enable you to control the size of the request body and headers: `LimitRequestBody`, `LimitRequestFields`, `LimitRequestFieldSize`, `LimitRequestLine`, and `LimitXMLRequestBody`.

Robots

Robots, *web spiders*, and *web crawlers* are names that describe a category of programs that access pages in your website, recursively following your site's links. Web search engines use these programs to scan the Internet for web servers, download their content, and index it. Real-life users use these types of programs to download an entire website or portion of a website for later offline browsing. Normally, these programs are well behaved, but sometimes they can be aggressive and swamp your website with too many simultaneous connections or become caught in cyclic loops.

Well-behaved spiders request a special file, called `robots.txt`, that contains instructions about how to access your website and which parts of the website won't be available to them. You can find the syntax for the file at http://www.robotstxt.org/.

By placing a properly formatted `robots.txt` file in your web server document root, you can control spider activity. In addition, you can stop the requests at the router or operating system level.

Implementing Virtual Hosting

The first generation of web servers was designed to handle the contents of a single site. The standard way of hosting several websites in the same machine was to install and configure separate web server instances for each site. As the Internet grew, so did the need for hosting multiple websites, and a more efficient solution was developed: virtual hosting. Virtual hosting allows a single instance of Apache to serve different websites, identified by their domain names or IP addresses. *IP-based* virtual hosting means that each domain is assigned a different IP address; *name-based* virtual hosting means that several domains share a single IP address.

Web clients use the DNS to translate hostnames into IP addresses and vice versa. Several mappings are possible:

▶ **One-to-one**—Each hostname is assigned a single, unique IP address. This is the foundation for IP-based virtual hosting.

▶ **One-to-many**—A single hostname is assigned to several IP addresses. This is useful for having several Apache instances serving the same website. If each of the servers is installed in a different machine, it is possible to balance the web traffic among them, improving scalability.

▶ **Many-to-one**—You can assign the same IP address to several hostnames. The client specifies the website it is accessing by using the `Host:` header in the request. This is the foundation for name-based virtual hosting.

When a many-to-one mapping is in place, a DNS server can usually be configured to respond with a different IP address for each DNS query, which helps to distribute the load. This is known as *round-robin DNS*. However, if you have the opportunity to use a load-balancing device instead of relying on a DNS server, doing so will alleviate any problems that may arise when tying your web server to your DNS server. Using a load balancer also eliminates the possibility that high traffic to your web server will bring down your DNS server.

IP-Based Virtual Hosting

The simplest virtual host configuration is when each host is assigned a unique IP address. Each IP address maps the HTTP requests that Apache handles to separate content trees in their own VirtualHost containers, as shown in the following snippet:

```
Listen 192.168.128.10:80
Listen 192.168.129.10:80

<VirtualHost 192.168.128.10:80>
    DocumentRoot /usr/local/apache2/htdocs/host1
    [other configurations specific to this host]
</VirtualHost>

<VirtualHost 192.168.129.10:80>
    DocumentRoot /usr/local/apache2/htdocs/host2
    [other configurations specific to this host]
</VirtualHost>
```

If a DocumentRoot or any other configurations are not specified for a given virtual host, the global setting, specified outside any <VirtualHost> section, is used. In this example, each virtual host has its own DocumentRoot. When a request arrives, Apache uses the destination IP address to direct the request to the appropriate host. For example, if a request comes for IP 192.168.128.10, Apache returns the documents from /usr/local/apache2/htdocs/host1.

If the host operating system cannot resolve an IP address used as the VirtualHost container's name and there's no ServerName directive, Apache complains at server startup time that it cannot map the IP addresses to hostnames. This complaint is not a fatal error. Apache still runs, but the error indicates that there might be some work to be done with the DNS configuration so that web browsers can find your server. You can use a *fully qualified domain name* (FQDN) rather than an IP address as the VirtualHost container name and the Listen directive binding (if the domain name resolves in DNS to an IP address configured on the machine and Apache can bind to it).

Name-Based Virtual Hosts

As a way to mitigate the consumption of IP addresses for virtual hosts, the HTTP/1.1 protocol version introduced the Host header, which enables a browser to specify the exact host for which the request is intended. This allows several hostnames to share a single IP address. Most browsers nowadays provide HTTP/1.1 support.

NOTE _____

> You cannot use SSL with name-based virtual hosts, except in tightly controlled circumstances. Please see http://httpd.apache.org/docs/2.4/ssl/ssl_faq.html#vhosts for more information. You can, however, use SSL with IP-based virtual hosts.

Listing 29.1 shows a typical set of request headers from the Mozilla Firefox browser. If the URL were entered with a port number, it would be part of the Host header contents as well.

LISTING 29.1   Request Headers

```
GET / HTTP/1.1
Accept: image/gif, image/x-xbitmap, image/jpeg, image/pjpeg, */*
Accept-Language: en-us
Accept-Encoding: gzip, deflate
Mozilla/5.0 (Windows NT 6.1; WOW64) AppleWebKit/535.7 (KHTML, like Gecko)
 Chrome/16.0.912.75 Safari/535.7
Host: host1.example.com
Connection: Keep-Alive
```

Apache uses the Host: header for configurations in which multiple hostnames can be shared by a single IP address—the many-to-one scenario outlined earlier this chapter—hence the description *name-based virtual hosts*.

Prior to Apache 2.4, using the NameVirtualHost directive enables you to specify IP address and port combinations on which the server receives requests for name-based virtual hosts. In Apache 2.2 and earlier, this is a required directive for name-based virtual hosts.

NOTE _____

> If you are using Apache 2.4, the NameVirtualHost directive is not used; instead, simply be sure you have matched the proper IP and ServerName in the VirtualHost container.

Listing 29.2 has Apache dispatch all connections to 192.168.128.10 based on the Host header contents.

LISTING 29.2   Name-Based Virtual Hosts

```
#Only use NameVirtualHost if pre-Apache 2.4
NameVirtualHost 192.168.128.10
Listen 192.168.128.10:80

<VirtualHost 192.168.128.10>
    ServerName host1.example.com
    DocumentRoot /usr/local/apache2/htdocs/host1
</VirtualHost>

<VirtualHost 192.168.128.10>
    ServerName host2.example.com
    DocumentRoot /usr/local/apache2/htdocs/host2
</VirtualHost>
```

For every hostname that resolves to 192.168.128.10, Apache can support another name-based virtual host. If a request comes for that IP address for a hostname that is not included in the configuration file, say host3.example.com, Apache simply associates the request to the first container in the configuration file; in this case, host1.example.com. The same behavior is applied to requests that are not accompanied by a Host header; whichever container is first in the configuration file is the one that gets the request.

An end user from the example.com domain might have his machine set up with example.com as his default domain. In that case, he might direct his browser to http://host1/ rather than the fully qualified http://host1.example.com/. The Host header would simply have host1 in it rather than host1.example.com. To make sure that the correct virtual host container gets the request, you can use the ServerAlias directive as shown in Listing 29.3.

LISTING 29.3   The ServerAlias Directive

```
#Only use NameVirtualHost if pre-Apache 2.4
NameVirtualHost 192.168.128.10
Listen 192.168.128.10:80

<VirtualHost 192.168.128.10>
    ServerName host1.example.com
    ServerAlias host1
    DocumentRoot /usr/local/apache2/htdocs/host1
</VirtualHost>

<VirtualHost 192.168.128.10>
    ServerName host2.example.com
    ServerAlias host2
    DocumentRoot /usr/local/apache2/htdocs/host2
</VirtualHost>
```

In fact, you can give ServerAlias a space-separated list of other names that might show up in the Host header so that you don't need a separate VirtualHost container with a bunch of common directives just to handle all the name variants.

HTTP 1.1 forces the use of the Host header. If the protocol version is identified as 1.1 in the HTTP request line, the request *must* be accompanied by a Host header. In the early days of name-based virtual hosts, Host headers were considered a trade-off: Fewer IP resources were required, but legacy browsers that did not send Host headers were still in use and, therefore, could not access all the server's virtual hosts. Today, that is not a consideration; there is no statistically significant number of such legacy browsers in use.

Mass Virtual Hosting

In the previous listings, the DocumentRoot directives follow a simple pattern:

```
DocumentRoot /usr/local/apache2/htdocs/hostname
```

where *hostname* is the hostname portion of the FQDN used in the virtual host's ServerName. For just a few virtual hosts, this configuration is fine. But what if there are dozens, hundreds, or even thousands of these virtual hosts? The configuration file can become difficult to maintain. Apache provides a good solution for cookie-cutter virtual hosts with mod_vhost_alias. You can configure Apache to map the virtual host requests to separate content trees with pattern-matching rules in the VirtualDocumentRoot directive. This functionality proves especially useful for *Internet service providers* (ISPs) that want to provide a virtual host for each one of their users. The following example provides a simple mass virtual host configuration:

```
#Only use NameVirtualHost if pre-Apache 2.4
NameVirtualHost 192.168.128.10
Listen 192.168.128.10:80

VirtualDocumentRoot /usr/local/apache2/htdocs/%1
```

The %1 token used in this example's VirtualDocumentRoot directive is substituted for the first portion of the FQDN. The mod_vhost_alias directives have a language for mapping FQDN components to filesystem locations, including characters within the FQDN.

If all the VirtualHost containers are eliminated and our configuration is simplified to the one shown here, the server serves requests for any subdirectories created in the /usr/local/apache2/htdocs directory. If the hostname portion of the FQDN is matched as a subdirectory, Apache looks there for content when it translates the request to a filesystem location.

Although virtual hosts normally inherit directives from the main server context, some of them, such as Alias directives, do not get propagated. For instance, the virtual hosts will not inherit this filesystem mapping:

```
Alias /icons /usr/local/apache2/icons
```

The FollowSymLinks flag for the Options directive is also disabled in this context. However, a variant of the ScriptAlias directive is supported.

The VirtualScriptAlias directive shown in the following snippet treats requests for any resources under /cgi-bin as containing CGI scripts:

```
#Only use NameVirtualHost if pre-Apache 2.4
NameVirtualHost 192.168.128.10
Listen 192.168.128.10:80
VirtualDocumentRoot /usr/local/apache2/htdocs/%1/docs
VirtualScriptAlias /usr/local/apache2/htdocs/%1/cgi-bin
```

Note that cgi-bin is a special token for that directive; calling the directory just cgi won't work; it must be cgi-bin.

For IP-based virtual hosting needs, there are variants of these directives: VirtualDocumentRootIP and VirtualScriptAliasIP.

Summary

This chapter provided information on Apache and operating system settings that can affect scalability and performance. In most cases, the problems in website performance relate to dynamic content generation and database access. Writing efficient scripts can help alleviate issues in those categories. Hardware-related improvements, such as high-quality network cards and drivers, increased memory, and disk arrays can also provide enhanced performance.

With regard to virtual hosting, you can configure Apache to handle virtual hosts in a variety of ways. Whether you need a large number of cookie-cutter virtual hosts, a varied set of different virtual host configurations, or the number of IP addresses you can use is limited, there's a way to configure Apache for your application. Name-based virtual hosting is a common technique for deploying virtual hosts without using up IP addresses. IP-based virtual hosting is another method when you have plenty of IP addresses available and you want to keep your configuration tidy, with a one-to-one balance of IP addresses to virtual hosts. In addition, if you cannot change your DNS configuration, you have the recourse of using separate port numbers for your virtual hosts.

Q&A

Q. *How can I measure whether my site is fast enough?*

A. Many developers test their sites locally or over an internal network, but if you run a public website, chances are good that many of your users will access it over slow links. Try navigating your website from a dialup account and make sure that your pages load fast enough, with the rule of thumb being that pages should load in less than three seconds.

Q. *How can I migrate an existing name-based virtual host to its own machine while maintaining continuous service?*

A. If a virtual host is destined to move to a neighboring machine, which by definition cannot have the same IP address, there are some extra measures to take. A common practice is to do something like the following, although many variations on these steps are possible:

1. Set the *time-to-live* (TTL) of the DNS mapping to a very low number. This increases the frequency of client lookups of the hostname.

2. Configure an IP alias on the old host with the new IP address.

3. Configure the virtual host's content to be served by both name- and IP-address-based virtual hosts.

4. After all the requests for the virtual host at the old IP address diminish (due to DNS caches expiring their old lookups), migrate the server.

Q. *Can I mix IP- and name-based virtual hosting?*

A. Yes. If multiple IP addresses are bound, you can allocate their usage a number of different ways. A family of name-based virtual hosts might be associated with each; just use a separate `NameVirtualHost` directive for each IP (if pre-Apache 2.4) or a controlled set of `ServerName` directives. One IP might be dedicated as an IP-based virtual host for SSL, for instance, whereas another might be dedicated to a family of name-based virtual hosts.

Workshop

The workshop is designed to help you review what you've learned.

Quiz

1. Name some Apache settings that might affect Apache performance.

2. Name some operating system settings that might limit scalability and performance.

3. Name some approaches to improve performance.

4. Is the `ServerName` directive necessary in a `VirtualHost` container?

Answers

1. Some of the Apache settings that might affect performance include `FollowSymLinks`, `SymLinksIfOwnerMatch` arguments to the `Options` directive, enabling per-directory configuration files, hostname lookups, having a scoreboard file, and statistics collection with `mod_status`.

2. Some operating system settings that might affect scalability and performance include limits for number of processes, open file descriptors, and memory allowed per process.

3. The following are some suggestions for improving performance: load distribution via a hardware load balancer or reverse proxy, data compression, caching, mapping files to memory, and compiling modules statically.

4. The `ServerName` directive is necessary in a `VirtualHost` container only when name-based virtual hosts are used. The `Host` header contents are compared to the contents of the `ServerName` directive. If a match isn't satisfied, the `VirtualHost` containers' `ServerAlias` directive value(s) are checked for matches.

## CHAPTER 30

Setting Up a Secure Web Server

In this chapter, you learn the following:

▶ The SSL/TLS family of protocols and the underlying cryptography concepts

▶ What secure certificates are and how to create and manage them

▶ How to activate the `mod_ssl` Apache module

This chapter explains how to set up an Apache server capable of secure transactions. If you are using shared server space with a hosting provider, you do not have access to these configuration options; the process of setting up a secure web server is specific to the provider and usually is not something you can do yourself. However, if you have root access to your server, this chapter will teach you the basics of securing your web server.

The Need for Security

Several types of Internet-related transactions require a high level of security. These include financial transactions, such as banking operations and electronic commerce, but also any exchange of sensitive information, such as medical records and corporate documents. Secure transactions over the Internet require three main elements:

▶ **Confidentiality**—If you are transmitting or accessing sensitive information such as your credit card number or your personal medical history, you certainly do not want a stranger to get hold of it.

▶ **Integrity**—Transmitted information must be protected from external manipulation—if you place an order online to buy 100 shares of stock, you don't want anyone to intercept the message and change it to an order to buy 1,000 shares.

▶ **Authentication**—You need to trust that the organizations or individuals you are communicating with are who they say they are.

The SSL Protocol

SSL stands for *Secure Sockets Layer*, and TLS stands for *Transport Layer Security*. These two families of protocols were originally designed to provide security for HTTP transactions, but they also can be used for a variety of other Internet protocols such as IMAP (*Internet Message Access Protocol*) and NNTP (*Network News Transfer Protocol*). HTTP running over SSL is referred to as *Secure HTTP*.

Netscape released SSL version 2 in 1994 and SSL version 3 in 1995. TLS is an IETF (*Internet Engineering Task Force*) standard designed to standardize SSL as an Internet protocol, but it is just a modification of SSL version 3 with a small number of added features and minor cleanups. The TLS acronym is the result of arguments between Microsoft and Netscape over the naming of the protocol because each company proposed its own name. However, the name has not stuck, and most people refer to these protocols simply as SSL. Unless otherwise specified, the rest of this chapter refers to SSL/TLS as *SSL*.

You specify that you want to connect to a server using SSL by replacing http with https in the protocol component of a URI (uniform resource identifier). The default port for HTTP over SSL is 443.

The following sections explain how SSL addresses the confidentiality, integrity, and authentication requirements outlined previously. You also learn a bit about the underlying mathematical and cryptographic principles at the core of SSL.

Addressing the Need for Confidentiality

The SSL protocol protects data by encrypting it. *Encryption* is the process of converting a message, the *plaintext*, into a new encrypted message, the *ciphertext*. Although the plaintext is readable by everyone, the ciphertext is completely unintelligible to anyone who might intercept it. Decryption is the reverse process, which transforms the ciphertext back into the original plaintext.

Usually, the encryption and decryption process involves an additional piece of information: a *key*. If both sender and receiver share the same key, the process is referred to as *symmetric cryptography*. If sender and receiver have different, complementary keys, the process is called *asymmetric* or *public key cryptography*.

Symmetric Cryptography

If the key used to both encrypt and decrypt the message is the same, the process is known as symmetric cryptography. DES, Triple DES, RC4, and RC2 are algorithms used for symmetric key cryptography. Many of these algorithms can have different key sizes, measured in bits. In general, given an algorithm, the greater the number of bits in the key, the more secure the algorithm is and the slower it will run because of the increased computational needs of performing the algorithm.

Symmetric cryptography is relatively fast compared to public key cryptography, which is explained in the next section. Symmetric cryptography has two main drawbacks, however. One is that keys must be changed periodically to avoid providing an eavesdropper with access to large amounts of material encrypted with the same key. The other issue is the key distribution problem: How do you get the keys to each one of the parties, and do so in a safe manner? This was one of the original limiting factors of symmetric cryptography; the problem was solved by periodically having people traveling around with suitcases full of keys. Then along came public key cryptography.

Public Key Cryptography

Public key cryptography takes a different approach than its symmetric predecessor. Instead of both parties sharing the same key, a pair of keys exists: one public and the other private. The public key can be widely distributed, whereas the owner keeps the private key secret. These two keys are *complementary*—a message encrypted with one of the keys can be decrypted only by the other key.

Using this method, anyone wanting to transmit a secure message to you can encrypt the message using your public key, assured that only the owner of the private key—you—can decrypt it. Even if an eavesdropper has access to the public key, he cannot decrypt the communication meant for you. In fact, you want the public key to be as widely available as possible so that more people can send encrypted messages to you. Public key cryptography can also be used to provide message integrity and authentication. People with public keys place these keys on public key servers or simply send the keys to others with whom they want to have secure email exchanges. Using the appropriate software tools, such as PGP or GnuPG, the sender encrypts the outgoing message based on the recipient's public key.

The assertion that only the owner of the private key can decrypt a message meant for her means that with the current knowledge of cryptography and availability of computing power, brute force alone will not break the encryption in a reasonable time frame; however, if the underlying algorithm or its implementation is flawed, such attacks are possible.

NOTE

Public key cryptography is similar to giving away many identical padlocks and retaining the master key. Anybody who wants to send you a message privately can do so by putting it in a safe and locking it with one of those padlocks (public keys) before sending it to you. Only you have the appropriate key (private key) to open that padlock (decrypt the message).

The SSL protocol uses public key cryptography in the initial handshake phase to securely exchange symmetric keys that can then be used to encrypt the communication.

Addressing the Need for Integrity

Data integrity is preserved by performing a special calculation on the contents of the message and storing the result with the message itself. When the message arrives at its destination, the recipient then performs the same calculation and compares the results. If the contents of the message changed, the results of the calculation will differ—and you'll know someone else has tampered with it.

Digest algorithms perform just that process: creating message digests. A *message digest* is a method of creating a fixed-length representation of an arbitrary message that uniquely identifies it (like a fingerprint). A good message digest algorithm should be irreversible and collision resistant, at least for practical purposes. *Irreversible* means that the original message cannot be obtained from the digest, and *collision resistant* means that no two different messages should have the same digest. Examples of digest algorithms are MD5 (*Message Digest*) and SHA (*Secure Hash*).

Message digests alone, however, do not guarantee the integrity of the message—an attacker could change the text *and* the message digest. *Message authentication codes*, or MACs, are similar to message digests, but incorporate a shared secret key in the process. The result of the algorithm depends both on the message and the key used. Because the attacker has no access to the key, he cannot modify both the message and the digest. HMAC (*Hash Message Authentication Code*) is an example of a message authentication code algorithm.

The SSL protocol uses MAC codes to avoid replay attacks and to ensure integrity of the transmitted information.

Addressing the Need for Authentication

SSL uses certificates to authenticate the parties in a communication. Public key cryptography can be used to digitally sign messages. In fact, just the act of your encrypting a message with your secret key guarantees the receiver that the message came from you. Other digital signature algorithms involve first calculating a digest of the message and then signing the digest.

You can tell that the person who created that public and private key pair is the one sending the message, but how do you tie that key to a person or organization that you can trust in the real world? It is plausible that an attacker could impersonate a sender's identity and distribute a different public key, claiming it is the legitimate one.

Trust can be achieved by using digital certificates. *Digital certificates* are electronic documents that contain a public key and information about its owner (name, address, and so on). To be useful, the certificate must be signed by a trusted third party (*certification authority*, or CA) who certifies that the information is correct. There are many different kinds of CAs, as described later in the chapter. Some of them are commercial entities, providing certification services to companies conducting business over the Internet. Companies providing internal certification services create other CAs.

The CA guarantees that the information in the certificate is correct, and that the key belongs to that individual or organization. Certificates have a period of validity and can expire or be revoked. Certificates can be chained so that the certification process can be delegated. For example, a trusted entity can certify companies, which in turn can take care of certifying its own employees.

If this whole process is to be effective and trusted, the certificate authority must require appropriate proof of identity from individuals and organizations before it issues a certificate.

By default, browsers include a collection of root certificates for trusted certificate authorities.

SSL and Certificates

The main standard defining certificates is X.509, adapted for Internet usage. An X.509 certificate contains the following information:

- ▶ **Issuer**—The name of the signer of the certificate
- ▶ **Subject**—The person holding the key being certified
- ▶ **Subject public key**—The public key of the subject
- ▶ **Control information**—Data such as the dates for which the certificate is valid
- ▶ **Signature**—The signature that covers the previous data

You can check a real-life certificate by connecting to a secure server with your browser. If the connection has been successful, a little padlock icon or another visual clue is added to the status bar of your browser. Depending on your browser, you should be able to click the representative icon to view information on the SSL connection and the remote server certificate. In the following example, the SSL certificate is examined for https://www.amazon.com/. You can see that the issuer of the certificate is VeriSign (see Figure 30.1). The page and its assets downloaded seamlessly because VeriSign is a trusted certification authority.

FIGURE 30.1
SSL certificate
in use at
www.amazon.
com.

In the case of the certificate in Figure 30.1, the Subject is an entity named Amazon.com, Inc. located in Seattle, Washington, United States. The common name of this entity is www.amazon.com.

C stands for *country*, ST for *state*, L for *locality*, O for *organization*, and CN for *common name*. In a website certificate, the common name identifies the *fully qualified domain name* (FQDN) of the website. This is the server name part of the URL; in this case, the www.amazon.com domain and the hostname www. If this address does not match what you typed in the location bar, the browser issues an error.

NOTE

> If the CN were *.amazon.com, the SSL certificate would be valid for any host on the amazon.com domain.

SSL Protocol Summary

You have seen how SSL achieves confidentiality via encryption, integrity via message authentication codes, and authentication via certificates and digital signatures.

The process to establish an SSL connection is the following:

1. The user uses his browser to connect to the remote web server.

2. The handshake phase begins—the browser and server exchange keys and certificate information.

3. The browser checks the validity of the server certificate, including that it has not expired, that it has been issued by a trusted CA, and so on.

4. Optionally, the server can require the client to present a valid certificate as well.

5. Server and client use each other's public key to securely agree on a symmetric key.

6. The handshake phase concludes and transmission continues using symmetric cryptography.

Obtaining and Installing SSL Tools

SSL support is provided by mod_ssl, an Apache module. This module requires the *OpenSSL library*—an open source implementation of the SSL/TLS protocols and a variety of other cryptographic algorithms. OpenSSL is based on the SSLeay library developed by Eric A. Young and Tim J. Hudson.

Because of the restrictions on the distribution of string cryptography and patented intellectual property worldwide, the installation of SSL-related tools varies in its ease from platform to platform. The following sections provide an overview for obtaining and installing SSL-related tools.

OpenSSL

You can find all the files and instructions necessary for installing OpenSSL at http://www.openssl.org/. Users of UNIX/Linux (and their variants) will find the installation of the OpenSSL software to be similar to installing other system tools. However, the casual Windows user will discover that there are currently no freely distributed precompiled binaries. As such, Windows users must compile the OpenSSL tools on their own. After you have installed the OpenSSL toolkit, you have all the necessary elements for creating and manipulating certificates and keys, as well as for interfacing with the mod_ssl Apache module.

Installation for Windows Users

Windows users familiar with the process of building their own binaries may do so with the OpenSSL source code provided at the OpenSSL website. The instructions for compiling OpenSSL on Windows are in the INSTALL.W32 file found in the source distribution. Restating these instructions is beyond the scope of this book; however, you will find they are comprehensive and well written. The required tools are ActiveState Perl for Windows and one of the following C compilers:

- ▶ Visual C++

- ▶ Borland C

- ▶ GNU C (Cygwin or MinGW)

Be sure to follow the instructions appropriate to your compiler of choice because they are different for each. You can also find tips from Apache for compiling OpenSSL as part of the Apache compilation instructions at http://httpd.apache.org/docs/2.4/platform/win_compiling.html.

Installation for UNIX/Linux Users

If you are running a recent Linux or FreeBSD distribution, OpenSSL might already be installed in your system. Should you need to install OpenSSL, you can download the source from the OpenSSL website. After you have downloaded the file, uncompress it and `cd` into the created directory (replace `-version` in the following commands with your particular current version of OpenSSL):

```
# gunzip < openssl-version.tar.gz | tar xvf -
# cd openssl-version
```

Complete installation instructions are found in the `INSTALL` file, but in short, the `config` script helps you build the software, which is followed by the `make` and `make install` processes.

The `mod_ssl` Apache Module

In the past, SSL extensions for Apache had to be distributed separately because of export restrictions. Currently, `mod_ssl` is bundled with Apache 2.2 and above, but only as part of the source distributions. Although this is not an issue for UNIX/Linux users, Windows users will find they must build Apache from source to build the `mod_ssl` module; `mod_ssl` is not distributed in the precompiled and distributed binaries. The `mod_ssl` module depends on the OpenSSL library, so a valid OpenSSL installation is required.

For Windows Users

When downloading the precompiled installation binaries, be sure to select the version with `openssl` in the filename. For instance, `httpd-2.2.22-win32-x86-openssl-0.9.8t.msi` is the name of the Windows installer for Apache 2.2.22.

NOTE

> At the time of writing, there was no Windows binary distribution for Apache 2.4. When there is, you can expect it to follow this naming convention.

If you want to build OpenSSL and Apache with `mod_ssl` from source, follow the Apache documentation found at http://httpd.apache.org/docs/2.4/platform/win_compiling.html. Again, restating these instructions is beyond the scope of this book, but they will provide you with all the information you need if you choose to go that route. The core requirements for building from source are as follows:

- Installed OpenSSL toolkit

- Microsoft Visual C++ 5.0 or higher

- The Windows Platform SDK

- The awk utility (awk, gawk, or similar)

For UNIX/Linux Users

The source distribution used in Chapter 3, "Installing and Configuring Apache," should already include the files necessary to use `mod_ssl`. Therefore, for UNIX/Linux users to use `mod_ssl`, you only need to follow the `configure` and `make`/`make install` process again, with the following addition as part of the `configure` command:

```
--enable-ssl --with-ssl=/usr/local/ssl/
```

This assumes that you installed OpenSSL in the listed location; if it resides in another directory on your server, just substitute the location in the preceding command.

If you compiled `mod_ssl` statically into Apache, you can check whether it is present by issuing the following command, which provides a list of compiled-in modules:

```
# /usr/local/apache2/bin/httpd -l
```

NOTE

> The preceding command assumes that you installed Apache in the `/usr/local/apache2` directory.

If `mod_ssl` was compiled as a dynamic loadable module, the following line must be added to or uncommented in the Apache configuration file (`httpd.conf`):

```
LoadModule ssl_module modules/libmodssl.so
```

When you have finished making changes to the `httpd.conf` file, restart Apache so that your changes take effect. If you look in your `error_log` after restarting, `mod_ssl` will be part of your server signature, as follows:

```
Apache/2.4.1 (Unix) mod_ssl/2.4.1 OpenSSL/0.9.8t PHP/5.4.0
```

Managing Certificates

After installing and configuring OpenSSL and `mod_ssl`, the next step for a working SSL server implementation is to create a server certificate. This section explains in detail how to create and manage certificates and keys by using the `openssl` command-line tool. If you are using SSL for an e-commerce site, encryption protects customer data from eavesdroppers, and the certificate enables customers to verify that you are who you claim to be.

The examples refer to the UNIX version of the command-line program `openssl`. If you are running under Windows, you need to use `openssl.exe` instead and change the paths of the examples to use backslashes rather than forward slashes. In addition, if you installed OpenSSL in a directory unlike the one listed here, simply substitute that directory in the examples.

Creating a Key Pair

You must have a public/private key pair before you can create a certificate request. Assume that the FQDN for the certificate you want to create is www.example.com. You can create the keys by issuing the following command:

```
# openssl genrsa --des3 -out www.example.com.key 1024
```

▶ The `genrsa` switch indicates to OpenSSL that you want to generate a key pair.

▶ The `-des3` switch indicates that the private key should be encrypted and protected by a pass phrase.

▶ The `-out` switch indicates where to store the results.

▶ `1024` indicates the number of bits of the generated key.

The result of invoking this command looks like this:

```
Generating RSA private key, 1024 bit long modulus
...............+++++
.....................+++++
e is 65537 (0x10001)
Enter pass phrase for www.example.com.key:
```

As you can see, you are asked to provide a pass phrase; choose a secure one. The pass phrase is necessary to protect the private key, and you are asked for it whenever you want to start the server.

TIP

> You can choose not to password-protect the key. This is convenient because you will not need to enter the pass phrase during reboots, but it is highly unsecure, and a compromise of the server means a compromise of the key as well. In any case, you can choose to unprotect the key either by leaving out the -des3 switch in the generation phase or by issuing the following command:
>
> ```
> # openssl rsa -in www.example.com.key -out www.example.com.key.unsecure
> ```

It is a good idea to back up the www.example.com.key file. You can learn about the contents of the key file by issuing the following command:

```
# openssl rsa -noout -text -in www.example.com.key
```

Elements of the key are then displayed to you.

Creating a Certificate Signing Request

To get a certificate issued by a CA, you must submit a *certificate signing request*. To create a request, issue the following command:

```
#  req -new -key www.example.com.key -out www.example.com.csr
```

You are prompted for the certificate information, something like this:

```
Using configuration from /usr/local/ssl/install/openssl/openssl.cnf
Enter PEM pass phrase:
You are about to be asked to enter information that will be incorporated
into your certificate request.
What you are about to enter is what is called a Distinguished Name or a DN.
There are quite a few fields but you can leave some blank
For some fields there will be a default value,
If you enter '.', the field will be left blank.
-----
Country Name (2 letter code) [AU]:US
State or Province Name (full name) [Some-State]:CA
Locality Name (eg, city) []: San Francisco
Organization Name (eg, company) [Internet Widgits Pty Ltd]:.
Organizational Unit Name (eg, section) []:.
Common Name (eg, YOUR name) []:www.example.com
Email Address []:administrator@example.com
Please enter the following 'extra' attributes
to be sent with your certificate request
A challenge password []:
An optional company name []:
```

It is important that the `Common Name` field entry matches the address that visitors to your website will type in their browsers. This is one of the checks that the browser performs for the remote server certificate. If the names differ, a warning indicating the mismatch issues to the user.

The certificate is now stored in `www.example.com.csr`. You can learn about the contents of the certificate using the following command:

```
# openssl req -noout -text -in www.example.com.csr
```

You can submit the certificate signing request file to a CA for processing. VeriSign, Thawte, and Network Solutions are two of those CAs, but many CAs are available. You can learn more about the VeriSign, Thawtem, and Network Solutions submission procedures at their websites for their products:

- ▶ **VeriSign**—http://www.verisign.com/ssl/
- ▶ **Thawte**—http://www.thawte.com/ssl/web-server-ssl-certificates/
- ▶ **Network Solutions**—http://www.networksolutions.com/SSL-certificates/

Creating a Self-Signed Certificate

You can also create a self-signed certificate. That is, you can be both the issuer and the subject of the certificate. Although this is not useful for a commercial website, it enables you to test your installation of `mod_ssl` and to have a secure web server while you wait for the official certificate from the CA:

```
# openssl x509 -req -days 30 -in
www.example.com.csr -signkey
www.example.com.key -out www.example.com.cert
```

You need to copy your certificate `www.example.com.cert` (either the one returned by the CA or your self-signed one) to `/usr/local/ssl/openssl/certs/` and your key to `/usr/local/ssl/openssl/private/`.

Protect your key file by issuing the following command:

```
# chmod 400 www.example.com.key
```

This command makes the key readable by only the root user.

SSL Configuration

The previous sections introduced the (not-so-basic) concepts behind SSL, and you have learned how to generate keys and certificates. Now you can configure Apache to support SSL. As you learned earlier in the chapter, the mod_ssl module must either be compiled statically, or, if you have compiled as a loadable module, the appropriate LoadModule directive must be present in the httpd.conf file.

Apache 2.2 and later ships with an "extra" configuration file specifically for running an SSL-aware server. To use this extra file, just uncomment this line in httpd.conf:

```
Include conf/extra/httpd-ssl.conf
```

Next, modify the standard configuration snippet in httpd-ssl.conf, replacing the information with your own, of course:

```
UseCanonicalName On
<VirtualHost www.example.com:443>
ServerName www.example.com
SSLEngine on
SSLCertificateFile /usr/local/ssl/openssl/certs/www.example.com.cert
SSLCertificateKeyFile /usr/loca/ssl/openssl/certs/www.example.com.key
</VirtualHost>
```

This snippet configures a new virtual host that will listen to port 443 (the default port for HTTPS); you enable SSL on that virtual host with the SSLEngine directive. The SSLCertificateFile and SSLCertificateKeyfile directives indicate where to find the server's certificate and the file containing the associated key.

Starting the Server

Previous versions of Apache required you to issue the apachectl startssl command when you wanted to start Apache in secure mode. However, given the configuration methods defined in the previous section, starting Apache in secure mode is no different from starting Apache without SSL: Issue the apachectl start command. As long as the httpd-ssl.conf file is included in httpd.conf via directive, per the earlier instructions, Apache starts the SSL-enabled server. If your server is already running and you restart it, you are prompted for your pass phrase if your key is protected by one. After you enter the correct pass phrase, Apache starts, and you should be able to connect securely to it using the https://www.example.com/ URL. Substitute your own domain name, of course. If you cannot successfully start your server, check the Apache error log for clues about what might have gone wrong. For example, if you cannot bind to the port, make sure that another Apache instance is not running already. You must have administrator privileges to bind to port 443.

Summary

This chapter explained the fundamentals of the SSL protocol and `mod_ssl`, the Apache module that implements support for SSL. You were given an introduction to installing and configuring OpenSSL and `mod_ssl`, and how to use the `openssl` command-line tool for certificate and key generation and management. You can access the `mod_ssl` reference documentation at http://httpd.apache.org/docs/2.4/mod/mod_ssl.html for in-depth syntax explanation and additional configuration information. Bear in mind also that SSL is just part of maintaining a secure server, which includes applying security patches, OS configuration, access control, physical security, and so on.

Q&A

Q. *Can I have SSL with name-based virtual hosting?*

A. A question that comes up frequently is how to make name-based virtual hosts work with SSL. The answer is that you currently cannot, as noted in Chapter 29, "Apache Performance Tuning and Virtual Hosting." Name-based virtual hosts depend on the `Host` header of the HTTP request, but the certificate verification happens when the SSL connection is being established and no HTTP request can be sent. There is a protocol for upgrading an existing HTTP connection to TLS, but it is mostly unsupported by current browsers (see RFC 2817, at http://www.rfc-editor.org/rfc/rfc2817.txt).

Q. *Can I use SSL with other protocols?*

A. The `mod_ssl` module implements the SSL protocol as a filter. Other protocols using the same Apache server can easily take advantage of the SSL.

Workshop

The workshop is designed to help you review what you've learned.

Quiz

1. Name three requirements to carry on secure communications on the Internet.

2. How do you start an SSL-enabled instance of Apache?

Answers

1. Confidentiality, integrity, and authentication.

2. Ensure that the `httpd-ssl.conf` file is included via a directive in the `httpd.conf` file, and issue the command `apachectl start`. As long as the `httpd-ssl.conf` file is included, any SSL-enabled instances will start along with non-SSL instances.

## CHAPTER 31

Optimizing and Tuning MySQL

In this chapter, you learn the following:

▶ Basic hardware and software optimization tips for your MySQL server

▶ Key startup parameters for your MySQL server

▶ How to use the OPTIMIZE TABLE command

▶ How to use the EXPLAIN command

▶ How to use the FLUSH command to clean up tables, caches, and log files

▶ How to use SHOW commands to retrieve information about databases, tables, and indexes

▶ How to use SHOW commands to find system status information

Proper care and feeding of your MySQL server will keep it running happily and without incident. The optimization of your system consists of proper hardware maintenance and software tuning.

> For additional methods of maintaining and administering your MySQL server, consider the MySQL Workbench product. You can find information and screenshots of this feature-rich graphical interface at http://www.mysql.com/products/workbench/.

NOTE

Building an Optimized Platform

Designing a well-structured, normalized database schema is just half of the optimization puzzle (albeit an important half). The other half is building and fine-tuning the server that will house your database. Think about the four main components of a server: CPU, memory, hard drive, and operating system. Each of these components must be up to speed or no amount of design or programming will make your database faster:

▶ **CPU**—The faster the CPU, the faster MySQL can process your data. There's no real secret to this, but a 3.0GHz processor is significantly faster than a 1.0GHz processor. With processor speeds consistently increasing, and with reasonable prices all around, it is not difficult to get a good bang for your buck.

▶ **Memory**—Put as much RAM in your machine as you can. You can never have enough, and RAM is cheap these days. Having available RAM can help balance out sluggish CPUs.

▶ **Hard drive**—The proper hard drive will be both large enough and fast enough to accommodate your database server and its traffic. An important measurement of hard drive speed is its *seek time*, or the amount of time it takes for the drive to spin around and find a specific piece of information. Seek time is measured in milliseconds, and an average disk seek time is around 8 or 9 milliseconds for desktop drives and 3 to 5 milliseconds for servers. When buying a hard drive, make sure that it is big enough to accommodate all the data you'll eventually store in your database and fast enough to find it quickly.

▶ **Operating system**—If you use an operating system that's a resource hog (for example, Windows), you have two choices: Buy enough resources so that it doesn't matter, or use an operating system that doesn't suck away all your resources.

Whether you're purchasing these components yourself to build a machine, or shopping for managed solutions of customized servers, if you put the proper pieces together at the system level, you'll have taken several steps toward overall server optimization.

NOTE

> The selection of MySQL table type—MyISAM or InnoDB—is also an optimization option. Depending on your selection, various additional optimizations will be available to you. I recommend taking a look at the table-specific optimization tips in the MySQL manual at http://dev.mysql.com/doc/refman/5.5/en/optimization.html, as well as the MySQL Performance Blog at http://www.mysqlperformanceblog.com/.

Benchmarking Your Database Server

You can perform a quick test of your server speed using the benchmark() MySQL function to see how long it takes to process a given expression. For example, you can make the test expression something simple, such as 10+10, or something more extravagant, such as extracting pieces of dates and performing advanced calculations.

No matter the result of the expression, the result of benchmark() will always be 0. The purpose of benchmark() is not to retrieve the result of an expression, but to see how long it takes to repeat the expression for a specific number of times. For example, the following command executes the expression 10+10 one million times:

```
select benchmark(1000000,10+10);
```

The result of this command on one of my test systems is this:

```
+--------------------------+
| benchmark(1000000,10+10) |
+--------------------------+
|                        0 |
+--------------------------+
1 row in set (0.04sec)
```

This command also executes the date extraction expression one million times:

```
select benchmark(1000000, extract(year from now()));
```

The result of this command on one of my test systems is as follows:

```
+----------------------------------------------+
| benchmark(1000000, extract(year from now())) |
+----------------------------------------------+
|                                            0 |
+----------------------------------------------+
1 row in set (0.09sec)
```

The important number is the time in seconds, which is the elapsed time for the execution of the function; the first test took 0.04 seconds, and the second took 0.09 seconds. You might want to run the same uses of benchmark() multiple times during different parts of the day (when your server is under different loads) to get a better idea of how your server is performing, and to try some benchmarks that put your server through more heavier processing than these simple examples.

MySQL Startup Options

MySQL administrators can fine-tune a wealth of server parameters, much of which the average user never needs to use. And frankly, if you are using MySQL in a virtual hosting environment, you cannot use the information except to ask for changes in your server setup. So as not to completely overwhelm you with information, this section contains only a few of the common startup options for a finely tuned MySQL server.

NOTE

> You can read more in the MySQL Manual at http://dev.mysql.com/doc/refman/5.5/en/server-system-variables.html.

When you start MySQL, a configuration file called `my.cnf` is loaded. This file contains information ranging from port number to buffer sizes but can be overruled by command-line startup options.

In the `support-files` subdirectory of your MySQL installation directory (or in the installation directory itself on Windows), you'll find sample configuration files, each tuned for a specific range of installed memory:

- ▶ `my-small.cnf`—For systems with less than 64MB of RAM, where MySQL is used occasionally.

- ▶ `my-medium.cnf`—For systems with less than 64MB of RAM, where MySQL is the primary activity on the system, or for systems with up to 128MB of RAM, where MySQL shares the box with other processes. This is the most common configuration, where MySQL is installed on the same box as a web server and receives a moderate amount of traffic.

- ▶ `my-large.cnf`—For a system with 128MB to 512MB of RAM, where MySQL is the primary activity.

- ▶ `my-huge.cnf`—For a system with 1GB to 2GB of RAM, where MySQL is the primary activity.

To use any of these as the base configuration file, simply copy the file of your choice to `/etc/my.cnf` (or wherever `my.cnf` is on your system) and change any system-specific information, such as port or file locations.

Key Startup Parameters

Two primary startup parameters affect your system the most: `key_buffer_size` and `table_cache`. If you get only two server parameters correctly tuned, make sure they're these two!

The value of `key_buffer_size` is the size of the buffer used with indexes. The larger the buffer, the faster the SQL command finishes and a result is returned. Try to find the fine line between finely tuned and overoptimized; you might have a `key_buffer_size` of 256MB on a system with 512MB of RAM, but any more than 256MB could cause degraded server performance.

A simple way to check the actual performance of the buffer is to examine four additional variables: `key_read_requests`, `key_reads`, `key_write_requests`, and `key_writes`. You can find the values of these variables by issuing the `SHOW STATUS` command.

A long list of variables and values are returned, listed in alphabetic order. Find the rows that look something like this. (Your values will differ.)

```
| Key_read_requests     | 10182771  |
| Key_reads             | 9326      |
| Key_write_requests    | 48487     |
| Key_writes            | 2287      |
```

If you divide the value of `key_reads` by the value of `key_read_requests`, the result should be less than 0.01. Also, if you divide the value of `key_writes` by the value of `key_write_requests`, the result should be less than 1. Using the previous values yields results of 0.000915861721998 and 0.047167281951863, respectively; well within the acceptable parameters. You could try to get these numbers even smaller by increasing the value of `key_buffer_size`, but these numbers are fine as they are.

The other important server parameter is `table_cache`, which is the number of open tables for all threads. The default is 64, but you might need to adjust this number. Using the `SHOW STATUS` command, look for a variable called `open_tables` in the output. If this number is large, the value of `table_cache` should be increased.

The sample configuration files included with your MySQL installation use various combinations of `key_buffer_size` and `table_cache`. You can use these combinations as a baseline for any modifications you need to make. Whenever you modify your configuration, you have to restart your server for changes to take effect—sometimes with no knowledge of the consequences of your changes. In this case, be sure to try your modifications in a development environment before rolling the changes into production.

Optimizing Your Table Structure

An optimized table structure is different from a well-designed table. Table structure optimization has to do with reclaiming unused space after deletions and basically cleaning up the table after structural modifications have been made. The `OPTIMIZE TABLE` SQL command takes care of this, using the following syntax:

```
OPTIMIZE TABLE table_name[,table_name]
```

For example, if you want to optimize the grocery_inventory table in the testDB database, use: **OPTIMIZE TABLE grocery_inventory**. You might see a status message that simply says "OK," or one that says " Table does not support optimize, doing recreate + analyze instead." These are both fine, as the outcome is the same—your table has been optimized.

Be aware that tables are locked while undergoing optimization, so if your table is large, perform the optimization during scheduled downtime or when little traffic is flowing to your system.

Optimizing Your Queries

Query optimization has a lot to do with the proper use of indexes. The EXPLAIN command examines a given SELECT statement to see whether it is optimized the best that it can be, using indexes wherever possible. This proves especially useful when looking at complex queries involving JOINs. The syntax for EXPLAIN is as follows:

EXPLAIN SELECT *statement*

The output of the EXPLAIN command is a table of information containing the following columns:

- **id**—The select identifier ID.
- **select_type**—The type of SELECT statement, of which there are several.
- **table**—The name of the table.
- **type**—The join type, of which there are several.
- **possible_keys**—This column indicates which indexes MySQL could use to find the rows in this table. If the result is NULL, no indexes would help with this query. You should then take a look at your table structure and see whether there are any indexes you could create that would increase the performance of this query.
- **key**—The key actually used in this query, or NULL if no index was used.
- **key_len**—The length of the key used, if any.
- **ref**—Any columns used with the key to retrieve a result.
- **rows**—The number of rows MySQL must examine to execute the query.

▶ **Extra**—Additional information regarding how MySQL will execute the query. There are several options, such as Using index (an index was used) and Where (a WHERE clause was used).

There's not much optimizing you can do with a "select all" query except add a WHERE clause with the primary key. The possible_keys column would then show PRIMARY, and the Extra column would show Where used.

When using EXPLAIN on statements involving JOIN, a quick way to gauge the optimization of the query is to look at the values in the rows column. Suppose that you have 2 and 1 as results; multiply these numbers together and you have 2 as your answer. This is the number of rows that MySQL must look at to produce the results of the query. You want to get this number as low as possible, and 2 is as low as it can go.

For a great deal more information on the EXPLAIN command, visit the MySQL Manual at http://dev.mysql.com/doc/refman/5.5/en/using-explain.html.

Using the FLUSH Command

Users with reload privileges for a specific database can use the FLUSH command to clean up the internal caches used by MySQL. Often, only the root-level user has the appropriate permissions to issue administrative commands such as FLUSH.

The FLUSH syntax is as follows:

```
FLUSH flush_option
```

The FLUSH command has nine different options, with these being the most common:

▶ PRIVILEGES

▶ TABLES

▶ HOSTS

▶ LOGS

You have used the FLUSH PRIVILEGES command before, after adding new users. This command simply reloads the grant tables in your MySQL database, enabling the changes to take effect without stopping and restarting MySQL. When you issue a FLUSH PRIVILEGES command, the Query OK response assures you that the cleaning process occurred without a hitch. For example, the process would look like this in the command-line interface:

```
mysql> FLUSH PRIVILEGES;
Query OK, 0 rows affected (0.10 sec)
```

The FLUSH TABLES command closes all tables currently open or in use and essentially gives your MySQL server a millisecond of breathing room before starting back to work. When your caches are empty, MySQL can better utilize available memory. Again, you're looking for the Query OK response:

```
mysql> FLUSH TABLES;
Query OK, 0 rows affected (0.21 sec)
```

The FLUSH HOSTS command works specifically with the host cache tables. If you cannot connect to your MySQL server, a common reason is that the maximum number of connections has been reached for a particular host, and it is throwing errors. When MySQL sees numerous errors on connection, it assumes that something is amiss and simply blocks any additional connection attempts to that host. The FLUSH HOSTS command resets this process and again allows connections to be made:

```
mysql> FLUSH HOSTS;
Query OK, 0 rows affected (0.00 sec)
```

The FLUSH LOGS command closes and reopens all log files. If your log file is getting to be a burden, and you want to start a new one, this command creates a new, empty log file. Weeding through a year's worth of log entries in one file looking for errors can be a chore, so try to flush your logs at least monthly:

```
mysql> FLUSH LOGS;
Query OK, 0 rows affected (0.04 sec)
```

For more information on FLUSH, visit the MySQL Manual at http://dev.mysql.com/doc/refman/5.5/en/flush.html.

Using the SHOW Command

The SHOW command has several different uses and produces output displaying a great deal of useful information about your MySQL database, users, and tables. Depending on your access level, some SHOW commands are unavailable to you or provide only minimal information. The root-level user can use all the SHOW commands, with the most comprehensive results. The common uses of SHOW include the following, which you soon learn about in more detail:

```
SHOW GRANTS FOR user
SHOW DATABASES [LIKE something]
SHOW [OPEN] TABLES [FROM database_name] [LIKE something]
SHOW CREATE TABLE table_name
SHOW [FULL] COLUMNS FROM table_name [FROM database_name] [LIKE something]
SHOW INDEX FROM table_name [FROM database_name]
SHOW TABLE STATUS [FROM db_name] [LIKE something]
SHOW STATUS [LIKE something]
SHOW VARIABLES [LIKE something]
```

The SHOW GRANTS command displays the privileges for a given user at a given host. This is an easy way to check on the current status of a user, especially if you have a request to modify a user's privileges. With SHOW GRANTS, you can check first to see that the user doesn't already have the requested privileges. For example, examine the privileges available to the joeuser user we created early in this book:

```
SHOW GRANTS FOR joeuser@localhost;
```

The results of this query are as follows:

```
+-------------------------------------------------------------+
| Grants for joeuser@localhost                                |
+-------------------------------------------------------------+
| GRANT ALL PRIVILEGES ON *.* TO 'joeuser'@'localhost' IDENTIFIED|
| BY  PASSWORD ' *13883BDDBE566ECEFF0501CDE9B293303116521A'    |
+-------------------------------------------------------------+

1 rows in set (0.00 sec)
```

If you're not the root-level user or the joeuser user, you get an error; unless you're the root-level user, you can see only the information relevant to yourself. For example, the joeuser user isn't allowed to view information about the root-level user:

SHOW GRANTS FOR root@localhost;

This query results in the following error message:

```
ERROR 1044: Access denied for user:'joeuser@localhost' to database 'mysql'
```

Be aware of your privilege level throughout the remainder of this chapter. If you are not the root-level user, some of these commands are not available to you or display only limited information.

Some popular SHOW commands follow; for more information, see the MySQL Manual at http://dev.mysql.com/doc/refman/5.5/en/show.html.

Retrieving Information About Databases and Tables

You have used a few of the basic SHOW commands earlier in this book to view the list of databases and tables on your MySQL server. As a refresher, the SHOW DATABASES command does just that—it lists all the databases on your MySQL server. Here is one result example:

```
+-------------------+
| Database          |
+-------------------+
| testDB            |
| mysql             |
+-------------------+
2 rows in set (0.00 sec)
```

After you've selected a database to work with, you can also use SHOW to list the tables in the database. This example is the result of running a SHOW DATABASES query after the testDB has been selected. (Your table listing may vary.)

```
+---------------------+
| Tables_in_testDB    |
+---------------------+
| grocery_inventory   |
| email               |
| master_name         |
| myTest              |
| testTable           |
+---------------------+
5 rows in set (0.01 sec)
```

If you add OPEN to your SHOW TABLES command, you get a list of all the tables in the table cache, showing how many times they're cached and in use:

SHOW OPEN TABLES;

A result looks something like this:

```
+----------+-------------------+--------+-------------+
| Database | Table             | In_use | Name_locked |
+----------+-------------------+--------+-------------+
| mysql    | procs_priv        | 0      | 0           |
| mysql    | db                | 0      | 0           |
| mysql    | host              | 0      | 0           |
| testdb   | grocery_inventory | 0      | 0           |
| mysql    | user              | 0      | 0           |
| mysql    | tables_priv       | 0      | 0           |
| mysql    | columns_priv      | 0      | 0           |
+----------+-------------------+--------+-------------+
7 rows in set (0.00 sec)
```

Using this information in conjunction with the FLUSH TABLES command you learned earlier in this chapter helps keep your database running smoothly. If SHOW OPEN TABLES shows that tables are cached numerous times but are not currently in use, go ahead and use FLUSH TABLES to free up that memory.

Retrieving Table Structure Information

A helpful command is SHOW CREATE TABLE, which does what it sounds like; it shows you the SQL statement used to create a specified table:

```
SHOW CREATE TABLE grocery_inventory;
```

The preceding command results in the following:

```
+-------------------+-----------------------------------------------+
| Table             | Create Table                                  |
|+------------------+-----------------------------------------------+
| grocery_inventory | CREATE TABLE 'grocery_inventory' (            |
|                     'id' int(11) NOT NULL auto_increment,         |
|                     'item_name' varchar(50) NOT NULL default ",   |
|                     'item_desc' text,                             |
|                     'item_price' float NOT NULL default '0',      |
|                     'curr_qty' int(11) NOT NULL default '0',      |
|                     PRIMARY KEY  ('id')                           |
|                     ) ENGINE=InnoDB DEFAULT CHARSET=latin1        |
+-------------------+-----------------------------------------------+
1 row in set (0.00 sec)
```

This is essentially the same information you get if you dump the table schema, but you can use the SHOW CREATE TABLE command quickly if you're just looking for a reminder or a simple reference to a particular table-creation statement.

If you need to know the structure of the table but don't necessarily need the SQL command to create it, you can use the SHOW COLUMNS command, as follows:

```
SHOW COLUMNS FROM grocery_inventory;
```

This query results in something like this:

```
+------------+-------------+------+-----+---------+----------------+
| Field      | Type        | Null | Key | Default | Extra          |
+------------+-------------+------+-----+---------+----------------+
| id         | int(11)     | NO   | PRI |         | auto_increment |
| item_name  | varchar(50) | NO   |     |         |                |
| item_desc  | text        | YES  |     |         |                |
| item_price | float       | NO   |     |         |                |
| curr_qty   | int(11)     | NO   |     |         |                |
+------------+-------------+------+-----+---------+----------------+
5 rows in set (0.01 sec)
```

NOTE

> The SHOW COLUMNS and DESCRIBE commands are aliases for one another and, therefore, do the same thing.

The SHOW INDEX command displays information about all the indexes present in a particular table. The syntax is

```
SHOW INDEX FROM table_name [FROM database_name]
```

This command produces a table full of information, ranging from the column name to the cardinality of the index. Table 31.1 describes the columns returned from this command.

TABLE 31.1   Columns in the SHOW INDEX Result

Column Name	Description
Table	The name of the table.
Non_unique	1 or 0.
	1 = Index can contain duplicates.
	0 = Index can't contain duplicates.
Key_name	The name of the index.
Seq_in_index	The column sequence number for the Index; starts at 1.
Column_name	The name of the column.
Collation	The sort order of the column, either A (ascending) or NULL (not sorted).
Cardinality	Number of unique values in the index.
Sub_part	On a partially indexed column, this shows the number of indexed characters, or NULL if the entire key is indexed.
Packed	The size of numeric columns.
Null	Displays whether the column can contain NULL values.
Index_type	The index method used.
Comment	Any additional comments.

Another command that produces a wide table full of results is the SHOW TABLE STATUS command, the syntax of which is as follows:

```
SHOW TABLE STATUS [FROM database_name] LIKE 'something'
```

This command produces a table full of information, ranging from the size and number of rows to the next value to use in an `auto_increment` field. Table 31.2 describes the columns returned from this command.

TABLE 31.2 Columns in the SHOW TABLE STATUS Result

Column Name	Description
Name	The name of the table.
Engine	The storage engine used for this table.
Version	The version of the table's *.frm file.
Row_format	The row storage format: fixed, dynamic, or compressed.
Rows	The number of rows.
Avg_row_length	The average row length.
Data_length	The length of the data file.
Max_data_length	The maximum length of the data file.
Index_length	The length of the index file.
Data_free	The number of bytes allocated but not used.
Auto_increment	The next value to use in an auto_increment field.
Create_time	The date and time when the table was created (in datetime format).
Update_time	The date and time when the data file was last updated (in datetime format).
Check_time	The date and time when the table was last checked (in datetime format).
Collation	The character set and collation type for the table.
Checksum	The checksum value of the table, if applicable.
Create_options	Any extra options used in the CREATE TABLE statement.
Comment	Any comments added when the table was created. In addition, InnoDB tables uses this column to report the free space in the tablespace.

Retrieving System Status

The SHOW STATUS and SHOW VARIABLES commands quickly provide important information about your database server. The syntax for these commands is simply SHOW STATUS or SHOW VARIABLES—nothing fancy.

More than 300 status variables will appear as the output of SHOW STATUS, but some of the most useful are as follows:

▶ **Aborted_connects**—The number of failed attempts to connect to the MySQL server. Anytime you see an aborted connection, you should investigate the problem. It could be related to a bad username and password in a script, or the number of allowable simultaneous connections could be set too low for the flood of traffic to your site.

▶ **Connections**—The aggregate number of connection attempts to the MySQL server during the current period of uptime.

▶ **Max_used_connections**—The maximum number of connections that have been in use simultaneously during the current period of uptime.

▶ **Slow_queries**—The number of queries that have taken more than long_query_time, which defaults to 10 seconds. If you have more than one slow query, it is time to investigate your SQL syntax!

▶ **Uptime**—The total number of seconds the server has been up during the current period of uptime.

You can find a comprehensive list of SHOW STATUS variables and an explanation of their values in the MySQL Manual, at http://dev.mysql.com/doc/refman/5.5/en/server-status-variables.html.

The SHOW VARIABLES command produces 325 results that control the general operation of MySQL and include the following useful tidbits:

▶ **connect_timeout**—Shows the number of seconds the MySQL server waits during a connection attempt before it gives up

▶ **max_connections**—The allowable number of simultaneous connections to MySQL before a connection is refused

▶ **port**—The port on which MySQL is running

▶ **table_type**—The table type for MySQL

▶ **version**—The MySQL version number

You can find a comprehensive list of the variables returned by the SHOW VARIABLES results and an explanation of their values in the MySQL Manual at http://dev.mysql.com/doc/refman/5.5/en/show-variables.html. After you know the values you have, you can change them in your MySQL configuration file or startup command.

Summary

Running an optimized MySQL server starts with the hardware and operating system in use. Your system's CPU should be sufficiently fast, and you should have enough RAM in use to pick up the slack when your CPU struggles. This is especially true if MySQL shares resources with other processes, such as a web server.

In addition, the hard drive in use is important because a small hard drive limits the amount of information you can store in your database. The seek time of your hard drive is important. A slow seek time causes the overall performance of the server to be slower. Your operating system should not overwhelm your machine and should share resources with MySQL rather than use all the resources itself.

Some key startup parameters for MySQL are the values of `key_buffer_size` and `table_cache`, among others. You can find baseline values in sample MySQL configuration files, or you can modify the values of these variables and watch the server performance to see whether you hit on the right result for your environment.

Beyond hardware and software optimization is the optimization of tables, as well as `SELECT` queries. Table optimization, using the `OPTIMIZE` command, enables you to reclaim unused space. You can see how well (or not) optimized your queries are by using the `EXPLAIN` command. The resulting output shows if and when indexes are used and whether you can use any indexes to speed up the given query.

Paying attention to your MySQL server ensures that it continues to run smoothly. Basic administration commands, such as `FLUSH` and `SHOW`, help you to recognize and quickly fix potential problems. All these commands are designed to give MySQL a millisecond of rest time and breathing room if it is under a heavy load. Numerous `SHOW` commands display structural information about databases, tables, and indexes, as well as how the system is performing.

Q&A

Q. *Can MySQL take advantage of multiple CPUs in a single server?*

A. Absolutely. If your operating system supports multiple CPUs, MySQL takes advantage of them. However, the performance and tuning of MySQL using multiple processors varies, depending on the operating system.

Q. *What permission level must I have to use the* `OPTIMIZE` *command?*

A. Any user with `INSERT` privileges for a table can perform `OPTIMIZE` commands. If a user has only `SELECT` permissions, the `OPTIMIZE` command will not execute.

Workshop

The workshop is designed to help you review what you've learned and begin learning how to put your knowledge into practice.

Quiz

1. Which MySQL function enables you to run an expression many times over to find the speed of the iterations?

2. Which SQL command cleans up the structure of your tables?

3. Which FLUSH command resets the MySQL log files?

4. To quickly determine whether MySQL has support for InnoDB tables, would you use SHOW STATUS or SHOW VARIABLES?

5. Write a SQL statement that enables you to see the SQL statement used to create a table called myTable.

Answers

1. The benchmark() function

2. OPTIMIZE

3. FLUSH LOGS

4. SHOW VARIABLES

5. SHOW CREATE TABLE myTable

Activities

1. If you have root-level access to your server, change the values of key_buffer_size and table_cache, and run benchmark() functions after each change to see how the execution times differ.

2. Use OPTIMIZE on all the tables you have created in your database to clean up any structural issues.

3. Use the SHOW STATUS command to retrieve information about your MySQL server, and then issue FLUSH commands to clean up the server. After each command, use SHOW STATUS again to see which commands affect which results in the SHOW STATUS results display.

CHAPTER 32

Performing Software Upgrades

In this chapter, you learn the following:

▶ How to keep up-to-date with new software releases

▶ How to upgrade between minor versions of MySQL

▶ How to upgrade between minor versions of Apache

▶ How to upgrade between minor versions of PHP

Throughout this book, you have been reminded to seek out information about new versions of PHP, Apache, and MySQL, and to be mindful of updates. Also, you have been shown how to add functionality to PHP at build time, but only in the context of installing the software. In this short chapter, you learn how to update your already installed software over the normal course of time, without wreaking havoc on your system.

Staying in the Loop

You should already have bookmarked the websites for Apache, PHP, and MySQL. It doesn't matter whether you have been using these technologies for 6 days or 6 years; there will always be a need to refer back to the sites. (I do, all the time!) If the primary reason for visiting the websites is to obtain information about updates, you could always subscribe to an announcements-only mailing list:

▶ For PHP announcements, go to http://www.php.net/mailing-lists.php and subscribe to the Announcements list.

▶ For MySQL announcements, go to http://lists.mysql.com/ and subscribe to the MySQL Announcements list.

▶ For Apache announcements, go to http://www.apache.org/foundation/mailinglists.html and subscribe to the Apache News and Announcements list.

When to Upgrade

As indicated in Part I, "Getting Up and Running" (the installation chapters), revision and minor version changes occur whenever the developers find it necessary to do so—not on any particular schedule. But just because a minor version change has occurred, that doesn't necessarily mean you should run right out and upgrade your software. Sometimes, however, you should upgrade as soon as possible.

TIP

> Software releases typically adhere to the format major.minor.revision; for example, PHP 5.4.0 would be major version 5, minor version 4, revision 0. It is true that changes in revisions may be "minor" in nature, but the release is referred to as a revision.

The primary instance in which you should immediately upgrade your software is when a security fix is announced. Usually, security issues are not discovered until they are exploited—sometimes in a testing environment, but sometimes by a rogue user who just wants to cause trouble for the world. After verification of a security issue, you can bet that it becomes the top priority for developers to fix, and quickly you will see an announcement of an upgrade. When that occurs, you should upgrade immediately, even if you don't use the particular element that is the cause of the security issue. A hole is a hole. Why leave it uncovered?

Here is an example of the Apache changelog documenting a change that occurred between version 2.0.61 and 2.0.63 (version 2.0.62 was not released to the public) that indicates a need to upgrade:

```
SECURITY: CVE-2007-6388 (cve.mitre.org)
mod_status: Ensure refresh parameter is numeric to prevent a possible XSS
attack caused by redirecting to other URLs.
```

A good rule of thumb is that if the word *security* appears anywhere in the changelog, you should upgrade. In the PHP 5 changelog, at http://www.php.net/ChangeLog-5.php, security-related fixes are grouped together and tend to be at the top of the list because of their importance.

However, if the release is just a maintenance release, meaning that it contains bug fixes and general enhancements that occur through normal development, you probably do not need to drop everything and upgrade your software. Here are some examples of maintenance items from the Apache and PHP changelogs, respectively:

```
mpm_winnt: Eliminate wait_for_many_objects.  Allows the clean shutdown of the
server when the MaxClients is higher then 257,  in a more responsive manner.
Fixed bug #43137 (rmdir() and rename() do not clear statcache).
```

If nothing in the list of changes is relevant to you, your work, or your environment, you could probably put off the upgrade until scheduled downtime or a rainy day. For example, if all the bugs fixed in a maintenance release of PHP have to do with the Windows platform and you run PHP on Linux, you can put the task aside, worry-free.

Even if you do not immediately upgrade your software, it is a good idea to stay at least within a few revisions of the current production version of the software. Anything past that and it becomes more likely that new features would be added or bugs fixed that are indeed relevant to your work or your environment.

Upgrading MySQL

Whether you use UNIX/Linux or Windows, upgrading versions of MySQL is simple: Install the new version as if the other version does not exist.

> Before upgrading to a new version of MySQL, always back up your existing databases.

CAUTION

Updates to MySQL are quite simple within the same base version; 5.4 is a base version, 5.5 is a base version, and so on. This means that upgrading any revision in the 5.5.x family is as simple as installing the new software on top of the old software. With the Windows Installer, this is all invisible to you but is exactly what occurs. UNIX/Linux users who install from the binary distribution simply relink the mysql symbolic directory to the new, unpacked distribution, as part of the installation process.

If you run into problems during the upgrade process, refer to the troubleshooting tips at http://dev.mysql.com/doc/refman/5.5/en/upgrading.html. However, upgrading minor versions of MySQL has always been a painless experience for me, on multiple platforms.

> If you change character sets when upgrading, you must run the following command to adjust the collation of your existing data:
> ```
> # myisamchk -r -q --set-collation=new_collation_name
> ```

NOTE

Upgrading Apache

As with MySQL, upgrading or rebuilding Apache follows the same process as installing the software in the first place. Windows users have the benefit of an installer application that automatically detects the previous version, removes core components, and installs new ones. The Windows Installer will, however, retain existing configuration files. You are responsible for upgrading any other version-specific modules that may be tied to specific versions of Apache.

For UNIX/Linux users, the process also follows the same path as the original installation. When you unpack your new distribution, it creates a directory named with the new version number. For example, if your previous version was 2.2.17 and you are upgrading to 2.4.1, your directories will be named `httpd-2.2.17` and `httpd-2.4.1`, respectively.

The actual installation directory for Apache is determined by you, when you run the `configure` script, as in this example:

```
# ./configure --prefix=/usr/local/apache2
```

After running the `configure` script to build the new version of Apache, just go through the `make` and `make install` process as you did when installing Apache in the first place.

Now, should you want to install your new version of Apache directly over your old version, you can—even with the old `httpd` binary still running. Just be sure to back up your configuration files in case something goes awry. However, if you are more comfortable installing your new version in a different directory, that's fine, too; you just have to move all your web-related files (that is, everything in the document root) to the new directory and make all appropriate edits to your fresh, new `httpd.conf` file. Whichever method you choose is up to you. (One method just requires more file movement and reconfiguration than the other.)

After upgrading Apache on UNIX/Linux, you should also rebuild your PHP module. Windows users do not have a module to rebuild but should ensure that the appropriate PHP-related changes are still present in the `httpd.conf` file related to loading the module residing in the PHP directory tree.

Modifying Apache Without Upgrading

Suppose that you need to add or remove functionality from Apache but are not upgrading to a new minor version. An example is to add a new module or to upgrade the version of OpenSSL used on your system.

In this case, UNIX/Linux users should go to the existing source directory (such as httpd-2.2.17, using the earlier example) and type **make clean** at the prompt. This will, essentially, reset the makefiles so that you can rebuild Apache without relying on previous, cached values. After the make clean command, run the configure script with your new parameters, and go through the make and make install process again. You do not need to rebuild the PHP module in this situation.

Windows users would activate the prebuilt modules by uncommenting the appropriate lines in httpd.conf or by adding the lines if they do not already exist.

Upgrading PHP

Given that UNIX/Linux users can add so much functionality to PHP through various build options, it is likely that you will upgrade or modify PHP more often than Apache or MySQL. Regardless of whether you are upgrading to a new revision or minor version or simply adding new functionality (or removing some you no longer need), the process for modifying an existing version is exactly the same as installing it in the first place: configure, make, make install. The make install step places the PHP module in the appropriate place in the Apache directory tree. When your new module is in place, restart Apache—the new version of PHP should be in use.

When you upgrade PHP to a new version, you will have a completely distinct directory tree when you extract the distribution archive, based on the new version number. Perform the configure, make, make install steps within this new directory structure, and a new PHP module will be built, independent of the other.

Windows users have a different set of tasks to perform: Adding new functionality to an existing module requires only that you activate the module by uncommenting its entry in php.ini and then restart Apache. Upgrading to a new minor version requires you to download a new distribution file. The contents of this file extract into a directory named for the version it represents. You must then follow the steps required for installation, regarding the configuration of php.ini, because each version produces a different file. Finally, change any PHP-related pathnames in the Apache httpd.conf file and restart the server. The new version of PHP should be in use.

Using PECL and PEAR to Extend PHP

You can obtain a wealth of user-created extensions and applications from PECL (the *PHP Extension Community Library*, at http://pecl.php.net/), and PEAR (the *PHP Extension and Application Repository*, at http://pear.php.net/). These sites are governed by rules and style guides, so everything you download from these sites is of high quality.

If you are looking for additional extensions for your PHP installation, look to PECL. If you are looking for a library of open source code to integrate in your application, look to PEAR.

Summary

This short chapter provided some guidelines for keeping your installations of MySQL, Apache, and PHP current. You learned where to look for updates and how to weigh the importance of upgrading to a new version. In addition, you learned the step-by-step processes for upgrading or modifying MySQL, Apache, and PHP.

Workshop

The workshop is designed to help you review what you've learned, and begin putting your knowledge into practice.

Quiz

1. How would you refer to software in which the major version is 3, the minor version is 4, and the revision is 14?

2. What is considered the primary reason for upgrading to a new minor version of any software?

3. What command cleans up previous `makefiles` and cached settings?

Answers

1. The full version number would be 3.4.14.

2. Security issues that have been found and fixed by the developers.

3. The `make clean` command.

Activity

By the time you read this chapter, it is very likely that one or more of PHP, MySQL, and Apache will have a different version number than the ones either included on the CD or that you downloaded and installed at the beginning of the book. So, if you have the permissions to upgrade (that is, if you are not using a virtual hosting environment), just pick one (or more) of the technologies and go through the upgrade process.

CHAPTER 33

Using Application Frameworks

In this short chapter, you learn, including the following:

▶ What an application framework is and how it can help you

▶ The basics of the model-view-controller pattern of software architecture

▶ Considering and installing some popular PHP application frameworks

This book has taught you the basics of creating dynamic functionality within a website, be it individual scripts used to increase functionality or display dynamic data or a series of scripts hooked together in some consistent fashion to produce a web-based application. When you are ready to move to larger projects, in which you are likely to want to use functionality that others most certainly have used in their projects but you have neither the time nor inclination to reinvent the wheel, an application framework will become your new best friend.

Understanding Application Frameworks

Getting to the heart of the matter, an application framework is nothing more than a set of libraries and templates that enable you to rapidly develop feature-rich dynamic sites and web applications without building every piece of the puzzle from scratch. If you recall, in the chapters in Part V, "Basic Projects," I was always careful to note that the examples showed but one of many ways to create scripts to achieve the overall goal. The use of an application framework allows you to say "I understand there are many ways to create a login sequence (or shopping cart, or discussion forum, and so on), and instead of starting from scratch, I will implement the [application framework] way of doing things."

Besides the obvious benefit of reusing a stable codebase for common functionality, using a framework also helps a developer adhere to a consistent software architectural pattern. In the case of PHP frameworks, that pattern is typically the model-view-controller (MVC) pattern, which you learn more about in the next section. Another aspect of adhering to a framework, and thus some sort of software architecture, is the ability to implement a stable and consistent three-tier architecture for your application. In a three-tier architecture, you have a physical tier to represent the client, and then an application and database under your control and management. In other words, a user's web browser or mobile device (client) connects directly to your application—and typically the presentation layer of it, or what you see in the browser—which in turn reaches back into the database to retrieve data to be presented.

It's important to understand that some content management systems—installable software packages in their own right, such as WordPress (http://www.wordpress.org), Drupal (http://www.drupal.org), and Joomla (http://www.joomla.org)—are not technically application frameworks, but it is possible to install and customize the applications in such a way as to create your own flavor of it while reusing their feature-rich codebase.

Using the MVC Pattern

One goal of any software architecture pattern is to provide consistent structures, elements, and properties and attributes among the constituent pieces so as to ensure the transparency of the inner workings of the application for those developing and maintaining it. Think about the situation where one person has been coding an application alone without adhering to any architectural pattern: What happens when a new person joins the team, or the original person leaves it? Without a fundamental and shared body of knowledge—such as the adherence to a general architectural pattern—enormous amounts of time will be spent getting the new person up to speed, and that doesn't even begin to touch on the issues he will have in consistently auditing, testing, and maintaining the hodgepodge code.

The MVC software architecture pattern is ready-made for web-based applications, and in fact many applications (or even just dynamic websites) adhere to some version of this pattern without even trying too hard. Figure 33.1 illustrates the MVC concept in a basic way, with solid lines indicating direct associations between each of the three components and dashed lines indicating what are sometimes indirect associations between some of the parts.

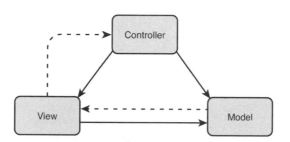

FIGURE 33.1
Visualizing the
MVC pattern.

In general, the three components can be defined like this:

- ▶ **Model**—Stores and separates data. It is not a database itself, but rather think about the parts of your scripts to date that reach back into the database and pull information out of it, before it is displayed to the user.

- ▶ **View**—The visual representation of data in the model. These are like the parts of your scripts to date that have done nothing but display data you have retrieved from the database.

- ▶ **Controller**—The way in which the user invokes an action in a system. Often referred to as the "brains" of the application, it determines how the model will be used to achieve a successful result of that action.

Here's another way of thinking about the flow in an MVC application. Assume that a user in an online store is viewing an item page and wants to add that item to her shopping cart:

1. The user presses a submit button on the page, with the mouse.

2. The controller accepts the form action and sends information to the model.

3. To show the user that an action and change in their data has occurred, the view communicates with the model to get data back out to show the user.

4. The controller waits for more user actions, when the cycle will repeat.

Each of the PHP frameworks discussed in this chapter enable you to easily apply an MVC pattern to your software applications. Many other PHP frameworks do as well, and although you might not choose to adhere to the pattern, it is recommended that you do so to enable easier testing, development, deployment, and ongoing maintenance of your applications.

For even more examples and explanations of the MVC pattern, see Jeff Atwood's clear and concise blog post "Understanding Model-View-Controller" at http://www.codinghorror.com/blog/2008/05/understanding-model-view-controller.html.

Installing and Using PHP Application Frameworks

At the time of this writing, developers worldwide use more than 30 PHP application frameworks. Selecting a few to discuss in general was no small feat, but the ones I'm calling out in this chapter have a (relatively) long history and an active developer community with considerable uptake. In fact, those are three features unrelated to the code itself that you should think about when evaluating a framework for your own purposes: Has it been around awhile and is it stable? Are people actively using it? Is the parent company or group of developers actively maintaining it?

Other considerations for selection include the following:

▶ Determining whether the framework is best suited for the type of application you are creating; some frameworks are great for e-commerce, some for content publication, and some for both.

▶ Determining whether the framework provides you with the opportunity to use a software architecture pattern, and if so, whether it is the one you want to use.

▶ Determining whether the framework requires additional PHP modules or server libraries. If it does, but you do not control your server and therefore cannot modify the libraries and modules installed, that framework cannot work for you.

The next few sections cover the three popular open source PHP application frameworks: Zend, CakePHP, and CodeIgniter. Again, these are not the only possible frameworks; in fact, Symfony (http://www.symfony.com/) and Yii (http://www.yiiframework.com/) could easily have been included in the "best of breed" list.

Wikipedia maintains a comprehensive list of PHP application frameworks at http://en.wikipedia.org/wiki/Comparison_of_web_application_frameworks#PHP.

Considering the Zend Framework

If you are developing enterprise-grade PHP applications, seriously consider starting with the Zend Framework (http://framework.zend.com/). You might have heard of Zend, the company behind the Zend Framework, as its founders have been contributors to the PHP language itself almost since its initial creation. The core PHP engine is often referred to as *the Zend engine*. In other words, if evaluating the Zend Framework according to the criteria I previously mentioned, you would be hard-pressed to find a framework that is more stable, has been around longer, or has more people actively developing the framework and applications with it.

Although the name of the software is the Zend *Framework*, and indeed it is a framework, you might also hear it referred to as a *component library* because it is possible to pick and choose from a set of loosely coupled components instead of implementing a structured, well-architected application. For example, Zend's separate components address database connections and profiling, internationalization and localization, authentication, authorization, and session management, consuming and exposing web services, and mail functions, to name a few.

That the framework is made of components is not a negative evaluation at all, but it does warrant a reminder that one of the goals of using frameworks and adhering to an architecture pattern is for the ease of maintenance—your application can be kept tidy, for lack of a better word. If your application includes a library of framework components and you are only using one of them, you might ask yourself if the overhead of maintaining the framework (updates, patches, and so on) is worth it. Your answers will vary, and only you will know which decision is right for you.

To download and install the Zend Framework with the existing PHP, Apache, and MySQL installation that you've been working with in this book, first go to the Requirements page at http://framework.zend.com/manual/en/requirements.introduction.html to ensure you have the correct version of PHP and any ancillary libraries and modules. If you do, go to http://framework.zend.com/download/latest for links to the Full or Minimal version of the software. After you have obtained the distribution archive in the format of your choice, just extract it according to the instructions included in the distribution. (In brief, you extract a directory and put it in your existing filesystem.) The Zend Framework QuickStart Guide, at http://framework.zend.com/manual/en/learning.quickstart.intro.html, walks you through the process of using the framework and its components through the creation of sample applications.

Considering CakePHP

Another of the long-standing and stable PHP application frameworks with a strong user and developer community is CakePHP (http://www.cakephp.org/). At its core, CakePHP is an MVC framework, with components for common functionality such as database connections, authentication, authorization, and session management, and consuming and exposing web services—all much like the Zend Framework and, in fact, numerous other frameworks.

One of CakePHP's greatest selling points is its ease of use (or ease of integration) while not allowing its simplicity to hinder feature-rich development and enterprise deployment. Like the Zend Framework, you do not have to deal with custom configuration files, and instead you just download and install the framework and get started with rapid development. From the perspective of the new user, CakePHP wins points for having detailed and user-friendly documentation as well as multimedia tutorials, in addition to the standard developer forums.

To download and install CakePHP with the existing PHP, Apache, and MySQL installation that you've been working with in this book, first go to the Installation page of the CakePHP Cookbook (also known as the documentation) at http://book.cakephp.org/2.0/en/installation.html to ensure you have the correct version of PHP and any ancillary libraries and modules. If you do, download the current version from links further down the page or on the main page of the site.

After you have obtained the distribution archive, just extract it into your web server document root. You have a few different options for using CakePHP in a development or production environment, all discussed in the Cookbook at http://book.cakephp.org/2.0/en/installation.html. Once CakePHP is installed, head to the QuickStart Guide at http://book.cakephp.org/2.0/en/getting-started.html for a walkthrough on using CakePHP to create some sample applications.

Considering CodeIgniter

Although CakePHP is billed as easy to use (and it is), CodeIgniter (http://www.codeigniter.com) is a good starting place for true beginners. While feature rich, its functionality is targeted at delivering content rather than commerce or other transactional processes. This is not at all a bad thing, because delivering content in an easy-to-use manner within architecturally sound software is always a plus. I might not use CodeIgniter in the enterprise, but many web developers make a fine living with numerous happy clients without ever entering the enterprise space. So again, pick the framework that is right for you.

In addition to being an MVC framework, CodeIgniter addresses common functionality such as database connections, authentication, authorization, and session management, localization, image manipulation, and consuming and exposing web services, among others—much like the other frameworks discussed in this chapter. Again, like the other frameworks discussed, installation consists of downloading and installing the framework and beginning to develop immediately (and rapidly). Like CakePHP, CodeIgniter wins points for having detailed and user-friendly documentation as well as multimedia tutorials, in addition to the standard developer forums.

To download and install CodeIgniter with the existing PHP, Apache, and MySQL installation that you've been working with in this book, first go to the Server Requirements page of the documentation at http://codeigniter.com/user_guide/general/requirements.html to ensure you have the correct version of PHP and any ancillary libraries and modules. If you do, download the current version from the Downloads page at http://codeigniter.com/downloads/.

Summary

This short chapter introduced you to the concept of using an application framework, and specifically one using the model-view-controller pattern of software architecture. Before reading about three popular PHP application frameworks (Zend, CakePHP, and CodeIgniter), you learned the basics of how to evaluate a framework for use in your own application development.

Workshop

The workshop is designed to help you review what you've learned and begin putting your knowledge into practice.

Quiz

1. What are some of the benefits of using an application framework?

2. In the MVC pattern, what does the model do?

3. Do you have to use an application framework?

Answers

1. Working with a stable codebase, adhering to a software architecture pattern, and not reinventing the wheel.

2. The model stores and separates data from the controlling and viewing components.

3. Not at all. In fact, nothing in this book—which covers fundamental aspects of developing with PHP and MySQL—relies on a framework.

Activities

1. Download and install at least one of the frameworks discussed in this chapter. (If you install more than one, delete the old ones first to avoid collisions.)

2. Follow at least one of the tutorials provided by the developers of these frameworks so that you can gain some practical knowledge of using a framework as well as the MVC pattern.

Index

Numbers

3D pie charts, creating, 269-270

Symbols

+ (addition operators), 85-87

&& (and operator), 91-92

[ ] (array operators), 140

= (assignment operators), 77, 86-89

* (asterisks), 305

   comments, 72

   wildcards, 32

\ (backslashes)

   directives, 45

   escaping string quotation marks, 113

   time stamp conversions, 184

. (concatenation operators), 87-88

/ (division operators), 87

$ (dollar signs), variable names, 76

… (ellipses)

   color fills, 266

   drawing, 264

= (equal to operator), 308

== (equivalence operators), 90

// (forward slashes), comments, 72

> (greater than operators), 91, 308

>= (greater than or equal to operators), 91, 308

=== (identical operators), 91

< (less than operators), 91, 308

<= (less than or equal to operators), 91, 308

% (modulus operators), 87

* (multiplication operators), 87

! (not operators), 92

!= (nonequivalence operators), 90

!= (not equal to operator), 308

|| (or operators), 91-92

() (parentheses), subqueries, 315

% (percent signs)

   conversion specifications, 160-162

   log-formatting directives, 510

   wildcards, 32

(pound signs)

   comments, 72

   directives, 45

   PHP/Apache integration, 62

"" (quotation marks)

   escaping strings, 113

   MySQL field names, 324

; (semicolons)

   instruction terminators, 76

   statements, 70

- (subtraction operators), 87

? (ternary operator), 105

A

%a format string option (DATE_FORMAT() function), 337

%A log-formatting directive, 510

ab (ApacheBench), 559-561

aborted_connects status variable, 602

abs() function, 121

abuse prevention, 563-564

accept mechanisms, 559

access

   authentication

      authoritative information, 494

      back-end storage, 494

      browsers, 493

      client, 492-493

      combining with access control rules, 500

      database file-based, 496-497

      defined, 491

      denying access, 494

      directives, 493-494

      etc/passwd file, 507

      file-based, 495-496

      realms, 493

      user management, 494

   authorization, 492

   class properties with object methods, 153

   constants, 94

   cookies, 214-215

   log files, 50

   global variables, 127

   reports, creating, 521-522

   restricting based on

      cookies, 502-506

      HTTP methods, 501

   rules

      clients, 498

      combining with authentication, 500

      domain names, 498

      environment variables, 498

      evaluating, 499-500

      implementing, 497-498

N